# Understanding Blanchot, Understanding Modernism

**Understanding Philosophy, Understanding Modernism**

The aim of each volume in **Understanding Philosophy, Understanding Modernism** is to understand a philosophical thinker more fully through literary and cultural modernism and consequently to understand literary modernism better through a key philosophical figure. In this way, the series also rethinks the limits of modernism, calling attention to lacunae in modernist studies and sometimes in the philosophical work under examination.

Series Editors:
Paul Ardoin, S. E. Gontarski, and Laci Mattison

Volumes in the Series:
*Understanding Bergson, Understanding Modernism*
*Understanding Deleuze, Understanding Modernism*
*Understanding Wittgenstein, Understanding Modernism*
*Understanding Foucault, Understanding Modernism*
*Understanding James, Understanding Modernism*
*Understanding Rancière, Understanding Modernism*
*Understanding Blanchot, Understanding Modernism*
*Understanding Merleau-Ponty, Understanding Modernism* (forthcoming)
*Understanding Nietzsche, Understanding Modernism* (forthcoming)
*Understanding Cavell, Understanding Modernism* (forthcoming)
*Understanding Derrida, Understanding Modernism* (forthcoming)

# Understanding Blanchot, Understanding Modernism

Edited by

Christopher Langlois

BLOOMSBURY ACADEMIC
NEW YORK • LONDON • OXFORD • NEW DELHI • SYDNEY

BLOOMSBURY ACADEMIC
Bloomsbury Publishing Inc
1385 Broadway, New York, NY 10018, USA

BLOOMSBURY, BLOOMSBURY ACADEMIC and the Diana logo
are trademarks of Bloomsbury Publishing Plc

First published in the United States of America 2018
Paperback edition published 2020

Cover design: Olivia D'Cruz
Cover image © Getty Images/WIN-Initiative

Library of Congress Cataloging-in-Publication Data
Names: Langlois, Christopher author.
Title: Understanding Blanchot, understanding modernism / Christopher Langlois [editor].
Description: New York, NY : Bloomsbury Academic, 2018. |
Series: Understanding philosophy, understanding modernism |
Includes bibliographical references and index.
Identifiers: LCCN 2017055534 (print) | LCCN 2017059721 (ebook) |
ISBN 9781501331398 (ePDF) | ISBN 9781501331381 (ePUB) | ISBN 9781501331374
(hardback)
Subjects: LCSH: Blanchot, Maurice. | Modernism (Literature) | Literature–Philosophy.
Classification: LCC B2430.B574 (ebook) | LCC B2430.B574 U53 2018 (print) |
DDC 194–dc23
LC record available at https://lccn.loc.gov/2017055534

ISBN: HB: 978-1-5013-3137-4
PB: 978-1-5013-6096-1
ePDF: 978-1-5013-3139-8
eBook: 978-1-5013-3138-1

Series: Understanding Philosophy, Understanding Modernism

Typeset by Integra Software Services Pvt. Ltd.

To find out more about our authors and books visit www.bloomsbury.com
and sign up for our newsletters.

# Contents

# Notes on Contributors

**Joseph Albernaz** is a PhD student at the University of California, Berkeley, where he is completing a dissertation on community and the everyday in Romanticism. His other academic interests include ecological thought and criticism, contemporary theory, German Idealism, political theology, revolutions, and contemporary poetry in French and English. His publications include essays and reviews on John Clare, photography, and French thought.

**William S. Allen** is an independent researcher at the University of Southampton, UK. He is the author of *Ellipsis: Of Poetry and the Experience of Language after Heidegger, Hölderlin, and Blanchot* (SUNY Press, 2007), *Aesthetics of Negativity: Blanchot, Adorno, and Autonomy* (Fordham University Press, 2016), and *Without End: Sade's Critique of Reason* (Bloomsbury, 2018).

**Kevin Bell** teaches at the Pennsylvania State University. He is the author of *Ashes Taken for Fire: Aesthetic Modernism and the Critique of Identity* (University of Minnesota Press, 2007). He is now completing *Drift Velocities: The Figural Curve of Radical Black Film and Literature,* a study of non-anthropocentric itineraries in black American writing and cinema since the mid-1960s.

**Jonathan Boulter** is Professor of English at Western University. He is the author of *Parables of the Posthuman* (2015); *Melancholy and the Archive: Trauma, Memory, and History in the Contemporary Novel* (2011); *Beckett: A Guide for the Perplexed* (2008); *Interpreting Narrative in the Novels of Samuel Beckett* (2001); and coeditor of *Cultural Subjects: A Cultural Studies Reader* (2005). His work has appeared in *Cultural Critique, Modern Fiction Studies, SubStance, Genre, Hispanic Review, Samuel Beckett Today/Aujourd'hui, Journal of Beckett Studies,* and *International Ford Madox Ford Studies.*

**Jeff Fort** is Associate Professor of French at the University of California, Davis. He is the author of *The Imperative to Write: Destitutions of the Sublime in Kafka, Blanchot and Beckett* (Fordham, 2014). He has translated numerous books by authors such as Maurice Blanchot, Jacques Derrida, Jean Genet, Jean-Luc Nancy, Philippe Lacoue-Labarthe, and Jacques Roubaud.

**Kevin Hart** is the Edwin B. Kyle Professor of Christian Studies in the Department of Religious Studies at the University of Virginia, where he also holds professorships in the Department of English and the Department of French. He is the author of *The Dark Gaze: Maurice Blanchot and the Sacred* (University of Chicago Press, 2004), the editor of *Clandestine Encounters: Philosophy in the Narratives of Maurice Blanchot* (Notre Dame University Press, 2010), and the editor, with Geoffrey Hartman, of *The Power of Contestation: Perspectives on Maurice Blanchot* (The Johns Hopkins University Press, 2004). His most recent scholarly publications are *Kingdoms of God* (Indiana University Press, 2014) and *Poetry and Revelation* (Bloomsbury, 2017). His poetry is collected in *Wild Track: New and Selected Poems* (Notre Dame University Press, 2015) and *Barefoot* (Notre Dame University Press, 2018).

**Leslie Hill** is Emeritus Professor of French Studies at the University of Warwick and the author of several books on the work of Blanchot and others, including *Beckett's Fiction: In Different Words* (1990), *Marguerite Duras: Apocalyptic Desires* (1993), *Blanchot: Extreme Contemporary* (1997), *Bataille, Klossowski, Blanchot: Writing at the Limit* (2001), *The Cambridge Introduction to Jacques Derrida* (2007), *Radical Indecision: Barthes, Blanchot, Derrida, and the Future of Criticism* (2010), and *Maurice Blanchot and Fragmentary Writing: A Change of Epoch* (2012). He has recently completed a forthcoming study of the controversy between Jean-Luc Nancy and Blanchot on the question of "community," and is currently working on a book exploring the writings of Pierre Klossowski entitled *Circulus vitiosus deus: Klossowski, Nietzsche, and the Deconstruction of Christianity*.

**Michael Holland** is a Fellow of St. Hugh's College, Oxford. He has published widely on Maurice Blanchot in both English and French. He published the first comprehensive bibliography of Blanchot's work. His *Blanchot Reader* (1995) brought together texts covering all of Blanchot's postwar writings. In 2012 he launched the *Cahiers Maurice Blanchot* in collaboration with the late Monique Antelme and Danielle Cohen-Levinas. In 2015 a collection of his articles in French appeared with the title *Avant dire. Essais sur Blanchot*. He is working on a book in English on Blanchot and narrative. He has translated Blanchot's *Chroniques littéraires 1941–1944* in four volumes for Fordham University Press. With Hannes Opelz, he is preparing a *Dictionnaire Maurice Blanchot* for Classiques Garnier.

**Michael Krimper** is a PhD candidate in the Department of Comparative Literature at New York University, where he is finishing a dissertation on the poetics and politics of inoperativity in modernism, with a particular focus on the writings of Blanchot, Bataille, Beckett, and Melville. One of his recent articles on Blanchot's concept of *désoeuvrement* has appeared in *SubStance*.

**Christopher Langlois** is Lecturer of English at Dawson College, Canada, and author of Samuel Beckett and the Terror of Literature (Edinburgh University Press, 2017). Some of his articles and essays have appeared in *Twentieth-Century Literature, College Literature, Mosaic, Modernism/ modernity, The Faulkner Journal, Samuel Beckett Today/Aujourd'hui,* and *European Journal of English Studies*. He is also guest-editing a forthcoming special issue of *ARIEL: A Review of International English Literature* commemorating the fortieth anniversary of Edward Said's *Orientalism*.

**Patrick Lyons** is a graduate student in the Department of French at the University of California, Berkeley.

**James Martell** is Assistant Professor of Romance Languages at Lyon College. He is the coeditor—together with Arka Chattopadhyay—of *Samuel Beckett and the Encounter of Philosophy and Literature* (Roman Books, 2013). His current book-length project focuses on modernism and matricide. He has published articles on Derrida, Deleuze, Beckett, and the cinema of Béla Tarr. His latest article on Derrida and tattooing has appeared in the December 2017 issue of *The Oxford Literary Review*.

**John McKeane** is Lecturer in French studies at the University of Reading. He is the author of *Philippe Lacoue-Labarthe: (Un)timely Meditations* (2015) as well as of articles on the work of Blanchot, Barthes, Derrida, and others. He coedited the collective volume *Blanchot romantique* (2011), and has translated various volumes, including Jean-Luc Nancy, *Adoration: The Deconstruction of Christianity, II* (2013), and Christophe Bident's biography of Blanchot (forthcoming).

**Aïcha Liviana Messina** is Professor of Philosophy in the Institute of Humanities at the Universidad Diego Portales. Her work is mainly focused on the relationship between violence and language, on political issues such as law, sovereignty, peace, and war, and on the relationship between critic, knowledge, and power. She is the author of a book on the living model, *Poser me va si bien* (P.O.L, 2005); an essay on Marx and love, *Amour/Argent. Le livre blanc des manuscrits de 1844* (Les cahiers du portique, 2011); and a monograph on Emmanuel Lévinas, *L'anarchie de la paix. Lévinas et la philosophie politique* (CNRS, forthcoming). She is currently working on the problem of innocence and Christianity in Blanchot's work and is leading two research projects funded by the National Funding for the Scientific and Technologic Development in Chile (Fondecyt 1140113 and 1179580).

**Hannes Opelz** teaches in the French Department at Trinity College, Dublin. His work focuses on theories of representation in Western thought and aesthetics, from Plato to Philippe Lacoue-Labarthe. He published a translation of Lacoue-Labarthe's book on Maurice Blanchot, *Ending and Unending Agony* (Fordham UP, 2015), and is coeditor of *Blanchot Romantique* (Peter Lang, 2011).

**Allan Pero** is Associate Professor of English and Acting Director of the Centre for the Study of Theory and Criticism at Western University, London, Canada. He is also chief editor of *English Studies in Canada*. He is coeditor (with Gyllian Phillips) and contributor to a volume entitled *The Many Façades of Edith Sitwell* (University Press of Florida, 2017). Recent publications include articles in *The Journal of Wyndham Lewis Studies, The Virginia Woolf Miscellany, Modernism/ modernity, Katherine Mansfield Studies*, and a forthcoming chapter on Ford's *The Good Soldier*. He is currently working on *An Encyclopedia of Cultural Theory*, with Dr. Kel Pero, for the University of Toronto Press, and a book-length project on camp and modernism.

**Jean-Michel Rabaté**, Professor of English and Comparative Literature at the University of Pennsylvania since 1992, a curator of the Slought Foundation, an editor of the *Journal of Modern Literature*, and a Fellow of the American Academy of Arts and Sciences, has authored or edited more than thirty-five books on modernism, psychoanalysis, and philosophy. Recent books include *Crimes of the Future, The Cambridge Introduction to Literature and Psychoanalysis, The Pathos of Distance, Think, Pig! Beckett at the Limit of the Human,* and *Les Guerres de Derrida.*

**Cosmin Toma** holds a PhD from the Université de Montréal, where he wrote a thesis on the literary absolute in the works of Samuel Beckett and Maurice Blanchot. His academic writing has appeared in the journals *Études françaises,*

*Formes poétiques contemporaines, The University of Toronto Quarterly, Les Cahiers Maurice Blanchot*, and *Word and Text*. He has also translated texts by Jacques Derrida.

**Audrey Wasser** is Assistant Professor of French in the Department of French & Italian at Miami University, Ohio. She is the author of *The Work of Difference: Modernism, Romanticism, and the Production of Literary Form* (Fordham 2016). Her work focuses on experimental modernism in connection with philosophically inflected accounts of literary form, as well as on contemporary French thought. She has published articles on Proust, Beckett, Deleuze, and Spinoza, and is currently at work on a book on literary judgment.

# Series Preface

*Understanding Philosophy, Understanding Modernism*

Sometime in the late twentieth century, modernism, like philosophy itself, underwent something of an unmooring from (at least) linear literary history, in favor of the multi-perspectival history implicit in "new historicism" or varieties of "presentism," say. Amid current reassessments of modernism and modernity, critics have posited various "new" or alternative modernisms—postcolonial, cosmopolitan, transatlantic, transnational, geomodernism, or even "bad" modernisms. In doing so, they have not only reassessed modernism as a category, but also, more broadly, they have rethought epistemology and ontology, aesthetics, metaphysics, materialism, history, and being itself, opening possibilities of rethinking not only which texts we read as modernist, but also how we read those texts.

Much of this new conversation constitutes something of a critique of the periodization of modernism or modernist studies in favor of modernism as mode (or mode of production) or concept. *Understanding Philosophy, Understanding Modernism* situates itself amid the plurality of discourses, offering collections focused on single key philosophical thinkers influential both to the moment of modernism and to our current understanding of that moment's genealogy, archeology, and becomings. Such critiques of modernism(s) and modernity afford opportunities to rethink and reassess the overlaps, folds, interrelationships, interleavings, or cross-pollinations of modernism and philosophy. Our goals in each volume of the series are to understand literary modernism better through philosophy as we also better understand a philosopher through literary modernism.

The first two volumes of the series, those on Henri Bergson and Gilles Deleuze, have established a tripartite structure that serves to offer accessibility to both the philosopher's principal texts and to current new research. Each volume opens with a section focused on "conceptualizing" the philosopher through close readings of seminal texts in the thinker's *oeuvre*. A second section, on aesthetics, maps connections between modernist works and the philosophical figure, often surveying key modernist trends and shedding new light on authors and texts. The final section of each volume serves as an extended glossary of principal terms in the philosopher's work, each treated at length, allowing a fuller engagement with and examination of the many, sometimes contradictory, ways terms are deployed. The series is thus designed to both introduce philosophers and rethink their relationship to modernist studies, revising our understandings of both modernism and philosophy, and offering resources that will be of use across disciplines, from philosophy, theory, and literature, to religion, the visual and performing arts, and often to the sciences as well.

# List of Abbreviations

## Selected Works of Maurice Blanchot Translated into English

BC      *The Book to Come*, trans. Charlotte Mandell (Stanford: Stanford University Press, 2003).

DS      *Death Sentence*, trans. Lydia Davis (Barrytown: Station Hill Press, 1998).

F      *Friendship*, trans. Elizabeth Rottenberg (Stanford: Stanford University Press, 1997).

FP      *Faux Pas*, trans. Charlotte Mandell (Stanford: Stanford University Press, 2001).

GO      *The Gaze of Orpheus and Other Literary Essays*, trans. Lydia Davis, ed. P. Adams Sitney (Barrytown: Station Hill Press, 1981).

IC      *The Infinite Conversation*, trans. Susan Hanson (Minneapolis and London: University of Minnesota Press, 1993).

IMD      *The Instant of My Death*, bound with Jacques Derrida, *Demeure: Fiction and Testimony*, trans. Elizabeth Rottenberg (Stanford: Stanford University Press, 2000).

LS      *Lautréamont and Sade*, trans. Stuart Kendall and Michelle Kendall (Stanford: Stanford University Press, 2004).

OWS      *The One Who Was Standing Apart from Me*, trans. Lydia Davis (Barrytown: Station Hill Press, 1993).

PW      *Political Writings, 1953–1993*, trans. Zakir Paul (New York: Fordham University Press, 2010).

SL      *The Space of Literature*, trans. Ann Smock (Lincoln and London: University of Nebraska Press, 1982).

SNB     *The Step Not Beyond*, trans. Lycette Nelson (Albany: State University of New York Press, 1992).

TO     *Thomas the Obscure*, trans. Robert Lamberton (Barrytown: Station Hill Press, 1988).

UC     *The Unavowable Community*, trans. Pierre Joris (Barrytown: Station Hill Press, 1988).

VE     *A Voice from Elsewhere*, trans. Charlotte Mandell (Albany: State University of New York Press, 2007).

WTC     *When the Time Comes*, trans. Lydia Davis, *Station Hill Blanchot Reader*, ed. George Quasha (Barrytown: Station Hill Press, 1999).

WF     *The Work of Fire*, trans. Charlotte Mandell (Stanford: Stanford University Press, 1995).

WD     *The Writing of the Disaster*, trans. Ann Smock (Lincoln and London: University of Nebraska Press, 1995).

## Selected Works of Maurice Blanchot in French

A     *L'Amitié* (Paris: Gallimard, 1971).

AM     *L'Arrêt de mort* (Paris: Gallimard, 1948).

AMV     *Au moment voulu* (Paris: Gallimard, 1951).

CAP     *Celui qui ne m'accompagnait pas* (Paris: Gallimard, 1953).

ED     *L'Écriture du desastre* (Paris: Gallimard, 1980).

EI     *L'Entretien infini* (Paris: Gallimard, 1969).

EL     *L'Espace littéraire* (Paris: Gallimard, 1955).

LV     *Le Livre à venir* (Paris: Gallimard, 1959).

PF     *La Part du feu* (Paris: Gallimard, 1949).

PA     *Le Pas au-delà* (Paris: Gallimard, 1973).

# Introduction: Against Praise of Maurice Blanchot

Christopher Langlois

In one of his early essays on Maurice Blanchot, "Pace not(s)," Jacques Derrida writes that Blanchot is "awaiting us, still to come, to be read, to be reread by those very same ones that do it ever since they knew how to read, and *thanks* to him."[1] Readers of Blanchot in English will recall not only that an excerpt of these lines appears on the back cover of Susan Hanson's translation of *L'Entretien infini*, *The Infinite Conversation*, but also that Derrida's identification of the community of readers anticipated by Blanchot is omitted. The omission is unfortunate, for what it robs from Derrida's assessment of Blanchot's projected legacy is the paradoxical designation of a community of readers who have unwittingly been reading Blanchot *ever since they first learned how to read*. Blanchot's increasingly growing reputation both inside and outside of France is owing in no small part to the recognition of the instrumental role his work—literary, critical, and philosophical—has played in transmitting to his early readers particular ways of writing and thinking that set the tone for how a generation of artists and intellectuals after the Second World War responded to the most pressing cultural, social, and political issues of the day. This generation came of age during the Algerian War of Independence (1954–62); the popular uprising in France in May 1968; the struggles for decolonization in Latin America, the Middle East, and Africa; and the Cold War. But while there is no denying that Blanchot, "as a writer," as he always insisted, was committed to the cause of freedom from political oppression, whether colonial, fascist, or totalitarian,[2] nevertheless it was

---

[1] Jacques Derrida, "*Pace Not(s)*," in *Parages*, trans. and ed. John P. Leavey (Stanford: Stanford University Press, 2011), 43; emphasis in the original.
[2] We need only point for evidence of this commitment to Blanchot's contribution drafting the "Declaration of the Right to Insubordination in the Algerian War," more popularly known as the

almost always through the crucible of literature—of the experience, work, and space of literature—that he framed and tested the ideas that are now associated with the signature of his thinking.

Through the emphasis he placed in his work on transgressing the boundaries that had hitherto kept literary and philosophical modes of thinking ideologically (and institutionally) apart, it is not surprising that Blanchot would come to be recognized as a pioneering architect of the poststructuralist (re-)engagement with history, politics, and culture. What made Blanchot so indispensable to the post-1968 revolution in poststructuralist thinking, as Derrida recognizes, is that readers who passed through the gauntlet of Blanchot's writing were initiated into a time and space of reflection and dialogue that fundamentally reimagined the relations that had delimited (and handicapped) the practices and possibilities of thinking *as such*. Indeed, readers of Blanchot are transported to a time bereft of time and to a space of radical exteriority wherein the border posts of signification, comprehension, and communication have not yet been firmly established. Blanchot seduces his readers with the clearest and most straightforward of prose. Once the seduction of his writing has taken effect, however, readers are very quickly overwhelmed by a tidal wave of uncertainty, fascination, and anxiety over just how to reconstruct and indeed *understand* the import and significance of what, in Blanchot's writing, they have just encountered. Reading Blanchot is to learn how to read (and think) for the first time *again*, and it is this experience of reading (and thinking) again for the first time that Derrida rightly identifies as definitive of Blanchot's always untimely contemporaneity.

Blanchot's thinking continues to demand a redrawing of the fault lines whereby literature is separated from philosophy, and both literature and philosophy are separated from the historical and political world where they acquire their (ethico-critical) significance in the first place. Blanchot's writing delivers us to a place of exile from the world, to a time outside of history where thinking *as such* begins (where it ends again and begins again), but in this beginning, in this ending, in this place beyond place and in this time outside of time, we begin to become singularly responsive to a demand—the demand of the future—that we continue thinking, a demand that taps into an infinite reserve of resistance against any and all images and concepts of closure to the

"Manifesto of the 121," which advocated for the "refusal to take arms against the Algerian people," the right "to bring help and protection to the oppressed Algerians," and the imperative to recognize that "that the cause of the Algerian people, which contributes to ruining the colonial system in a decisive way, is the cause of all free men" (PW 17).

future that awaits us. Derrida was one of the first serious readers of Blanchot to properly diagnose the indefatigable defense of the future that Blanchot's writing mounts. In this recognition, however, Derrida is cautious to praise Blanchot for so vigilantly keeping watch over the future that inscribes new meanings, new knowledges, and new dialogues as the ineluctable promise of the unknown always still yet to come. In fact, Derrida *cannot* praise Blanchot without simultaneously ascribing to his work the ambivalent distinction of prophesying knowledge or salvation of a future that can never be ours to possess; rather, it is imperative to recognize (as Derrida does) that Blanchot's thinking proceeds from a position of absolute passivity in the face of the future that it knows from the outset it can neither grasp nor tame. "If there were," Derrida explains, "which I don't believe, some pertinence to praise" Blanchot "for this, if there weren't in that a coarse attribution of mastery and if *Le pas au-delà* did not make such a metaphor out of date in advance, I would say that never have I imagined him so far in front of us as I have today."[3] We are all anachronistic in the encounter with Blanchot, but herein resides his unmistakable (perhaps timeless) appeal. Blanchot demands the impossible of his readers, which is that they become the contemporaries of a future that can be accessed only *via* the unending postponement of its arrival.

The question that Blanchot asks of the work of Samuel Beckett in *The Infinite Conversation* is therefore relevant for being asked of the work of Blanchot himself: "would we dare promise it to posterity? Would we even wish to praise it?" (IC 328). Does praise not imply that one has first learned how to read, how to understand, indeed how to master the work that is thus deemed praiseworthy? Can we praise that which we do not yet know how to read? Again like Beckett (whose name crops up often, and for good reason, in several of the chapters collected here), Blanchot is not easy to read, particularly if what we understand by reading, in the words of Blanchot, is that "often too-wise completion that risks betraying the still unaccomplished movement to which one should respond" (328). Blanchot's writings, both literary and critical, belong to that category of works, like Sade's, Mallarmé's, Hölderlin's, Kafka's, Artaud's, Char's, or Beckett's, "that go unrecognized more through praise than through disparagement: to deprecate them is to come into contact with the force of refusal that has rendered them present and also with the remoteness that gives them their measure" (328). This is why, in seeking to understand Blanchot, we should not shy away from

---

[3]  Derrida, "*Pace* Not(*s*)," 43.

affirming the (poetic) ambiguity that circulates, and in circulating enriches, Blanchot's writing. We should not, in other words, be overly wary of the refusal, in Blanchot's thinking, of investing the terms and notions with which he navigates the experience of literature, philosophy, history, and politics with the power of mastery and comprehension requisite for these to become concepts, to become complicit in the metaphysical violence of the concept *as such* (the Hegelian *Begriff*). Rather than articulating a conceptual understanding of literature, for instance, Blanchot insists on pursuing an experience of literature that would be predicated on its essential recalcitrance to conceptual capture, its strangeness in relation to cultural measures of normalcy and knowledge, and its spirit of resistance and refusal against mobilizations of power seeking to foreclose the future of reading.

Reading Blanchot requires a recalibration of what reading is and does, but the secret to the act of reading through the experience of literature as Blanchot understands it can be accomplished only by already having joined the conversation *about* literature and literary work that Blanchot's writing prescribes. When we read Blanchot's reflections on thinkers like Hegel, Heidegger, Bataille, Levinas, or Foucault, or his criticism (never simply exegetic or evaluative) of writers like Hölderlin, Mallarmé, Rilke, Kafka, Stein, Duras, Char, Celan, Artaud, or Beckett, we encounter a way of both reading and thinking that says as much about itself as it does about the texts of such modern writers and thinkers that attract its gaze in the first place. Trying to understand Blanchot is predicated on understanding Blanchot's own protocols of understanding the work of those writers and thinkers who similarly demand, as Derrida puts it *apropos* of Blanchot, to be read and reread in the future still to come of the time of their understanding. Until the time of our understanding of Blanchot arrives, in other words, a time that Blanchot's writing ceaselessly defers, all that we can do with Blanchot is strive to join him in the conversation with and about literature that his writings invite.

Indeed, this word, *conversation*, or *entretien*, is indispensable to the task of reading that Blanchot has set before us and to which the chapters in this volume respond, "for what is undertaken" in this "conversation," not only with Blanchot but also "with oneself, with the very pursuit of conversation," Jean-Luc Nancy reminds us, is "the ever-renewed relationship of speech to the *infinity* of meaning that shapes its truth."[4] In praising Blanchot we would risk putting an end to

---

[4]   http://this-space.blogspot.ca/2007/09/maurice-blanchot-1907-2003-by-jean-luc.html.

this conversation and deciding that the time of reading Blanchot as Blanchot demands to be read is over, that having arrived at an understanding of Blanchot, of the proper import and influence of his thinking, we are now in a position to assign Blanchot his rightful (though not uncontroversial) place in intellectual posterity after Hegel, Nietzsche, and Heidegger (Blanchot's avowed precursors). But Blanchot is not so easily praised. Blanchot is not so easily understood. Nevertheless, the demand of understanding Blanchot does not disappear simply because the task must be infinite, and so one of the responsibilities of reading Blanchot is to decide, to simply, impossibly decide on a way into his work, and it is the wager of this volume of chapters that we could do much worse than name *modernism* one such pathway.

Approaching an understanding of Blanchot through the double lens of understanding modernism and of understanding modernism through Blanchot as this volume of chapters pledges to do, however, is to confront from the outset the very real problem that the word "modernism" is conspicuously absent from the lexicon of Blanchot's literary and philosophical criticism. If "modernism" is absent from Blanchot's vocabulary, if such readymade concepts as "modernism" do not sit well with his understanding and critique of the literature and literary works most commonly associated with modernism, then it is perhaps because both the literature canonized by the name "modernism" and the reflections on modernist writing that are authorized under the name "Blanchot" are too overburdened by an essential relation with the experience of absence to be straightjacketed in this way by the intellectually suffocating grip of categorization. Blanchot leads us to think that perhaps a conversation with the literature of modernism would be more ably conducted through a conversation with the experience of absence in the work that the word "modernism" has come to name. Conversely, perhaps we can better understand Blanchot by understanding just how thoroughgoing is his critique of absence, just how invested his thinking and writing are in the aesthetics of the experience of absence in the time of modernity. The aesthetic task of modernism, which Blanchot enables us to articulate as the study (in and through art, literature, and also philosophy) of what is essentially hidden or disappears from view in our experiences of the world; of what is occluded in our perceptions of ourselves and of our surroundings and environments (social, political, and cultural); and of what goes unthought and unreflected— unknown and unknowable—in our consciousness and in our interpretations of the discourses and ideologies that shape (and misshape) our everyday existence, is a task demanded by writing's essential fascination with absence.

Through Blanchot, then, we can put forward a provisional definition of the work of modernism, of modernist writing and thinking, one that predicates of modernism a constitutive aesthetic relation with the (non-)experience of absence. Accordingly, it just might be possible to arrive at an understanding of modernism through Blanchot by understanding the work of absence, again through Blanchot. But presenting a concept like "absence" as in some way constitutive of Blanchot's encounter with the modernist work of literature is to risk falling back into the trap of conceptualization and foreclosing access to the intricate, limpid, always mesmerizing, always disquieting labyrinths of reflection that Blanchot's singular way of thinking about absence opens up (and into which, Orpheus-like, it bravely descends). And yet, when Blanchot interrogates literature over the question of its experience of absence, he inevitably confronts the law of what he calls "the absence of the work," "the absence of the book," which sets down a law of writing that no work can evade if it takes itself seriously as the work of literature:

> the absence of the book: the prior deterioration of the book, its dissident play with reference to the space in which it is inscribed; the preliminary dying of the book. To write: the relation to the other of every book, to what in the book would be de-scription, a scriptuary exigency outside discourse, outside language. To write at the edge of the book, outside the book.
>
> This writing outside language: a writing that would be in a kind of originary manner a language rendering impossible any object (either present or absent) of language. This writing would never be the writing of man, that is to say, never God's writing either; at most the writing of the other, of dying itself. (IC 427)

The thought of absence is in many ways constitutive (and simultaneously disintegrative) for Blanchot not only of what it means to be thinking in the space of literature, but also of what it means to be committed to (and simultaneously exiled from) what he calls, citing Stéphane Mallarmé, "*this insane game of writing*" (422; italics in the original). Whether the experience of absence or the law of the absence of the book translates for Blanchot through the aconceptual idioms of the neuter, the narrative voice, absolute negativity, the *il y a*, the outside, the essential solitude, plural speech, the fragmentary imperative, or the writing of the disaster, all of which are subjected to patient analysis by the contributors to this volume, there is a disarming consistency to how Blanchot sets about exposing absence to the infinite work of its disclosure and displacement. It is precisely this inconspicuous ethic of consistency, one oriented by a rigorous, yet always differentiated, thinking of absence and a thoroughgoing interrogation of the multiple forms of absence that recognizable works of modernism distinguish themselves by harboring, that enables the chapters in this collection to come coherently together around so capacious and precise, so fragmentary and disorienting an *oeuvre* as Blanchot's.

As with the preceding volumes in this series, *Understanding Blanchot, Understanding Modernism* is divided into three sections: "Conceptualizing Blanchot," "Blanchot and Aesthetics," and an extended "Glossary." The first section, "Conceptualizing Blanchot," includes chapters by Cosmin Toma, Hannes Opelz, James Martell, Leslie Hill, Christopher Langlois, and Aïcha Liviana Messina. These chapters offer close readings of Blanchot's more seminal critical texts, namely, *Faux Pas* (1943), *The Work of Fire* (1949), *The Space of Literature* (1955), *The Book to Come* (1959), *The Infinite Conversation* (1969), and *The Step Not Beyond* (1973), respectively. The purpose of these chapters is to pay careful attention to how Blanchot's decades-long engagement with both modern works of art and literature and the cultural, political, and historical experience of modernity is reflected in his critical-theoretical writing after 1941 (i.e., when, during the German Occupation of France, Blanchot began publishing articles of literary and intellectual criticism in the *Journal des Débats*).

Toma's opening chapter on *Faux Pas*, "Critical First Steps," begins with reference to Blanchot's cameo in Jonathan Littell's controversial masterpiece, *The Kindly Ones*, which has its protagonist, SS officer Max Aue, stumble upon Blanchot's *Faux Pas* at a bookseller in Paris during the Second World War. For Toma, this scene "subtly recalls Blanchot's questionable contributions to Maurrassian newspapers and magazines throughout the 1930's."[5] What rescues Blanchot from suffering the same ignominious fate as Heidegger or Paul de Man, or even Ezra Pound or W. B. Yeats, for that matter, as a sympathizer of far-right nationalist politics (and fascism) is that Blanchot would go on to spend a lifetime writing in order that the missteps of his political past as a contributor to (but never collaborator with) right-wing, anti-Semitic journals in France not succumb to the disastrous risk of repetition. Tactfully and refreshingly, Toma refuses to hang around for any longer than a paragraph or so on the controversy surrounding Blanchot's politico-journalistic writings in the 1930s, a question

---

[5]  Blanchot himself would later concede, in a letter or Roger Laporte dated December 24, 1992, in which he goes "immediately to the worst," that "in March 1942 one pronounces the name of Maurras (particularly when nothing in the context demands a name such as this," as Blanchot had regretfully done in an article published in the *Journal des débats* entitled "La Politique de Sainte-Beuve," "is detestable and inexcusable" (210). Maurice Blanchot, "A Letter," trans. Leslie Hill, in *Maurice Blanchot: The Demand of Writing*, ed. Carolyn Bailey Gill (London and New York: Routledge, 1996).

which has already been interrogated and all but definitively decided in favor of Blanchot in a number of previous studies of Blanchot's work during this period;[6] rather, Toma proceeds to guide us ably through what the significance of a faux pas is for Blanchot's early understanding of what the work of literature and the experience of writing entails, that is to say, of what the experience of literature *is* as the experience specifically of "*spacing*, in a post-Mallarméan and pre-Derridean sense."

Whereas Toma takes us on a comprehensive journey across the essays that Blanchot collected in *Faux Pas*, Hannes Opelz, writing on Blanchot's second collection of essays, *The Work of Fire*, devotes the bulk of his chapter, "Thus Spoke Literature," to the single and indeed singular text, "La Littérature et le droit à la mort," or "Literature and the Right to Death," that many Blanchot critics, including several appearing in this volume, take to be foundational of Blanchot's more mature understanding of how literature relates to both itself and the world. Casting this text in the role of serving far more than as a master key for understanding Blanchot's evolving conception of the work of literature for decades to come, Opelz boldly asserts, agreeing (though not without qualification) with Philippe Lacoue-Labarthe's estimation of Blanchot as "'an absolutely mythical figure of the modern writer,'" that "if Beckett's *Comment c'est* can be described as 'our epic,'" as it is by Blanchot in *The Infinite Conversation*, then "it would be no exaggeration to claim that 'La Littérature et le droit à la mort' is the epic of modern literary criticism …, literary criticism's *Zarathustra*." Opelz's decision to devote the entirety of his chapter to this one text in *The Work of Fire* is a shrewd one, for it shows readers why confronting the formal complexity of any one of Blanchot's critical writings is necessary in order to understand what that writing is trying to say, and not just about the experience of literature.

The next chapter in this volume, James Martell's "Absolute Modernism and *The Space of Literature*," opens by citing the fragment that Blanchot situates at the preliminary threshold of *The Space of Literature*. Martell uses this fragment, which begins by announcing that "A book, even a fragmentary one, has a center which attracts it," to orient his chapter around the significance for Blanchot of the mythical figure of Orpheus. For Martell, uncovering the

[6]   The two major studies that have taken aim at Blanchot and sought to discover evidence of anti-Semitism in his writing both before and after the Second World War include Jeffrey Mehlman, *Legacies of Anti-Semitism in France* (Minneapolis: University of Minnesota Press, 1983) and Steven Ungar, *Scandal and Aftereffect: Blanchot and France since 1930* (Minneapolis: University of Minnesota Press, 1995).

"absolute modernism" of *The Space of Literature*—"absolute" construed "in the etymological," but also fragmentary "sense of separation (*ab-solvo*)," as Toma had already demonstrated—hinges around this provocation of searching for the putative center of the experience and work of literature, for the object of the gaze of Orpheus that refuses to capitulate to the death and disappearance of Eurydice. While Martell does not waver on figuring the myth of Orpheus, particularly as Blanchot understands it, as "the mysterious origin of poetry," as poetry's "'sacrificial point'" of origin, it is ultimately the figure of Eurydice that intrigues Martell the most, not least because it is through Eurydice that something like the *absolute* modernism of *The Space of Literature* is exposed. Martell's reflections on the spectral presence of Eurydice in *The Space of Literature* lead him to conclude that, Eurydice notwithstanding, "the absence of a female voice in *The Space of Literature* is conspicuous, and troubling." Troubling though it is, Martell suggests, such an absence is nevertheless symptomatic of what renders *The Space of Literature* a work of absolute modernism, for better or worse, that is to say, the failure on the part of Blanchot that paradoxically rescues his work from the pitfalls of totality. Thus it is, for Martell, that "the constant displacement of the centre is what constitutes *The Space of Literature* as a work of absolute modernism."

In his chapter on *The Book to Come*, Leslie Hill accounts, in a way that counterintuitively reinforces Martell's reading of *The Space of Literature*, for why such periodizing categories as "modern," "modernity," and "modernism" tend to be rejected by Blanchot. For Blanchot, Hill claims, these categories, that is, categories that Fredric Jameson proposes we cannot do without in reflecting on intellectual and cultural history,[7] "were irretrievably and unacceptably teleological. They were, in other words, fundamentally prescriptive, and at some risk of entirely misunderstanding or misrepresenting what future or futurity lay beyond literature's present horizon." By distancing Blanchot principally from both Jean-Paul Sartre and Roland Barthes (and also Hegel) on the question of accounting for just what it is that makes modern literature

---

[7] Jameson would concur even as he would disagree with the conclusion to be drawn from this reading of Blanchot's deep antipathy toward periodization. Indeed, Blanchot's antipathy toward periodization is partly responsible for why Jameson accuses Blanchot of promoting the idea of the ahistorical autonomy of literature by replicating it "in the form of the existential or the political, which promotes it to something like a supreme value …, leaving an ambiguous situation in which modernist affirmation can still be endowed with political or existential justification when need be, but where existential commitment and political praxis to come (May '68) are somehow already suspiciously 'aestheticized', as Benjamin put it in a memorable pre-war moment" (188). Fredric Jameson, *A Singular Modernity: Essay on the Ontology of the Present* (London and New York: Verso, 2002).

"modern," particularly in the cultural milieu of postwar Europe and France, Hill is able to uncover the idea, quintessentially Blanchotesque, that "literature's essence was disappearance." The understanding of literature as the experience of disappearance, or absence, has implications not only for the act of writing, but for the act of reading and thinking about literature too. By predicating literature as disappearance, thereby separating literature from its identity as an object present to the gaze of aesthetic or theoretical reflection, Blanchot presents literary theory with a perhaps insurmountable problem. This "is why it is misleading," Hill contends, "to consider Blanchot in any sense to be a theorist of literature, since for Blanchot there is no theoretical object that is identifiable as 'literature' 'as such' which might then be theorised. Literary theory, in this sense, is but a metaphysical aberration."

In my own chapter focusing on Blanchot's *The Infinite Conversation*, "Literature Outside the Law," I follow Blanchot through several of the more prominent encounters in this text with such towering thinkers and writers about the experience of modernity as Schlegel and Novalis, Nietzsche and Mallarmé, Kafka and Bataille, and Breton and Char. Blanchot is interested in these figures because he finds in their work the experience of what writing can and should be made to do when and where it coincides with historical crisis. Simply put, my chapter frames Blanchot's understanding of the ethico-historical task of writing as one that is first and foremost responsible (and responsive) to the unknown. *The Infinite Conversation* is where Blanchot becomes explicit about the responsibility of modern literature to adopt the form of the fragment in defense not only of the unknown but also of the future from which the unknown *as such* originates. By reading Blanchot reading the writers and texts that he sees responding most intimately to the crises of modernity, particularly in the twentieth century, my chapter seeks to understand why the question of the future, which doubles for Blanchot as the question of the unknown, occupies such a central place in Blanchot's thinking about both the ethical and formal imperatives of literature and the work of writing.

Following my contribution on *The Infinite Conversation* is Aïcha Liviana Messina's chapter on *The Step Not Beyond*, " 'Exacerbating the Self-Critical Tendency': Ethics and Critique in *Le pas au-delà*," which questions Blanchot's insistence on the disappearance (or erasure) of the "self" in philosophical "self-criticism" over its involvement in both the metaphysical and epistemological demands of modernism. For such theorists of modernism as Clement Greenberg, Messina reminds us, the bourgeoning "self-critical tendency" of modern art and literature at the beginning of the eighteenth century owes a debt to Kant, the "first real modernist," in Greenberg's view, but only insofar as this tendency is understood in terms of consolidating the epistemo-metaphysical power of the self in relation to the philosophical performance of self-criticism. For Blanchot, on the other hand, if the distinction of the "first real modernist" belongs to any one thinker, then it would have to be to Socrates, not Kant. As Messina explains, it was Socrates who first intuited that writing and thinking are predicated on the death and not the empowerment of the self. But whereas Socrates is content with thinking the negativity of death as the origin of critical self-dialogue, Blanchot restlessly seeks to understand death as the beginning of a truly ethical "encounter with alterity." The emphasis Messina places on the (non-)phenomenon of death assures that her chapter will be required reading for understanding how and why writing and dying are inextricably linked in the act of thinking as Blanchot performs it.

The second section of *Understanding Blanchot, Understanding Modernism*, "Blanchot and Aesthetics," begins with Jean-Michel Rabaté's "*Nescio Vos*: The Pathos of Unknowing in *When The Time Comes*," the only chapter in the volume to engage in such depth with one of Blanchot's fictional *récits*. Rabaté reads *When the Time Comes* as a narrative that is in continuous approach of "the limits of hospitality." Readers will be interested to learn from Rabaté that Blanchot relied on memories from his own biography, and particularly from his friendship with Bataille and Denise Rollin, to interweave a series of riddles about the experiences of writing, desire, ecstasy, and death (and mourning) into the complex, "tenuous plot" of *When the Times Comes*. Moreover, by figuring *When the Time Comes* (1951) as "the central panel in [Blanchot's] novelistic triptych, next to *Death Sentence* (1948) and *The One Who Was Standing Apart From Me* (1953)," Rabaté accomplishes far more than explicating the riddles of just this one narrative; rather, he is able to introduce readers into the ways that Blanchot's abstract reflections on the experience of literature influenced the composition of several of his more straightforwardly literary texts (fascinatingly peculiar though they no doubt are), obliging us to remember that when Blanchot comments philosophically on the work of literature, he does so always from the perspective of one who has lived this experience (of writing, but perhaps also of dying) intimately.

After noting Blanchot's debt to Kafka for the writing of *Thomas the Obscure* (1941) and *Aminadab* (1942) as narratives exploring questions of alienation and authority, writing and shame, and the representational failures of symbol and allegory, Michael Holland, in his chapter "Writing as *Überfluss*: Blanchot's Reading of Kafka's *Diaries*," proceeds to provide readers with a characteristically penetrating analysis of why Kafka, specifically, "becomes a regular point of reference in Blanchot's critical writing" after the Second World War. Kafka is exceptional for Blanchot, according to Holland, because his writing, whether in diary or novel form, excludes the possibility that literature not be an all-consuming ordeal for maintaining the subjectivity of the writer, day and night. Both the originality and indispensability of Holland's chapter to this volume more generally become strikingly apparent as soon as he enters into the discussion about why Blanchot opted to privilege Kafka's *Diaries* over his novels. The reason why "Blanchot will return repeatedly to the *Diaries*, pursuing his resistance to Kafka's use of *I* at one level, while at another, discovering in the *Diaries* the promise of a new and original literary mode," is that in this phenomenon of indecision that surrounds the belonging of the "I" in Kafka's writing and worldview, Blanchot discovers "something akin to a gasp, a stutter, a cry of simultaneous agony and relief at being able to bring suffering into language." For Holland, it is difficult to adequately understand Blanchot without also understanding why Kafka remains so pivotal to his evolving reflections on the experience of literature from *The Work of Fire* to *The Writing of the Disaster*.

The next chapter in this volume, Kevin Hart's "'I Hear My Destiny in the Rustling of an Oak': Blanchot's Char," approaches another of the writers who Blanchot gives pride of place in his reflections on modern literature and the writers most adept at responding to the weighty demands on writing in the time of modernity, René Char. Hart observes that while Blanchot may have easily turned to "Char's collaborations with Braque, Kandinsky, Klee, Matisse, Miró, and Picasso, now all secure figures in the canon of modernist visual art," as evidence of Char's responsiveness to the historico-cultural demands of modernism, or to "Char's schooling in surrealism, a movement [Blanchot] greatly prizes, as a prime credential for his standing in the pantheon of the avant-garde or as a representative of what we would tend to call these days 'late modernism,'" the truth is that, for Blanchot, according to Hart, the contemporary value of Char is figured best "by way of the philosophical, ancient and modern, and the political, with reference to the sacred." Blanchot finds in Char a kindred intellectual spirit who is fiercely committed to severing our ontological relation with regressive ideals of unity and exclusionary images of being. Through Char, writing after the Second World War, and after Charles De Gaulle's extraordinary, but troubling, ascendency to power in France, Blanchot detects a new destiny (understood "as that which diverts from every destination") for poetry, one that is neither celebratory nor powerful, neither monumental nor revelatory; rather, poetry inherits the work of the sacred (and is thus reliant on sacrifice of the self, the "je" or "I"), which is undertaken in order not to manifest but to acknowledge what approaches from outside presence or power, and in acknowledging what approaches from the outside, offer the chance of breathing new life into it, into that which "the known and the ordered have long hidden."

Jonathan Boulter, in his chapter "Neutral Conditions: Blanchot, Beckett, and the Space of Writing," sets for himself the straightforward (not to say simple) task of figuring "the neutral" in the work of Blanchot and Beckett. Needless to say, the straightforwardness of this task is quickly undermined by the inherent difficulty of explication that "the neutral" poses, for part of what makes "the neutral" so significant to Blanchot's thinking, and above all about literature, is that it points to what simultaneously lures and defies signification and presence. Or, as Boulter defines it in the opening paragraph of his chapter, "the neutral is a category of being that can only ever mark the effacement of ideas like 'category' and 'being'; the neutral is not ever quite like Heidegger's notion of the 'placeholder of being,' but as a space of neither one thing nor another (as Blanchot reminds us is the etymology of the word), the neutral never quite is, never quite is not." The value of leveraging "the neutral" for understanding Blanchot and for reading Beckett, and particularly Beckett's *How It Is*, is readily apparent across the entirety of Boulter's chapter. Boulter aids readers in considering that what Blanchot means by "the neutral" occupies nothing less than "a critical place as the (aporetic) grounds of writing," the burden of which it is the honor of Beckett to have accommodated in and through the narratives and narrative voices of his texts. Beckett is therefore an unavoidable traveling companion of Blanchot as both are in search of the point where writing, in the words of Blanchot cited by Boulter, "is put to the test of impossibility. There," the place where Beckett's books are written, where they originate and where their writing tends, "language does not speak, it is; in it nothing begins, nothing is said, but it is always new and always begins again."

Before proceeding to explore the centrality of "the image" to Blanchot's reflections on literature and modernity, Jeff Fort, in his chapter "The Look of Nothingness: Blanchot and the Image," contends that if Blanchot's postwar work "up to the early 1960s," and here he is thinking specifically about *The Space of Literature* and *The Book to Come*, that is, Blanchot's critical writing prior to the more fragmentary experiments of *The Infinite Conversation, The*

*Step Not Beyond*, and *The Writing of the Disaster*, as well as Blanchot's postwar novelistic and "recitical" output (*Thomas the Obscure, Aminadab*, and *The Most High*), "can be said to fall within some lineage of modernism, this is because it stretches the latter's terms and limits to an extreme point of rupture, if not outright destruction." Fort situates Blanchot here at the terminal point of modernist anxiety over whether or not its signature works can discover or produce images that would not be immediately co-opted into the dialectical regressions of technological reproducibility, or "captured in the egological gears of psychology," and in the process is able to distinguish Blanchot from other philosophers interested in the problem of the image as a distinct problem (if not *the* problem) of modernity, most notably Sartre and Heidegger (but also Walter Benjamin, however obliquely). The starting point for Blanchot in the time of modernity, accordingly, which Fort demonstrates convincingly as well as provocatively throughout, can be understood as the search for "the possibility of such an image, or inversely its fatality."

Allan Pero's chapter, "The Call of the Anterior: Blanchot, Lacan, and the Death Drive," begins with surprise that so little has been written on either the affinities or differences between Blanchot and Jacques Lacan given their close intellectual and geographical proximity in postwar France. To make up for this missed opportunity, Pero proceeds to demonstrate that "Blanchot's well-known fascination with death, as a site of (im)possibility, of limit experience, of an experience veiled by pulsions like repetition, by the blandishments of errancy, finds its intellectual antecedents not only in writers like Mallarmé, Sade, Levinas, and Bataille, but also in psychoanalysis." For a volume of chapters devoted to modernism, the value of Pero's approach to Blanchot cannot be overstated given the impact psychoanalytic studies has had (and continues to have) on the contemporary study of modernism, particularly through the psychoanalytic discourse on mourning and trauma. Inspired by Blanchot's fascination with the myth of Orpheus and Eurydice, and thus resonating in interesting ways with Martell and Fort's contributions, Pero advances the idea "that mourning is an ethical duty that one cannot avoid." On the way to uncovering what he rightly identifies as "one of the profound truths" of the Orphic myth, its ethical demand for the impossible work of mourning, the overcoming of death through desire, Pero takes readers meticulously through several other points of contact between Blanchot and Lacanian psychoanalysis: death's space and the death drive; the space of writing and the space of analysis; *l'autrui* and *objet a*. Bringing Blanchot into proximity with Lacan in this way profitably exposes readers to new angles of entry into Blanchot's critical writings, as well as Lacan's, that will do much to further our understanding of their significance (actual and potential) for both posing and responding to questions of desire, death, law, transgression, ethics, and mourning that remain pertinent to modernist studies today.

For the final chapter in this section, "'Unmade According to his Image' or, Night for Day: Blanchot and the Blacknesses of Cinema Figure," Kevin Bell makes an impassioned, lyrical defense of the need to consult Blanchot, not for the all too commonplace insight that "we finally know nothing of death, aside from the bar of finitude it imposes on the living," but for the far more disquieting intuition, interwoven throughout the fragmentary crevices of Blanchot's writing, that "we appear to know even less of freedom." In order to account for why Blanchot would be an indispensable interlocutor in the always ongoing dialogue over how modern and contemporary literature and art are to represent spaces of radical freedom and oppression without trampling all over the essential unrepresentability that adheres to such experiences (the one disappointingly rare, the other all too tragically prevalent), Bell juxtaposes "several of Blanchot's critical instruments" with "experimental constellations of black-diasporic film and writing": Chris Marker's essayistic documentary *Sans Soleil*, Christopher Harris's documentary *Still/Here*, Claudia Rankine's multi-genre text *Don't Let Me Be Lonely*, and George Jackson's prison letters, *Soledad Brother*. Readers will come away from Bell's chapter, and perhaps from *Understanding Blanchot, Understanding Modernism* as a whole as well, knowing that the time of Blanchot's thinking is not now nor has it ever been past. Blanchot, Bell insists, echoing Derrida and in unison with all the contributors to this volume, is still ahead of us, pointing the way, without knowing the destination, to an experience of radical freedom that inheres in the unknown future from where the ethical call of the unknown and the other *as such* originates. When Blanchot reads and thinks about the work and experience of literature, in other words, it is this call, above all others, that he works so doggedly, if not impossibly, to articulate.

Part One

# Conceptualizing Blanchot

# 1

# Critical First Steps: On *Faux Pas*

Cosmin Toma

On leave in Nazi-occupied Paris after miraculously surviving the Battle of Stalingrad, Max Aue, the protagonist of Jonathan Littell's novel *The Kindly Ones*, picks up a copy of Maurice Blanchot's *Faux Pas* while rummaging through the booksellers' stalls along the Seine. Aue, a Franco-German SS officer, tellingly singles out the names of Louis-Ferdinand Céline and Pierre Drieu la Rochelle among the books on display, further observing that "they were openly selling Kafka, Proust, and even Thomas Mann; permissiveness seemed to be the rule."[1] In keeping with *The Kindly Ones*' transgressive aims, the remark is as provocative as it is thought-provoking. Indeed, where are we to situate Blanchot among this motley assortment of figures? When Aue describes him as "a critic from the *Journal des débats*, some of whose articles I had read with interest before the war,"[2] the latter clarification subtly recalls Blanchot's questionable contributions to Maurrassian newspapers and magazines throughout the 1930s. Yet insofar as *The Work of Fire, The Space of Literature, The Book to Come*, and *The Infinite Conversation* contain penetrating commentaries of Kafka, Proust, and Mann, Littell's vignette kindles a vague sense of malaise, one that Blanchot's name still occasionally elicits to this day.

It is difficult, when retracing the beginnings of Blanchot's oeuvre and its thorny relationship with politics,[3] to avoid remarking that his first book of criticism bears a rather suggestive title. Read in this light, *Faux Pas* is a palinode, an avowal that mistakes have been made that will not be repeated. After all, a faux pas is a tactless blunder, an embarrassing gesture that

---

[1] Jonathan Littell, *The Kindly Ones*, trans. C. Mandell (Toronto: McClelland & Stewart, 2010), 499.

[2] Ibid., 499.

[3] For a recent discussion of Blanchot's politics, see the "*Politique*" section of Michael Holland, *Avant dire: Essais sur Blanchot* (Paris: Hermann, 2015).

sometimes leaves an indelible stain on one's psyche—or one's public image. In French, however, it is simultaneously more and less than that. Besides its figurative meaning, it denotes a literal misstep, conjuring up the Beckettian trope of someone aimlessly ambling along a purgatorial path, unable to secure a lasting foothold, yet stirring still. Its significance is thus (at least) twofold: as a *gradus, Faux Pas* implies that error is the inevitable price of self-awareness; as a deliberate reprise of said error, it attenuates the phrase's sententious connotations, neutralizing them, as it were. On the face of it, however, the value judgment passed on these articles, all of which had previously appeared in *Le Journal des débats* (with the notable exception of "From Anxiety to Language,"[4] conceived as a prelude), is frankly disconcerting: have they not been handpicked by the author himself? Were they merely the least unseemly of his lapses? And now that they have been gathered in book form, stamped with Gallimard's seal of approval, can we credibly continue labelling them "missteps"?

Much like the later notion of "disaster," which "ruins everything, all the while leaving everything intact" (WD 1), that of "faux pas" is a *pas de côté*, a sidestep that forces us to reexamine our immediate understanding of its meaning. More specifically, it exemplifies Blanchot's uncanny grasp of negation beyond its Hegelian-Kojèvian framework, foreshadowing the neuter. Etymologically speaking, *faux pas* presupposes the erasure of negation by negation, the transition from *ne* to *pas* as preferred negatory adverb in the French language, as though every "no" were also an "on"[5]—or perhaps neither. The *pas* of negation can therefore be construed as a false (*faux*) "not," with the proviso that the quality of falseness is itself subverted by this para-dialectical mode of thinking. And the subterranean semantic network *Faux Pas* adumbrates becomes more abyssal still when we consider its homophony with *faut pas*, a colloquial elision of *il ne faut pas* (you/one must not), where the vanishing *il* mutely points toward Emmanuel Levinas's *il y a*[6] no less than toward the pivotal role of the *il* alongside the *on* in Blanchot's writings on the neuter. As such, *Faux Pas* is both a solemn commandment and its parody,

---

[4]  Charlotte Mandell translates *angoisse* as "anguish," which strikes me as excessive. *Angoisse* is a more versatile term than either "anguish" or "anxiety," but the latter appropriately emphasizes its everydayness.

[5]  Samuel Beckett relentlessly picks this palindrome apart in *Worstward Ho*.

[6]  Levinas notably says of the *il y a* (there is) that it is a "fear of Being" rather than a "fear for Being." In Emmanuel Levinas, *Existence and Existents*, trans. A. Lingis (The Hague: Martinus Nijhoff, 1978), 20.

the harsh letter of the law and its more lenient spirit, an injunction and an infraction, bringing to mind Blanchot's contemporaneous novels *Aminadab* and *The Most High*.

***

Although *Faux Pas* ostensibly doubles down on some of Blanchot's missteps by turning them into a book—with all the architectonic unity, coherence, and staying power such an appellation entails, including when it is disavowed—it makes no secret of its journalistic origins. Even as they seek literature's nocturnal core, these disparate texts remain beholden to the idiom of day, which at this point in Blanchot's career refers not only to the demands of an ever-shifting present but also to industriousness and operativeness in general. A double bind is at work here: on the one hand, literary criticism must defer to the atemporal language of night[7] if it is to do justice to literature's singularity; on the other hand, no critical piece can shirk the task of shedding light on the work's secret, of transposing art into the productive discourse of a given time and place. *Faux Pas* thus marks the onset of a tension that informs almost all of Blanchot's writings, instantiating what Jacques Derrida would later call "the undecidable."

Blurring the lines between literature as *res (literaria)*—the object of a public debate, be it aesthetic or political or other still—and literature as *Ding an sich*—the work of art in itself—*Faux Pas* recalls early German Romanticism's willingness to collapse the distinction between poetical and critical language, prefiguring the fragmentary synthesis attempted in *The Step Not Beyond* and *The Writing of Disaster*. At times, Blanchot's commentaries lead us to literature's *imagined center* even more readily than the literary works they examine, undermining the very divide between night and day on which so much of his pre-1960s work operates (TO 3). Granted, it seems natural to think of *Thomas the Obscure*—whose extended, maze-like first version was published in 1941, two years before *Faux Pas*—as a creature of blackest night, utterly alien to a piece such as "The Criticism of Albert Thibaudet," which seeks to elucidate the very act of elucidation. Yet despite their obvious differences, it is perhaps a mere question of degree (*gradus*), as if a few steps in either direction could tip the scale toward the "literary" or the "critical," respectively. *Faux Pas* thus bears witness to a series of attempts at subverting these boundaries by writing *literary* literary

---

[7] In *The Space of Literature*, Blanchot argues that "to write is to surrender to the fascination of time's absence" (30).

criticism, so to speak, even if the literariness of literature may well turn out to be an eidolon, devoid of consistency or essence, leaving us in the throes of an unbearably ambiguous predicament.

"Do not separate the no from the yes," advises "Speak, you too," a poem by Paul Celan[8] that Blanchot would later translate in *A Voice from Elsewhere* as "The Last to Speak." Somewhat anachronistically, the poet's suggestion can be said to govern *Faux Pas* as a whole, starting with "From Anxiety to Language," one of Blanchot's key meditations on ambiguity. A threshold of sorts, it shapes our reading of the *membra disjecta* that follow, all of which lie somewhere between affirmation and negation, arranged according to a half-orderly, half-chaotic compositional principle. In addition to "From Anxiety to Language," which also lends its title to the volume's opening section, we are offered "Digressions on Poetry," "Digressions on the Novel," and "A Miscellany of Digressions." Roughly speaking, the sequence goes from philosophy to poetry to the novel before its ostensible *telos* fizzles out, as if the goal were to set up a semblance of systematicity the better to unravel it. After all, the original title of the fourth and final section is "Digressions sans suite," a quasi-tautology that one could also translate as "Non sequiturs," underscoring the book's ultimately fragmentary provenance. Waltzing to and fro, from yes to no and the obverse, these steps and missteps also augur *The Step Not Beyond*'s more arduous rhythms, hinting at a writerly music that, although rarely identified as such, goes a long way toward explaining the fascination exerted by Blanchot's anonymous, yet inimitable, sense of phrasing.

In writing, such musically oriented effects are often lauded, perhaps paradoxically, for their literariness—a trait that has remained inextricably tied to the author's legacy in no small part due to the ubiquitous autobiographical sketch appended to his publications[9]—yet "From Anxiety to Language" almost never calls literature by its proper name, and when it does, its implied working definition is unusually broad, even porous. While it is true that *Faux Pas* primarily discusses works that are widely deemed to be literary, it also teases out the potential literariness of *corpora* that do not traditionally fall under this umbrella, such as those of Meister Eckhart, Leonardo da Vinci, or Alain. Indeed, if literature is to be literary at all, it must run the risk of dissolving into vaster

---

[8]  Paul Celan, *Selections*, ed. Pierre Joris (Berkeley and Los Angeles: University of California Press, 2005), 54.

[9]  "Maurice Blanchot, novelist and critic, was born in 1907. His life is entirely devoted to literature and to the silence that is proper to it (or to him)."

waters, even as it resists its absorption by envisioning itself, to quote Jean-Luc Nancy and Philippe Lacoue-Labarthe, as an absolute, that is, as that which cannot be subsumed into a greater whole—into *relation* as such.

Presaging *The Space of Literature*'s post-Rilkean exploration of the work of art's solitude, Blanchot kicks off "From Anxiety to Language" by reflecting on what it means to write the words "I am alone," noting that "it is comical to be aware of one's solitude while addressing a reader, making use of means that keep one from being alone" (FP 1). There is thus a sense in which language radically precludes isolation, no doubt because it appears to be the most "correlationist" (as Quentin Meillassoux would have it) medium of all, a space where absence is continuously woven into presence and presence into absence.[10] But if there is no denying language's reticular sway, perhaps some degree of withdrawal is achievable *within* its mesh. Indeed, such a claim becomes defendable once we dispense with the expectation that language be a conveyor of unadulterated truth. Might one not suggest, instead, that speech's essential mendacity—its literariness—gestures toward a different kind of truth, albeit one that is a mere shadow of itself?[11] Indeed, in this penumbra, the act of writing "I am alone" flutters between self-annulment (the writer is never alone) and apotheosis (no one is more alone than the writer), unable to settle on one or the other.

The solution to this dilemma is seemingly simple: "the writer could of course not write" (FP 5). Yet silence, whether forced or willed, solves nothing. On the contrary, Blanchot's claim is that withdrawal requires a foil in order to fulfill its solitary essence (or lack thereof)—a split that is exemplarily brought about by the act of writing. Even the Latin *absolutus*—that is, that which has been freed from relation—is a pleonasm of sorts, since the three morphemes that constitute it—*ab*, *se*, and *luo*—all hinge on the selfsame loosening, as though absolute singularity could not express itself outside of what *The Infinite Conversation* calls "plural speech" (IC 80). And this radical ambiguity, which distantly echoes Blanchot's childhood realization, retold in *The Writing of the Disaster*, that the sky's superficiality and transparency secrete no more and no less than the nothingness of all there is, is in evidence as early as *Faux Pas*, giving his work its characteristically neutral heft. To put it differently, writing is *spacing*, in a post-Mallarméan and pre-Derridean sense.

---

[10]    See Quentin Meillassoux, *After Finitude: An Essay on the Necessity of Contingency*, trans. Ray Brassier (London and New York: Continuum, 2008).

[11]    As Paul Celan writes: "Speaks True, Who Speaks Shadows," in Celan, *Selections*, 54.

To write "I am alone" is thus to self-reflexively refract the act of writing "I am alone," to engender a *Doppelgänger* not only in the person of the writer, who is consequently dispossessed of his I, but also in the notion of aloneness itself, which now oscillates between word (a relation) and thing (the absolute). Much like Beckett, Blanchot argues that every entity conceals a pseudo-couple: "it is not the one who is alone who experiences the feeling of being alone; this monster of desolation needs another for his desolation to have meaning" (FP 2). And in the writer's case, this partition isn't merely incidental, since there appears to be a privileged connection between the act of writing, the anxiety of solitude, and their *dédoublement*. Indeed, as Heidegger had already intuited in "What Is Metaphysics?," *Angst* is the state where nothing is likeliest to manifest itself as a thing, where the tension between affirmation and negation reaches its apex—a coming and going, "from impenetrable self to impenetrable unself by way of neither," that Blanchot believes to be characteristic of literary writing.[12] The fundamental distinction between *rien* (nothing) and the *res* (thing) from which it stems is thus abolished, anticipating Beckett's *Three Dialogues*[13]: "the writer finds himself in the increasingly ludicrous condition of having nothing to write, of having no means with which to write it, and of being constrained by the utter necessity of always writing it" (3). Better yet: it is *because* the writer is tongue-tied that language can be fictively liberated as literature.

Unlike Heidegger before him, Blanchot does not ground his inquiry in language or thought, but in the groundlessness of writing as such. On the one hand, it goes without saying that anxiety can befall any *Dasein*, this unsettled being that we are insofar as our being is always in question. On the other hand, Blanchot claims that there is a fundamental difference between the way a cobbler and a writer experience anxiety, respectively. While the former would be hard-pressed to describe his anxiety "as the condition of a man who mends shoes," the latter "sometimes seems strangely as if anguish [*angoisse*] were part of his occupation and, even more, as if the fact of writing so deepens anguish that it attaches itself to him rather than to any other sort of person" (3–4). In truth, the accursed privilege afforded to the writer by Blanchot is highly debatable,

---

12   Samuel Beckett, *The Complete Short Prose, 1929–1989*, ed. S. E. Gontarski (New York: Grove Press, 1995), 258.

13   Beckett speaks of "the expression that there is nothing to express, nothing with which to express, nothing from which to express, together with the obligation to express" (142). In Samuel Beckett, *Disjecta: Miscellaneous Writings and a Dramatic Fragment*, ed. Ruby Cohn (London: John Calder, 1983).

and not just in relation to other kinds of artisans or artists.[14] Regardless, his insistence on anxiety, as well as on the ambiguity it begets, speaks volumes about the way he conceives the relationship between the writer and his work. Like anxiety, the work "is this very indifference to that which creates it, although it may seem at the same time to rivet its victim to the cause it has chosen" (4). Perhaps counterintuitively, the ambiguity of anxiety and the anxiety of ambiguity thus originate from the same apathy, that is, from the work of art's neutral (no) thingness, somewhere between *res* and *rien*.

It is the very same indifference or neutrality that underlies art's inhuman autonomy, the fact that it is in a world of its own, indifferent to its own (in) difference, and all the more moving for it. Blanchot begins by framing this question conventionally, in terms of usefulness versus uselessness.[15] Indeed, if the literary work of art is indifferent to the aims imposed upon it by its author or reader, it cannot be reduced to the status of a mere tool. This is an old argument, of course, which in the French tradition notably hearkens back to the concept of *l'art pour l'art* (art for art's sake). Rather than declare the issue resolved, however, Blanchot exacerbates its complexity by focusing on what he describes as "a profitable operation of transformation of energy" whereby "the author has produced something more than himself" (6). Yet Blanchot does not simply theorize art as sheer excess: echoing the work of his friend, Georges Bataille, he also intimates the pure loss that such a transformation fatally impels. Since he is given over to anxiety—according to the etymology, an ever-straitening path—the writer is unable to distinguish the surfeit of energy he produces from the black hole into or out of which it is channeled. As such, the Kafkan promise of a soteriological instance of writing that could absolve him of his uselessness is bound to be ruined by the ever-renewed, dread-inducing indifference of anxiety; by its eerily aesthetic, overwhelming absence of destination. Once again, from anxiety's oppressively neutral perspective, everything appears to be nothing and nothing inexplicably manifests itself as a thing.

---

[14]  The composer's or the painter's anxiety can also be a direct consequence of the artistic process. And to dismiss the cobbler so swiftly is facile.

[15]  A resolutely "modern" distinction according to Blanchot: "On this point modern aesthetics has brought us all kinds of insights. To summarize them, in two words, it is enough to recall that beside language, as a value of practical exchange, one supposes another form of language that does not tend toward action, that is not determined by meaning and that, rather than the useful substitute of an idea or an object, is a sum of physical effects and patent possibilities. That is clear, too clear" (FP 137). This "modern" take is self-evident, yet overly so—Blanchot isn't entirely comfortable with the term.

Even as it bewilderingly enables them, ambiguity thus halts all projects by default, including aesthetic ones. We cannot outdistance the throw of the die, which always precedes the work in a Heideggerian sense; it is as *geworfen* as we are, just as it reminds us of our own *Geworfenheit*. Moreover, like the sky's pellucid emptiness, this revelation of arbitrariness is itself arbitrary, hinging on pure chance or *hasard*.[16] This is why Mallarmé speaks of (literary) writing as a *jeu insensé* (senseless game): it is a nerve-wracking instance of play wherein "the feeling of the uselessness of what I am doing is linked to this other feeling that nothing is more serious."[17] Every subject thus "become[s] a player who has a vested interest in playing and who by this interest in the game makes the game impossible (it is no longer a game)" (FP 13). Seemingly ludic, even ludicrous, in nature, the ambiguity and uselessness of literary writing turn out to be nothing less than a grave ontological problem, akin to what Meillassoux would later call "the necessity of contingency."[18] And works of literature are perhaps the most emblematically undecidable sites of all:

> Does the absurd page, by dint of being sensible, actually make sense? Perhaps it doesn't have the least sense; how are we to decide? Its character is linked to a change of perspective, and there is nothing in it that allows one to fix it in a definitive light. (One can always say that its meaning lies in allowing the two interpretations, in coloring itself sometimes as good sense, sometimes as non-sense, and thus that it can be determined as a nondetermination between these two possibilities; but even that betrays its structure, for one cannot say that its truth is to be sometimes this or sometimes that; on the contrary, it is possible that it is only this or only that; it imperiously demands this choice; it adds to the indeterminacy in which one would like to grasp it the claim to be absolutely determined by one of the two extremes between which it oscillates). (FP 9)

To recapitulate, if a given ambiguous statement is made up of two opposing terms, we may focus on their juxtaposition in and of itself, but in so doing we fail to do justice to the antagonism that drives them. Strife is insuperable: if ambiguity is to occur "as such," it must be actively threatened from within by both of its individual components. In other words, there is always an *absolute* chance that the "solution" to the predicament of ambiguity is to be found in one of its two terms, exclusively. "Gregarious loneliness," for example, is

---

[16]  The word—French for "chance," more or less—happens to be haunted by the Arabic *az-zahr*, which means "dice." And in German, *geworfen* is cognate with *Würfel*, which also means "dice."

[17]  Stephane Mallarmé, *Œuvres complètes* (t. 2), ed. Bertrand Marchal (Paris: Gallimard, 2003), 23.

[18]  Meillassoux, *After Finitude*.

necessarily more than an oxymoron, since we can never wholly dismiss the prospect of loneliness trumping gregariousness and vice versa, like when we fall for Joseph Jastrow's duck–rabbit illusion. As in Beckett's fiction, whenever a zero-sum game is set up, it is quickly undercut by an unforeseen imbalance, by the "neither this … nor that" of the neuter, which ensures both the system's eternal return and its continuous failure, the ever-lasting reign of ambiguity and its imminent ruin.

***

Although "From Anxiety to Language" decisively weds the ambiguity of anxiety to the experience of writing, the pieces that follow—sequentially if not chronologically—bear the mark of a hesitation on Blanchot's part. Granted, he tends to devote his attention to writers or at the very least to thinkers who are noted for their sustained interest in language. After all, his own writing style, with its studiedly paradoxical turns of phrase, is inseparable from his thought. Nevertheless, his early interest in mysticism betrays a longing for a "genuinely" extra-linguistic experience. Søren Kierkegaard's diary, for example, is primarily taken as an opportunity to discuss the author's life, which Blanchot regards, following Paul Valéry, as that of "an extraordinary mind [*esprit*]" (17). Although he highlights the significance of writing for the Danish philosopher's autobiographical process of revelation and dissimulation, it remains an incidental issue in *Faux Pas*. Likewise, it is the transcendental equivocality of Meister Eckhart's sermons that speaks to Blanchot, regardless of their textual status. Continuing in this theological vein, the short piece on William Blake's *The Marriage of Heaven and Hell* readily paints the poet as an *esprit* endowed with a superior understanding of ambiguity, confirming once again Valéry's hold on Blanchot at this point in his career. And even his review of Bataille's *The Inner Experience* describes the latter as an "authentic translation" (41), as though writing were but a means to a spiritual end.

This neo-Romantic yearning for that which lies beyond the veil of words also haunts the subsequent pieces on Proust and Rilke, yet a notable shift occurs here. While *In Search of Lost Time* shows us that "art is not possible without a nonrational revelation" (42), his epiphany only matters insofar as it impels the work's ulterior advent. The author's "mysterious states" are hence to be understood as stimuli, not as ends in themselves: they "seem to have been offered to him only so that this work could be written" (46). The mystical revelation is now one with its work, in every sense of the term. Similarly, although Blanchot notes that it is legitimate to speak of Rilke in conjunction with esoteric symbolists such as Stefan George, Gabriele d'Annunzio, Maurice Maeterlinck and William Butler Yeats, he reminds us that, much like Proust's narrator, Malte Laurids Brigge, can only make himself known through his notebooks, including when he is unable to transcribe his observations. Indeed, Blanchot notes this failure—"he rejects words that unravel and meanings that come undone" (52)—and implicitly condemns the protagonist's unwillingness to give himself completely to the experience of death that further note-keeping would purportedly precipitate.[19] The inability to write is thus analyzed from the perspective of writing, which is now understood as an absolute necessity, even unto death—a fatal demand or *exigence*.

Through writing, Blanchot silently, stoically advocates a form of existential heroism in the face of dread, even as he openly distances himself from his contemporaries Jean-Paul Sartre and Albert Camus. In the latter's *Myth of Sisyphus*, for example, the then-novel concept of absurdity is lambasted on account of the special status granted to it by the author: "he makes a key for himself from the fact that there is no key; outside of the terrible bonds of the absurd he keeps the absurd itself" (58). It thus comes as no surprise when Sartre's play *The Flies* is criticized in turn for its protagonist's supposed faintheartedness. In Blanchot's eyes, Orestes's actions fall short of actual sacrilege, for his attempt at transgression fails to live up to the law that he seeks to overturn. Of course, the two reproaches go hand in hand, prolonging his take on Malte: in each of these instances, Blanchot disparages the writer's desire to have his cake and eat it too, to put it coarsely, which is why *Faux Pas* reserves most of its praise for sacrificial figures that are willing to lose themselves completely in their quest for the absolute, a fatalism that comes to the fore most plainly in his review of Thierry Maulnier's *Lecture de Phèdre*, which dwells on Phaedra's wordless acknowledgment of the Fates' omnipotence.

Considering his admiration for the terrifying laws of destiny, one is almost tempted to paint Blanchot as a twentieth-century Racine, all the more so when we consider the potentially disturbing continuity between his political views in the 1930s and his absolutist aesthetics in the 1940s. Yet that is far too simplistic a reading, not least because the word "destiny" is indicative here of an ever-transgressive, increasingly more strenuous demand: for every apparent absolute there is a more exigent one still, a greater requisite that calls unto

---

[19] This presupposes a privileged link between writing and death, one that underlies Blanchot's oeuvre as a whole.

us and whose clearest—and always *provisional*—appellations at this stage of Blanchot's career are "anxiety" and "ambiguity."[20]

***

In "How Is Literature Possible?," also published as a stand-alone book by José Corti in 1942, the ambiguity of writing is further deepened, this time from an explicitly literary angle. The volume under review is Jean Paulhan's *The Flowers of Tarbes; or, Terror in Literature*, which pits two diametrically opposed stylistic exigencies against each other. The first is both "terrorist," as per Paulhan's term, and thoroughly modernist: it espouses the struggle against clichés; its objective is to make it new. The second is classicist and self-effacing: it aims for simplicity and lucidity. Maintaining his analytic distance, Paulhan stresses that both approaches inevitably lead to their own undoing. Indeed, language is an obstacle to the terrorist because it is never expressive enough, but it is irrelevant to the classicist, for whom it ultimately disappears in its own transparency. In both instances, and as "Literature and the Right to Death" would soon demonstrate, language thrives on its own vanishing point, not to mention on the impending death of the things it names. What primarily interests Blanchot, however, is Paulhan's "Copernican revolution," which "consists of causing language no longer to revolve around thought but rather to imagine another very subtle and complex mechanism in which thought, in order to rediscover its authentic nature, revolves around language" (83). In spite or because of its exorbitance—a term that also brings to mind the de-centering of an orbit—perhaps this is the most literary notion of all.

From a literary point of view, nowhere does the problem of language appear more crucial than when it is tackled in relation to poetry. *Mutatis mutandis*, poetry is the state of literature where language is likeliest to manifest itself heliocentrically, that is, as an autonomous thing endowed with an existence and a gravitational force of its own. This is compounded by our quasi-proverbial, at times subconscious, conception of poetry as that most *literal* of literary genres. The widespread custom of learning poems by heart as children illustrates this traditional definition: in poetry, every word, every line, every punctuation

---

[20] William S. Allen sees in Blanchot's treatment of this question a contribution to the debate on transcendence: "what is compelling about Blanchot's response to this problem is the way that he transforms it by reading it in terms of literature, but doing so does not reduce its philosophical or metaphysical complexity; instead, literature seems to make the issue of transcendence more profound by problematizing the nature of the limit that is seemingly being overstepped." In William S. Allen, *Aesthetics of Negativity: Blanchot, Adorno, and Autonomy* (New York: Fordham University Press, 2016), 93.

mark matters. Prosaic prose—as opposed to poetic prose, which is still poetry by any sensible yardstick—is indeed perceived to be looser, because its main function is to act as a carrier for extra-linguistic meaning. Prose thus appears to be less literally minded, *pace* stylists such as Gustave Flaubert, who coined *le mot juste*. Granted, this conceptual model is not without its flaws (which will not be discussed here) but it is precisely the one that Blanchot espouses in "Is Mallarmé's Poetry Obscure?," a caustic review of Charles Mauron's *Mallarmé l'Obscur*, which attempts to translate the poet's work into plain speech.

The obstacles to such an experiment are innumerable. As Blanchot is quick to point out, Mauron's basic assumption that prose and poetry are utterly heterogeneous is problematic in and of itself: "we guess that such transposition, thought inadmissible if it concerns a poem, is just as void of meaning for prose works like *Maldoror* or *Aurélia*" (108). Whether they visually manifest themselves as continuous prose or discontinuous poetry, such works have "a meaning whose structure is original and irreducible" (108). They are *sui generis*, possessed of a nonpareil singularity: "this meaning cannot be compared to the sense that forms the basis of practical intelligibility, and … any attempt to grasp it while neglecting this structure is as absurd as the study of a dog, a barking animal, would be for the knowledge of the Dog, the night sky constellation Canis" (108). Almost two decades before Paul Celan's *Meridian*, which famously states that "the poem is lonely,"[21] Blanchot theorizes its incomparable, incompatible solitude.

In many ways, Blanchot's claim is reminiscent of New Criticism, though it is more than likely that he developed his stance independently of his American peers. Regardless, there is an unexpected kinship between, say, Archibald MacLeish's oft-quoted suggestion that "a poem should not mean/But be,"[22] and Blanchot's categorical definition of "poetic meaning" as that which is "linked, without possible change, to the language that manifests it" because "what the poem signifies coincides exactly with what it is" (108). Seen in this light, the poem's body is immutable[23] due to its sheer literalism or thingness, which guarantees its specificity or singularity: "in nonpoetic language we know that we have understood the idea whose presence discourse brings us when we can express it in various forms… On the contrary, if poetry is to be understood, it demands total acquiescence to the unique form that it proposes" (108). Due to

---

[21]   In Celan, *Selections*, 164.
[22]   In Archibald MacLeish, "Ars poetica," in *Collected Poems 1917–1954* (Boston: Houghton Mifflin, 1962), 50–51.
[23]   Yet not its spirit, infused as it is with ambiguity, turning interpretation into a never-ending task.

its rejection of paraphrase, poetry is an instance of writing that is utterly devoid of style[24]: none other than *this* or *that* variant is valid. To put it differently, the poem is a *hapax legomenon*, signifying the impossibility of rewriting; it is the ephemeral essence of writing *qua* writing.

Although it is not a volume of poetry by any stretch of the imagination, perhaps this helps us gain a better understanding of *Faux Pas*'s title. Once again, if we allow that Blanchot seeks to write *literary* literary criticism—and not merely a discourse *on* literature that takes its cues from philosophy, critical theory, sociology, history, neurology, psychology, geography, politics, and so on—it is tempting to think of these missteps as having a value wholly their own, bearing witness to singular readings of equally singular works of art. In that sense, to expurgate or edit them in any way, shape, or form[25] is to maim or at the very least transform their tentative, shadowy truth. As we know all too well, there can be no unambiguously correct interpretation of a given instance of literary writing, and Blanchot acknowledges that to discuss these works is to falter, even when taking the most careful and circuitous of paths, as he so often does. In other words, since criticism is assigned the burden of commenting on that which withdraws from its grasp,[26] it has no choice but to paraphrase and even translate the literary work; it must fail as literature ("literal-ture") to succeed as literary criticism. From this perspective, perhaps Mauron's greatest mistake was that he did not self-reflexively recognize the impossibility of his experiment rather than the fact that he conducted it in the first place.

Blanchot's barbs lose something of their sting, however, when set next to his own rewriting of *Thomas the Obscure*, a spectacular self-transgression of the work's law, as well as a triumph of its spirit over its letter. After all, *Thomas the Obscure* is nothing if not a poetically inflected ocean of hypnotic prose, an instantiation of the absolute novel that Blanchot repeatedly called for in the early 1940s. In "Mallarmé and the Art of the Novel," for example, he draws a parallel between the French poet's impossible Book and the novelistic form, noting that

---

[24] Beckett explained his switch to French in strikingly similar terms.

[25] Which isn't to say that these articles were all reproduced *verbatim et literalim* in *Faux Pas*, but they don't appear to have been thoroughly overhauled.

[26] Leslie Hill sheds light on this aspect of *Faux Pas*: "the text inserted by Gallimard into *Faux Pas* in December 1943, which is more than likely to have been written by Blanchot himself, concludes as follows: 'Each and every book of some significance conceals a secret that makes it better than what it may be [*supérieur à ce qu'il peut être*]. This secret is what every critic aims to approach but always misses, distracted by the need to inform readers of books about to appear. The critic advances, but goes nowhere, and remains rooted to the spot. And if the journey sometimes reaches its goal, it does so only by taking a false step [*un faux pas*]'" (382–83). In Leslie Hill, *Radical Indecision: Barthes, Blanchot, Derrida, and the Future of Criticism* (Notre Dame: University of Notre Dame Press, 2010).

"it is curious that no novelist has discovered in Mallarmé's remarks a definition of the art of the novel or an allusion charged with glory to the work he is called to do" (166). The true novelist hence embarks on a paradoxically poetic endeavor that implies the composition of pure prose: "the true language of the novel, if it is always secretly ordered by an order of images and words of a rigorous necessity, can very well bring to the reader, as metaphor, nothing but a complete absence of metaphors, of sought-out turns of phrase, of fortunate words" (170–171). In terms reminiscent of Beckett, once again, who had yet to experience his postwar anti-epiphany, Blanchot strangely points to Joyce as that exemplary novelist whose language "becomes impoverished and withered. It seems to lose at once its body and its soul. It is there, as a warning, to provoke the reader, thanks to a power that cannot be analyzed, to the feeling of tragic fictions that it touches on" (171). As such, the ideal novel's idiom is a deliquescent image of the absolute—of the Great Equalizer itself.

Such statements notwithstanding, Joyce's influence on Blanchot appears to have been marginal. Instead, his early novels (especially *Thomas the Obscure*) are modeled in no small part after Lautréamont's *Songs of Maldoror*, which *The Work of Fire* would soon describe as a light-absorbing monolith—one of the most literal things there is. More specifically, Isidore Ducasse's one-off is for Blanchot "a novel whose main subject is its creation as a novel" (173). It possesses an autonomy borne out of self-reflexivity, whose purposeless purpose is to accomplish its own nothingness; it is a literal *mise en abyme*, a descent into the abyss. *The Songs of Maldoror* thus profoundly realizes the negative promise of literature as such: "all that constitutes the subject matter of the novelist is abolished by Lautréamont's purifying action. It is outside of any so-called story, any recourse to characters, any acquiescence to life that the novel establishes [as] its domain" (173). And to the extent that the novelist's task is necessarily hopeless, he must live up to that impossibility by embracing it, thus becoming the anxious, even anguished, instrument of his own unmaking, the nothing that brings about the thing, ex nihilo.

A similarly hyperbolic logic is at play in the article on *Moby-Dick*, no less admirable than *The Songs of Maldoror* in that it "tries to be a total book, expressing not only a complete human experience but offering itself as the written equivalent of the universe." Blanchot sees in Melville's work an attempt at accounting for everything that is, and *Moby-Dick* enacts this ontological, even ontic, pretention by consorting with the sky's arbitrarily constellated emptiness: "it is, in a certain way, one of those books that help us to understand the supreme ambition of

Mallarmé when he wanted to 'raise a page to the power of the starry sky'" (239). Although Melville's novel exhibits the trappings of allegory, it is "condemned finally to silence … by the simplicity of its mystery" (243), that is also to say by its sheer superficiality and literality, which for Blanchot are the literary secret's best hidden secrets, as *The Instant of My Death* would later make plain.[27]

∗∗∗

Yet of all the guises ambiguity assumes throughout *Faux Pas*, perhaps the most obvious and most mysterious is that of *hasard* versus *destin*: an antagonism that admits no reconciliation, instead compelling the writer to aggravate both antipodes until each reaches its zenith. One need look no further than Blanchot's review of Camus's *L'Étranger*, partly exempt from the criticisms leveled at *The Myth of Sisyphus*. As expected, Blanchot praises Camus for the blankness of his prose, anticipating the notion of *écriture blanche*: "it rejects any exterior beauty, and the only metaphor with which it allows itself to be enriched is the very story that offers an invisible idea the chance for exact and moving expression" (217). Here, language does not draw attention to itself, since it is meant to act as a mere catalyst for the novel's narrative, yet Blanchot interprets this semantic transparency as a paradoxical prerequisite for the most extreme form of literalism. Despite their glaring differences, *L'Étranger* shares *Moby-Dick*'s surface secrecy, just as it too acts as a meeting point for fatefulness and randomness. Glossing the protagonist's iconic murder, Blanchot provocatively argues that "in social life to be the plaything of chance is not possible without crime," to which he adds: "chance becomes fate [*Le hasard y devient le destin*]" (220). Such appears to be the point where the worthiest literary works converge according to *Faux Pas*'s implicit system of values.

It would be misleading, however, to assume that this running thread thwarts the book's latent fragmentation. Even when openly discussing intertextual continuity, as is the case in his piece on Charles Baudelaire's *The Flowers of Evil*, Blanchot stresses discontinuity.[28] And it is no coincidence that this particular

---

[27]  See Ginette Michaud, *Tenir au secret (Derrida, Blanchot)* (Paris: Galilée, 2006).

[28]  Referring to early German romanticism's influence on Blanchot's oeuvre, Gisèle Berkman rightly states that "Blanchot à la fois inaugure bien une certaine façon inédite, en France, de lire la littérature, et s'en dissocie du même coup, déjouant toute généalogie, toute filiation" (71). In other words, "Blanchot inaugurates an unprecedented manner of reading literature in France, even as he dissociates himself from it, foiling genealogy and filiation in the process." In Gisèle Berkman, "'Une histoire dans le romantisme?' Maurice Blanchot et l'*Athenaeum*," in *Blanchot romantique*, ed. John McKeane and Hannes Opelz (Bern: Peter Lang, 2011).

problem underpins *Faux Pas*'s most sustained inquiry into modernism, a term that calls for a few words of caution. Indeed, despite its self-avowed international aspirations, the "-ism" of "modernism" is inseparable from English-language literature and criticism. Its cousin, the French *modernité*, roams farther afield, not least because it does not automatically call to mind aesthetics, art, and/or literature, having a broader and perhaps more enigmatic scope, often historiological in its application. "Modernism" is thus simultaneously relevant and irrelevant to Blanchot, which is why we may only speak of *le modernisme de Blanchot* as an expression of his anachronistic poetics of rupture, and on the condition that we keep in mind his own nuanced observations regarding Baudelaire, often considered to be the first modern writer in the French canon.

Reviewing a newly published critical edition of *The Flowers of Evil*, Blanchot pays tribute to editors Jacques Crépet and Georges Blin's extensive critical apparatus, shrewdly noting—more than two decades before the debate on the death of the author or even his own embrace of anonymity—that "the hypothesis that definitively separates the man from the author and leaves whoever wants to enjoy a poem with only its bare text" is too neat to be thoroughly persuasive (157). Indeed, such a stance "makes creation into an absolute that is prodigiously sheltered from chance and accident," in effect violating the laws of tension and fatefulness that are integral to Blanchot's deliberately ambiguous conception of literature (157). Granted, "the work remains the essential thing," but its obstinate singularity is such that it allows and even encourages critical and/or theoretical elucidation, as if to prove that no amount of exegesis will ever bring its buried secret to light (157).

That includes, of course, Crépet and Blin's encyclopedic glosses, aimed at relating Baudelaire back to his precursors: Poe, Maturin, Sainte-Beuve, Hugo, Hoffmann, De Quincey, Byron, Gray, Longfellow, Rabbe, Cazotte, Swedenborg, de Maistre, Gautier, and others. Yet this litany of names hardly amounts to a sum total bearing the title *The Flowers of Evil*. Instead, Blanchot argues that, for Baudelaire, as for Lautréamont and Rimbaud, "poetry can completely stop being new without ceasing to be original … its efficacy, its purity, its original force are not necessarily broken in the vice of reminiscences and under the weight of what has already been said" (162). Here, then, is a conception of modernism that has much in common with that set forth by Hugh Kenner in *The Pound Era*: insofar as "a poet sometimes succeeds in expressing himself in a way that is unique to him by expressing himself as another," the writer's signature style is necessarily imitable, just as classicism was designed to be reiterated ad infinitum and yet differently every single time (162). No matter how literalist, each and every utterance runs the risk—one is tempted to say, this time in English, the *hazard*—of being rewritten, including when the words that constitute it remain intact. A peculiar paradox, to be sure, and one whose amphiboly Blanchot knowingly, anxiously exacerbates throughout *Faux Pas*, and beyond.

*⁎⁎⁎*

In my fatally fragmentary attempt at writing about *Faux Pas*, I have only touched on a handful of its imagined centers. Nonetheless, although it lacks an overarching theme—even as, mirroring literature itself, it unceasingly, teasingly suggests that it might have one—*Faux Pas* stands out among Blanchot's books, and not just for chronological reasons. As expected, it lays the groundwork for his subsequent writings, but it also highlights certain tendencies that he would soon seek to erase. In lieu of a conclusion, I would like to briefly develop one of these faux pas, namely, his unbounded admiration for heroic literary figures, which gives credence to a subjectivist vision of writing that he came to disavow in the 1960s.

Mallarmé's oeuvre in particular impels uncharacteristically gushing paeans on Blanchot's part.[29] Indeed, the essay titled "The Silence of Mallarmé" adopts a tone reminiscent of some of the less cautious texts from *Le Journal des débats* that were not reprinted in *Faux Pas*. From the outset, Blanchot bemoans that "the purest writers are not entirely inside their works; they have existed; they have even lived. One must resign oneself to that" (99). Nevertheless, he takes comfort in presuming that Mallarmé "was affable, wonderfully well bred, and at the same time of an intransigence and a determined rigor of which stringency could give no idea … he knew himself as … a demiurge, since he did nothing less than deify the written word" (99)—qualities that Blanchot himself manifestly pursues in his early writings. He marvels at the poet's ambition, convinced that, having transcended the mystics discussed in the first section of *Faux Pas*, Mallarmé "truly grasped the absolute" (100). What is more, even the Book's failure is read here as a baffling sign of its success, since the poet's *esprit*—a term that once again speaks to Valéry's formative influence—"had expressed itself completely on its own, had said itself and had seen itself completely," attaining an elusive degree of autonomy and perfection of which his poems are merely the evanescent traces

---

[29]    These never fully abated. One need look no further than *The Book to Come*, which praises Mallarmé (alongside Cézanne) in only slightly less feverish terms.

(106). Indeed, Mallarmé's name doesn't operate as a metonymy of his writings in "The Silence of Mallarmé"; even as the writer writes in the hope of erasing his identity, such a gesture ultimately glorifies his abnegatory courage rather than his workless work.

In line with his critical takes on Sartre, Camus, and Rilke, the pieces on Péguy, Nietzsche, and Montherlant from "A Miscellany of Digressions" make the same point: solely the subject who is willing to risk self-annihilation is worthy of literature's highest mantle, recalling T. S. Eliot's quip that "only those who have personality and emotions know what it means to want to escape from these things."[30] Likewise, from the work's monstrous, inhuman perspective, first comes *l'œuvre*, then its *désœuvrement*—always in this order at this point in Blanchot's career—which is why an exacting law must be decreed prior to its heroic infringement, lest the experience be too placid, too insipid. Such is perhaps the main lesson of *Faux Pas*: literature demands that the author keep pace with the absolute in its essential ambiguity, in its possible-impossible promise. Everything is required of the sacrificial figure who withdraws in the name of the work, even nothing "itself." It is the most radical of demands, and although it would soon be mitigated by the resolutely neutral, anti-heroic bareness of anonymity, its call quietly subsists in all the writings that follow.

---

[30]   T. S. Eliot, "Tradition and the Individual Talent," in *Selected Prose*, ed. Frank Kermode (New York: Farrar, Straus and Giroux, 1975), 43.

# 2

# Thus Spoke Literature

Hannes Opelz

*Alle mythische Bedeutung sucht Geheimnis.*

Walter Benjamin

*Mythologie blanche—la métaphysique a effacé en elle-même la scène fabuleuse qui l'a produite et qui reste néanmoins active, remuante, inscrite à l'encre blanche.*

Jacques Derrida

*Surface et profondeur, dialogue et mythe ne s'opposent pas comme deux concepts antithétiques mais comme deux forces dont l'une est destinée à conjurer l'autre.*

Sarah Kofman

"La Littérature et le droit à la mort" (1947–48) belongs to that category of texts where every return visit is both a discovery and a disillusion—the discovery of a myriad of heretofore unsuspected lines of inquiry, and the disillusion arising from the impossibility of exploring them all, let alone reconciling them. As a rule, such texts are destined to acquire near-mythical status. Blanchot's essay is no exception—and with every new commentary, the mythical aura shrouding it only thickens. That even deconstructive readings have all but left it intact should give us pause, raising questions not just for "La Littérature et le droit à la mort," but perhaps more importantly, for deconstruction itself. Given the scope of such questions, there is no room to flesh out each and every one of them here, much less answer them. But that should not prevent us from making attempts, however provisional, at formulating at least some of them as clearly as possible. Perhaps the most obvious—but by no means least demanding—of these could be articulated as follows: is the mythical standing of Blanchot's essay merely the result of its reception, as I have hastily just suggested? Before pointing the finger at its readers and commentators (no matter how tempting and justified that might be), should we not be asking ourselves whether its mythical powers may lie elsewhere, namely, in the text itself? And if so, how, exactly, does it wield them?

With these questions in mind, and at the risk of being once again disillusioned but with the prospect that some discovery may be in store, I would like to revisit Blanchot's essay—more precisely, by taking as a starting point what is perhaps the last of Philippe Lacoue-Labarthe's powerful intuitions: that Blanchot's experience of literature, as he put it in an interview soon after the author's death, "allowed him to construct ... the *modern myth of the writer*," before adding, no less emphatically, that Blanchot himself had become "an absolutely mythical figure of the modern writer."[1] It was, of course, much more than an intuition. Much of what Lacoue-Labarthe had written up until then—not just on Blanchot but also, in other contexts, on myth and the figure, on the modern and the absolute—made the observation practically inevitable. But it was, evidently, the event of Blanchot's death that sanctioned it in its brutal simplicity, as if death were not simply a catalyst but also a developer of myth.

What, then, underpinned Lacoue-Labarthe's claim? In its most succinct form, it is the idea, formulated a decade earlier, that "the impossible experience of death is the *authorization* of Literature."[2] To be sure, the degree of clarity achieved in such a formulation is extraordinary. In fact, it is so transparent that we risk losing sight of what is taking place on the surface of Blanchot's text. For, my suspicion is that, if myth can be said to operate in Blanchot, and if he came to embody it "absolutely" in the process, it is not so much (or only) because his writings *contain* the lethal law of literature abolishing its subject—what Blanchot would famously term *le mourir* or *la mort impossible nécessaire*—as because of the *formal* devices employed by Blanchot to present it. In other words, it is because Blanchot very deliberately and meticulously composes a fable—that is to say, a discourse that offers itself as a bearer of an unverifiable truth, a truth too difficult or obscure to

---

[1]  Philippe Lacoue-Labarthe, *Ending and Unending Agony* (2011), trans. Hannes Opelz (New York: Fordham University Press, 2015), 1 (Lacoue-Labarthe's emphasis); *Agonie terminée, agonie interminable*, ed. Aristide Bianchi and Leonid Kharlamov (Paris: Galilée, 2011), 10.

[2]  Lacoue-Labarthe, *Ending and Unending Agony*, 65 (Lacoue-Labarthe's emphasis); *Agonie terminée, agonie interminable*, 125. In a similar vein, Lacoue-Labarthe also writes (speaking again of Blanchot): "The experience of death—that pure impossibility—would thus be the condition, end, and origin, if not the categorical imperative (the unconditional 'one must [*il faut*]'), of literature and, equally, of thought" (*Ending and Unending Agony*, 48; *Agonie terminée, agonie interminable*, 95).

enunciate directly or demonstrate logically and as such requiring the detour of a fiction—that the modern myth of the writer becomes fully operable.

It is, I would argue, at the level of "form," therefore, rather than "content"—assuming provisionally such a distinction can be usefully maintained—that myth operates most effectively, which is to say more or less unconsciously. This entails that deconstruction of Blanchot's myth (in both the objective and subjective sense of the genitive) only truly begins when we start paying attention to his work's mode(s) of presentation or exposition, and that so long as we keep reading him for content, for a hidden truth or meaning waiting to be unveiled, interpreted, or deconstructed, we will remain vulnerable to the myth in question, if not complicit in its erection. Besides, as far as content is concerned, Blanchot's text is perfectly capable of *thinking* deconstructively on its own—supposing, for now, that what goes under the name of *désœuvrement* in Blanchot lies somewhere between Heidegger's *Destruktion* and Derrida's *déconstruction*.

"La Littérature et le droit à la mort" is exemplary in this regard. And if it continues to enthrall even its most vigilant commentators, it is precisely, and paradoxically, because its de(con)structive movement is deployed through—or subsumed in—mythic configurations. Put differently, de(con)struction in Blanchot's essay takes the *form* of myth. (Which is one of the reasons why the use of the term "deconstruction" to describe Blanchot's work is problematic.) It is not until a decade or so later that attempts in Blanchot to deconstruct the very form of (his own) critical discourse become apparent—with the *entretien* and the *fragmentaire*, for instance—and that myth is *formally* exposed.[3] From this

---

[3]  This is not to suggest that myth no longer operates in Blanchot's later writings; in fact, one could show that mythic devices are still at work there (see, for instance, Hannes Opelz, "La Précipitation du désastre," in *Penser en commun? Un "rapport sans rapport,"* ed. Isabelle Ullern and Pierre Gisel [Paris: Beauchesne, 2015], 31–62]). Nor is it to suggest that the *entretien* or *fragmentaire* do not produce their own mythic power, giving rise, as they have, to appropriations by new generations of thinkers and writers, including such deconstructively attentive readers as Derrida, Lacoue-Labarthe, or Nancy (see Jacques Derrida, "Pace Not(s)" (1976), in *Parages*, trans. John P. Leavey et al. (Stanford: Stanford University Press, 2010), 11–102; "Pas," in *Parages* (Paris: Galilée, 1986), 19–116; Philippe Lacoue-Labarthe, "Dismay" (1978; 2000), in *Ending and Unending Agony*, 111–14; "L'Émoi," in *Agonie terminée, agonie interminable*, 153–59; Philippe Lacoue-Labarthe and Jean-Luc Nancy, "Noli me frangere" (1982), in *The Birth to Presence*, trans. Brian Holmes et al. (Stanford: Stanford University Press, 1993), 266–78; "Noli me frangere," *Europe* 973 (May 2010): 32–42; and Jean-Luc Nancy, "Un plaisir immense," in *Blanchot dans son siècle*, ed. Monique Antelme et al. (Lyon: Parangon, 2009), 15–24). In the case of "Noli me frangere," the sheer complexity, at the level of form, of its—parodic? deconstructive?—imitation of Blanchot's *entretien* and *fragmentaire*, integrating dialogue (*à la* Schlegel) and quotation (Schelling) along the way, not to mention its explicit questioning, at the level of content, of Blanchot's formal operations, denotes an abyssal mode of mimesis intent on interrupting or unravelling processes of mythification. Regardless of whether or not their text succeeds in this, Lacoue-Labarthe and Nancy (but Lacoue-Labarthe to a greater degree perhaps than Nancy, and certainly than Derrida) are among the few to have perceived Blanchot's engagement with form *as* the problem of myth.

perspective, Blanchot's relentless formal innovations (whether in his critical/ theoretical or fictional/narrative writings, insofar as such distinctions can be said to hold in his case, and nothing, from the late 1950s and early 1960s onward, is less certain) suggest just how acutely aware he was of the fact that the secret of what is at stake in literature—"the end of myths" (WD 47; ED 80), to borrow a phrase from *L'Écriture du désastre* (1980)—lies in the form. An awareness that must have been agonizing—and certainly marks him out as agonizingly *modern*.

Now, Lacoue-Labarthe, too, was well aware that the formal apparatus of Blanchot's work (of any given work, for that matter) plays a vital role in enabling (or disabling, as the case may be) its potential for mythification. His reference, for example, to the *figure* (of the modern writer) in the passage quoted in the opening makes this plain.[4] Only, despite laying the groundwork for a formal engagement with Blanchot, Lacoue-Labarthe never systematically engages with the form of his critical writings—not, that is, as far as the earlier Blanchot of, say, *Faux pas* (1943) or *La Part du feu* (1949) is concerned. At any rate, there is in Lacoue-Labarthe no sustained engagement, formal or otherwise, with "La Littérature et le droit à la mort." And yet it is here, I would suggest, rather than, say, in *L'Espace littéraire* (1955) and the Orphic tradition within which Lacoue-Labarthe squarely situates Blanchot's figuration of the writer,[5] that the *mythical* figure of the writer emerges—and not just, it might be added, on account of figuration, which is only the more visible symptom of the myth-making operations at work in Blanchot's seminal essay.

In any event, my only pretension here is to sketch out some of the implications of Lacoue-Labarthe's insight into Blanchot and the question of (his) myth by inquiring into the rhetoric—rather than, say, the poetics—of "La Littérature et le droit à la mort." A poetics, it certainly is, which also explains why it has been variously received, and rightly so, as a kind of manifesto or program for Blanchot's aesthetics as a whole. Its rhetorical strategies, however, are no less deserving of our attention, all the more so if they can help us understand the ways in which Blanchot's nonfictional work is capable of producing fascination (to revert to his own language), not to say fantasy (to borrow the language of a field that, with the notable exception of a few ambiguous but decisive words

---

[4]	Not to mention, in addition to what is at play in *"Noli me frangere,"* his discussion in *Agonie terminée, agonie interminable* of Blanchot's fragmentary writing, namely, in relation to *L'Écriture du désastre* (see *Ending and Unending Agony*, 71–82; *Agonie terminée, agonie interminable*, 131–51).

[5]	See Lacoue-Labarthe, *Ending and Unending Agony*, 1, 22, 42, 52, 64, 81; *Agonie terminée, agonie interminable*, 9, 50, 85, 102, 122, 150.

in Jacques Lacan's seminar on identification, has yet to come to terms with Blanchot). A fascination or fantasy that readers have often helplessly pointed out but determinedly failed to critique—at the peril of all the mythifying and identificatory mechanisms this implies.[6]

My hypothesis is that the *fictionizing* framework in Blanchot's essay responsible for producing what Lacoue-Labarthe calls the "modern myth of the writer" is governed by the articulation and combination of the following formal devices, assuming for the purposes of exposition that they can be so neatly distinguished: mimesis, prosopopoeia, citation, figuration. (In fact, one could argue that the Latinate latter are merely technical effectuations or consummations of the Greek former, as is so often the case in Rome's agon with Greece.) But before setting out to demonstrate this, some clarifications are in order. To begin with, I have no intention to engage in an exercise in tropology. Far from it. Nor do I hope to claim that a master trope commands all of Blanchot's work. If resorting to (what used to be called) rhetoric is indispensable here, it is merely because it intersects crucially with a long-standing problem in (what used to be called) metaphysics, particularly in relation to (what used to be called) aesthetics: the question of (re)presentation. As Lacoue-Labarthe has shown time and again,

---

[6] The most recent (and perhaps only) serious attempt to engage explicitly with Blanchot's rhetoric and the fascination it produces is Yves Gilonne's *La Rhétorique du sublime dans l'œuvre de Maurice Blanchot* (Paris: L'Harmattan, 2008). Notwithstanding obvious differences in approach, leading to divergences that cannot be explored here (regarding figuration, for example: the question, I would argue, is not limited to whether, or to what extent, figuration in Blanchot partakes of the sublime— it certainly does, as Gilonne reminds us—but entails also, and perhaps more importantly, asking whether, or to what extent, it partakes of the beautiful), Gilonne raises a number of issues that broadly coincide with those I hope to raise here as well as elsewhere. Despite passing references to some of its formal features, however, Gilonne never fully engages with "La Littérature et le droit à la mort." Few commentators do, besides, and when they do, their commentaries tend to operate almost exclusively at the level of content, of what Plato calls *logos* (i.e., at the level of *what* Blanchot says about literature, language, death, terror, etc.), rather than at the level of form, of *lexis* (i.e., at the level of *how* Blanchot speaks of literature, language, death, terror, etc.); see, among many other examples paying more or less attention to Blanchot's essay, Andrzej Warminski, "Dreadful Reading: Blanchot on Hegel," *Yale French Studies* 69 (1985): 267–75; Rodolphe Gasché, "The Felicities of Paradox," in *The Demand of Writing*, ed. Carolyn Gill (London: Routledge, 1996), 34–69; Christopher Fynsk, "Crossing the Threshold," in *The Demand of Writing*, 70–90; Simon Critchley, *Very Little ... Almost Nothing: Death, Philosophy, Literature* (1997) (London: Routledge, 2004), 56–77; Gerald Bruns, *Maurice Blanchot: The Refusal of Philosophy* (Baltimore: Johns Hopkins University Press, 1997), 34–55; Leslie Hill, *Blanchot: Extreme Contemporary* (London: Routledge, 1997), 103–14; James Swenson, "Revolutionary Sentences," *Yale French Studies* 93 (1998): 11–29; Jacques Derrida, *Parages* (Paris: Galilée, 2003), 267–300; Michel Collot, "Enquête sur une double disparition," in *Maurice Blanchot: Récits critiques*, ed. Christophe Bident and Pierre Vilar (Tours: Farrago/Léo Scheer, 2003), 259–69; Vanghélis Bitsoris, "Blanchot, Derrida: du droit à la mort au droit à la vie," in *Blanchot dans son siècle*, 179–93; Étienne Balibar, "Blanchot l'insoumis," in *Blanchot dans son siècle*, 289–314; Dominique Rabaté, "La Littérature comme question," in *Les Cahiers de l'Herne: Maurice Blanchot*, ed. Éric Hoppenot and Dominique Rabaté (Paris: L'Herne, 2014), 261–66; Étienne Pinat, *Les Deux morts de Maurice Blanchot* (Bucarest: Zeta Books, 2014), 25–34, etc.

this question cannot easily be separated from the question of myth, inasmuch as (re)presentation—including, and perhaps especially, philosophy's own mode of presentation—can be shown to be inextricably bound up with what is known since Lacoue-Labarthe as "onto-typo-logy,"[7] that is to say, the typifying function at work in Western modes of (re)presentation, instantiating figural—and, by extension, mythic—schemata of thought construed to reveal the truth—being, essence, origin, nature, identity or any other concept making transcendental claims—of the matter in hand. Hence the broader question I propose to put to Blanchot's essay: to what extent might it be shown to be onto-typo-logical, if not, by extension, onto-mythological?

Naturally, such a question cannot be answered in the space provided here, as even the slightest extent would compel us to rethink some of our most enduring assumptions about Blanchot and his legacy—for instance, the assumption, as Jean-Luc Nancy put it (to question it), that Blanchot was a "slayer [*pourfendeur*] of myth."[8] At any rate, the question is not simply whether Blanchot's text deposes myth or signals its return (as I have been suggesting, it does both—the former at the level of content, the latter at the level of form); rather, it has to do with determining the conditions that allow the question of myth not only to emerge but to be left unresolved.

## Mimesis

That Blanchot's essay holds a distinctive place in *La Part du feu*—given its exceptional length, title page, italic script, and placement as a kind of afterword to the collection—is well known. That it opens, unlike any other essay collected in the volume, with a *scene* is perhaps less remarked on but just as significant:

> Does a writer, who watches his pen form letters, does he even have a right to lift it and say to it: "Stop! What do you know about yourself! Why are you moving forward? Why can't you see that your ink isn't making any marks, that although you may be moving ahead freely, you're moving through a void, that the reason you never encounter any obstacles is that you never left your starting place? And yet you write …" (WF 300; translation modified; PF 293)

---

[7]  See Philippe Lacoue-Labarthe, "Typography" (1975), trans. Eduardo Cadava, in *Typography: Mimesis, Philosophy, Politics* (1989), ed. Christopher Fynsk (Stanford: Stanford University Press, 1998), 43–138; "Typographie," in *Mimesis des articulations*, ed. Philippe Lacoue-Labarthe et al. (Paris: Flammarion, 1975), 165–270.

[8]  Jean-Luc Nancy, "Fin du colloque," in *Maurice Blanchot: Récits critiques*, 631 (my translation).

... and so on, until the end of the paragraph. To borrow Plato's terminology and transpose it to literary criticism (leaving aside, for now, the questions raised by the transposition itself), the opening of the essay is thus not merely diegetic, that is, involving the narration of an action (namely, that of a puzzled writer watching his pen as he writes), but also mimetic, that is, the enunciator (Blanchot, the critic) delegates his enunciation (to an imagined writer), or, put differently, he is not speaking in his own name but through a character ("a writer") called up for the occasion.

This is not the first time that Blanchot uses such a device—"the device of myth itself,"[9] as Lacoue-Labarthe once put it—in his critical writings to dramatize the experience of literature. The device in question is already at stake, albeit in less elaborate form, in "De l'angoisse au langage" (1943), the equally distinct and programmatic essay that prefaced, five years earlier, *Faux pas*:

> "I do not want to achieve something," the writer says to himself. "Instead I want this thing that I am when I write to come, by the fact that I write, to nothing, in any shape or form. It is essential to me to be a writer who is infinitely less great in his work than in himself, and to be so with the full and honest use of all his means. I want this possibility of creating, by becoming creation, not only to express its own destruction but also ..." (FP 7; translation modified; FP 14-15)

... and so forth, until the end of the paragraph. The difference, however, between this passage and the one from "La Littérature et le droit à la mort" is that the former is a "fictional monologue" (as Blanchot himself describes it in the subsequent paragraph), whereas the latter is a fictional *dialogue*—or more exactly, *implies* the fictional schema of a dialogue insofar as, in addressing his pen, the writer-character confers upon it an agency that would in theory enable it to be in a position to receive the question and, presumably, reply (not to mention its inferred ability to "know" or "see": "What do you *know* about yourself?," "Why can't you *see* that your ink isn't making any marks?"). Either way, regardless of whether or not the pen is capable of responding and engaging in conversation, the opening of "La Littérature et le droit à la mort" meets all the requirements of a scene, whether one defines it, perhaps most fundamentally, as the fiction of mimetic enunciation, in other words, of an address,[10] or, in more structural

---

[9]  Philippe Lacoue-Labarthe, "The Horror of the West" (1996), trans. Nidesh Lawtoo and Hannes Opelz, in *Conrad's* Heart of Darkness *and Contemporary Thought*, ed. Nidesh Lawtoo (London: Bloomsbury, 2012), 111–22 (113); "L'Horreur occidentale," in *La Réponse d'Ulysse et autres textes sur l'Occident*, ed. Aristide Bianchi et Leonid Kharlamov (Paris: Lignes/IMEC, 2012), 57–70 (60).

[10]  See Philippe Lacoue-Labarthe and Jean-Luc Nancy, "Dialogue sur le dialogue" (2005), in *Scène* (Paris: Bourgois, 2013), 75–76.

terms, as a triangular configuration where an observer (in this case, the reader of Blanchot's essay) witnesses the interaction between two agents (the writer and his pen).[11]

Although there are other rhetorical devices that contribute to the fictionizing framework of the essay's opening and that would merit attention in this context (the most apparent being the pen's traditional function as a metonymy for literature, corroborated by the oft-cited opening of the following paragraph: "Let us suppose that literature begins at the moment when literature becomes a question" [WF 300; PF 293]), I would like to move on and explore the mimetic apparatus of Blanchot's text in more detail. Indeed, the use of mimetic speech is not confined to the opening. After describing at some length the plight of the writer, we encounter another scene, far more sophisticated, mimetically speaking, than the previous one:

> The writer must respond to several absolute and absolutely different commands at once, and his morality is made up of the confrontation and opposition of implacably hostile rules.
>
> One of them says to him: "You will not write, you will remain nothingness, you will keep silent, you will not know words."
>
> The other rule says: "Know nothing but words."
>
> "Write to say nothing."
>
> "Write to say something."
>
> "No works; rather, the experience of yourself, the knowledge of what is unknown to you."
>
> "A work! A real work, recognized by other people and important to other people."
>
> "Obliterate the reader."
>
> "Obliterate yourself before the reader."
>
> "Write in order to be true."
>
> "Write for the sake of truth."
>
> "In that case, be a lie, because to write with truth in mind is to write what is not yet true and perhaps never will be so."
>
> "It doesn't matter, write in order to act."
>
> "Write, you who are afraid to act."
>
> "Let freedom speak in you."
>
> "Oh! do not let freedom become a word in you."

---

[11]  See Philippe Ortel, "Vers une poétique des dispositifs," in *Discours, Image, Dispositif* (Paris: L'Harmattan, 2008), 33–58 (46–49).

Which law should be obeyed? Which voice be heard? But the writer must obey them all! What confusion, then! Isn't clarity his law? Yes, clarity, too. He must therefore oppose himself, deny himself even as he affirms himself, go find the depth of the night in the facility of the day, the sure light that cannot end in the shadows that never begin. He must save the world and be the abyss, justify existence and allow what does not exist to speak; he must be at the end of time in the universal plenitude, whilst being also the origin, the birth of what does nothing but come into being. Is he all that? Literature is all that, in him. (WF 312–313; translation modified; PF 303–304)

The dialogic mode employed here does not merely inscribe Blanchot's essay in a very long tradition—in what is perhaps tradition itself, as far as Western aesthetics is concerned: as is known, from Plato to Schelling, through Shaftesbury to Diderot, and even up to Valéry (the reference in Blanchot's text to *Eupalinos* is no accident), dialogism has been a privileged form of discursive exposition, to the point of becoming a genre unto itself. The very presence of the dialogic form in Blanchot's essay also poses the question of literary criticism's—or, if one prefers, theory's—own mode of presentation, just as it had for philosophy.[12]

This question, however, is never explicitly raised, formulated, or explored by Blanchot here. And although the text already appears to upset the philosophical (Socratic) function of dialogue—instead of being dialectically resolved or subsumed into some unifying form of knowledge or truth (what Blanchot would much later refer to as "the paradise of decorous idealism" [IC 81; EI 114]), the contradictory statements made by the "rules" of literature lead the writer to confusion ("What confusion, then!"), and in the longer run, to irreducibly paradoxical demands ("deny himself even as he affirms himself," "go find the depth of the night in the facility of the day," etc.)—the dialogic form itself is more a practical expedient, readily abandoned after use (it never returns in the essay), than a theme or object of reflection. In fact, as I briefly suggested earlier, despite implying its importance throughout the postwar era (if not already before), the question—or *problem*—of literary criticism (or theory), of its discourse and of how it presents (and relates to) its subject matter (namely, literature), would not be posed as such by Blanchot until the early 1960s: as mere points of reference, let's say, at the level of content, with "Qu'en est-il de la critique?" (1963), where, besides, he notes that "the dialogue between critical speech and 'creative' speech is strange" (LS 2; translation modified; LS 10); and at the level of form (and

---

[12]  See Philippe Lacoue-Labarthe and Jean-Luc Nancy, "Le Dialogue des genres," *Poétique* 21 (1975): 148–75.

content), with "Les Paroles doivent cheminer longtemps" (1961), where the notion, and, more importantly, the form of dialogue reappear but where both decisively question, if not altogether reinvent, the form (dialogic or otherwise) of critical discourse.[13] In any event, dialogism in "La Littérature et le droit à la mort"—however nondialectical its function (which is in keeping, more broadly, with the aporetic force of so many of the essay's statements), however limited its use (after all, it represents only a very small portion of the essay as a whole), and however asymmetrical the exchange (admittedly, what we have is less an actual dialogue between two or more characters taking turns to address each other than the *mise-en-scène* of a dialogic framework in which two or more voices ("Which *voice* should be heard?") address in the imperative a character who remains silent)—serves the purpose of dramatizing the experience of the writer.

## Prosopopoeia

But the fictionizing configuration of the scene in question is not attributable to mimetic enunciation alone; it is more specifically contingent upon Blanchot's recourse to one of the most ancient of rhetorical devices: prosopopoeia. Indeed, if the essay's opening already presented, albeit in embryonic form, the key characteristics of the trope in question—namely, that of conferring human agency (typically, speech) upon an insentient, absent, deceased, or non-human being, such as an inanimate object, an animal, a fictitious or mythical character, the dead, an abstract entity, and so on: in this case, the pen's implied ability to reply[14]—this scene fully puts it into effect: not only do we have the fiction of mimetic speech (and this time, an effectuated—rather than merely inferred—agency) but the subject of enunciation is *literature* (an abstract entity), or rather, in a reference—intended or not—to Plato's *Crito*, its *laws*.

As readers of Blanchot's essay will recall, this is not the only instance in which we find literature speaking (mimetically): "Literature," we read later on, "says, 'I no longer represent, I am; I do not signify, I present'" (WF 328;

---

[13]  See Maurice Blanchot, "Words Must Travel Far," in *The Infinite Conversation*, 326–31; "Les Paroles doivent cheminer longtemps," in *L'Entretien infini* (Paris: Gallimard, 1969), 478–86.

[14]  Paul de Man, for instance, defines prosopopoeia as "the fiction of an apostrophe to an absent, deceased or voiceless entity, which posits the possibility of the latter's reply and confers upon it the power of speech"; see *The Rhetoric of Romanticism* (New York: Columbia University Press, 1984), 75–76.

PF 317).[15] And the term *parole*, appearing regularly throughout the essay—not to say throughout Blanchot's critical œuvre—is only a symptom, at the content level, of the prosopopoeic schema governing Blanchot's essay, if not his thought on literature more generally. In truth, the relationship between literature and speech is all but catachrestic in Blanchot: for those who are familiar with his work, to speak of the *parole* of literature—or, from 1960s onward, the *parole* of writing—is like speaking of the face of a mountain or the legs of a table. Literature, for Blanchot, *speaks*—and not just "in a manner of speaking"; it is, literally, *fabulous*—no matter how *ineffable* its content. (What's more, literature's agency is not limited to speech: literature, we are told at various moments in the course of Blanchot's text, "looks," "wants," "refuses," "thinks," "learns," "knows," "evades," "finds," "names," "sympathizes," "distrusts," "searches," "accuses," "condemns," "admires," "works," "plays," "recognizes," "tries," "realizes," and so on. For all its destabilizing, ambiguous essence (literature, we are reminded on more than one occasion, is drawn "to an unstable point where it can indiscriminately change both its meaning and its sign" [WF 342; PF 329]), literature in Blanchot's essay thus acquires all the formal attributes of a figure, of a *dramatis persona*, with which/whom the writer is made to wholly identify ("Literature is all that, in him"), in spite of the irreducible contradictions that thoroughly corrode such an identity from within.)

Like all fables, the fable of literature speaks a truth—an enigmatic truth that holds in an enigmatic sentence (a sentence, incidentally, with which the first part of Blanchot's essay practically concludes,[16] as if to sum up, in an impenetrable nutshell, everything that preceded it):

> Literature contemplates itself in revolution, it finds its justification in revolution, and if it has been called *Terror*, this is because its ideal is indeed that moment in history when "life endures death and maintains itself in it" in order to gain from death the possibility and the truth of speech [*la possibilité et la vérité de la parole*]. (WF 321–322; translation modified; PF 311)

---

[15] One might add, in passing, that "art" (very much an equivalent, in the context of Blanchot's essay, of "literature") receives the same prosopopoeic treatment: "What is art's complaint about everyday speech? 'It lacks meaning,' it *says*: art *feels* it is madness to think that in each word some thing is completely present through the absence that determines it" (WF 332–33; translation modified; my emphasis; PF 321).

[16] As is known, Blanchot's essay was originally published in two parts in *Critique*, respectively entitled "Le Règne animal de l'esprit" (November 1947) and "La Littérature et le droit à la mort" (January 1948).

That what we are faced with is of the order of an enigma, of a fundamental, universal question far exceeding the individuality of this or that subject—"this question," we recall from the opening of the essay, "is not the same as a writer's doubts or scruples" (WF 300; PF 293)—is further confirmed by the next sentence, the very last of the essay's first half: "This is the 'question' that seeks to pose itself in literature, the 'question' that is its essence" (WF 322; PF 311).

## Citation

Answering without answering, as myths are prone to do, the question with which *it all began* ("Let us suppose that literature begins at the moment when literature becomes a question"), the questioning essence that makes up literature is, moreover, shored up by a quotation: "that moment in history when 'life endures death and maintains itself in it' in order to gain ..." Now, most readers—whether reading Blanchot's essay today or in the late 1940s—would be familiar with Hegel's well-known phrase from the *Phenomenology of Spirit*. But Blanchot's use of quotation here is striking in more than one respect: not so much because—this should no longer surprise us—Blanchot makes use of yet another prosopopoeic (mimetic) device (after all, what is citation but the practice of making an absentee speak?) as because (1) the phrase remains anonymous (at no point does Blanchot explicitly name Hegel as the author of the quoted phrase); (2) it is repeated, like a mantra and with peremptory resolve, throughout the second part of the essay—not once, nor twice, but three times after its first occurrence[17]; and (3) in its penultimate and final occurrences, it loses its quotation marks and changes to italics (actually, to roman, given the entire essay is already italicized), as though its continued repetition entailed the disappearance of (the voice of) its author *into* Blanchot's text, thereby emphasizing the phrase's—rather than its author's—authority.

Almost exactly the same process is triggered in the following lines with another quotation of another well-known phrase, on which the second part of Blanchot's essay opens:

> Literature is bound to language. Language is reassuring and disquieting at the same time. When we speak, we gain control over things with an ease that satisfies

---

[17]    See Maurice Blanchot, *The Work of Fire* (Stanford: Stanford University Press, 1995), 327, 336, 343; *La Part du feu* (Paris: Gallimard, 1949), 316, 324, 330.

us. I say, "this woman," and she is immediately available to me, I push her away, I bring her close, she is everything I want her to be, she becomes the place in which the most surprising sorts of transformations occur and actions unfold: speech is life's ease and security. We cannot do anything with an object that has no name. (WF 322; translation modified; PF 311–312)

Once again, readers will have recognized that Blanchot's phrase—"I say, 'this woman'"—is calqued on Mallarmé's "I say, 'a flower!'" from *Crise de vers*. And once again, the phrase is impersonalized, recurring, and in its last iteration, devoid of quotation marks and romanized for emphasis. Impersonalized, not merely because Blanchot never plainly states that his phrase is drawn from Mallarmé (besides, as with the Hegel quotation, there was no need, given its glaring recognizability) but because he makes every effort to universalize it—in at least two ways: by modifying it, and as such by indicating that regardless of what the targeted signified of its content is ("a flower" or "this woman"), its elocutionary form ("I say, ' … ' ") performs the same function (the "reassuring" and yet "disquieting" act of naming, the demonstration of which is noted enough not to recall it here),[18] and by contending, in substance, that the phrase could just as well have been Hölderlin's or that of any other poet worthy of the name, or more exactly, "whose theme is the essence of poetry" (WF 322; PF 312). Like the Hegel quotation, the phrase is also recited several times after its first use,[19] as if it were an unassailable precept. Finally, in the last of its occurrences, quotation marks are dropped and type changes (to roman) for emphasis again, but this time, the phrase regains its verbatim form ("*I say a flower!*"), as though the original could only return, emphatically, divested of its (marks of) originarity.

In both cases, Blanchot's technique of citation—anonymization, declaratory repetition, eventual removal of quotation marks and replacement with emphasis—suggests that the function of "La Littérature et le droit à la mort" is not merely expository; it is also, to put it bluntly, mythic. For, in Blanchot's essay, Hegel's or Mallarmé's phrase no longer belongs to Hegel or Mallarmé; it belongs to the experience of literature itself—or rather, to its *myth*. (And it is of course no accident that five years after the publication of "La Littérature et le droit à la mort," Blanchot should choose Homer to exemplify the disappearance of the

---

[18] That said, the modification brought to Mallarmé's phrase deserves far more attention than can be spared here, not least because of its implications for Blanchot's figuration of the feminine (and gender, more broadly), here as elsewhere, and both in his criticism and fiction.

[19] See Blanchot, *The Work of Fire*, 322, 323, 327; *La Part du feu*, 312, 313, 316.

author as the very question and condition of narration.[20]) By definition, a myth has no author—because it *is* the authority, or what amounts to the same thing: it has no origin because it *is* the origin. And that is precisely what Blanchot's essay says of literature, and what all his work seeks to expiate in one way or another. In any case, by transferring the mythical power—the authorial originarity—of Hegel's and Mallarmé's words to literature, the citational operation performed by Blanchot entails that quotation itself is no longer necessary: citation has been subsumed, as it were, into the impersonality of literature. And to win out over citation, as Lacoue-Labarthe once remarked, has always been the task of literature:

> To write, "to go in for writing [*faire de la littérature*]," is—and has always been—
> to undertake to win out over citation [*regagner sur la citation*], or, if one prefers,
> to cite myth itself, as itself, in its own element (language), or even: to create myth
> (the Greeks called this *mythopoiesis*)—in short, to *re-cite* myth.[21]

In other words, in citing and reciting what Blanchot very aptly calls, in another well-known essay from *La Part du feu*, "the myth of Mallarmé" (i.e., the (poetic, literary) experience of language) (WF 63; PF 68), in citing and reciting the myth of Hegel (i.e., the (philosophical, speculative) experience of death), not to mention other instances of mythic (re-)citation (the "*Lazare, veni foras*" [WF 326; PF 316], for example, which, like the Hegelian and Mallarméan myths, returns in *L'Espace littéraire*), Blanchot's essay *produces* the myth of literature. Put differently, "La Littérature et le droit à la mort" is the critical *mythopoiesis* of modern literary experience, obliterating the subject of literature ("Literature," observes Blanchot, "now dispenses with the writer" [WF 328; PF 317]). Paradoxically, however, the dissolution of authorship into literature's myth becomes the very condition for the subject to (re-)emerge. If "to write," as Lacoue-Labarthe was saying, is "to *re-cite* myth," mythical re-citation is also, he adds, "to invent oneself as a *subject*":

> To write ... is ... to *re-cite* myth. Which is the best way not to cite it at all—one is
> too busy transcribing or fashioning it, regardless of whether or not it is dictated

---

[20]    "What would happen," writes Blanchot in "Le Chant des Sirènes" (1954), "if ... Homer drew his ability to narrate [*pouvoir de raconter*] exclusively from the fact that, under the name of Ulysses, ... he goes toward that place where the ability to speak and narrate [*pouvoir de parler et de raconter*] seems promised to him on the condition that he disappears in it? [§] That is one of the strange qualities, or should we say pretensions, of narration [*récit*]" (BC 7; translation modified; LV 14).

[21]    Philippe Lacoue-Labarthe, "Précis," *Critique* 357 (February 1977): 148 (my translation; emphasis in the original).

by the Muses—but to tear oneself away from its law, to claim an autonomy for oneself, to give oneself authority and power: to invent oneself as a *subject*, that is to say, as an *author*. A subject of myth, if you will—provided one understands therewith that the subject, freeing itself from myth, installs itself as myth [*s'instaure lui-même en mythe*] and that literature never ceases to produce itself, every time, as the *myth of the subject*.[22]

This, then, might go some way into explaining why Blanchot himself has become, as Lacoue-Labarthe suggested, "an absolutely mythical figure of the modern writer," why he has come to embody "Literature itself," why "his voice … was the Authority," and why, for so many of Blanchot's contemporaries, that authority "taught [them] Myth."[23]

## Figuration

But the myth of the writer cannot merely be put down to the essay's citational apparatus; it is also, and we are now approaching what is perhaps the most obvious fictionizing device in Blanchot's essay, the result of figuration—more precisely (or more philosophically), of an onto-typo-logy, which is to say, a logic whereby the (re)presentation of a given object—in this case, literature—is consummated by an emblematic figure, construed to typify the being—truth, essence, meaning, and so on—of the object in question, it being understood that in Blanchot's case, as commentators have shown time and again, the "onto-" is undermined from the outset (an "onto"-typo-logy, then).[24]

Although this is not the place to discuss in any detail the well-known analogy drawn in Blanchot's essay between literary experience and revolutionary terror, readers will recall his contention that revolutionary action—in other words, the modern (romantic) experience of politics (history), in which, Blanchot argues, absolute freedom (death) is realized—is "in every respect analogous" to what takes place in literature (WF 319; PF 309). Eventually, the analogy

---

[22] Ibid., 148.

[23] Lacoue-Labarthe, *Ending and Unending Agony*, 1, 67; *Agonie terminée, agonie interminable*, 10, 128.

[24] As I argue elsewhere (see "La Figure du politique," *Cahiers Maurice Blanchot* 3 (Autumn 2014): 84–103), there are elements in Blanchot's *thought* that also explicitly undermine the "typo-" (and indeed much of its originality and forcefulness rests precisely in this), but that does not prevent the figural from operating on a *formal* level. On the contrary.

enables Blanchot's argument to move between "The writer [who] sees himself in the Revolution" and "Literature [that] contemplates itself in revolution"—that is to say, between the (political) "event" in which a citizen claims his right to death (history) and the (poetic) "ideal" in which language is undergone as an experience of death (literature) (WF 321; PF 311). Formally speaking, however, what effectuates Blanchot's analogy is the enlistment of a figure—and not just any figure, but the figure of a writer, and not just any figure of the writer, but a figure of "the writer par excellence":

> In *1793* there is a man who identifies himself completely with revolution and the Terror. He is an aristocrat clinging to the battlements of his medieval castle, a tolerant man, rather shy and obsequiously polite: but he writes, all he does is write, and it does not matter that freedom puts him back into the Bastille after having brought him out, he is the one who understands freedom the best … He is also the man for whom death is the greatest passion and the ultimate platitude, who cuts off people's heads the way you cut a head of cabbage …, and yet no one has been more acutely aware that death is sovereign, that freedom is death. Sade is the writer par excellence, he combines all the writer's contradictions. (WF 321; translation modified; Blanchot's emphasis; PF 311)

It is worthwhile noting here that, of all the figures that Blanchot could have chosen to emblematize literature (Mallarmé, Hölderlin, Lautréamont, Ponge, Kafka, to mention only the most obvious candidates appearing in Blanchot's essay), it is Sade—in other words, a writer who was also, Blanchot insists, "a public figure and an important politician" (WF 321; translation modified; PF 311)—who is singled out and literally elevated ("par *excellence*"). Not only, then, is Blanchot's "onto"-typo-logical presentation of literary experience also, to borrow another term from Lacoue-Labarthe, "onto-steleo-logical"[25]—in other words, determined by a ("onto"-typo) logic of erection—or I should say, more cautiously, "onto"-steleo-logical; it is also distinctly tied to a political (namely, revolutionary) determination.[26] In truth, from a purely formal perspective, it is as if literature can only be fully presented from the figural standpoint of a

---

[25]   See Lacoue-Labarthe, "Typography," 43–138 (63–94); "Typographie," 165–270 (190–224); and Philippe Lacoue-Labarthe, "La figure (humaine)" (1992), in *Écrits sur l'art*, ed. Leonid Kharlamov and Aristide Bianchi (Dijon: Les presses du reel, 2009), 189–99.

[26]   And this operation can also be found elsewhere in Blanchot's critical writings at the time (see Opelz, "La Figure du politique," 84–103) and in fact extends, albeit in increasingly complex ways, to his later work (see Opelz, "La Précipitation du désastre," 31–62).

political experience (namely, of death—that is to say, according to Blanchot, of history itself). It is no surprise therefore that Blanchot should explicitly employ the language of myth to account for what is at stake here:

> Such periods [i.e. when *absolute* freedom becomes an event] are given the name Revolution. In that moment [*À cet instant*], freedom aspires to be realized in the *immediate* form of *everything* is possible, everything can be done. A fabulous moment [*moment fabuleux*]—and no one who has experienced it can completely recover from it, since he has experienced history as his own history and his own freedom as universal freedom. Fabulous moments indeed [*Moments fabuleux en effet*]: in them, fable speaks [*en eux parle la fable*]; in them, the speech of fable becomes action [*la parole de la fable se fait action*]. That the writer should be tempted by them is completely justified. (WF 318–319; translation modified; Blanchot's emphasis; PF 309)

He is tempted by them because in them, experience itself becomes mythic; he is fascinated by them because they are "the time in which literature becomes history" (WF 321; translation modified; PF 311). Blanchot adds (resorting once again to mimetic enunciation): "Any writer who, by the very fact of writing, is not led to think: 'I am the revolution, only freedom allows me to write,' is not really writing" (WF 321; translation modified; PF 311). In other words, the (mythic) experience of literature implies identification: "I *am* the revolution." And that, as Thomas Mann put it, is "the formula of myth,"[27] and what the figure of Sade is enlisted to present.

✳✳✳

Perhaps more so than its (truth) content—say, "the impossible experience of death is the *authorization* of literature," to recall Lacoue-Labarthe's claim with which I began—it is the (fictionizing) form of Blanchot's essay—mimesis, prosopopoeia, citation, figuration—that gives rise to myth. No matter how "insidious" literature's truth (WF 333; translation modified; PF 322), no matter how instable, how changing its substance ("It is as though at the very heart of literature and language ... a place of instability [*un point d'instabilité*], a power to transform its substance [*une puissance de métamorphose substantielle*], were

---

[27] Thomas Mann, "Freud and the Future" (1936), in *Essays of Three Decades*, trans. H. T. Lowe-Porter (New York: Knopf, 1947), 424 (translation modified); "Freud und die Zukunft," in *Gesammelte Werke in 13 Bänden* (Frankfurt: Fisher Verlag, 1974), 496.

reserved" [WF 343; translation modified; PF 330], writes Blanchot), in short, no matter how de(con)structive Blanchot's thought of literature, its mythical force not only survives at the formal level but absolves itself, as it were. For, if the content of Blanchot's essay (or to borrow the language of linguists, its *énoncés*) gives the impression that myth has been deposed, that by obstinately attacking the very basis upon which it could rise to presence, Blanchot has emptied literature of all mythical substrata, and that in doing so, mythification has been preemptively defused or the question of myth forestalled, myth remains secretly active at the level of form (of the essay's *énonciation*), inscribing itself invisibly on the surface of the text. Put differently, because the essay never really questions its own (mythifying) mode of presentation, because it presents what it has to say transparently, giving unfettered access to its content, and because that content's de(con)structive (demythifying) movement is all there is to see, not only does myth not emerge as a problem but even assuming it would, it would almost instantly be neutralized, pointing instead to an absence of myth. But "the absence of myth," as Georges Bataille observed in the same year as Blanchot's essay was first published, "is also a myth."[28] "The only *true* one,"[29] he went on to conclude ... but also, one might add, the most invisible, the most secretive, the most operative—in other words, an *absolute* myth. From this perspective, what Blanchot's essay offers is not so much a deconstruction of myth as its effacement.

The very clarity—or transparency—of the form, then, is what deceives us. And this deception is what makes literature speak, turning it into a fable. Philosophically speaking, the (re)presentation of literature in Blanchot's essay is governed by what might be called, for convenience's sake, an "onto"-prosopo-logy—that is to say, a logic deploying a prosopopoeic fiction of enunciation (which, after all, is none other than what Blanchot famously described in *L'Espace littéraire* as "the liberating passage from the first to the third person" [SL 73; EL 86]), capable of revealing the "being" of literature or whatever it "is"—be it nothingness, absence, lack, non existence, unreality, and so on—that the *parole* of literature is said to reveal, even if the revelation in question reveals itself to be unrevealing ("the revelation," remarks Blanchot, "of what revelation destroys" [WF 328; PF 317]). More simply put, criticism is a kind of rhapsody, through which literature speaks and repeats itself: "The critic," Blanchot would observe much later in *L'Entretien infini* (1969), "is a kind of rhapsode" (IC 390; EI 572).

---

28  Georges Bataille, "L'absence de mythe" (1947), in *Œuvres complètes*, XI (Paris: Gallimard, 1988), 236 (my translation).

29  Ibid., 236 (my translation; emphasis in the original).

And if "the critic's judgement," he would add, "has only the *form* of judgement," it is because "[that judgement], too, is literature; it *says* literature, which *says* nothing" (IC 328; translation modified; my emphasis; EI 480).

In Blanchot's endeavor to speak from the place where literature speaks, to be the *voice* of literature itself (what the Ancients called the Muse) addressing the writer (the poet) or speaking through him (the rhapsode), in his determination to echo the speech of literature in what he would later refer to as "critical *speech* [*la* parole *critique*]" (LS 2; translation modified; my emphasis; LS 10) or "the *speech* of commentary [*la* parole *de commentaire*]" (IC 389; my emphasis; EI 570), one is reminded of Nietzsche's oft-quoted posthumous fragment on Plato's dialogues: "Plato's philosophical drama belongs to neither tragedy nor comedy … It is far more epical, and in the spirit of Homer. It is Antiquity's novel. Destined, above all, not to practical ends but to reading: it is a rhapsody. It is literary drama."[30] If Beckett's *Comment c'est*, as in turn Blanchot argues, can be described as "our epic" (IC 329; EI 482), it would be no exaggeration to claim that "La Littérature et le droit à la mort" is the epic of modern literary criticism —or, since I have summoned Nietzsche, literary criticism's *Zarathustra*. (But Nietzsche, like Beckett, knew parody.)

What this means in Blanchot's case, at any rate, is that the essay's form has not yet caught up with its content: the text fundamentally destabilizes *what* it speaks of (literature) but not the fact *that* it speaks (for literature). On the contrary, it installs—instantiates—literature (and the discourse on literature) as *parole*. But this is where reading Blanchot historically becomes decisive. Indeed, it would only be a matter of time before Blanchot addressed the contradiction—between (mythifying) form and (demythifying) content— inhabiting his critical writings. This he did by developing, from the early 1960s onward, at least two interrelated formal innovations, perhaps the most important of his career as a critic, if not of twentieth-century literary criticism and theory as a whole: the *entretien*, whereby Blanchot revives but in order to deconstruct the mimetic (dialogic) mode of what had been since Plato a privileged form of discursive exposition, and the *fragmentaire*, whereby he revives but again in order to deconstruct the fragmentary mode of what had been, notwithstanding the Pre-Socratics and the Jena Romantics, a neglected

---

[30] Friedrich Nietzsche, "Posthumous Fragment Group 1 [108] (1869)," in *Kritische Gesamtausgabe Werke*, III: 3, ed. Giorgio Colli and Mazzino Montinari (de Gruyter: Berlin, 1978), 38 (my translation).

form of philosophical expression. With these innovations, the prevailing mode of criticism or commentary was essentially interrupted, thereby interrupting in the process, if not myth, at least its absolution. In other words, deconstruction in Blanchot had found its form, and with that discovery, the *question* of form was given its due. At least in principle.

Whence, also, the unashamedly superficial reading of Blanchot's essay given here. Foregrounding its surface—or its screen, as Lacan would have said—no doubt does an injustice to it. But such an injustice must be measured against the rarely averted danger of drowning in the abyssal clarity of Blanchot's thought.

# 3

# Absolute Modernism and *The Space of Literature*

James Martell

*A book, even a fragmentary one, has a center which attracts it. This center is not fixed, but is displaced by the pressure of the book and the circumstances of its composition. Yet it is also a fixed center which, if it is genuine [véritable], displaces itself, while remaining the same and becoming always more central, more hidden, more uncertain and more imperious. He who writes the book writes it out of desire for this center and out of ignorance. The feeling of having touched it can very well be only the illusion of having reached it. When the book in question is one whose purpose is to elucidate, there is a kind of methodological good faith [loyauté] toward what point it seems to be directed: here: seems to be directed: here, toward the pages entitled "Orpheus" Gaze. (SL v)*

## Centers

At the threshold of *The Space of Literature* we find the aforementioned lines, which could be described as an epigraph, an introduction, or even as instructions telling us how to read or understand the book. They talk about a center, or rather *the* center of the book, located in a subsection of its Vth section, *Inspiration*, called "Orpheus's Gaze". The lines present: "*a fixed center which … displaces itself*." They describe, in a book "*whose purpose is to elucidate,*" a certain "*methodological good faith* [loyauté méthodique]" that dictates that one must tell to what point the book seems to *go* (or to direct its course). Here, in the book called *The Space of Literature*, the direction seems to be toward those eight (or five in the English translation) pages called "Orpheus's Gaze". But, according to this introduction, this is still just an appearance, and Maurice Blanchot himself, the putative writer of the book, could never have known—as the writer of it—where was this center. The proof of his ignorance is the book itself, which, according to these lines at the threshold, was written precisely because of his ignorance and desire of the book's center.

But what exactly is this center, "Orpheus' Gaze"? In Ovid's version of the story in *The Metamorphoses*, after Orpheus' wife, Eurydice, is bitten by a viper and dies, Orpheus crosses the Styx into the Underworld, and convinces Hades and Persephone to let him bring Eurydice back. However, as a condition, they tell him "he must not turn his eyes behind him, until he emerged from the vale of Avernus, or the gift would be null and void." Here is the moment where everything—life and death—turns:

> Afraid she was no longer there, and eager to see her, the lover turned his eyes. In an instant she dropped back, and he, unhappy man, stretching out his arms to hold her and be held, clutched at nothing but the receding air. Dying a second time, now, there was no complaint to her husband (what, then, could she complain of, except that she had been loved?). She spoke a last "farewell" that, now, scarcely reached his ears, and turned again towards that same place.

Blanchot's version of this scene performs a series of substitutions that make— at least apparently—of *The Space of Literature* a work of literary criticism and not of literary fiction. According to the text, for Orpheus "Eurydice is the extreme that art can reach, … she is the profoundly obscure point toward which art and desire, death and night, seem to tend" (SL 171; translation modified). That "point" (Eurydice) is what Orpheus' work, his *oeuvre*, must bring back to the light of day. As with Ovid's version of the story, Blanchot's Orpheus "is capable of everything, except of looking this 'point' in the face, except of looking at the center of night in the night" (171; translation modified). However, as one enters further into "Orpheus' Gaze," both this "point" (Eurydice) and Blanchot's substitutions of the characters for concepts continue moving, shifting, turning, making of Orpheus' act of "turning away" (*detour*), a "turned towards"; of Eurydice's death, Orpheus' own; and of his impatient desire to see and possess her—instead of just *singing her*—the patience that will "seek to master [the absence of time] by making of it another time, measured otherwise" (173). The scene keeps turning thus until—when "Orpheus' Gaze" remarks its belonging to the section called *Inspiration* through a subsection with the same name—this very act of looking at Eurydice "without regard for the song, in the impatience and imprudence of desire which forgets the law" is declared to be inspiration itself (173). But what exactly does inspiration do here? Like a center, it "turns [*tourne*] Orpheus and propels him through an irresistible movement toward [Orpheus'] failure and [the] insignificance [and void of night]" (173; translation modified). In this way, inspiration produces both Orpheus' and his work's (*oeuvre*) failure. In contrast with Classical and Romantic versions of it, inspiration here guarantees neither the success nor the survival of the work. Thus, through the inspired gaze produced by desire, "the work is lost" (174).

Given all these conceptual substitutions, what exactly does Orpheus desire in Eurydice, as the object of his gaze—and thus as the center of *The Space of Literature*? This gaze, as "desire's measureless movement," brings—or at least attempts to do so—the work toward itself in its origin (174). Consequently, Eurydice's disappearance figures the disappearance or the "eclipse" of the work itself, "the nostalgic return to the uncertainty of the origin" (174). Now, does this center of *The Space of Literature*, with all its turns and movements, have only *one* origin? At the end of this putative center, in its last subsection, "The Leap," Blanchot describes the difficulty of determining any one origin or true beginning of writing—and literature: "one writes only if one reaches that instant which nevertheless one can only approach in the space opened by the movement of writing. To write, one has to write already" (176).

Let us gaze now into another center. *The Space of Literature* was published in 1955. Two years before, Samuel Beckett's *Watt* appeared.[1] Within this other book, written by the most terminal of modernists, a similar, (un)fixed, hidden because exposed center appears. This center is part of a painting that the character Watt finds in the room of one of the servants of Mr. Knott, Erskine. This painting is not described in a detached manner; rather, it is presented as inseparably attached to Watt's sight of it. In an analogous way as the introductory lines describing the center of *The Space of Literature*, this painting with its center presents itself together with that which it affects as center: a gaze. Within this fragment we see and experience thus not only what is within the frame, but also Watt himself, and through him, the whole book that bears his name. In other words, as a metonymy of the character—and of what is most essential in him, since this experience melts Watt at the core, transforming his vision into tears—and of the

---

[1] While at the moment of writing *The Space of Literature*, it is very unlikely that Blanchot had read *Watt*, it is well known the importance that Beckett would play later in Blanchot's writing. This is epitomized by Blanchot's juxtaposition of both his and Beckett's words in "Oh All to End," trans. Leslie Hill, in *The Blanchot Reader*, ed. Michael Holland (Oxford: Blackwell, 1995), 298–300.

book as a whole, this (un)fixed center presents us with *Watt*'s, the book's origin: the desire and ignorance of its center. Here is the passage:

> The only other object of note in Erskine's room was a picture, hanging on the wall, from a nail. A circle, obviously described by a compass, and broken at its lowest point, occupied the middle foreground, of this picture. Was it receding? Watt had that impression. In the eastern background appeared a point, or dot. The circumference was black. The point was blue, but blue! The rest was white … Watt wondered how long it would be before the point and circle entered together upon the same plane. Or had they not done so already, or almost? And was it not rather the circle that was in the background, and the point that was in the foreground? … And he wondered what the artist had intended to represent (Watt knew nothing about painting), a circle and its centre in search of the other, or a circle and its centre in search of a centre and a circle respectively, … or a circle and a centre not its centre in search of a centre and its circle respectively, in boundless space, in endless time (Watt knew nothing about physics), and at the thought that it was perhaps this, a circle and a centre not its centre in search of a centre and its circle respectively, in boundless space, in endless time, then Watt's eyes filled with tears that he could not stem, and they flowed down his fluted cheeks unchecked, in a steady flow, refreshing him greatly.[2]

As we contemplate the centers of these two works, we are faced with a series of questions not unrelated to the possibilities contemplated by Watt in front of the painting. First, philosophically speaking, does a circle always accompany a center? In other words, does the idea of center always entail the idea of circle, of an eternal or sempiternal figure, simultaneously inside and outside the structure, inside and outside of time? In order to start considering the modernism of *The Space of Literature*, we can begin by asking: when Blanchot decides to open his book with an explanation of the centers of literary texts, is this a quintessential modernist gesture? Is a center a modern(ist) object or notion? In other words, does the idea of center, as it is developed in modern thought, and/or in modern politics, art, geometry, or history, determine in a particular way the notion of center within literature? Etymologically, a center—*centrum* in Latin, κέντρον in Ancient Greek—designates a spur, a spike, or the point of the compass: the center of the circle. Its geometrical traits and conceptual markers give it certain particularities that, while recognizing it as part of a structure, separate it from all other regular parts. It is "equidistant," the "middle point," that around which

---

2   Samuel Beckett, "Watt," in *Samuel Beckett, The Grove Centenary Edition. Volume I Novels*, ed. Paul Auster (New York: Grove Press, 2006), 272–73.

"everything rotates," a "source," the "principal point," and so on. It includes thus the idea of *some*-thing related but different to *every*-thing else (i.e., equidistant). When we think about Renaissance's theories of perspective, or Neo-platonic spheres, the role of the center and circle—as complex as it can be—appears clear and crucial. But when we talk about modernism, and modernist literature or modern thought, can we easily define its circles and centers, or even its regular and irregular parts and structures? *The Space of Literature*'s first line suggests this difficulty, when it says: "*A book*, even a fragmentary one, *has a center which attracts it.*" How does a fragmentary work, a work that has neither regular parts, nor regular relations between its parts, have a center? And if it, notwithstanding its fragmentarity, has a center, does this make it more or less modern or modernist? Especially when both Romanticism (as defined by Jean-Luc Nancy and Philippe Lacoue-Labarthe in *The Literary Absolute*) and modernism—and perhaps, at the end, all epochs as ἐποχή or suspension—can be said to have fragmentarity as one of its essential literary and artistic principles.[3] Before we answer this, let us believe and follow the epigraph, the instructions of *The Space of Literature*, and examine its avowed center.

## Eurydice: The point

*Von einem gewissen Punkt an gibt es keine Rückkehr mehr. Dieser Punkt ist zu erreichen.*

Kafka.

As mentioned before, "Orpheus' Gaze" is a subsection of section V. *Inspiration*. Before we reach this point in the book, we have already gone through the main sections: I. *The Essential Solitude*, II. *Approaching Literature's Space*, III. *The Work's Space and Its Demand*, and IV. *The Work and Death's Space*; and after V.

---

[3]    The question of fragmentarity in Blanchot, and for modernism in general, is too complex to develop it here sufficiently. However, it does underscore a problem of periodization, and thus, complicates any clear distinction between the romantic and modernist fragments. As Leslie Hill shows, through the fragment as an essential trait of writing, all epochs are interrupted, but at the same time, they interrupt their own interruption: "An epoch is what begins or ends. But it is also what can never begin or end. And this is why, as Blanchot explains in *L'Écriture du désastre*, all writing, under the aegis of the fragmentary—and all writing, suggests Blanchot, partakes in the fragmentary—not only interrupts history, but, just as importantly, interrupts its own interruption" (50). In Leslie Hill, *Maurice Blanchot and Fragmentary Writing. A Change of Epoch* (London: Continuum, 2012). This interruption of the interruption as history is what I will call in what follows Blanchot's "absolute modernism."

*Inspiration*, we will read VI. *Communication and the Work*, and VII. *Literature and the Original Experience*. Afterward we find three short annexes that are referenced throughout the book. Before we reach the mythological figures of Orpheus and Eurydice, the question of the literary space is examined mainly through the works of Mallarmé, Kafka, and Rilke. After this center, the book does not focus on any particular author, until the very end; or we should say after the end, since "Hölderlin's Itinerary" is part of the annexes, and not of the main text. Other authors, both writers and philosophers, are mentioned and quoted throughout the book: Hugo von Hofmannsthal, Breton, Gide, Valéry, Rimbaud, Nietzsche, Hegel, René Char, Dostoyevsky, Goethe, Lautréamont, and others, as well as artists like Cézanne, Goya, Giacometti, and Van Gogh, making the space of literature a space that includes the visual or plastic arts, or, in other words, a "literary" space that is not necessarily discursive or linguistic. For example, in the threshold between Part II and Part III, writing is described as the finding of a point that Blanchot describes through an encounter with Giacometti's sculptures. As with *Watt's* painting, the spectator here is taken away, outside of her limits, through perception:

> When we look at the sculptures of Giacometti, there is a point where they are no longer subject to the fluctuations of appearance or to the movement of perspective. One sees them *absolutely*: no longer reduced, but withdrawn from reduction, irreducible, and, in space, masters of space through their power to substitute for space the unmalleable, lifeless profundity of the imaginary. This point, whence we see them irreducible, takes us to infinitum; it is the point at which here coincides with nowhere. To write is to find this point. No one writes who has not enabled language to maintain or provoke contact with this point. (SL 48)

This point, like the center in Watt's picture, comes and goes, appearing and disappearing through the analyses of the authors. It marks the centrality of ambiguity in Mallarmé's work ("This point is ambiguity itself" [44]), as well as the goal and limit of writing: "The need to write is linked to the approach toward this point at which nothing can be done with words" (52). Fundamentally, as an evanescent center ("The Central Point"), it describes the space of literature as the writer's always-already begun search for writing's origin. Because writing then is its search for its own origin as center, *The Space of Literature* is approached mostly in *spatial* terms, with descriptions and analyses of the physical or empirical conditions of the writer/reader (essential solitude), their movement toward the space (approaching), and the literary space's relation to other delimitations (death's space). Thus, while before the center called "Orpheus' Gaze," we are approaching this space; after the center—but it is already there at the beginning, in the lines at the threshold, as the search of its beginning and center—we as readers are already deep within the literary space, and the question becomes, what does this space as literature do for (or to) the reader(s), art, communication, and experience in general?

But why exactly is Orpheus' Gaze the center of *The Space of Literature*? Why are these two figures, Orpheus and Eurydice, and their last encounter, used as the center or pivotal point of the book? The question of this encounter, or the place where such a question appears, is also split in—at least—two parts, confirming what the lines at the threshold announced to us, *"the feeling of having touched [the center] can very well be only the illusion of having reached it."* Before "Orpheus' Gaze," Orpheus has appeared already in connection to Rilke's work in section IV, subsection III ("Rilke and Death's Demand") in two separate parts: "Song as Origin: Orpheus" and "Orphic Space." However, in "Orpheus' Gaze" there is a mention of neither Rilke nor of his *Sonnets to Orpheus*. While they are certainly influenced by the preceding analysis of Rilke's Orpheus, these versions of Orpheus and Eurydice are strictly Blanchot's and *The Space of Literature*'s own figures. They are not anymore the literary creations, adaptations, or characters of Rilke's work. They are the figures and events, the metamorphosing center of Blanchot's fragmentary book. However, because one of the traits of Blanchot's fragmentary writing is precisely its porosity (even if *The Space of Literature* is not as overtly fragmentary as later work like *L'attente l'oubli* or *Le pas au-delà*), there is no clear limit between his figures of Orpheus and Eurydice, and the ones he analyzes earlier in the work of Rilke. For instance, the metamorphoses of *The Space of Literature*'s Orphic center are foreseen in one of the sections focused on Rilke's Orpheus, "Song as Origin: Orpheus":

> Orpheus is the act of metamorphoses: not the Orpheus who has conquered death, but he who always dies, who is the demand of disappearance, and who disappears in the anguish of this disappearance, an anguish which becomes song, a word which is the pure movement of dying. Orpheus dies a little more than we do, he is we ourselves bearing the anticipated knowledge of our death, knowledge which is dispersion's intimacy. (142–143; translation modified)

Thus, through Orpheus the links between the spaces of literature and death appear clearly. The work (*l'œuvre*), poems, and art are connected—and somewhat confused—with the space of death. Rilke shows thus the essential link between the spaces of death and literature—just like Kafka, Mallarmé, and Dostoyevsky, albeit each in a different manner, with a different set of figures according to the need of their work. It is in Rilke's Orphic space where *The Space of Literature* shows the essential link between "Death's Space and the Word's." This shared topography is "The Open." This is the space of the poem, "the Orphic space to which the poet doubtless has no access, where he can penetrate only to disappear" (142). This is why Orpheus, disappearing through his gaze with Eurydice, is we ourselves, but dying more, charged with the anticipated knowledge of our death. He is, however, here still a literary creation, not so much a sonnet or any poem, but a poem if this one could become a poet. Yet he is not a finished poem. He is rather the mysterious origin of poetry, the "sacrificial point."

> Orpheus would be the poem, if the poem could become a poet, the ideal and example of poetic plenitude. Yet he is at the same time not the completed poem, but something more mysterious and more demanding: the origin of the poem, the sacrificial point which is no longer the reconciliation of the two domains, but the abyss of the lost god, the infinite trace of absence, a moment to which Rilke comes closest perhaps in these three lines://O you, lost god! You, infinite trace!/ By dismembering you the hostile forces had to disperse you/To make of us now hearers and a mouth of Nature. (143; translation modified)

According to this passage, Rilke's poetry "comes closest" in these verses to Orpheus, but the latter disappears again in adherence to his essence (being "the demand of disappearance"). When he reappears in the book, this time as the avowed center of *The Space of Literature*, he is, in its cyclical appearing/disappearing, the circle in search of its center. As we know, this center or point is Eurydice, and she is for Orpheus "the extreme that art can reach, … the profoundly obscure point toward which art and desire, death and night, seem to tend" (171). Eurydice is thus the point of the circle, the center of the center of *The Space of Literature*. She is the extreme or limit of art, the obscure point where art, desire, death, and night collide. However, as a center of this fragmentary work, she is also already the circle, the periphery, or limit looking for itself as center. If the avowed center of the book is titled "Orpheus' Gaze," it is because, as we saw in *Watt*'s painting, the center is a point that, even when fixed, continues changing place. The center is this constant movement, the appearing and disappearing of itself as center through the experience of (s)he[4] who is looking for it. It is the writer's or artist's contemplation that starts the movement and existence of *a* center and *a* circle, or *their* center and *their* circle, in the first place.

But is this really the causality of this movement? Can we say for certain that the writer precedes the search for the center, that it is only their desire that brings to existence the center of (their) writing? When the center, Eurydice, is the point toward which art, desire, death, and night seem to tend, can we say that the subject who is searching for them (the writer) exists before them? The work of art, of writing, is different from work as the Hegelian transformation of nature. The work of art, writing itself, begins with Orpheus' gaze. But as we saw in the last section of "Orpheus' Gaze," "The Leap," in order to reach this point, this beginning, Orpheus needed to have already arrived there: "*To write, one has to write already*" (176; my italics). In the movement of causality of writing, we are faced thus with a circle again. As we see, this circular movement is essential to the construction of *The Space of Literature*. Consequently, this circle is also its center, in the sense of source, the point from where it starts, and around which it turns its thought. Earlier in the book, this center had already appeared in the subsection "Death as Possibility," within a subsection titled "The Circle": "Whenever thought is caught in a circle, this is because it has touched upon something original, its point of departure beyond which it cannot move except to return" (93).[5] But if temporality is circular in this space, how can something be "original," according to what sense of linearity, or to what kind of interruption? Is this a modern or modernist temporality, a modernist origin, or the modernist erasure of all origins?

## The modern ghosts

In *The Pathos of Distance*, Jean-Michel Rabaté revisited the question of modernism in relation to French literature: "'Modernism' is a loaded word when understood in a French context, whereas its meaning is relatively clear in an Anglo-Saxon context … If we agree that there is room for a specific French

---

[4]  The question of gender in *The Space of Literature* extends beyond the limits of this article, as well as beyond the fact that there is not one mention of a female writer or artist in the book. Through the notions of the mother and maternity, this question is connected with the idea of the "origin" of the artist, as well as of the work of art. We will explore this question on the one before the last section of this chapter.

[5]  *SL*, 93.

modernism, I would like to explore how it displays a specific pathos of distance as opposed to proximity."[6] Twenty years earlier, in *The Ghosts of Modernity* (twenty-three if we consider the original French edition, *La penultième est morte*), Rabaté had already touched on this subject, the existence of French modernism, albeit in a less direct fashion. He had not examined it as a separate possibility, but rather as part of a wider phenomenon that, beginning with the Enlightenment, continued with contemporary literature, and was represented— in this narrative—by three French-speaking writers: "Modernism postulates both the necessity and the impossibility of mourning—and my contention is that this applies not only to high modernism but also to a wider history that begins with the Enlightenment, reaches its heights with Mallarmé, and finally informs the history of postmodernity, from Beckett to contemporary writers such as Blanchot and Derrida."[7] According to this description, modernism was neither a simple reaction to tradition, nor an unambiguous search for the new. For Rabaté and other readers of Blanchot, like Derrida, modernism was not just a historical or literary event, but also one of the most drastic questions posed to history and historicity. Modernism's postulation of "the necessity and the impossibility of mourning"—in resonance with Blanchot's own aporetic "pas au-delà," or with Orpheus' refusal of Eurydice's death, and with her subsequent, and through literature, cyclical, "double death"—showed an irresolution with regard to temporality itself, and, thus, to the ideas of both origin and ending. Like Derrida in *Specters of Marx*—where he quotes *La penultième est morte*— Rabaté showed how the temporality of modernism is that of the specter or spectral, an instance or figure "never contemporaneous with itself," a projection that "anticipates, and returns to mythical origins, but that also teaches us more about the 'present', which it historicizes."[8]

But why is it then that, while High or Anglo-American modernism are readily accepted, French modernism is something we still need to agree on? If one of the main traits of modernism, with its "stylistic experimentation" and efforts "to restate ancient cultural themes,"[9] is its ghostly temporality that, returning from the totality of the past, haunts the present with unforeseeable futures, is not Blanchot's *The Space of Literature*, and his whole oeuvre, one of the most

---

[6]  Jean-Michel Rabaté, *The Pathos of Distance: Affects of the Moderns* (New York: Bloomsbury, 2016), 41.
[7]  Jean-Miche Rabaté, *The Ghosts of Modernity* (Gainesville: University Press of Florida, 2001), xvi.
[8]  Ibid., 3.
[9]  Rabaté, *The Pathos of Distance*, 41.

extreme examples of modernist literature? If modernist literary texts construct an interruption of temporality and history, where a spectrographic suspension haunts any possibility of a present, would not Blanchot's literary space—as the space of the circular search for the ultimate origin of both work and poet, an origin that, like the point or center (Eurydice), disappears and reappears without end—present to us the ultimate example of modernism? Let us consider, for instance, a description of the neuter—from *The Infinite Conversation*—as an essential trait of literature:

> Neuter might be a way of describing the literary act that participates neither in affirmation nor in negation [*ni d'affirmation ni de négation*] and (in the first instance) releases meaning as a ghost [*comme fantôme*], a haunting obsession [*hantisse*], a simulacrum of meaning, as though it was in literature's nature to be spectral, not haunted by itself, but because we think of it as supplying the prerequisite of all meaning [*ce préalable de tout sens*] which is its haunting obsession [*sa hantise*].[10]

If the neuter is indeed one of literary modernism's main traits, then the modernist "literary and stylistic revolution"[11] described by Rabaté would have invaded not only the genre of prose, but also all discourse, and the possibility of meaning in general. In other words, if Rabaté among others could propose a wider modernism crossing national, historical, and linguistic boundaries, it is because the "stylistic experimentation" and efforts "to restate ancient themes" were not the cause of the modernist drive, but some of its consequences. They were the outcome of the literary act's ghostly "neither affirmation nor negation" status, of its haunting possibilities, not only as literature or prose, but also and primarily as the preconditions of all meaning, all discourse, and all writing in general.

As a consequence, if Blanchot's fragmentary writing is the primary example of this modernist questioning of the preconditions of all writing, discourse, and meaning in general, it is because his work performs an analogous, but more radical, suspension of meaning than Husserl's phenomenological epoché (ἐποχή). While it also suspends everyday experience, it does not do so in order to, as Leslie Hill explains it, uncover "a new scientific domain." It goes a step further:

---

[10]  Maurice Blanchot, *The Infinite Conversation*, trans. S. Hanson (Minnesota: University of Minnesota Press, 2012), 304. Translation modified and quoted by Hill, *Maurice Blanchot and Fragmentary Writing*, 61–62.

[11]  Rabaté, *The Pathos of Distance*, 41.

In Blanchot, however, the epochal experience of writing was more radical. It was not conditioned by the strategic ambition of uncovering "a new scientific domain," as Husserl called it. It therefore not only set aside the world and its activities, not only suspended everyday psychological experience; it went a step further in neutralising all certainty, including the transcendental claim … that a first or last ground might thus be reached, embodied in what Husserl, deploying the phenomenological reduction as the gateway to understanding of the constitution of the world as such, articulated as "pure consciousness in its own absolute being."[12]

In other words, if Blanchot's criticism of modernist literature exposes the preconditions of discourse, of writing, and of experience in general, it does so by not stopping at any certainty, and especially not at the philosophical certainty of a present subject—transcendental or otherwise. The suspension that Blanchot's sui-generis *epoché* performs—what I call here his *absolute* modernism, in the etymological sense of separation (*ab-solvo*)—creates a temporality where no subject, no philosophical or empirical voice can ultimately affirm itself. "The Essential Solitude" that is necessary for entering *The Space of Literature* demands a spectralization of both time and self that precludes any possibility of the present, and consequently, of any given presence:

> The writer's solitude, that condition which is the risk he runs, seems to come from his belonging, in the work, to what always precedes the work. Through him, the work comes into being; it constitutes the solidity of the beginning. But he himself belongs to a time ruled by the indecisiveness inherent in beginning anew. (SL 24)

In other words, in the modernist circle's eternal search of a/the center, the subject—just as Watt—disintegrates in its (or a) sempiternal return. This is the return of what never is (or was) present, of what has always already passed and thus can only come back. This is the modernist ghost, where all knowledge is just a recognition, a constant uncanny remembering of nobody that ruins all possibility of delimiting a self, and with it, any period or epoch, literary or otherwise.

What distinguishes, for example, this *absolute* modernism, from the modernism identified with an epoch like "modernity," as the one proposed by Fredric Jameson, is precisely this focus on the beginning (or what comes before it), and through it, on the condition of possibility of time and history

---

[12]   Leslie Hill, ibid., 57.

themselves. In comparison, a non-absolute modernism (a modernity), defined by a historical epoch and its material conditions would be, paradoxically, circumscribed ultimately not through time but rather through a concrete series of spaces (countries, metropoles, colonies, etc.).[13]

## Modern origin(s)

Now, if due to our modernist ghosts, every possibility of delimiting a subject, a self, or a period is doomed from the beginning, does this mean that literature has always been the same? The authors and artists analyzed and mentioned in *The Space of Literature* all belong to modern times (e.g., Hugo von Hofmannsthal, Breton, Gide, Valéry, Rimbaud, Nietzsche, Hegel, René Char, Dostoyevsky, Goethe, Lautréamont, Cézanne, Goya, Giacometti, Van Gogh), but what is it that defines their—and Blanchot's—own modernism, that distinguishes it from previous literary epochs where the modernist drive has already appeared? Linking the question of modernism with the questions of modernity and modern thought—and thus pointing as well to the complex relations between the French terms "moderne," "modernité," and "modernisme"[14]—the modern epoch is described in *The Space of Literature* as a double movement, a "perpetual play of exchange between an existence that becomes an increasingly pure, subjective intimacy and the ever more active and objective conquest of the world according to the aims of the realizing mind and the productive will" (SL 215). According to this description, what modernity marks is the beginning of a constant split, a play where, after the gods are gone—and even the memory of their abandonment

---

[13] As an example, in "Modernism and Imperialism" Jameson decides to read modernism's "hesitation" "between the contingency of physical objects and the demand for an impossible meaning," or its "substitution of a spatial or perceptual 'meaning' (whatever now that is) for the other kind (whatever that was, or might be in the future)" always in terms of a space or concrete location (160). This is in line with his need to limit, in this text, the meaning of "Imperialism" to a defined epoch of modern times. "Modernism and Imperialism," in *The Modernist Papers*, ed. Fredric Jameson (London: Verso, 2007), 152–69.

[14] As we know, the history of the concepts of modernism and modern(ities) is complex and different according to the language and countries. Jean-Michel Rabaté gives a good overview of the origin of the term "modernism": "The concept of modernism was invented for an Anglo-Saxon corpus in a promotion by academics for academics; this took place in the 1950s and was retroactively applied to works from the 1920s. Such a periodization is not relevant if we consider the French cultural scene or its Spanish counterpart. However, the concept of modernism has begun to be used by French literary critics. If an influential review in English speaking countries is *Modernism/Modernity*, its French equivalent is simply called *Modernités*," since this is "the term that was felt to be more relevant was that of 'modernity'—a *modernité* encompassing a tradition of the new taking Baudelaire, Mallarmé, Lautréamont, and Jarry as its beacons" (41). In Rabaté, *The Ghosts of Modernity*.

has been forgotten—humankind is divided between a retreat within the subject's innermost essence, and the working and transformation—the conquest—of the world through the will. It is according to this division that we can distinguish the different kinds of art and literature developed in modern times. On the one hand, there is the dwelling on interiority, "the formal devotion which nineteenth-century writers stress," focusing on the artist and their "états d'âme" (SL 236). On the other, there is work, transformation, and "the values upon which the world is built" (220).

Thus, with the gods gone, and together with them, the transcendent absolute, modernity is the moment

> when the absolute tends to take the form of history, when the times have concerns and interests no longer in harmony with the sovereignty of art, when the poet yields to the belletrist [*litterateur*] and he to the chronicler of the day-to-day—at the moment when through the forces of the times art disappears. (220; translation modified)

But what exactly happens with art or literature when the absolute takes the form of history? The direct answer is that it becomes modern. But it is not until it becomes self-conscious, self-reflexive of this moment, of this interruption, and, as a consequence, that it interrupts all history—including its own—separating itself from any linear conception of time—including and especially that of Romanticism, and any "end of times"—that it becomes modern*ist*. Absolute modernism would be thus this irruption of the absolute in history *as history*, or what Leslie Hill defines in Blanchot as "epoch," that is, the moment when "all writing, under the aegis of the fragmentary—and all writing, suggests Blanchot, partakes in the fragmentary—not only interrupts history, but, just as importantly, interrupts its own interruption."[15]

We have thus the definition: the modernist literature of *The Space of Literature* is the conscious, self-reflective moment of the absolute incarnating itself in history *as* history (something akin to Nietzsche's affirmation of all history through its negation in the Eternal Return of the Same). According to Hegel, this moment marks art's realization of its own demise. After this, the artist must retreat in its utmost interiority, or leave his/her place to the "littérateur," and he to the chronicler of the day-to-day, the everyday man, whose work will empirically transform the world. Nevertheless, for Blanchot, it is here that art appears:

[15] Hill, *Maurice Blanchot and Fragmentary Writing*, 50.

as a search in which something essential is at stake, where what counts is no longer the artist, or his "états d'âme" or the close appearance of man, or active labor or any of the values upon which the world is built or even any of the other values upon which formerly the beyond opened. (220; translation modified)

This search for "something essential" would be the search for the fragmentary, transparency, or the neuter as that which—suspending, placing it in the absolute of parenthesis—precedes being: "the neuter of what we call being, which already places being in parenthesis and in some sense precedes it, having always already neutralized it less by a nihilating operation than by a non-operative operation" (IC 303; translation modified). This double suspension, beyond any phenomenological epoché, is absolute modernism, the modernism of Hölderlin, Mallarmé, Rilke, Breton, Kafka, Char, and others—as theorized and practiced by Blanchot, Derrida, and others. But can we say then that our own search is over, that we have delineated Blanchot's literary space—of absolute modernism?

> Why, instead of dissipating itself in pure enjoyable satisfaction [*satisfaction jouissante*], or in the frivolous vanity of an escapist ego, has the passion of art, whether it be in Van Gogh or in Kafka, become absolutely serious? Why has it become passion for the absolute? … This is not an easy question to answer; perhaps it cannot yet be perceived in its *true light* [*sous son vrai jour*]. (SL 216; translation modified; my italics)

How are we going to answer it then? Is there any way of answering a question not "in its *true* light/day," or in other words, not as a question of truth?

In the last section of the book, Blanchot asks, "Could the nontrue be an essential form of authenticity? In that case, we do, then, have the work? We have art?" (247; translation modified). In the next paragraph the text comments: "To this question there can be no response. The poem is the answer's absence" (247). However, at the end of the first question ("could the nontrue … "), a number sends us to the last footnote of the book. In this footnote, art's uselessness, its demise in front of the world's history is put into question. Here, the "nontrue" of the work of art can still be related to "historical actuality." In fact, here, the work of art, in its absolute modernist stance, is a consequence, a reaction, or at least a response to modernity's strive for fulfilment, that is to say, to the world's attempt at full meaning under the mastery of humankind. In response to the world's logical development toward "the broad daylight of truth" the poet and the artist have a mission: to remind us, and what is more, to bring us back to *that point*, to error, to the meaningless, from where—perhaps—the source, *the center* of all authenticity springs.

the more the world is affirmed as the future and broad daylight of truth, where everything will have value, bear meaning, where the whole will be achieved under the mastery of man and for his use, the more it seems that art must descend toward *that point where nothing has meaning yet*, the more it matters that art maintain the movement, the insecurity and the grief of that which escapes every grasp and all ends. The artist and the poet seem to have received this mission: to call us obstinately back to error, to turn us toward that space where everything we propose, everything we have acquired, everything we are, all that opens upon the earth and in the sky, returns to insignificance, and where what approaches is the nonserious and the nontrue, as if perhaps thence sprang the source of all authenticity. (247; my italics)

## The sex of the ghost

What is this space "where everything we propose, everything we have acquired, everything we are, all that opens upon the earth and in the sky, returns to insignificance"? Is this the space of the modernist ghost? Or, the spectral temporality of absolute modernism, where nothing really happens, but everything happens *again*, everything recurs, as the past haunts the future without any possibility of an actual, isolated present? If this is the space of the neuter, where the literary act "releases meaning as a ghost, a haunting obsession, a simulacrum of meaning,"[16] who or what are these ghosts? Are ghosts still a "who," or a "what," or perhaps neither, a "where"?[17] Is this still the ghost of Eurydice as the center of *The Space of Literature*? While modernity is the epoch inaugurated by the departure of the gods, as modernism it is also the time of the

---

[16] Blanchot, *The Infinite Conversation*, as quoted in Hill, *Maurice Blanchot and Fragmentary Writing*, 62.

[17] The centrality of the question of "where" for certain absolute modernism or "absolute writing" linking Flaubert, Kafka, Joyce, Blanchot, and others, like Clarice Lispector, is well described by Cixous: "Writing pushed to an absolute degree differs from that of human and mercantile dimensions. We can verify this by taking as the main question the locus of *writing* and not that of art. Flaubert advanced in this dilemma to the point of madness. For him, the question is not who but where, from where? In the course of the journey, Flaubert—like Kafka—got lost" (2). In Hélène Cixous, *Readings: The Poetics of Blanchot, Joyce, Kafka, Kleist, Lispector, and Tsvetayeva*, ed. and trans. Verena Andermatt Conley (Minneapolis: University of Minnesota Press, 1991). As I have mentioned elsewhere [*Samuel Beckett and the Encounter of Philosophy and Literature*, ed. Arka Chattopadhyay and James Martell (London: Roman Books, 2013)], the importance of locality for writing was underscored by Beckett in his translation of *L'innommable/The Unnameable*, since of the three questions with which the text starts, "Où maintenant?"/"Where now?" is the only one, and the first, that does not change place between the two versions.

spectral, the epoch of ghosts. But whose ghosts are these, and of whom? Of the gods', Eurydice's, Orpheus', Blanchot's? Let me conjure Rabaté's voice yet again:

> What is, then, a ghost? As noted by Spinoza, this question cannot be dissociated from the question regarding the sex of ghosts. The question "what is a ghost?" could be untenable, the impossible interrogation par excellence, to the extent that it presupposes an enunciative mechanism from which it can never isolate itself.[18]

Thus, the question "what is a ghost" cannot be separated from "who asks the question of/to the ghosts," who summons them? And from where? Within *The Space of Literature*, who summons all these ghosts, both the names within the book, as well as the words called forth by these names, that is to say, the words and traces that become works written, sculpted, or painted by ghosts? Let us look again at most, if not all, of them: Hugo von Hofmannsthal, Breton, Gide, Bataille, Flaubert, Heidegger, Bergson, Goethe, Valéry, Ponge, Rimbaud, Malraux, Nietzsche, Hegel, René Char, Novalis, Michaux, Heraclitus, Dostoyevsky, Picasso, Rodin, Tolstoy, Keats, Proust, Goethe, Lautréamont, Nerval, Cézanne, Goya, Giacometti, Van Gogh, and others. As far as I can tell, besides Eurydice—and a certain Freudian mother—there are no female ghosts within the book, or at least there are no female *authors* of ghosts. This is why, when earlier we described the center, following our analogy with Watt, we had difficulties not gendering (s)he who perceives it: Orpheus, Watt, Blanchot, Beckett.

The absence of a female voice in *The Space of Literature* is conspicuous, and troubling. In an analysis that examines the conflation of Eurydice and the mother within the book, Lynn Huffer has drawn very important consequences, not only for Blanchot studies, but also for modernist studies in general. In her reading, Blanchot's "purportedly neutral workings of figural language rely on an ideologically-charged, value-laden structure of meaning embedded in the politics of sexual difference. Those politics, to put it simply, erase the feminine so that the masculine may speak."[19] In other words, according to Huffer, even if Blanchot's project in *The Space of Literature* was to present the neutral and fragmentary space of literature beyond or before the instauration of meanings that create a politics of sexual difference, the literary space does not hinder the instauration of these meanings, and what is more, it is itself construed upon them. In Huffer's reading, by having as its center Orpheus' gaze, what

[18]   Rabaté, *The Ghosts of Modernity,* 228.
[19]   Lynne Huffer, *Maternal Pasts, Feminine Futures* (Stanford: Stanford University Press, 1998), 51.

*The Space of Literature* performs is "the transformation of the void at the center of figuration in the voice of a speaking subject … That void is feminine—Eurydice, the mother—and that voice is masculine—Orpheus, the son."[20] But how do these figures work exactly? According to Huffer,

> the heterosexual couplings of Eurydice-Orpheus and mother-son thus function—in the terms of a binary logic of complementary halves—as the internally divisible but inseparable markers of a nonhuman relational movement. The feminine half of these couplings—Eurydice or the mother—names the void or lack—the loss—at the center of the relation through which those apparently symmetrical opposites are produced.[21]

This description of "Orpheus' Gaze" as a "nonhuman relational movement" of signification begs the question: how nonhuman is this relation? Or in other words, how human, ultimately, are Eurydice and the mother? And are they the same? Huffer links the mother—and, as a consequence, Eurydice—to this nonhuman relational movement through the subsection "The Image" in Part I. The Essential Solitude, where Blanchot writes:

> Perhaps the force of the maternal figure borrows its brightness from the very force of fascination, and one might say then, that if the mother exerts this fascinating attraction it is because, appearing when the child lives altogether in fascination's gaze, she concentrates in herself all the powers of enchantment. It is because the child is fascinated that the mother is fascinating … Fascination is fundamentally linked to neutral, impersonal presence, to the indeterminate They ["On"], the immense, Someone without figure. (SL 33; translation modified)

However, for Huffer, this "They ['On'], the immense, Someone without figure" has to be the mother. By linking her to Eurydice (constructing the conceptual pairs Mother-son/Eurydice-Orpheus) Huffer concludes that the nonhuman structure appearance/disappearance within *The Space of Literature* is essentially linked to a gendered dialectic. In other words, that because this relational, nonhuman structure must include the figure of the mother, the tropes of *The Space of Literature* are essentially nostalgic. As a consequence, for Huffer, through the workings of both, trope and nostalgia, "the unattainable center of those movements of turning and return remains an irrecuperable void or point of loss."[22] But what exactly is this center in her reading? Is it a nonhuman void

---

20   Ibid., 51.
21   Ibid., 50.
22   Ibid.

still, or a nostalgic point of human loss? Or is it Eurydice, or the mother? Is it first the mother (the real, empirical one, mentioned in Huffer's title for this chapter: "Blanchot's Mother"), or Eurydice as the mythological and heterosexual representation of desire? Or is it first the nonhuman point, origin, or trope (τρόπος) as movement, that is to say, the circle around which everything turns, or the act of turning itself around a center or puncture?

According to Huffer, the "result [of this relational structure at the center of *The Space of Literature*] is a "poetics of pure figure" where language is completely self-reflective and removed from meaning or truth."[23] However, as she remarks, "meaning must and does occur."[24] But how exactly does this leap occur, from the poetics of a *pure* figure to an *empirical* or *realistic* meaning and truth? How do we go from a nonhuman "void or point of loss" to Eurydice or the mother, Orpheus or the son? Is the spectrality as figure of Eurydice or the mother enough for such a leap? Or is it because of Blanchot's masculine voice that the conjuration of such female ghosts is inevitable? More importantly: is sexual difference (at) the center of this leap from figure to the empirical? Huffer's own movement from the real, empirical mother, and the heterosexual object of desire (Eurydice), to the nonhuman relation between terms—and back—is affected by the essential underdetermination of the center. While she states that: "Blanchot's mother—'the fascinating … mother … of early childhood'—is neither an original space nor an originary time, but is rather the continual movement of a relation between terms."[25] She qualifies this statement, by adding that "however, in Blanchot, her appearance as a figure vested with meaning marks the *inevitable* humanization of the movement of loss that is itself the condition of the possibility of writing."[26] As support, she quotes one of the annexes of *The Space of Literature*, "The Two Versions of the Imaginary": "In this way the image fulfils one of its functions, which is to quiet, to humanize the formless nothingness pressed upon us by the indelible residue of being" (SL 255). But this "humanization" is not a "making human" in the sense of literally transforming the nothingness into an empirical being. As a matter of fact, this "humanization" consists rather in—as Blanchot continues—allowing "us to believe, dreaming, the happy dream which art too often authorizes, that, separated from the real and immediately behind it, we find, as pure pleasure and superb satisfaction, the transparent eternity of the unreal"

---

[23] Ibid.
[24] Ibid., 51.
[25] Ibid., 49.
[26] Ibid., my italics.

(255). Therefore, while it is true that in *The Space of Literature* "to write is to make oneself the echo of what cannot cease speaking ... the giant murmuring upon which *language opens and thus becomes image*," Blanchot qualifies this image, un-defining, or blurring its contours: "becomes image, becomes imaginary, becomes a speaking depth, an indistinct plenitude which is empty" (27). In other words, the image in *The Space of Literature* can indeed represent an object or subject (the desired heterosexual image/the mother), but, as it is described within "Two Versions": "it is nonetheless with the bottom or abyss [le *fond*] that the image is allied—with the fundamental materiality, the still undetermined absence of form (the world oscillating between adjective and substantive), before foundering in the formless prolixity of indetermination" (255; translation modified). Thus, are "the transparent eternity of the unreal," "the abyss" [le *fond*], "the indistinct plenitude which is empty," and the "formless prolixity of indetermination" images—however undetermined, or even undetermining, that is to say, erasing all limits and contours—that we can ally with a heterosexual (or not) object of desire (Eurydice), as well as with the mother? Certainly. But as Huffer states, this is just "one such meaning,"[27] based upon one reading of *The Space of Literature*, or in other words, upon only one of its centers.

Nevertheless, the lack of any female author within the text remains not only troubling, but it is also symptomatic. The only space where a female writing hand appears is in the context of letters or love interests: the countess of Solms-Laubach and Clara for Rilke; Regine Olsen for Kierkegaard; and Milena Jesenka and Dora Dymant for Kafka. What is more, as the analogy between Eurydice, "art and desire, death and night" suggests—as well as the link between Eurydice and the Freudian mother that Huffer disclosed—there are connections between the obscurity of the center of *The Space of Literature* (or "the opacity of transparency" in *The Infinite Conversation*), the feminine, and motherhood (171). I believe that these links are part of what made Hélène Cixous say—in a statement quoted by Huffer—that "to write on, to talk on women, on the corpses of dead women ... is one of the recurrent motives in Blanchot's texts."[28]

I do not have the space here to continue the research on Blanchot, women, and motherhood, done by Huffer, Cixous, and Larysa Mykata, among others. I would like to suggest, however, two points within the book where the questions, not only of the centers of *The Space of Literature*, but also of the centers of

---

[27]   Ibid., 51.
[28]   Ibid., 52.

absolute modernism and modernist writers in general, in their relation to women, feminity, maternity, and matricide, might appear. One is a short verse from Rilke that appears in the subsection "The Task of Dying and the Artistic Task," when, analyzing Rilke's reflections on death, Blanchot quotes "Das Buch von der Armut und vom Tode" from *Das Studen-Buch*: "And grant us now (after all women's pains) the serious motherhood of men" (125). Here the "after" or *nach* (*nach aller Weiber Wehen*) could point out, not only a question of temporal priority, but also of modelling, mimesis, and order, translated perhaps as "*in the guise of* all women's pains."[29] The other point involves also a matricide that is both literary—like the effacement of women implied in "the serious motherhood of men"—but also literal, since it portrays the actual killing of a mother—one of the first ones of our Western tradition. When in the subsection "The Work and History" Blanchot is considering the relation between the work of art and the language of its birth, he uses as an example *The Oresteia*, specifically, *The Eumenides*. As we know, these are the divinities formerly known as the Erinyes, whose name changed after the mythical matricide of Clytemnestra by Orestes was forgiven:

> It is sometimes said regretfully that the work of art will never again speak the language it spoke when it was born, the language of its birth, which only those who belonged to the same world heard and received. Never again will the Eumenides speak to the Greeks, and we will never know what was said in that language. This is true. But it is also true that the Eumenides have still never spoken, and that each time they speak it is the unique birth of their language that they announce. Long ago they spoke as enraged and appeased divinities before withdrawing into the temple of night—and this is unknown to us and will ever remain foreign. Later they spoke as symbols of the dark forces that must be combated in order for there to be justice and culture—and this is only too well known to us. Finally, one day, perhaps they will speak as the work in which language is always original, in which it is the language of the origin. And this is unknown to us, but not foreign. (206–207)

Looking at these two points together, we can ask, where exactly would this "motherhood of men" appear if it were granted? Would this motherhood be the male authors' original language, the language of the author's, or of the work's origin? Would this language include, through the author's origin, his own mother, the maternity that bore him, and/or what the Eumenides, the Erinyes

---

[29]   I want to thank Scott Roulier here for remarking this other possibility to me.

themselves could say if they spoke? How would a female author, in her own right and gaze, shift the circles and centers within *The Space of Literature*? Perhaps as Cixous—reading Blanchot—or as Lispector—not reading him—did? As we know, all leaps, all substitutions and displacements within the work—the literary space—must be guaranteed by the work's center, that is to say, by its pivotal point. But, as Derrida remarked, the center "is the point at which the substitution of contents, elements, or terms is no longer possible. At the center, the permutation or the transformation of elements … is forbidden."[30] But what exactly is a center?

## The center is not the center

In 1966, Derrida read "Structure, Sign and Play in the Discourse of the Human Sciences" at Johns Hopkins University. At the beginning of this foundational text and lecture, he started his analysis of a radical change in the modern concept of structure by examining what founds and determines all structures: a center. But like what happens in front of *Watt*'s painting, and with "Orpheus' Gaze," in this inaugural text the center started—through Derrida's voice and in the audience's eyes—quickly moving, shifting, metamorphosing. Here, the center

> is the point at which the substitution of contents, elements, or terms is no longer possible. At the center, the permutation or the transformation of elements … is forbidden … [T]he center is, paradoxically, *within* the structure and *outside* it. The center is at the center of the totality, and yet, since the center does not belong to the totality (is not part of the totality), the totality *has its center elsewhere*. The center is not the center … Successively, and in a regulated fashion, the center receives different forms or names.[31]

Given the center's signification as origin (*archè*), as well as its own origin as a product of desire ("the desire for a center"[32]), it is easy to see how the leap can be made from a "non human relation" to the mother and Eurydice, especially given that Blanchot was an empirical man. This meaning takes place, but the book, the literary space within it, and their center(s) do not stay there. The constant displacement of the center is what constitutes *The Space of Literature* as a work of absolute modernism. But what is that "something essential" that

---

[30]  Jacques Derrida, "Structure, Sign and Play in the Discourse of the Human Sciences," in *Writing and Difference*, trans. Alan Bass (Chicago: University of Chicago Press, 1978), 279.
[31]  Ibid., 279.
[32]  Ibid.

absolute modernism seeks? As Rabaté explains: "modernism is defined in terms of an attempt to fuse form and content ... Wherever this fusion takes place, real modernism is reached."[33] "Real modernism" would be, then, "absolute modernism" in the sense of a real interruption, an affirmation of the interruption of history *as history*, what allows any phenomenon, in the opacity of its transparency—form and content fused—to occur. In his contribution to *Our Exagmination Round His Factification for Incamination of Work in Progress*, Beckett had already remarked the point where Joyce's modernism became absolute: "Here form *is* content, content *is* form. You complain that this stuff is not written in English. It is not written at all. It is not to be read—or rather it is not only to be read. It is to be looked at and listened to."[34] The center is this point where form and content fuse. When they fuse, the center is lost, it has moved, it has become the circle, and the circle is not there anymore. Yet they are both there, searching for each other (like the series of remembrances and resonances in Proust's *In Search of Lost Time*, and the broken circle of its ending and beginning; or like the riverrun of meaningless sound and silent signification in *Finnegans Wake*), or for some other center, for some other circle, exhausting the combinations until the divide between subject and object disappears—for a moment.

Where this fusion happens, literature becomes—as Beckett remarked, and performed—unreadable. Perhaps this is what Derrida—another French absolute modernist—meant about the "blindness that opens the eye."[35] The modernist center is where "the eye would be destined not to see but to weep."[36] Thus, always already, in front of all of the center's possibilities, but most importantly, in front of the impossibility of the center, that is to say, of our ignorance and desire of a center (that might always not be our own, and which might be looking also for us, or for somebody else), "in boundless space, in endless time," at the thought of this desire that makes us write, Watt's, Blanchot's, Orpheus', Rabaté's, Derrida's, but also Cixous's, Woolf's, Stein's, Irigaray's, and all our eyes "filled with tears that [we] could not stem, and they flowed down [our] cheeks unchecked, in a steady flow, refreshing [us] greatly."[37]

---

[33] Rabaté, *The Ghosts of Modernity*, 206.
[34] Samuel Beckett, "Dante ... Bruno. Vico ... Joyce," in *Modernism, an Anthology*, ed. Lawrence Rainey (Malden: Blackwell, 2005), 1067.
[35] Jacques Derrida, *Memoirs of the Blind*, trans. Pascale-Anne Brault and Michael Naas (Chicago: University of Chicago Press, 1993), 126.
[36] Ibid.
[37] Beckett, "Watt," 273.

# 4

# Writing the Future: Blanchot's *Le Livre à venir*

## Leslie Hill

In July 1953, some seven months after assuming his position as a regular contributor to the *Nouvelle Revue française* (or *Nouvelle Nouvelle Revue française* as the recently relaunched monthly was now known, having finally served out the years of suspension imposed for being implicated in collaboration with the Nazis under the editorship of the fascist writer Pierre Drieu La Rochelle), Blanchot published the first of a series of essays that would culminate six years later in his fifth book of literary criticism, *Le Livre à venir* (*The Book to Come*). Containing a sequence of chapters devoted to modern (or not so modern) and contemporary writing or, more accurately, to the question of literature's future, the collection would be the first to be entirely made up of articles that initially appeared in the revived journal.[1] The title of Blanchot's July 1953 article, which provided the book with its central theme, was in any case both timely and simple: "Where," it asked, "is literature going?"[2] This was a common enough question in France at the time. The political, ideological, and constitutional upheavals of the postwar years had resulted in a significant cultural sea-change. Many established reputations were consigned to the past; unfamiliar names had begun to emerge; and in the theater, poetry, and the novel, in painting and in film, in literary criticism and philosophy, innovative ideas were already making their mark. Jean-Paul Sartre, for many the leading intellectual of the period, faced with the tabula rasa of first defeat, then victory, was not the only observer (even if in his case the point was also to dismiss such potential rivals as Bataille and Blanchot) to define a new aesthetics and to affirm a renewed belief in literature's possible relevance in the much changed circumstances of the postwar world. "There is no

---

[1] Maurice Blanchot, *Le Livre à venir* (Paris: Gallimard, 1959); *The Book to Come*, trans. Charlotte Mandell (Stanford: Stanford University Press, 2003).

[2] Maurice Blanchot, "Où va la littérature?," *La Nouvelle Nouvelle Revue française* 7 (July 1953): 98–107.

guarantee that literature is immortal," he insisted in his landmark manifesto of 1948, *Qu'est-ce que la littérature? (What Is Literature?)*; but "its chance, today," he added, "its sole chance, is Europe's chance, for socialism, democracy, and peace. This is a card we have to play; if we waste it, we writers, so much the worse for us. But so much the worse for society too."[3]

In the wake of France's liberation, many were the voices, of diverse political and ideological persuasions, that competed for attention in the hurly-burly of the intellectual marketplace. This they did through numerous, sometimes precarious or short-lived journals. As the Occupation ended, Blanchot is reported as writing in a letter to Pierre Prévost, there were already near 150 such publications about to appear.[4] In time, very few would survive. Of those that did, the best known and most influential during the early postwar period was *Les Temps modernes*, founded in October 1945 by Sartre, de Beauvoir, Merleau-Ponty, and others, with the idea of filling the gap left by the still-banned *Nouvelle Revue française*. This was an astute move, for in the years that followed it was clear that the ever-increasing public presence of Sartrian existentialism had as much to do with the success of the journal as a forum for politically engaged intellectual debate as it did with Sartre's own work as a philosopher, novelist, or dramatist. *Les Temps modernes*, however, was not alone. Bataille, too, alongside Prévost, and with the assistance of Blanchot and Éric Weil, attempted something similar the following year with *Critique*, a journal far less willing however to identify itself with a particular ideological tendency, and one that aimed instead to engage more generally with a wide range of contemporary philosophical, literary, and political issues. But despite early financial difficulties, which at one point, between September 1949 and October 1950, caused it to cease publication, *Critique* too, in time, flourished.[5]

In launching these journals, Sartre and Bataille were evidently eager, as were others, to set the agenda for postwar debate. The same was no doubt also true of Blanchot, whose impressively single-minded efforts to establish himself as a distinctive literary critical voice after the war led him to contribute to a bewildering array of publications. Naturally enough, these included *Critique*, which, between 1946 and 1953, carried more than a dozen articles by the writer,

---

[3]  Jean-Paul Sartre, *Qu'est-ce que la littérature?* (Paris: Gallimard folio, 1948), 293; *What Is Literature?*, trans. Bernard Frechtman (London: Methuen, 1967), 220; translation modified.

[4]  See Pierre Prévost, *Rencontre Georges Bataille* (Paris: Jean-Michel Place, 1987), 117.

[5]  For a detailed history of the journal's first half-century, see Sylvie Patron, *Critique, 1946–1996: une encyclopédie de l'esprit moderne* (Paris: éditions de l'IMEC, 1999). On Bataille's initial plans for the journal and Blanchot's early involvement, see Prévost, *Rencontre Georges Bataille*, 119–49.

and *Les Temps modernes* which in 1947 and 1952 similarly published a further four substantial texts. At the same time, Blanchot also sent reviews to such varied or relatively little-known journals or magazines as *L'Arche* (1945–47), *Paysage dimanche* (1945), *Carrefour* (1946), *Saisons* (1946), *Cahiers de la Pléiade* (1947–49), *Cahiers d'art* (1948–53), and *L'Observateur* (1950),[6] even as he also continued his career as an author of fiction, bringing out between 1945 and 1950 not only his third and final novel, *Le Très-Haut* (*The Most High*), but also a series of shorter texts (notably the two prewar stories collected as *Le Ressassement éternel* [*Vicious Circles*], *L'Arrêt de mort* [*Death Sentence*], what would later be called *La Folie du jour* [*The Madness of the Day*], and the abridged version of *Thomas l'Obscur* [*Thomas The Obscure: new version*]).

But it was only in January 1953, when the *Nouvelle Revue française* was able to reappear under its ironic new title that Blanchot was given the opportunity, thanks to its editor Jean Paulhan, now restored to the position he had held prior to June 1940, to comment on a regular monthly basis, in relative freedom, and in uniquely authoritative fashion, on developments in the literary world. It was a slot he would occupy with distinction almost without interruption, as health issues and political distractions permitted, for some fifteen years. Throughout that whole period he was able, as a result, significantly to shape the reception of literary texts in France and to support the output of an impressive range of writers, both young and less young, from Robbe-Grillet to Duras, Beckett to Bataille, Laporte to Char. That Blanchot did this on the authority of his own writing, and without the recognition or prestige that might have come from something resembling university status, is not unimportant. Admittedly, it was at the time far from unusual. Many leading thinkers of the period, Sartre himself, as well as de Beauvoir or Camus, similarly derived a living from their writing or, like Bataille and (in the first instance) Levinas, from other professional or administrative occupations. This ensured a degree of intellectual independence, but it was not without constraints of its own. As Blanchot was only too keenly aware, literary journalism often made conflicting demands. It was necessary for instance to respond at short notice to new books, even before they had arrived in bookshops, and whose appearance was largely a function of the vagaries of the publishing cycle rather than of any considered program of study or debate. At the same time, given France's fiercely competitive intellectual environment, it was also essential to comment on these volumes in decisive and arresting fashion,

---

[6] For a comprehensive listing of Blanchot's critical writing during these postwar years, see the bibliography available on the Espace Maurice Blanchot website (www.blanchot.fr).

such as to address major literary or other issues rather than simply contenting oneself with inconclusive short-term value judgments.

Many, then, of the texts or topics tackled in Blanchot's regular pieces in *La Nouvelle Nouvelle Revue française* were in some measure dictated by circumstances or by conjuncture, and this is reflected in turn in the composition of his various essay collections. *Le Livre à venir* is a case in point. At first sight, the selection of texts discussed seems almost accidental. There is for instance only occasional mention of such crucially important figures as Hölderlin, Kafka, Rilke, or even Heidegger, who in diverse ways had loomed so large in *La Part du feu* (*The Work of Fire*) or *L'Espace littéraire* (*The Space of Literature*). Sade and Lautréamont, too, are conspicuous by their absence. The apparent commitment to literary history implied by the book's title is similarly half-hearted. Artaud (1896–1948) rubs shoulders with Rousseau (1712–78), Joubert (1724–1824) with Claudel (1868–1945), and Beckett (1906–89) with Mallarmé (1842–98). There are authors represented who, in the France of the 1950s, were little known, while others were already exceedingly canonical. Some were controversial, others much less so. There are essays on French writers, but also on authors, British or American, who originally wrote in English; several others, German, Swiss, or Austrian, who wrote in German; and one, Borges, who did so in Spanish. And by the time Blanchot's book appeared, only a minority were even actively producing new work. In this sense, far from endorsing some overarching plan, the essays contained in *Le Livre à venir*, having for the most part been prompted by the publication of a new critical study, a new text or edition, or simply a translation, seemed much rather to reflect the relatively haphazard churning of events characteristic of daily goings-on in the literary world.

The challenge Blanchot set himself in his critical writing, however, was that of discerning in the contingent the essential, and it is in this regard no surprise that, in considering Mallarmé's "Un coup de dés" alongside the recently published drafts and fragments of the poet's notoriously unfinished Livre (or Book), it is this strange reciprocity between chance and necessity, by which "the one and the other are held in check by the force of disaster," that Blanchot chose to foreground (BC 233–234 / LV 284). It was not, however, a matter of disregarding the contingent in favor of something supposedly timeless or universal, but rather of affirming the singular co-intrication of the two. For if it was indeed the case, as Mallarmé's poem and Blanchot's criticism confirmed, that "a dice-throw never will abolish chance [*un coup de dés jamais n'abolira le hasard*]," then it followed that chance and necessity, far from being diametrically opposed, were but the two sides of a single tossed coin. There was, in other words, nothing essential that was not also contingent, and nothing contingent that was not also essential. Both concepts, then, were little more than placeholders for something other, more akin to what Blanchot, partly quoting Mallarmé, as he does here, would later call: disaster, a word, he suggests, that implied nothing negative, but rather, neutralizing immanence and transcendence alike, announced a "work which is therefore not there, but present in its sole coincidence with that which is always beyond" (234/284; translation modified). This in turn was to emphasize that critical writing, even as the minor branch of philosophical reflection it took itself to be, had no more privileged access to truth than its putative object. It too was exposed to the same difficulties as that which it claimed to dominate, which was nothing other than the very impossibility of fulfilling the task allocated to it. For what was most disastrous in a text, most singular and distinctive, so to speak, was not what was most easily assimilable in it, but, on the contrary, what most obstinately resisted assimilation, what made reading less a finite act than an infinite challenge, not a possibility, in other words, but an impossibility, such that it was in its very failure to reach a conclusion that the virtue and the value of the activity called criticism were to be found. "On the difficult practice of criticism," Blanchot began an essay on the use of dialogue by Duras, James, and several others. "The critic," he went on,

> almost never reads. It is not always for lack of time; but he cannot read while thinking only of having to write, and if he makes things simple, at times by making them more complicated, if he awards plaudits or brickbats, if he hurriedly rids himself of the simplicity of the book by replacing it with the correctness of a verdict or with the generous assertion of his deep understanding, it is because impatience is driving him, because, being unable to read a book, he must not have read twenty or thirty others, and because this multiple failure to read, which on the one hand absorbs him, on the other is irrelevant to him, merely inviting him to move on ever more quickly from one book to the next, from one book he scarcely reads to another he thinks he has already read, in order to reach that moment when, having read nothing of any book, he will perhaps come up against himself, in that state of worklessness [*désœuvrement*] which might finally allow him to begin reading, if only he had not in turn long ago become an author. (150/185; translation modified)

The possibility of reading, then, was never self-evident. For if some texts obstinately resisted reading, others seemed to have always already let it take place. But either way, if it were properly to occur at all, reading, like writing, could only do so not in the present, but in the future. In arranging the disparate essays that went to make up *Le Livre à venir*, this was clearly one of the criteria Blanchot had uppermost in his mind. For by the judicious use of subtitles and by changing the sequence in which the essays were originally written (the first, for instance, published in July 1953, now appears more than 200 pages into the book, while the last, from November 1958, is to be found more than a hundred pages earlier), the volume offered a digressive or dilatory narrative of its own, having less to do with a desire to issue finite literary judgments as such than with the iterative movement of its own thinking. By way of explanation the publisher's blurb for the book, which Blanchot most likely drafted himself, began by listing the four sections into which the book was divided: "I. The Song of the Sirens (the secret of writing); II. The Question of Literature (literature as exigency and as meaning); III. On an Art Without Future (literature and the novel); IV. Where Is Literature Going? (the book to come)." It then added: "From the juxtaposition of these titles and the sequence of these essays comes the feeling and, as it were, the story [*récit*] of a migration, almost like the odyssey that took Ulysses in sight of the island where the Sirens were singing. And it is indeed by the force of a movement, both purposeful and directionless, free but insistent, that we are drawn through this evolving reality that is literature, in which Mallarmé, or Proust or Breton represent perhaps what to History (at least according to ancient narrative) was the Fall of Constantinople." "But perhaps," the blurb concluded, "what is at stake here, rather than authors and their books, is the movement from which all books come, and which, in still hidden fashion, holds the future of communication or communication as future."

By evoking in this way, on the one hand, the Sirens, whose inhuman futural song is recalled in Blanchot's opening pages, and, on the other, the fall of the Roman Empire, the memory of which foreshadows the inevitable defeat of other dictatorships, including more recent ones intimated in the book's closing chapters, Blanchot's blurb emphasized how any history of literature, like any narrative, from Homer to the present, necessarily implied its own writing or rewriting, its own invention or reinvention. Even as it framed its own reading for the benefit of its future audience, then, Blanchot's book bore silent witness to something that was properly unavailable to any narrative, whether fiction or non fiction, grounded in myth or in the archive—this was no doubt the reason for choosing such seemingly mismatched emblems as the Sirens' Song and the fall of Constantinople—which was the possibility of its inscription as such. This, of course, was writing's secret, as Beckett's *L'Innommable* (*The Unnamable*) would later testify, and the reason it was both infinitely discreet and infinitely garrulous. History was plainly not nothing. But, at the same time, whatever its imperious claim to say all there was, it was not everything either. It was separated from itself, in other words, by that which made it possible, on which it depended and which it forcibly could not contain, and which only manifested itself as lying necessarily beyond its reach, that is, as an aporia or paradox or hiatus, here by the morphing of song into silence, there by the morphing of time into epochal discontinuity. And insofar as writing in its turn preceded, traversed, and exceeded history as such, so for Blanchot it belonged to history only insofar as it forcibly escaped it, just as history was what it was only by dint of that which was inaccessible to it—which was the very possibility of its articulation or inscription at all.

The implications of this deconstructive reading of the relationship between history—in particular the history of literature, if such exists—and the possibilities and impossibilities of its writing are many. They are clearly apparent in Blanchot's choice of critical vocabulary. For in his account of what today, in the work of so many other literary critics, theorists, or commentators, would be quite routinely described as modernity or modernism, it is revealing that Blanchot uses the first of these two (and its cognates) only very sparingly, while the second is consistently ignored or tacitly rejected. This was no mere idiosyncratic terminological decision. At stake was a deep-seated skepticism regarding periodization and any attempt at purely historical or sociological explanation of that which the term "modern," insofar as it was worth preserving at all, served to address. All such explanations, Blanchot implied, as on the part of such important and influential contemporaries as Sartre or Roland Barthes, were irretrievably and unacceptably teleological. They were, in other words, fundamentally prescriptive, and at some risk of entirely misunderstanding or misrepresenting what future or futurity lay beyond literature's present horizon.

For the Sartre of *Qu'est-ce que la littérature?*, for instance, following a well-established Marxist tradition, literary modernism, so-called, was nothing futural at all, merely the negative corollary of a specific historical failure, that of the 1848 Revolution—this repetition of tragedy that was nothing short of farce, as Marx famously quipped—which, by forcing history in France down a blind alley, excluded the progressive bourgeoisie as well as the industrial proletariat from political power, and as a result left the bourgeois writer—Flaubert, for Sartre, was the prime example of this—with little option than to opt to retreat into pseudo-aristocratic isolation, able only to intervene into the social sphere in ironic, destructive, subjective, and irresponsible fashion. The difficulty of modern or modernist writing, Sartre concluded, was in this sense little more than an exercise in sterile negativity, with Beckett, during the postwar years, being cast in the familiar role of counterrevolutionary bogeyman. "All *Godot's* themes," Sartre declared in an interview in 1955, "are bourgeois themes: solitude, despair, clichés, incommunicability, they are all the product of the inner solitude of the bourgeoisie."[7]

This was admittedly not the only way to account for the appearance of literary modernism at the end of the nineteenth century and the beginning of the twentieth, or the only way to judge its postwar legacy or present-day actuality. Barthes, in *Le Degré zéro de l'écriture* (*Writing Degree Zero*), while adopting broadly the same post-Marxist historical scenario as Sartre, with the work of Flaubert once more being identified as a key turning point, saw the implications of literary modernity in very different terms. For Barthes, what occurred in the novels of Flaubert, and led to what he described as the subsequent "Flaubertisation of writing,"[8] was that the novelist, having become excluded from history, so to speak, thereby acquired a sharper, critical awareness of both the language of politics and the politics of language, and of the extent to which words, being no longer transparent, were endowed with a historical thickness requiring ideological critique. The effect, Barthes suggested, in a bold extrapolation, was to change the reader from a passive consumer of single meaning to an active producer of plural meanings. From this perspective, then, though it was still thought to have grown out of a crisis in social cohesion and still thought to bear the scars of its difficult birth, modernity or modernism was a largely affirmative development which, from the jaws of historical defeat, was able to snatch something resembling artistic victory. Now, Barthes observed, "every time the writer writes down a knot of tangled words, the very existence of Literature itself is called into question; what modernity gives us to read in the plurality of its writings is the impasse of its own History."[9]

---

[7]   Jean-Paul Sartre, *Un théâtre de situations*, ed. Michel Conta and Michel Rybalka (Paris: Gallimard, 1973), 75.

[8]   Roland Barthes, *Œuvres complètes*, ed. Éric Marty, revised edition, 5 vols. (Paris: Seuil, 2002), I, 211; *Writing Degree Zero*, trans. Annette Lavers and Colin Smith (New York: Hill and Wang, 1968), 66.

[9]   Barthes, *Œuvres complètes*, I, 208; *Writing Degree Zero*, 61; translation modified.

Sartre and Barthes in the 1950s disagreed about many things, in particular about the political implications of at least some kinds of avant-garde or experimental writing. They differed most markedly, for instance, in their response to Brecht, who at the time was France's most frequently staged modern dramatist, for whom Barthes displayed boundless enthusiasm, while Sartre remained deeply unmoved. But what the two thinkers shared was no less significant. For both retained the implicit assumption, at least throughout the 1950s and 1960s, that the relationship between what was modern and what was not was one of verifiable opposition, and that one kind of writing, that is, communicative transparency for Sartre, sensuous linguistic plurality for Barthes, was either politically or aesthetically superior to its so-called opposite. In Sartre's case, since words, he argued, were actions, this meant promoting the idea of ethico-political commitment in prose writing (though not in poetry or other media) to the detriment of so-called self-indulgent experimentalism. In the case of Barthes, on the grounds that words only ever referred to other words, with which they were always in critical dialogue, it meant consigning to the past a literature that was merely readable, and as such either nauseous or pleasurable (or both), and affirming a modern idiom that, being only writeable, was exhaustingly and vibrantly plural.

In this general context, what is perhaps most distinctive about Blanchot's approach to so-called modern or modernist literary works is that he subscribes to neither of these ultimately dogmatic models. This in turn explains why he was equally critical of aspects of both. When Sartre in *Qu'est-ce que la littérature?* asserted for instance that "a writer's function is to call a spade a spade [*appeler un chat un chat*]" and, citing as sheer nonsense Bataille's emblematic poetic expression, "butter horse [*cheval de beurre*]," insisted that "if words are sick, it is the duty of the writer to cure them," Blanchot demurred, pointing out that what Sartre was minded to call the sickness of language was in fact indistinguishable from its rude health, and that, in any case, whenever a writer sought to subordinate fiction to ethico-political ends, all that resulted was that those ends ironically became fictitious ones.[10] Commitment in writing, in other words, as reception of Sartre's work persistently showed, and as the writer himself was ultimately forced to acknowledge, tended almost invariably to culminate in the

---

[10]  Sartre, *Qu'est-ce que la littérature?*, 281; *What Is Literature?*, 210. On Bataille, see Jean-Paul Sartre, *Situations I* (Paris: Gallimard: folio, 1947), 179. For Blanchot's rejoinder, see *La Part du feu* (Paris: Gallimard, 1949), 188–203, 302; *The Work of Fire*, trans. Charlotte Mandell (Stanford: Stanford University Press, 1995), 191–207, 310.

reverse of what it intended, making the contrast between one kind of language and another, however principled, quite simply untenable.

Blanchot's reply to *Le Degré zéro de l'écriture*, which was subsequently included in the final section of *Le Livre à venir*, was admittedly more nuanced. It too, however, raised doubts regarding the teleology inherent in Barthes's attempted periodization, by virtue of which, it was claimed, modern or modernist writing was fundamentally different from the normative, seemingly universal literary idiom that preceded it. "Literature," Blanchot objected, "is not more diverse than in previous times, it is perhaps more monotonous, in the same way that night-time may be deemed more monotonous than the day" (BC 205; translation modified). "The diversity, originality, and anarchy of what is being tried out today," he went on, replying to the central claim of Barthes's book, "are not what turn literature into a world dispersed. We need to find a different formulation, and say: the experience of literature is exposure to dispersion itself, the approach to that which escapes unity, and the experience of that which is without shared understanding, without agreement, and without law—error and the outside, the ungraspable and the irregular" (205/249-50; translation modified).[11]

As the literary thinking of both Sartre and Barthes implicitly suggests, and as Blanchot himself was keenly aware, most theories of the modern are theories of Romanticism. After all, was it not Baudelaire, this belated Romantic in the era of high capitalism, who in France first reintroduced the word "modernity," in its modern sense, and gave it its distinctive conceptual form? What the painter of contemporary life was after, Baudelaire explained, as he sought high and low, here, there, and everywhere, he wrote, was "something I may be allowed to call: modernity [*la modernité*]" "What this involves," he went on, "is for the artist to extract from fashion [*la mode*] whatever poetry is contained in the historical, and to draw the eternal from the transitory." "Modernity [*La modernité*]," he went on, "is the transient, the fleeting, and the contingent, the one half of art, of which the other half is the timeless and the unchanging."[12] No matter

---

11   Blanchot's review originally appeared under the slightly more critical title, "Plus loin que le degré zéro [Further Than Zero Degree]," *La Nouvelle Nouvelle Revue française* 9 (September 1953): 485–94. The problem of periodization remained a troublesome one for Barthes, and caused him in his later work to shift the emphasis of his thinking quite significantly. For an overview of some of the difficulties Barthes encountered in the 1950s and 1960s, see my *Radical Indecision: Barthes, Blanchot, Derrida, and the Future of Criticism* (Notre Dame, Indiana: Notre Dame University Press, 2010), 71–119.

12   Charles Baudelaire, *Œuvres complètes*, ed. Y.-G. Le Dantec and Claude Pichois (Paris: Gallimard, 1961), 1163.

that what was invoked here by Baudelaire was less a stable synthesis than an aporetic collision of irreconcilables, what counted, and continued to count, for Blanchot, nearly a century later, was that the artwork was henceforth forever divided against itself, no longer fully present, in other words, and by that very token bereft of all foundation or self-evidence. If literature began when literature itself became a question, Blanchot suggested in 1947, it remained, *pace* Sartre, as a question without an answer, or, paradoxically, as a question for which the answer, perhaps unexpectedly, was deceptively straightforward.[13] "Where is literature going?," Blanchot had asked in 1953. His reply was immediate: "Yes, the question is a surprising one, but what is most surprising is that, if there is an answer [*s'il y a une réponse*], it is easy: literature is going towards itself, towards its essence which is disappearance [*la disparition*]" (BC 195/LV 237; translation slightly modified).

To explain what was at stake here, Blanchot turned to probably the most famous of all philosophical claims from the early nineteenth century regarding the present and future state of art, Hegel's notorious pronouncement in the *Lectures on Aesthetics* of 1820–21 to the effect that "art considered in its highest vocation is and remains for us a thing of the past [*ein Vergangenes*]."[14] As Blanchot hastened to explain, this was not an empirical observation. Indeed, the early decades of the nineteenth century in Germany were a time of particularly intense cultural, philosophical, and literary activity. Hegel's verdict needed to be seen, rather, as a speculative or essential one. Its point was that, in an age of secular enlightenment, art had forfeited its "authentic truth and vitality [*die echte Wahrheit und Lebendigkeit*]."[15] It had lost, so to speak, its teleological mission, and parted company with history, truth, reality. Worldly action, science, philosophy had taken its place. The present and future belong, then, not to art, but to action in the world, and if there is a book to be written in these modern times, Blanchot quips, that book is most likely not *War and Peace* but *Das Kapital*. At any event, according to Hegel, for the first time in its existence, art was now merely an object of aesthetic, critical contemplation, which is also to say that, in the eyes of those who came after, it was now for the first time properly constituted *as* itself, *as* art. Blanchot,

---

[13]   Blanchot, *The Work of Fire*, 300; *La Part du feu*, 293.

[14]   Hegel, *Werke*, XIII, 25; *Aesthetics*, I, 11; translation modified.

[15]   G. W. F. Hegel, *Werke*, ed. Eva Moldenhauer and Karl Markus Michel, 20 vols. (Frankfurt: Suhrkamp, 1970), XIII, 25; *Aesthetics*, trans. T. M. Knox, 2 vols. (Oxford: Clarendon Press, 1975), I, 11.

at least up to a certain point, could not do other than concur. For such, he argued, was the familiar condition of art in general from Hegel's time to the present. "Art," he therefore agreed, "is no longer capable of sustaining the need for an absolute. What counts absolutely is henceforth the achievement of the world, the seriousness of action, and the task of real freedom. Art is close to the absolute only in the past, and it is only in the Museum that it still has value and potency. Or else, in what is a more worrying disfavour, it lapses in our estimation into becoming mere aesthetic pleasure, auxiliary to culture" (195/237; translation modified).

Faced with Hegel's influential diagnosis, the vast majority of modern literary critics or literary theorists have tended to adopt one of two general approaches. Some, while accepting the evidence of art's divorce from history, have nevertheless sought to find in art a continuation of worldly action by other means, treating art, on the one hand, as an activity whose function was primarily social or sociological or ethico-political and asked to be judged positively or negatively on explicitly ideological grounds, or, on the other, as one that was nevertheless still capable of making an indirect intervention into society, not least because the unreconciled negativity of the artwork, by supplying it with a dialectical, oppositional vantage-point, enabled it to reflect critically on social change, and, in resisting history, testify to all that remained unresolved by it or within it. Others, however, have drawn the opposite conclusion from Hegel's thesis, and argued that art's forced retreat from worldly action meant that its primary, even its sole, object was henceforth nothing other than itself, and that what therefore defined the artwork was its self-reflexive autonomy, as reflected in the unfettered subjective perceptions it embodied and the special status of its language, which differed in essential ways from the language of everyday communicative interaction. There are, of course, many possible variations on these two lines of thought, and many opportunities for crossovers between them. But, taking them together, it would not be hard to see in them most of the key assumptions that continue to inform current theories of the modern, of modernity or of modernism, nor would it be hard to see what both owed to the legacy of Hegel, which is their sometimes inadvertent, but always implicit, teleology. For whether in the guise of the totalizing, but untotalizable artwork or under the auspices of the autonomy of aesthetic language, what each supposed was that art in the end was always subordinate to the disclosure of a particular given truth.

What is most distinctive about Blanchot's account of so-called modern or modernist literature is that he subscribes to neither of these models. However revealing he found Hegel's dictum, Blanchot was not content to take the philosopher at his word. For Hegel had his undoubted blind spots, and history's verdict on the relative insignificance of art, Blanchot objected, was at best somewhat crude. For there was an alternative dimension, not grounded in philosophy, but to be heard in the experience of writers and artists, both preceding and following Hegel. "Art," from this perspective, Blanchot maintained, "does not negate the modern world, nor the world of technology [*technique*], nor the effort of liberation and transformation that bases itself on technology, but expresses and arguably brings to completion relations that *precede* all objective, technological accomplishment" (197/240; emphasis in the original; translation modified). And it was this countertemporal aspect of artistic production that allowed Blanchot, in the second section of *Le Livre à venir*, alongside numerous subsequent writers, to include essays, surprisingly enough, on Goethe and, in recognition of an important new study by the critic Jean Starobinski, on Rousseau. Rousseau, obviously enough, was no modernist. He was nevertheless, as Derrida in *De la grammatologie* (*On Grammatology*) would later confirm, a writer in whom the desire to write raised an obstinate, intractable, and painful question. "Rousseau," Blanchot put it in June 1958, "this man of beginnings, of nature and of truth, is also the man who can fulfil these relationships only by writing; in writing, he can but make them deviate from the certainty he has; in this deviation that causes him to suffer, and which he repudiates with energy and with despair, he helps literature to become aware of itself in being released from antiquated conventions, and to shape for itself, in contestation and amid contradictions, a new rectitude" (41/53-54; translation modified).

Even more important for Blanchot's meditation on the limits of historical reason was of course the work of Hölderlin, Hegel's one-time fellow student in Tübingen, who had himself earlier drawn attention to poetry's plight by famously describing its time as a time of distress, a time when the gods were no more and were yet still to come, and when the question of poetry's purpose or even of its very existence was more acute than ever. For in that in-between time, when time itself, belonging neither to the present nor to eternity, becomes what Blanchot calls the time of the absence of time, the fate that befalls the poet, as Blanchot puts it, quoting a famous passage from Hölderlin's poem "Brot und Wein (Bread and Wine)," is "to wander from country to country in holy darkness," not however in the hope of reaching any destination, nor with the promise of finding truth (SL 238/EL 250; translation modified). For "the risk that awaits the poet," writes Blanchot,

> and, behind the poet, anyone who writes in the sway of an essential work, is error. To err means to wander, to be unable to call anywhere home any more, because, wherever one is, the conditions for a decisive here are lacking; in this place, what happens does not possess the clarity of an event from which something solid might be made and, consequently, what happens does not happen, but nor does it pass either, for it is never past, but happens and recurs without cease, is the horror and the confusion and the uncertainty of endless recapitulation. Here, it is not this or that truth that is lacking, nor is it truth in general; but nor is it doubt leading us nor despair rooting us to the spot. Whoever is wandering has no truth that may be called home, but only exile, and lives outside, *on this side*, way off, where the depths of dissimulation reign, that elemental darkness that admits of no approach and, because of that, is the unapproachable itself. (238/249-50; emphasis in the original; translation modified)

The predicament, in Blanchot's eyes, was not limited to Hölderlin. Mallarmé, too, he notes, merely "by hollowing out the poem [*creusant le vers*]," "enters into that time of distress which is that of the absence of the gods." "Whoever hollows out the poem," he went on, "escapes all certainty of being, encounters the absence of the gods, lives in the intimacy of this absence, becomes responsible for it, assumes the risk, and bears its favour" (38/30; translation modified).

If, in deploying itself as what many would call a crisis in legitimation (though Blanchot never uses the term), such a time shows some similarity with Hegel's epochal pronouncement regarding art's ending and its beginning, its implications are however very different. Again it is Mallarmé who provides Blanchot with a crucial insight into the stakes of poetic experience. "What is the artwork?," Blanchot asked. "What is language in the artwork?," he also asked. "When Mallarmé wonders: 'Does something like literature [*les Lettres*] exist?,'" he replied, much as he had in 1947, that "that question is literature itself, literature when it has become a concern [*souci*: Blanchot obviously has Heideggerian care or *Sorge* in mind] for its own essence." Mallarmé, Blanchot went on,

> had the most profoundly tormented sense of the specific nature of literary creation. The artwork reduces itself to being. That is its task, to be, to render

present "the very word: *is*", "the whole mystery is there," he claims. But, at the same time, it cannot be said that the artwork belongs to being or that it exists. On the contrary, what must be said is that it never exists in the manner of a thing or an entity in general. What must be said, in answer to our question, is that literature does not exist [*n'existe pas*] or, if it takes place at all, it does so as something "not taking place in the way of any object that does exist." (43/35-36; translation modified)

Literature, then, did not exist; the work was not all; and the language of the artwork was no different from ordinary language, save that it knew that it was nothing, knew that it made things disappear, knew that it could disappear in its turn into the void thereby created.

When Blanchot argues, then, that literature's essence was disappearance, this was not to bind literature to any negative dialectic or dialectic of negativity; nor was it to identify writing with the autonomy of the artwork or poetic language; nor indeed, despite appearances, was it to define writing ontologically. Far more radically, it was to deprive it of all identity and all foundation, all presence and all permanence, and to determine it merely as a fleeting, inconsistent trace without inside or outside, beginning or end, *archè* or *telos*. And this is why it is misleading to consider Blanchot in any sense to be a theorist of literature, since for Blanchot there is no theoretical object that is identifiable as "literature" "as such" which might then be theorized. Literary theory, in this sense, is but a metaphysical aberration. And this is also why what comes first for Blanchot is not "the world," which it might then be thought to be literature's task to depict, or imitate, or express, but writing as a ceaseless questioning of its own possibility and impossibility and of the possibility and impossibility of any world. For as Blanchot explains,

> it is precisely the essence of literature to escape any determination of its essence, any assertion which might stabilise it or even turn it into a reality: literature is never given, but remains always to be rediscovered or reinvented. It is not even certain that the word "literature", or "art", corresponds to anything real, or possible, or important.

And he adds,

> Whoever affirms literature in itself affirms nothing. Whoever seeks it seeks only that which slips away; whoever finds it finds only what falls short of literature or, even worse, what lies beyond it. This is why, in the end, it is non-literature

that each book pursues as the essence of what it loves and yearns passionately to discover. (BC 201/LV 244; translation modified)

But art, literature, writing, for Blanchot, still had everything to do with experience. The word, admittedly, is a problematic one. As Derrida rightly argues, experience has almost always been thought as a mode of presence: of the presence of a subject to his or her experience, the presence of experience before the world, the presence of language to itself as a form of direct expression. Blanchot's use of the term, like that of Bataille, is, however, very different. This is apparent in numerous essays of the 1950s, on Mallarmé, Rilke, Kafka, and others. And from the opening chapters of *Le Livre à venir* it similarly informs Blanchot's reading of Proust, with little doubt the novelist most closely associated in modernist criticism with the recovery or resurrection of lived experience in the present through the phenomenon of involuntary memory. Blanchot's interpretation of Proust's "experience of imaginary time" offers, however, a radically alternative perspective, more consistent with the circularity of *A la recherche du temps perdu* as a perpetually recursive object of reading and rewriting, in which no beginning is in fact a beginning, and the only ending an unmasterable return to the beginning. "As a metamorphosis of time," Blanchot commented, Proust's experience

> first metamorphoses the present in which it appears to take place, drawing it into the indefinite abyss in which the "present" rebegins the "past", but in which the past opens onto the future it repeats, so that what comes always comes again, and again, and again. Admittedly, the revelation takes place here, now, for the first time, but the image that is present to us here and for the first time is the presence of an "already other time", and what it reveals is that "now" is "long ago", and that here is another place, a place always other where whoever believes they can calmly witness this transformation from the outside can transform it into potency only if they let themselves be drawn out of themselves and be dragged into the movement in which a part of oneself, beginning with the hand that is writing, becomes imaginary. (17/25; translation modified)

Who then was Proust? "We say Proust," Blanchot replied, some 200 pages later, "but we know it is the entirely other who is writing, not only someone else, but the very demand of writing, a demand that takes Proust's name, but does not express Proust, which expresses him only by disappropriating him, by making him Other" (208-209/254; translation modified).

It is of course an abiding critical cliché that subjectivity is the preeminent theme of all modern novels. From Blanchot's perspective, however, this was little more than a dubious and outdated assumption. And here was another reason why he was unwilling to linger with Hegel and his contemporaries, the writers of the early Sturm und Drang, or the Romantics Novalis and Eichendorff, all of whom, Blanchot argued, had reacted to history's damning verdict by promoting instead the individual subjectivity of the artist as demiurge or genius. Far more important, Blanchot argued, was the radically other experience of Mallarmé and Cézanne. This was not just to swap French names for German ones, and nor was it simply to accept for a moment that Marxist political frame for which the decisive turning point was 1848. More importantly, it was to challenge the potent legacy of Romanticism itself. For what manifested itself in Mallarmé and Cézanne, Blanchot argued, was no glorification of the artist, nor any proud belief in the transcendence of the artwork, but rather abiding and fundamental doubt, expressed with modesty and sobriety: "an obscure quest, difficult and tormented," Blanchot put it. "An experience of essential risk," he went on, "in which art, the work, truth, and the essence of language are called into question and enter into risk" (197/240; translation modified). And if what this entailed, prior to the completion of any artwork, outside truth, and far from the so-called certainties of language, and what Blanchot occasionally called worklessness, or *désœuvrement*, it was not to make of *désœuvrement* the occasion for another incompletely complete work—"the work of the absence of work," Blanchot called it—as Schlegel and others had done, but to experience the radical impossibility of doing so, the ordeal of being forever exposed, as Blanchot has it of Beckett's *L'Innommable*, to that place without place where "speaking does not speak, but is, where nothing begins, nothing is said, but is always anew and always begins again" (216/263; translation modified).[16]

When *Le Livre à venir* appeared in 1959, it did so amid significant political upheaval. The Algerian War, though not named as such by the French authorities until 1999, was slowly reaching its dramatic climax. The year before Blanchot's book, partly as a result of events in Algeria, the French Fourth Republic,

---

[16] I examine Blanchot's reading of Beckett in more detail in my "'Poststructuralist' Readings of Beckett?," in *Palgrave Advances in Samuel Beckett Studies*, ed. Lois Oppenheim (New York: Palgrave Macmillan, 2004), 68–88.

founded after the war, finally collapsed, allowing De Gaulle to take control—
many, including Blanchot, thought so illegitimately—and establish the Fifth
Republic which remains in power today. Until 1958, notwithstanding his prewar
career as a political journalist, Blanchot opted to keep his opinions to himself.
At Dionys Mascolo's invitation, however, he now publicly committed himself to
the campaign against De Gaulle and against the pursuit of the Algerian war. He
explained his thinking in a word. The word was "Le Refus [Refusal]," as glossed
in a brief text published in Mascolo's broadsheet *Le 14 Juillet*, and republished,
in slightly modified form, in *L'Amitié* (*Friendship*) thirteen years later.[17] Blanchot
explained what was at stake in the closing chapter of *Le Livre à venir*, "La
Puissance et la gloire [The Power and the Glory]." There was no contradiction
between what Blanchot had argued elsewhere in his 1959 book and the political
decisions he took at the time. For if the future of literature was synonymous
with the refusal of power and authority and with the multiple exigencies that
arise from an absence of foundation, Blanchot argued, so the same was forcibly
also the case in the realm of the political too. In the years that followed it would
be what Blanchot in his writing and in his political actions would endeavor to
affirm.

---

[17]  See Maurice Blanchot, *L'Amitié* (Paris: Gallimard, 1971), 130–31; *Friendship*, trans. Elizabeth
Rottenberg (Stanford: Stanford University Press, 1997), 111–12. I discuss Blanchot's postwar
political thinking in more detail in my *Maurice Blanchot and Fragmentary Writing: A Change of
Epoch* (New York: Continuum, 2012), 231–53.

# 5

# Literature Outside the Law: Blanchot's *The Infinite Conversation*

## Christopher Langlois

Blanchot concludes the "Note" that opens *The Infinite Conversation*, which consists of a mixture of dialogic, fragmentary, and essayistic texts that first appeared in *La Nouvelle Revue française* between 1954 and 1969,[1] by proposing that "writing is the greatest violence, for it transgresses the law, every law, and also its own" (IC xii). The notion of the law plays a pivotal role in Blanchot's understanding of the work of literature and writing. The law exists, and not only in relation to literature and writing, in order to ensure continuity of operation in whatever genre or regime of discourse is vulnerable to suspension, and it is through that very function of defending continuity against discontinuity that the law, all law, necessarily presupposes and indeed thrives on the prospect of its own transgression. The law, as Blanchot appears to be using it here, can therefore be taken to represent a power that sanctions, in both senses of this wonderfully ambiguous word, any and all acts seeking to subvert the continuity of discourse that the law constitutively upholds. Blanchot is all too aware that behind the authority of the law is a long-standing cultural investment in the discrete metaphysical principles that have historically grounded the law's essentially conservative power. Such metaphysical principles that have grounded the otherwise empty authority of the law, tempting the forces of its transgression to act in the name of the discontinuation of the law, include Unity, Identity, and Truth, but also Man, the State, and God. Principles such as these supplement the law by providing it with the metaphysical cover needed for legislating that continuity of discourse and preservation of culture be defended, always under

---

[1] Blanchot then revised several of these texts before they were republished in the context of *L'Entretien infini*.

penalty of death,[2] against the anarchic violence implicit in acts that haunt, if not outright assault, the law with the forces aspiring to its imminent transgression.

The metaphysical law that concerns Blanchot most explicitly in *The Infinite Conversation*, however, is "the *law* of the book" (426; emphasis in the original). Dialectical promise of Hegel, intoxicating, impossible dream of Mallarmé[3] prefiguring the modernist desire for a totality of knowledge and an immediacy of representation through the perfected work of art and literature, the concept of the book is predicated on the supposition that the value of "the book" *qua* "repository and receptacle of knowledge" vastly exceeds the value commonly attached to the empirical book "found in libraries, that labyrinth where all the combinations of forms, words and letters are rolled up in volumes" (423). More than this, "the book is the Book. Still to be read, to be written, always already written and thoroughly penetrated by reading, the book constitutes the condition for every possibility of reading and writing" (423). Blanchot is not interested, either here in *The Infinite Conversation* or elsewhere in his political activity "as a writer," as he empathically puts it,[4] in establishing an oppositional, combative, and therefore dialectically redemptive relation between the law and the transgressiveness of writing. Writing and the law are, on the contrary, essential accomplices in demarcating a place of exteriority prior to all writing and all law, a place that Blanchot identifies as the "outside" and that legislates the possibility of the one in relation to the other (writing in relation to the law and

---

2  As Blanchot will write in one of the fragments in *The Step Not Beyond*, "the law kills. Death is always the horizon of the law: if you do this, you will die. It kills whoever does not observe it, and to observe it is already to die, to die to all possibilities" (25).

3  Notably, this impossibility of the Mallarméan dream is what makes all the difference in distinguishing Mallarmé from Hegel: "a difference evidenced by their different ways of being anonymous in the naming and signing of their work. Hegel does not die, even if he disavows himself in the displacement or turning about of the System: since every system still names him, Hegel is never altogether nameless. Mallarmé and the work are without relation, and this lack of relationship is played out in the Work, establishing the work as what would be forbidden to this particular Mallarmé, as it would be to anyone else bearing a name, and as it would be to the work conceived as the power of accomplishing itself in and through itself" (IC 429).

4  Blanchot, reflecting on his co-authorship and public endorsement of the Declaration of the Right to Insubordination in the Algerian War, or more commonly known as the Manifesto of the 121, and which was released on September 6, 1960, in *Vérité-Liberté*, that is, contemporaneously with several of the texts that would go on to comprise *The Infinite Conversation*, insists that it is precisely "as a writer" that he "signed this text, not even as a political writer, nor as a citizen engaged in political struggles, for I do not participate in them, but as a nonpolitical writer led to comment seriously and firmly on essential problems" (26). Blanchot elaborates on the passivity of writing in another response to his actions against France's persecution of The Algerian War, explaining that "writing is, at the limit," and again it is as a writer that Blanchot signs the Manifesto of the 121, "always in search of a nonpower, refusing mastery, order, and the established order above all, preferring silence to the speech of absolute truth, thereby contesting things and contesting them incessantly" (117). See *Maurice Blanchot: Political Writings, 1953–1993*, ed. Paul Zakir (New York: Fordham University Press, 2010).

vice versa). We only know of this place of exteriority beyond knowledge, speech, and light—this lawless place of the outside where presence never reigns—because its contravention of the authority of the law ceaselessly reinforces the law's prohibition against its trespass and traversal.

This place where no Self comes into being and where there is no hope of crossing the distance that frames it is the site of an originary experience of writing that guarantees only violence and terror without end (an experience of the impossibility of experience). This is "a region," in other words, as Blanchot depicts it *via* his defense of the absurd in the work of Kafka and Camus, that is "approached in life by all who, having lost the world, move restlessly between being and nothingness: a swarming mass of inexistence, a proliferation without reality, nihilism's vermin: ourselves" (179). What we gain from subjection to the law and the concomitant invitation into community and culture, namely, possession of the world and salvation from the disaster of "alterity itself" (432), however, we pay for with the forfeiture of a future that would be exterior and exempt from all continuity of discourse promised by the law's "essentially theological" securities of transcendence (428). This is why Blanchot does not call upon writing simply to abolish the law or amend its prohibitions, but instead to keep vigilant watch over the approach of exteriority that upsets the law's totalitarian proclivities, even and perhaps especially in light of the knowledge that "the law is what saves us from writing" (432).

In the essay "The Absence of the Book," which concludes *The Infinite Conversation* and that Blanchot had considered as an alternative title for the project as a whole,[5] Blanchot registers the need for distinguishing between a "first" and a "second" mode of writing. He does so in recognition that the writing inscribed in the pages of the empirical book, the annals of culture, is always too legible for it to coincide with the writing of exteriority prior to the law. It is when writing "accepts taking form in language by giving rise to the book," to "written discourse," however, that exteriority appears as that which writing cannot express free of the cultural trappings of language that invariably dissimulates the essential hostility of exteriority to representation, knowledge, and experience (of presence). What Blanchot labels "first" writing, in other words, is a "writing exterior to the knowledge that is gained through reading, and also exterior to the form or the requirements of the Law" (431). When

---

[5] For an excellent genetic reading of "The Absence of the Book" and its significance to the overall development of Blanchot's thinking leading up to *The Infinite Conversation*, see John McKeane, "Change in the Archive: Blanchot's *L'Entretien infini*," *Forum for Modern Language Studies* 50, no. 1 (2013): 69–81.

the impulse of writing originating from exteriority inevitably passes over into language, when writing metamorphoses into the legibility of "second" writing—from the clamorous murmuring of silence into the communicable discourse of speech—it is then that "the Law is writing itself, writing that has renounced the exteriority of interdiction [*l'entre-dire*] in order to designate the place of the interdict" (431). What this means for the work of literature when it is exposed to the rogue exteriority of writing, and thus exiled to a place of interminable transit back and forth between the legitimacy and illegitimacy of writing-become-law and law-become-writing, is that its proper place, the space wherein the labor of literature is secretly (not primordially) conducted, is one of perpetual detour and fragmentation, unfolding "*outside speech*, and as turned only toward the *outside*" (431; emphasis in the original).

What would therefore be "at stake in the fact that something like art or literature exists," as Blanchot speculates in the prefatory "Note," or that "since Mallarmé, … [e]ssays, novels, poems seem only to be there, and to be written in order to allow the labor of literature (now considered as a singular force or a position of sovereignty) to accomplish itself" (xi), is that the most suffocating, murderous laws of historico-political closure that continue to haunt the future of modernity, particularly after the Second World War, are precluded from having the last word on how the infinite approach of exteriority, of writing turned toward and turning perpetually about the outside, is to instigate and instigate always the transgression of such laws that make of history, in the words of Joyce's Stephen Daedalus, "a nightmare from which I am trying to awake."[6] To do this, however, art and literature, which is now to say writing, must risk denouncing all the metaphysical principles of the law that they have been historically complicit in servicing. They must declare, through the transgressive illegality of writing,

> the end and also the completion of everything that guarantees our culture—not so that we might in idyllic fashion turn back, but rather so we might go beyond, that is, to the limit, in order to attempt to break the circle, the circle of circles: the *totality* of the concepts that founds history, that develops in history, and whose development history is. Writing, in this sense—in this direction in which it is not possible to maintain oneself alone, or even in the name of all without the tentative advances, the lapses, the turns and detours whose trace the texts here brought together bear (and their interest, I believe, lies in this)—supposes a radical change of epoch: interruption, death itself—or, to speak hyperbolically, "the end of history." (xii)

6  James Joyce, *Ulysses* (London: Penguin Books, 2000), 42.

Blanchot's ambitious declaration of what writing must accomplish in relation to the dialectical law of historical development entails that writing must likewise envision and therefore become complicit in the very end of history, the completion of the totality of the concepts that found history, that it is otherwise called upon from the outside of the law to repetitively transgress. To become the sovereign force equal to the task of transgressing the totality of the concepts of history, the force of writing, that is, the neutral, fragmentary force of a literature separated absolutely from history and culture, must double as the force of its own sovereign exception. Writing is thus doubly violent because it is committed to an endless reciprocity of transgressive suspensions and relegislations of the law, all laws, and especially its own at the interminable turning point of the end of history. The law of a literature contemporaneous with the nightmarish closures of history that punctuated the violence of the twentieth century is one obliged to stipulate that literature is, from now on, a literature of the fragment. The time is therefore now, in light of the permanently untimely breach of the contemporary, to think not only about the modern task of art and literature, but also about what philosophy and criticism can do in the space and time *beyond* philosophy and criticism, beyond the Whole of philosophical knowledge where writing dwells outside the law (outside the law of laws, the law of the Book).

We can begin to speculate that part of Blanchot's purpose in collecting the diverse texts of *The Infinite Conversation* into a single volume of essays-*cum*-chapters adding up to a book is to open up the spaces between the moving intervals that separate the work of writing and reading literature from thinking philosophically about literature, history, politics, culture, and, of course, philosophy itself. Blanchot leads us to believe that it is here, in the spaces of transit between literary, critical, and philosophical experience where the weightiest problematics of ethics and politics, literature and philosophy, and culture and history have the best chance of being addressed in response to the imperative (and impossibility) of their resolution if not also their redemption.[7] Indeed, one of the principal tasks Blanchot sets for himself in *The Infinite Conversation*

---

[7]   It would be more accurate to say that, for Blanchot, the Second World War is not solely responsible for what, in the short essay "War and Literature" collected in *Friendship*, he describes as "the change undergone by the concept of literature," which "is not in immediate relation to the 'Second World War,' having been in the process of becoming long before; however, it found the accelerated confirmation of the fundamental crisis in the war, the change of an era that we do not yet know how to measure for lack of a language" (109). *The Infinite Conversation* is very much engaged in the search for a language that would be capable of measuring the crisis of history, politics, philosophy, and literature that has been germinating since the inauguration of European modernity at the end of the eighteenth century.

is to measure the extent to which the ambitious project of both literary and philosophical modernity, the post-romantic commitment to fragmentary writing, has negotiated precisely the problematic of making common cause with forces of violence at the always pernicious, but sometimes utopian, detours of history.

The philosophical task of modernity, in Blanchot's view, is one of attuning the movement of thinking to a relation that the speech of modern poetry (Friedrich Hölderlin's, Paul Celan's, and perhaps above all René Char's), specifically, remains the most adept at approaching. Blanchot's question throughout *The Infinite Conversation*, which is the question that philosophical thinking must begin seriously to contemplate if it is interested in thinking the problematic of violence amid the (ethical and political as much as ontological and metaphysical) conditions of historical closure, is the question of how to enter into "a relation with the obscure and the unknown that would be a relation neither of force [*puissance*], nor of comprehension, nor even of revelation" (48). How do we, in experiencing the crises and violence of modernity at the limits of experience, begin speaking on the basis of "the secret decision of every essential speech in us: *naming* the possible, *responding* to the impossible" (48) (emphasis in the original)?[8] If philosophical thinking is to pose this question decisively, it will first have to purge itself of the tendencies that have defined its subservience to the revelatory movements of thinking demanded for so long by the metaphysics of presence and the law of the book, namely, such tendencies as its drive to illumination, clarity, and reason, not the least of which is its tendency to uphold "the optical imperative … through which it is suggested that, to speak truly, one must think according to the measure of the eye" (27). Modern philosophical thinking therefore has a profound, and profoundly unsettling, lesson to learn from what Blanchot will later describe, reflecting on Antonin Artaud, as the "cruel poetic reason" of fragmentary writing, that is, of writing according to the fragmentary imperative whereby the work of literature is circumscribed by "a space not of words but of the relations of words that—always preceding them

---

[8] It would be difficult to underestimate the service Susan Hanson performs in her translator's foreword for understanding what is at stake in *The Infinite Conversation* by turning the reader's attention to this proposition that "essential speech" begins by "naming the possible, responding to the impossible" (48). For Hanson, this proposition crystallizes Blanchot's intention, in writing *The Infinite Conversation*, to mark "a time between speaking wherein the world for an instant falls silent, and in whose disarming silence the reader is claimed by the appeal, the presence of something radically *other*" (xxxiii; emphasis in the original). To this I would only add that, for Blanchot, marking such a time is not free of a danger threatening the person who thinks under the weight of this proposition with the destruction of "his power to be still himself (lost in anguish, we say)" (50).

and nonetheless given by them—is their moving suspension, the appearance of their disappearance …; that is, the experience of being that is image before it is object, and the experience of an art that is gripped by the violent difference that is prior to all representation and all knowledge" (295).

Blanchot's understanding of fragmentary writing marks a significant advance in how the literary fragment had been hitherto approached in the history of its theorization and use. More often than not, the fragment is articulated almost exclusively in terms of the unities, continuities, and authorities it either obstructs or outright subverts. Not so for Blanchot, who starts from the perspective that if fragmentary writing is to stop itself from elapsing into yet another programmatic law of literary, aesthetic, or philosophical comportment, then it must cease always presupposing that such unities, continuities, and authorities it targets for transgression are always already present, are always simply *there* awaiting the dislocating encounter with the fragment. But this is not easy to do owing to all of the dialectical baggage that attaches itself to the concept of the "fragment" after romanticism:

> Whoever says fragment ought not to say simply the fragmenting of an already existent reality or the moment of the whole still to come. This is hard to envisage due to the necessity of comprehension according to which the only knowledge is knowledge of the whole, just as sight is always a view of the whole. For such comprehension, the fragment supposes an implied designation of something that has previously been or will subsequently be a whole—the severed finger refers back to the hand, just as the first atom prefigures and contains in itself the universe. Our thought is therefore caught between two limits: the imagining of the integrity of substance and the imagining of a dialectical becoming. But in the fragment's violence, and, in particular, the violence of which René Char grants access, quite a different relation is given to us—at least as a promise and as a task. "*What is reality without the dislocating energy of poetry?*" (307; emphasis in the original)

The fragment's particular violence, as Blanchot understands it here, is a force of infinite dislocation and transgression that simultaneously severs and sutures part and whole, image and ground, and word and thing to whatever structural Whole the fragment posits for tearing asunder. The poetry of René Char, in particular, leads Blanchot to think that "a new kind of arrangement" is possible as the structuring principle of the space of writing, one "not entailing harmony, concordance, or reconciliation, but that accepts disjunction or divergence as the infinite center from out of which, through speech, relation is to be created" (308).

This act of acceptance, this willingness to affirm "disjunction or divergence," cannot be made in the register of an absolute, sovereign declaration of the law of writing; rather, it requires constant renewal under the dogged, dialectical pressure of its negation and reversal. It cannot be made as an absolute (timeless, placeless) declaration of the law of writing, moreover, because writing is not its primal site of possibility. The fragment belongs to a dimension of language that simultaneously (and paradoxically) eludes without avoidance and seduces without seduction any and all attempts at its conceptual or representational capture. "*And to write*," as Blanchot puts it in the first of seven "Parentheses" appended to "The Fragment Word," would thus be "*to bring this unalluring attraction into play, to expose language to it and to disengage language from it through a violence that will once again deliver language over to it—to the point of the fragment word*" (311; italics in the original).

Blanchot reserves this ambivalent distinction of the place and play in language where writing becomes an infinite fragmentary force of dislocation for what he terms "the neutral," which cannot be thought separately from trying to think or say (to experience) the unknown *qua* unknown: "the unknown is always thought in the neuter. Thought of the neuter or the neutral is a threat and a scandal of thought" (299). Blanchot's understanding of what writing pursues in proximity of the "neutral," under the sway of its insistence on separation and spacing, recalls us once again to the double violence of writing, its scandal and its threat to the law, without which neither the act of writing nor what is written would have any purchase on what is demanded of literature at the detours of history. Through Char, Blanchot links the philosophical problematic of the unknown with the more literary problematic of "the neuter, the neutral," suggesting that each of these discourses (literature and philosophy), however different are their methods and aims of creative operation, converge around the same question of how to give voice and lend thought to a movement of alterity that articulates, we can only ever suspect, as the silent suspension of speaking and thinking (298). "By a simplification that is clearly abusive," Blanchot readily concedes, "the entire history of philosophy" can be interpreted according to the effort, beginning with Aristotle and Plato (who were equally responsible for sending philosophy astray from the thought of the neutral first intuited by Heraclitus), Hegel and Kant, and then continuing into the present epoch of philosophical modernity through Heidegger and Sartre, "either to acclimatize or to domesticate the neuter" (299).

Blanchot's turn away from the philosophical legacy of detaining the neuter so as to tame the free play of its separating (fragmenting) movement is the cause and consequence of discovering a relation with the unknown that translates not into a relation of power, but of infinite welcome and hospitality toward everything concealed and even everything potentially threatening about the unknown. This is a discovery that Blanchot attributes to Char and to a use of poetic speech that lets the neuter itself speak:

> To speak the unknown, to receive it through speech while leaving it unknown, is precisely not to take hold of it, not to comprehend it; it is rather to refuse to identify it even by sight, that "objective" hold that seizes, albeit at a distance. To live with the unknown before one (which also means: to live before the unknown, and before oneself as unknown) is to enter into the responsibility of a speech that speaks without exercising any form of power; even the power that accrues to us when we look, since, in looking, we keep whatever and whomever stands before us within our horizon and within our circle of sight—thus within the dimension of the visible-invisible. Here let us recall René Char's now long-standing affirmation, which will bring forth everything we have just tried to say: "*A being of which one is ignorant is a being that is infinite—capable, in intervening, of changing our anguish and our burden into arterial dawn.*" The unknown as unknown is this infinite, and the speech that speaks it is a speech of the infinite. (302)

There is a supple, shrouding quality to poetic speech that renders it uniquely suitable for contact with the unknown. Devoid of grammatical personality, aware that it is never "I" who speaks in poetry, but language as such that speaks through the poetic word, the poetic speech of René Char strikes Blanchot as exemplary of the force of resistance to power that modern poetry, symptom of the crises, closures, and detours of history, singularly represents. At its best, poetry accepts its condition of passivity and powerlessness in proximity with the unknown, and paradoxically this act of acceptance of passivity is what indicates the supremacy of its power as a power of the refusal to power. While ordinary, non poetic speech acquiesces to the negativity of language, its power to efface the being of the things and persons language names, poetic speech aligns itself with what is lost in representation, that is, the unknown because unknowable itself. Without this poetic response to the demand of the neuter, the world would be deprived of everything that makes the experience of newness and the mystery of existence possible. The neuter is what disarms us of the power (if it does not become that power itself, for such is the ambiguity of the neuter *qua* anonymous placeholder of radical contingency) that forgets the experience of newness in the world, that makes culture possible, and that makes the taming of nature and the subjugation of other persons and existences prerequisites of our civilization (our barbarism). Char, whose name is inseparable in French literary history from the spirit of resistance to fascist occupation, is the poet who most excelled at readying the passivity of poetry for dealing with the historical crises and violence of the twentieth century and beyond.

Before being taken to the limit of the possibility of poetry by Char, however, it was the literature (writing) and theory (thinking) of German romanticism that Blanchot credits with having placed the first serious wager on the value of the fragment. Romanticism bets virtually everything that literature and poetry are capable of saying on the idea that the only form of writing and thinking equal to the task of actualizing an experience of absolute freedom outside the law, of declaring the sovereign right always to transgress the law, is a form of writing communicated only in and through fragmentary form. But romanticism, in secretly conservative deference, Blanchot suspects, of the dialectical "orientation of history, which, become revolutionary" after 1793 in France, "places at the forefront of its action work that is undertaken in view of the whole," closed literature off, in the splendor and solitude of the perfected fragment, from opening onto the future that arrives only through the intervals, detours, and discontinuities of the outside of the law that fragmentary writing was supposed to be tasked principally with orchestrating (359).

In the aesthetic, avant-garde hands of romanticism, the fragment became a totality unto itself, an aphoristic circumscription of the center of writing that would be severed from all relation with the surrounding world beyond the romantic fiefdom of literature. Signing off on "the closure of the perfect sentence" as enthusiastically as the principal theoretical architects of romanticism ended up doing, and particularly Friedrich Schlegel and Novalis, as Blanchot reads them as necessary, yet insufficient, precursors to modern poets like Char, led to texts and to a theory of texts that had their centers concentrated within "rather than in the field that *other* fragments constitute along with it" (359; emphasis in original). Because romanticism could not imagine the realization of its ambitions other than by totalizing its discoveries and concentrating all that it would write and think in a closeted, aphoristic form of the fragment, in other words, it ensured, paradoxically, that it would never complete the essentially incompleteable revolutionary task of infinite transgression that from now on would be the exclusive, incalculable measure of contemporary literature (and thus the promise of its repeated incompletion and failure). No sooner did romanticism lay down a new law for the future of writing, the law of the fragment, then did writing, the "first" writing outside the law, outside *all* law, respond by turning against the fragment itself. Blanchot anticipates Jean-Luc Nancy and Philippe Lacoue-Labarthe's *The Literary Absolute* in celebrating romanticism for its pioneering theory of literature, but noting, just as importantly, that it was precisely by submitting its *work* of literature to its *theory* of literature that romanticism was destined to betray the very outlawed freedom of writing that it was the first to so thrillingly declare. Romanticism fails, in Blanchot's eyes, because it declined to repeat the transgression of the law of literature that its fragmentary writings were now sovereignly responsible for legislating.

While it was the honor of German romanticism to have taken the first step toward asking the all-important question of the fragmentary detour of speech, the "question of discontinuity or difference as a question of form," its failure to pursue this question any further than settling on the aphoristic totality of the fragment ended up "consigning" the question "to Nietzsche and, beyond Nietzsche, to the future" (359). Indeed, it was Nietzsche's recourse to a more thoroughgoing mode of fragmentary writing, taken in order to express the necessary hazards of "a venturous thought, a thought that realizes itself in fragments," that eventually compelled him to philosophize outside the institutionally, professionally sanctioned space of the university (fearful as it was and still is of any thought that refuses the law of non contradiction), for "Nietzsche, too, was a professor" (4). Nietzsche's criticism of philosophical thinking stretching back all the way to Plato was damning not because it reversed the substitution of ontology with metaphysics, but because it discovered a way of neutralizing all power of thinking that derives its energy from the astral metaphors of light, the "imperialism of light," that have made philosophy into a discourse that dialogues only with what it crudely renders visible to its deadly powers of comprehension (162).

Under the Platonic paradigm of philosophical thinking there could be no experience of the unknown that does not commence from the a priori metaphysical desire to see it submitted to the diurnal light of comprehension. This, Blanchot argues, is what drove Nietzsche to perpetrate what was nothing less the "scandal of scandals," namely, the disengagement of philosophical thinking from "every optical reference" (160):

Fragmentary speech is not a speech in which the site would already be designated, as though in filigree—white on white—where the overman would find his place. Fragment speech is speech of the *between*-two. This between-two is not the intermediary between two times, the time of man already disappeared—but does he disappear?—and that of the overman in whom the past is to come—but does it come, and by what coming? The speech of the fragment does not form a joinder from one to the other, it rather separates them; as long as it speaks, and in speaking remains silent, it is the moving tear of time that maintains, one infinitely distant from the other, these two figures wherein knowledge turns. (158)

Fragmentary speech is thus able to become the "scandal of scandals" insofar as it is predicated on a commitment to relations of juxtaposition that can no longer be reconciled according to a (phenomenologically and epistemologically) measurable distance yet to be crossed. The goal of this speech is not to traverse the distance between the unknown and the known, the other and the self, or the depth and surface of representation (*pace* Blanchot's subtle criticism of Malevich's *White on White* in the excerpt above); rather, it is to circumscribe a space in language wherein the power of negativity, the luminosity of reason, is neutralized always in advance, cut off from apprehending this space as a temporary interlude of darkness, the repose of a night soon to be relieved by the dawning light of the day. With Nietzsche the fragment becomes a truly outlaw force of separation rather than a newly minted plenipotentiary of the optical imperative. This was perhaps Nietzsche's greatest gift to the literature and philosophy of the twentieth century as it became rightfully obsessed amid the dehumanizing technologies of politics, culture, and war (and most presciently through the work of Walter Benjamin, we know now in hindsight) with the irremediable fragility of historical experience.

Blanchot's close affinity (and friendship) with Georges Bataille, whose thinking made discoveries in this historical context of inestimably more importance than the spectacles for which he is all too popularly remembered of "engag[ing] in irreligion, prais[ing] debauchery, replac[ing] Christianity with Nietzscheanism and Nietzscheanism with Hinduism, after having hung around with surrealism," gives a clue into what Blanchot envisions as the novel horizon of twentieth-century philosophical thinking after Nietzsche (202–203). As it tends hubristically toward absolute knowledge, particularly under the omnipresent gaze of Hegelianism, modern philosophical thinking approaches a moment of historical crisis when it must suddenly contemplate and decide where thinking can possibly go and what it can possibly think in the event that it expends all of its reserves of negativity by seizing on the dialectical truth that nothing is unthinkable so long as thinking is guided by what Blanchot, echoing Bataille, calls "the passion of negative thought" (204). Is there an undiscovered frontier of thinking beyond the dialectical totality of the thinkable? What would it mean to escape the whole, the totality of concepts that found history, and thus to redraw the territorial boundaries of what remains to be conquered and dominated by the greedy power of dialectical negativity? What would the experience of thinking be, finally, when the power of negativity that drives its hunger for knowledge is exhausted by there being nothing left that thinking has not already digested?

Blanchot calls this experience of thinking at the dialectical end of history the "limit-experience," that is to say, "the experience of what is outside the whole when the whole excludes every outside; the experience of what is still to be attained when all is attained and of what is still to be known when all is known: the inaccessible, the unknown itself" (205). This is not to suggest that the limit-experience, as Blanchot defines it here in proximity and in debt to Bataille, represents the overcoming of negativity and the cessation of negative thought; on the contrary, because "the [limit-] experience is not an outcome," does not ultimately have the authority to sign off on the end of dialectical thinking (207), it is inextricably tied to negativity as a restless *movement* of thinking, a movement that delivers thinking over to "the ecstatic 'loss of knowledge,'" or "the grasping seizure of contestation at the height of rupture and dispossession" (207). The "intellectual importance of the limit-experience" (207) for Blanchot's understanding of what is most desperately needed of philosophical thinking in the interminably dying days of modernity, the crisis-ridden turning point of the "end of history," is precisely that it names the possibility of transgressing the totality of knowledge, of beginning to exist, "as Georges Bataille expresses it with the most simple profundity, ... in a state of 'negativity without employ' " (205).

It is here, in his reflections and commentary on Bataille, that Blanchot confronts most directly the perhaps insurmountable philosophical "problem brought forth by the limit-experience": "how can the absolute (in the form of totality) still be gotten beyond? Having arrived at the summit of his actions, how can man—he the universal, the eternal, always accomplishing himself, always accomplished and repeating himself in a Discourse that does no more than endlessly speak itself—not hold to this sufficiency, and go on to put himself, as such, in question? Properly speaking, he cannot" (207). Given that these two interrelated questions are posed in the context of reading Bataille, we would be wise not to ignore that the universal image of "man" that Blanchot has in mind is the one that Bataille conceded as the only anthropological image compatible with the posthistorical epoch anticipated by the Kojèvian-Hegelian dialectic of history.[9] Bataille's primary concern in this historical context in the 1930s was less on the validity of the diagnosis than it was on what was to be done with forces of negativity being faced with the unprecedented historical prospect of their superfluousness (destined for expenditure through eroticism, mysticism, etc.). Blanchot is invoking this universal image of posthistorical existence not in order to endorse it, but to use it to push thinking to the absolute, truly nightmarish extremity of what is thinkable. Only by entertaining in all seriousness the hypothesis that history has irreversibly entered the time of endless, meaningless repetition does it become possible to confront an experience of what such an apocalyptic vision of the future can never, in fact, contain[10]:

> an experience that is not lived, even less a state of our self; at most a limit-experience at which, perhaps, the limits fall but that reaches us only at the limit: when the entire future has become present and, through the resolution of the decisive Yes, there is affirmed the ascendency over which there is no longer any hold.
>
> The experience of non-experience.
>
> Detour from everything visible and invisible. (210)

What occurs on the precipice of the end of history, of "man" having accomplished himself and of continuing to accomplish this heroic image of himself accomplishing himself ad infinitum, is nothing as decisive as an epochal eclipse of ontological and historical stagnation, or the evental beginning of a new time or a new man. The sacrifice of lived, livable experience does not promise a return of this experience, if only because what is lost is nothing less, but nothing more than the consoling metaphysical illusion that "man did not in some sense already belong to this detour" (210). The detour that Blanchot has in mind is the detour introduced into existence by speech, but notably only insofar as "speaking is not seeing," as though, in this detour at the limit of experience, of modernity at the

---

[9]   In his English translator's introduction to Blanchot's *Le Très Haut*, "Death at the End of History," Allan Stoekl draws attention to a letter Bataille sent to Kojève in December 1937. Bataille: "I grant (as a likely supposition) that from now on history is ended (except for the dénouement). However, I picture things differently (I don't attribute much importance to the difference between fascism and communism; on the other hand, it certainly doesn't seem impossible that, in some very distant time, everything will begin again)" ("Letter to X., Lecturer on Hegel …," in *The College of Sociology: 1937–1939*, ed. Denis Hollier (Minneapolis: University of Minnesota Press, 1988), 90.

[10]  Blanchot's indebtedness to Nietzsche for the idea of the Eternal Return of the Same cannot be overstated (or underestimated), for as far as Blanchot is concerned, it was Nietzsche who first made the discovery that the hypothesis of the completion of time, the end of history, that was required to think the Eternal Return, is what leads to a thought of infinite spacing, separation, and rupture, a thought of the fragmentary imperative that it is the responsibility of literature and philosophy to keep always in play whenever history is threatened with closure.

end of history and "man" after the disappearance of "man," *pace* Nietzsche and now Bataille, "we were turned away from the visible, without being turned back round toward the invisible" (27).

After Nietzsche and in light of Bataille, only acts of discontinuity that exacerbate the "scandal of scandals" of fragmentary, neutral writing will do. Indeed, one of the reasons why Blanchot places so high a value on the writings of Franz Kafka (his novels, parables, diaries, and letters), accordingly, is that Kafka did more and went further than any other writer of prose fiction in the twentieth century in being "able to bring into image" the philosophically unthinkable idea (owing to the tyranny of Aristotelian logic so aggressively spurned by Nietzsche) "that all thought of non-signification, as soon as it is expressed, lives by way of a contradiction. 'Manage, if you can,' Kafka says, 'to make yourself understood by the wood louse. If you once succeed in questioning him on the goal of his work, you will by the same stroke have exterminated the population of wood louses' " (182).

Blanchot is attracted to this image of the extermination of the wood louse for at least two reasons. The first reason is that it clarifies the principle that the economy of dialogue, stripped bare to the presence of two solitary existences exchanging speech, is never one that operates between equal partners engaged peaceably, nonviolently in discourse; on the contrary, "all speech is a word of command, of terror, of seduction, of resentment, flattery, or aggression; all speech is violence—and to pretend to ignore this in claiming to dialogue is to add liberal hypocrisy to the dialectical optimism according to which war is no more than another form of dialogue" (81). Between the wood louses and ourselves, only the latter fetishize understanding (as a will to power), and it is for this reason that Blanchot can say that the "would-be dialogue with the population of wood louses entails a language in which solely our will to clarity speaks—a will to clarity that is a will to exterminate" (182). The second reason why Blanchot is drawn to Kafka's image of the wood louses being murderously subjected to speech is that it makes clear in what way language threatens the unknown *qua* unknowable with the forced metamorphosis into the knowable. It is but a short step from enacting the will to clarity expressed through language to carrying out the will to extermination expressed through wordless violence: "there is in Kafka's image something that brings to light a disquieting violence. It is a matter of exterminating, of doing away with, and speech would be what brings death to the inhuman, that which is in possession of nothingness and destruction … This would be a speech in which the vermin disappear, *but precisely because it is this very disappearance that defines vermin*, just as it defines speech, or at least a certain, strange speech" (182; my emphasis).

It is here in his reflections on this image and parable of Kafka's that Blanchot expresses his conviction in the starkest possible terms that there is nothing innocuous or innocent in the event that two incommensurable existences come into contact and engage in dialogue and speech. We underestimate the power of speech by thinking that its only effect is to bring to signification that which was previously unsignified, or to communicate that which had not yet been given the chance to communicate with others. Blanchot is not denying that speech has this power, and indeed this sociopolitical value in the building and maintenance of community, but he wants also to emphasize that speech is in possession of a far more primordial, unworkable power, namely, the power to speak "outside all power to represent or signify" (182). Inviting persons or communities persecuted as vermin to prove (always condescendingly), by participating in dialogue and speech, that they are not in fact vermin, are not after all inhuman, does nothing to rid the world of the oppressive language of civilization according to which there must be vermin in order for there to be the civilized non-vermin. Like the portrait of Kafka handed to us from Deleuze and Guattari's *Kafka: Toward a Minor Literature*, the Kafka we receive from Blanchot is one who confronts literature with the question, the impossible question, as Deleuze and Guattari put it, "of seeing and speaking like a beetle, like a dung beetle,"[11] or, returning to the words of Blanchot, of liberating "a language that does not push hell back, but makes its way into it, speaking at the level of the abyss and thereby giving word to it; giving a hearing to what can have no hearing" (183–184).

The violence of language, in the scenario of words wiping out the population of wood louse vermin, consists in that the existences language celebrates itself for rescuing from inhumanity by inviting to participate in the speech of civilized discourse are existences that are inhuman only in light of the speech that would thrust the manufactured signs of humanity upon them. Prior to speech, Blanchot suspects, we all inhabit "a region" of existence, are all subject to "an experience" where our essence is predicated precisely according to the impossibility of absolute, remainderless predication. This is a region, a place of absurdity *par excellence*, that does not simply disappear when it is effaced by dialogue or speech. As Blanchot explains by invoking

---

[11]   Gilles Deleuze and Félix Guattari, *Kafka: Toward a Minor Literature*, trans. Dana Polan (Minneapolis: University of Minnesota Press, 1986), 47.

a similar, "yet nonetheless different" parable of Kafka's—"*Crows claim that a single crow could destroy the sky. This is no doubt so, but it proves nothing about the sky for the sky signifies precisely: the impossibility of crows*' " (182; italics in the original)—"the pretentious 'logical' and 'humanist' thought that asserts that a single thought will destroy the absurd" misjudges the degree to which the absurd, this region of experience outside all power of experience, is fundamentally indifferent "to the thought in which the power of logos speaks" (182–183). Through Kafka (and Camus, in this part of *The Infinite Conversation*), Blanchot exposes a space where "speech would disclose itself as that which lays bare this limit of man that is no longer a power, not yet a power. A space from which what is called man has as if in advance always already disappeared" (183).

The decisive test of literature is whether or not writing can be made to keep open this desert-space of being "where there reigns the absence of relations," a "region always other, a space of emptiness and dispersion …: hell, the horror of absence, the boundlessness of the night that is *other*" (183; emphasis in the original). Literature's fundamental concern, in other words, is not with opening spaces where the voice, body, or face of the other would be empowered with outlets showcasing its humanity (*contra* Emmanuel Levinas, another of Blanchot's closest interlocutors and friends). The space that Blanchot advocates as becoming constitutive of modern literature is, rather, a place where all communication is spoken through words that denounce the establishment of a cohesive community, that reject communities predicated on the elimination of difference, and thus through words opening up a future that "no power—that is to say, no comprehension—no human or divine presence can anticipate" (187). Blanchot wants to preserve the space of literature, out of a strong sense of ethico-historical necessity after the catastrophic shock and surprise of the Second World War, in particular, as perhaps the last space where a voice of absolute refusal to power speaks.

When Blanchot returns to Kafka later in *The Infinite Conversation* under the chapter headings of "The Narrative Voice (*the 'he,' the neutral*)" and "The Wooden Bridge (*repetition, the neutral*)," it is to again credit Kafka with going the furthest toward demonstrating, "even if this formulation cannot be directly attributed to him," that the future of storytelling (narrative) hinges on bringing "the neutral into play" (384). Blanchot notes that any literary commentators can be excused if the "austerity" of style that marks Kafka's novels leads them to "rank" Kafka as one of the twentieth-century descendants of Flaubert. "Yet," Blanchot insists, "everything is different" (383), for what Kafka's novels represent, and this is especially the case with *The Castle*, is the inscription at the center of the novel of an "infinite vanishing point from which the speech of narrative, and within it all narratives and all speech about narrative, would receive and lose their perspective" (396). What distinguishes Kafka from Flaubert is that, for Kafka, literature must no longer be content to leave unquestioned the dividing lines (the ideological contours of aesthetic disinterestedness) separating the outside of literature (reality) from the inside of literature (fiction), or the self of narrating speech from speech become the voice of the narrative other:

> the distance—the creative disinterestedness (so visible in Flaubert inasmuch as he must struggle to maintain it)—which was the writer's and the reader's distance from the work and authorized contemplative pleasure, now enters the work's very sphere in the form of an irreducible strangeness. No longer questioned or reestablished as something denounced, as in Thomas Mann (or Gide), this distance is the medium of the novelistic world, the space in which the narrative experience unfolds in its unique simplicity—an experience that is not recounted but is in play when one recounts. This distance is not simply lived as such by the central character who is always at a distance from himself, just as he is from the events he experiences or the beings he encounters (which would still only be the manifestation of a singular self); this distance keeps him aloof from himself, removing him from the center, because it is constantly decentering the work in an immeasurable and indiscernible way, while at the same time introducing into the most rigorous narration the alteration occasioned by another kind of speech or by the other as speech (as writing). (383–384)

Writing from out of the self-decentering center of literature—"the emptiness of literature that constitutes it" (390)—as resolutely as does Kafka sets the tone for what the future of literature, if literature is to have future (and nothing could be less certain), must from now on set itself the task of pursuing. Literature risks the domestication of its transgressive force if it produces works in ignorance of Kafka (of what literature *is*, or, better yet, as Deleuze and Guattari may have preferred to put it, of what literature can be made to *do* after Kafka). For Blanchot, then, the impact on the future of literature "of modern works that are their own commentary," and that comment on themselves as ruthlessly and thoroughly as do Kafka's to the point that all of us, in the encounter with such literature, join in the terrifying experience of Josef K. before the law in Kafka's

*The Trial*, cannot be underestimated (391).[12] These are works that, in refusing to take the question of what literature *is* or what literature can *do* for granted any longer, expose literature to the future it may never in the end confront. Writers such as Kafka, in other words, sacrifice the work of literature without knowing beforehand whether or not the sacrifice will be redeemed, whether or not the future of literature will be automatically secured with payment of its loss.

Blanchot uses the occasion of the penultimate chapter of *The Infinite Conversation*, "Tomorrow at Stake," to extract from the memory of surrealism, and above all from the work of André Breton, particularly from his enigmatic, quasi-autobiographical novel *Nadja*, "a book 'always in the future' " (419), the discovery that if literature, and not only the literature of surrealism is to have a future (as we now know from reading Blanchot reading Kafka), if it is to be remembered as a literature not only *in* the future but also, and more profoundly, *of* the future, it will be by having put "*tomorrow into play* and as a player" (420; emphasis in original). The experience of surrealism is one that confronts the radical futurity of tomorrow only after having dislodged the work of surrealism from any measurable continuity with the past. In putting tomorrow into play, surrealism works to disempower the past as a power that would tame the radical alterity (the radical futurity) of the future. Where the future is calculated through the measureable odds of what it will bring, whether this be friendship or betrayal, or hospitality or violence, that is, calculations of what is to come made on the basis of what is projected through the memory and experience of the past, it is not the future that is welcomed, not the alterity or futurity of the future, but only the future such that its arrival will be knowingly tolerated.

Breton's decision to circumscribe the fictional narrative of an autobiographical memory around the presence of an absence, the presence of Nadja's absence, or rather the absence of this woman named "Nadja," succeeds in communicating an encounter only with what takes the place of what is missing from the narrative of the encounter:

---

[12]   In her influential 2008 essay, "Two Paths for the Novel," Zadie Smith argues that "all novels attempt to cut neural routes through the brain, to convince us that down this road the true future of the novel lies. In healthy times, we cut multiple roads, allowing for the possibility of a Jean Genet as surely as a Graham Greene" (72–73). It is this possibility that the future of literature belongs to multiple paths that Blanchot is seeking to defend here, and not on a prophetic vision of literature that would in any way prescribe that novels be written by author-clones of Kafka. See Zadie Smith, "Two Paths for the Novel," in *Changing My Mind: Occasional Essays* (New York: The Penguin Press, 2009), 72–96.

The encounter with Nadja is the encounter with encounter, a double encounter. Naturally, Nadja is real [*vraie*] or, more precisely, she is not real [*vraie*]; she remains apart from every interpretable truth, signifying only the unsignifying particularity of her presence; and this presence is that of encounter—brought forth by chance, taken back again by chance, as dangerous and fascinating as it is, and finally vanishing in and of itself, in the frightening *between-two* opened by the aleatory between reason and unreason. But this encounter that necessarily takes place in the continuity of the world is given precisely in such a way that it breaks this continuity and affirms itself as interruption, interval, arrest, or opening. *Real*, this young woman without a name, very shabbily dressed, walking with her head held high and so fragile that she scarcely touches the ground as she goes. (413; emphasis in the original)

The encounter about which *Nadja* is the recollection in narrative, as Blanchot reads it, is therefore not an encounter with this woman named "Nadja," but nor is it an encounter simply with her absence (a narrative mourning her disappearance). There is an encounter in *Nadja* only with the withdrawal of an encounter, and the narrative of this encounter is only the narrative of the "exhausting pursuit" that keeps the narrator riveted to the space of non-encounter where the one absent from the encounter, the unknown itself, figures only as "an interloper, that is, a third party in default, ever exterior to the horizon against which it seems to stand out, always different from the enigma by which, enigmatic, it would give itself over to knowledge" (416). Nadja is not a figure who has not yet appeared, nor is she a figure for whom the narrator impatiently awaits the right time for her appearance (in memory and in narrative). Figuring her in this way would deprive her figuration of its allegiance to non-presence, which is to say, its allegiance to an experience of the unknown that does not even enjoy the epistemological luxury of attributing to the unknown its hypothetical vulnerability to either appearance and representation or understanding and knowledge. "Where no understanding is possible," Blanchot writes, in thinking about the image of Nadja, "where all that happens happens outside understanding and is therefore fascinating—terrible or marvelous—and with no relation other than the intimacy of the absence of relation, it is here that the experience of encounter deploys its dangerous space: a field that is non-unified, non-legalized, and without set paths, where life is no more given at the level of the real than writing, accomplice of life, is present in the language where the real is articulated" (417).

With *Nadja*, we are in the presence of one of only a handful of modern novels and narratives, like Kafka's *The Castle* or Beckett's *The Unnamable*, that Blanchot risks crediting with opening "a new path for literature," but only on condition that the path on which literature finds itself pacing is one that sends it vainly yet dutifully in search of "the absence of work that designates itself as the work's center .... This absence—already aimed at by the thinking, writing in which it becomes necessity (and presence) through chance—is such that it changes the possibility of every book, making of the work what always ought to put itself out of work, unworking itself as it modifies the relations between thought, discourse, and life" (419). When writing approaches the pivotal force of separation through which it inserts itself between what is negated and named by language, or between what is visible and invisible before the blindnesses of philosophical and artistic vision, it is then that it approximates what writing (and thinking) is, what it has become, or what it is always in the process of becoming according to the doubly violent, infinitely transgressive law of the fragment. The law of the fragment is the law of a future separated from the temporality of history, the law that is history's only possibility of survival when it is threatened from within by powers tirelessly desiring its domestication and closure.

With *The Infinite Conversation*, we have in our hands a peculiar hybrid of narrative *récit*, literary criticism, and philosophical critique. No doubt the rich formal and thematic diversity of the texts Blanchot included in *The Infinite Conversation* is as a result of his gradual erasure of the walls between literary and philosophical, and creative and critical writing, but also of an acute awareness that in order to aptly respond to what Blanchot perceived as the most pressing questions of the day, a new means of communication was required that did not limit itself to a univocal mode of expression. *The Infinite Conversation* is Blanchot's most rigorous, committed attempt, before *The Step Not Beyond* and *The Writing of the Disaster*, to facilitate the putting into play of the neutral, the fragmentary, guardians of the alterity of the future that is always, unknowingly, to come.

# 6

# "Exacerbating the Self-Critical Tendency": Ethics and Critique in *Le pas au-delà*

Aïcha Liviana Messina

In "Modernist Painting," Clement Greenberg assimilates modernism to "the intensification, almost the exacerbation, of [a] self-critical tendency."[1] So understood, modernism is not a movement confined to an artistic project. Quite the contrary. For Greenberg, the project of carrying out a critique of knowledge using only the means of knowledge makes Kant "the first real Modernist."[2] Yet, if modernism is not a tendency proper to art, if philosophy, in its critical dimension, is its first expression, it is up to art to continue the philosophical project and, more precisely, the properly critical project of philosophy. In fact, insofar as it is capable of reflecting on its own materials, of experiencing itself in being exhibited, art, in its modernist phase, "intensifies" and "exacerbates" the "self-critical tendency." Modernism is thus a way for art not so much to practice philosophy as to *renew the conditions of possibility for this exercise*. Art's "self-critical tendency" renews the critical task of philosophy.

There is no doubt that the work of Maurice Blanchot is inscribed within this "self-critical tendency." More (and even entirely other) than a literary critic, Blanchot is a writer who ceaselessly reflected (upon) what the act of writing involved, and (upon) what made it possible or impossible.[3] For Blanchot,

---

[1] Clement Greenberg, "Modernist Painting," in *The Collected Essays and Criticism: Volume 4*, ed. John O'Brian (Chicago: University of Chicago Press, 1993), 85.

[2] Ibid.

[3] This process of self-reflection (of self-critique) corresponds to what Frederic Jameson calls "the autonomy of art." For Jameson, there is no doubt that Blanchot is inscribed within this "tendency" since, in continuing Mallarmé's and Valéry's projects of reflecting the act of writing, he in a sense pushes them further by making this reflection an act that does not remain at the level of the project. In Blanchot, in this sense, self-critique is not only a reflection that takes writing for its *object*; it is not only a reflection "upon." Writing is at once object and subject of the reflection. See Fredric Jameson, *A Singular Modernity: Essay on the Ontology of the Present* (New York: Verso, 2002), 185–86. However, while this process of self-reflection has an aesthetic dimension for Jameson, I would like to show that critique in Blanchot has an at once ethical and philosophical dimension.

indeed, writing relates to what cannot be totalized by language. Writing depends upon language since it deals with words, but it can also play with language inasmuch as it can take it as an object. As the writer can suspend language in its functionality (in the work of its meaning), writing happens both within language and at its limits. Blanchot's critical gesture thus concerns *both* language as a milieu necessary for the constitution of sense and on which the writer always depends *and* writing as what touches the limits of language. With Blanchot, however, self-critique is, in a way, also critiqued in its condition of possibility. If, as Greenberg says, modernism is characterized by an immanent method of critique—"Modernism," we read in "Modernist Painting," "criticizes from the inside, through the procedures themselves of that which is being criticized"[4]— then Blanchot's critical gesture consists precisely in calling into question the clear distinction between inside and outside and, thus, the pure coincidence between the object of critique and its procedures. To be sure, Blanchot reflects (upon) language from the perspective of language, but his work reflects what escapes language even as it constitutes language. As Blanchot shows from his first writings, the signifying totality of language is made on the basis of what resists the work of sense, on the basis of an emptiness of sense that cannot be totalized in turn. Thus, the act of writing does not come down to reflecting an object but, rather, to turning toward emptiness.[5] Reflection, then, is not a return upon oneself or a view constituted in grasping an object but, rather, the shimmering of an emptiness in which the subject of critique becomes abyssal and critiqued in turn—critiqued not by itself, however, but rather by what escapes it.[6] There is in Blanchot a "self-critical tendency," but it is not characterized by grasping an object; it is produced as a hetero-critique in which the self is before the Other that calls it into question.

   In *Le pas au-delà*, first published in 1973, this slippage into hetero-critique or into the critique of critique takes at least two forms of "intensification" or

---

[4]   Greenberg, "Modernist Painting," 85.

[5]   Already in 1949, for instance, in "Literature and the Right to Death," Blanchot exposes two sides of language, one where it appears as a means for naming the thing, the other where it itself becomes a thing deprived, however, of sense. See "Literature and the Right to Death," in *The Work of Fire*, trans. Charlotte Mandell (Stanford: Stanford University Press, 1995), 300–44.

[6]   Thus, in "The Most Profound Question," Blanchot critiques a questioning that would only be a questioning "of" or a question "addressed to." For Blanchot, following Levinas (but only in a sense), one must speak of "the other question, the question of the Other, but also a question that is always other," that is to say, the question that escapes its character as a question. See Maurice Blanchot, *The Infinite Conversation*, trans. Susan Hanson (Minneapolis: University of Minnesota Press, 1993), 440, note 3.

"exacerbation." On the one hand, *Le pas au-delà* exhibits the negativity that constitutes language, that is, the death at work at the origin of sense, to speak in the Hegelian terms used by Blanchot in the 1950s.[7] Speech, Blanchot recalls in *Le pas au-delà*, "carries death" (SNB 31). The first words of *Le pas au-delà*— "Let us enter into this relation" (1)—are an invitation to take a step into this negative, into the death that haunts language. In this sense, indeed, we are here in the scenario of an oeuvre thoroughly defined by self-critique. On the other hand, however, *Le pas au-delà* is an invitation. Its first word—*entrons* (let us enter)—refers at once to a movement (one must take a step in order to enter), to a localization (the French verb *entrer* bears the word *entre*, "between"), and to a community (*entrons*, "let us enter": in question is an invitation made in the first person plural, which engages an "us" subsequently repeated in the first fragment of the book: "To death we are not accustomed" [1]). The *incipit* of *Le pas au-delà* in this sense says a lot about the critical gesture that it exacerbates from its first words. In question is taking a *step* into the negativity that constitutes language while knowing, however, that this step has no proper place[8] (it is a question of entering into the indetermination of "this relation" that perhaps, moreover, does not even have an entrance), and that this negativity implicates *us* and calls, perhaps more than any other negativity, for experiencing the ordeal [*épreuve*] of precisely this relation, this us, or an us.[9] *Le pas au-delà* is therefore a step from self-critique to hetero-critique, or to the dimension of alterity required in every critique. It is a critique of critique (conceived as *self-critique*) that exacerbates, intensifies, what is required in every critique (namely, as we will see more precisely, the ordeal of alterity).

---

[7]   The text "Literature and the Right to Death" explicitly alludes to Hegel in order to develop the question of writing. Indeed, Blanchot recalls that to write, for Hegel, is a contradiction (even an aporia) because it requires two antithetical qualities: to write, one needs talent, that is, something inexplicable and prior to any act, but to write is also an action. It is, indeed, in writing that the writer is realized as a writer. It is through their work that writers can become conscious of what makes them writers: "Let us suppose that the work has been written: with it the writer is born," Blanchot affirms, clearly in the wake of Hegel (WF 305). Thus, writing is indeed a work of annihilation. Before writing, the writer is nothing. The writer becomes such only in writing. Yet, in writing, the writer then experiences the ordeal of nothingness. Thus, "to borrow an expression of Hegel's," one can characterize writing (and the writer) as a "nothingness working in nothingness" (WF 304).

[8]   In this sense, this step is also a step into the impossibility of going forward, beyond. It is a step into immobility. On the double sense that the step has in *Le pas au-delà*, see footnote 18.

[9]   On the use of pronouns in *Le pas au-delà* and in particular on the way it gives place to a thought of community, see Christopher Fynsk, *Last Steps: Maurice Blanchot's Exilic Writing* (New York: Fordham University Press, 2013). For Fynsk, the process of the reflection of writing in *Le pas au-delà* is also a process of the reflection of community. This idea joins the idea that critique is an ethics, but it also engages the political dimension of writing (a perspective that I will not develop in this study).

## The "step beyond"—critique

Like all of Blanchot's writings, *Le pas au-delà* does not adhere to a particular genre. At the limit, one can say that it is a fragmentary work (*Le pas au-delà* is composed of fragments of different lengths)—but only by immediately adding that perhaps all of Blanchot's writings are, in their way and in their different forms, fragmentary.[10] However, if *Le pas au-delà* is neither a story nor a philosophical work, it is nevertheless not dissociable from either. Indeed, the *incipit* of *Le pas au-delà* situates us from the start in the philosophical problem of the thought of death, even if it is a matter precisely of confronting thought with the fact that death is not an *object* of thought: "The thought of death," we read in the second fragment of the writing, "does not give us death as something to think" (SNB 1). Yet, because death is not an object of thought, it can be the object of an invitation. As that which cannot be subsumed by the categories of thought, death relates to the strange or foreign, to the "non-familiar," to the "unaccustomed." "Let us enter into this relation" is thus an invitation to take a step Outside, where there is no longer anything familiar, nothing that can be interiorized. At this stage and from this *incipit*, the philosophical problem of death, which no longer lends itself to the solidity or coherence of a philosophical treatise, is not completely purified of a narrative dimension. Indeed, there is something strange or foreign about death that intrigues; it attracts from an unknown region. According to this double valence of death, *Le pas au-delà* thus alternates between fragments of which the tendency seems rather theoretical, and fragments of which the tendency seems rather narrative (often marked by italics).[11] It alternates between fragments on such themes as time, thinking, the Law, transgression, or repetition, and fragments that evoke impossible

---

[10]  In this connection, one must recall the crucial difference that Leslie Hill brings into relief between the fragment and the fragmentary. The fragment, insofar as it has limits, still refers to a unity; it is therefore comprehended with reference to a totality. The fragmentary, by contrast, pertains to what cannot be totalized and, hence, to the infinite. Hill thus characterizes the fragmentary, unconfined to limits, as a "non-phenomenal, spectral event" about which one can speak only as "a radical futural trace irreducible to presence" (9). See Leslie Hill, *Maurice Blanchot and Fragmentary Writing: A Change of Epoch* (New York: Continuum, 2012). Now, if the fragmentary pertains to the trace, to the infinite, then one can say that Blanchot's fragmentary writings are not limited to those characterized by a juxtaposition of fragments. Insofar as it is constructed entirely around the idea of an infinite deferral, *The Infinite Conversation* certainly pertains to the fragmentary. On this subject, see also the important "fragment" in *Le pas au-delà* that proposes thinking "the demand of the fragmentary" in the difference between limit and limitation, that is (I will return to this later), on the basis of what, in finitude itself, cannot be understood as finite determination (SNB 44).

[11]  On the alternation between characters and the plot that it stages, I refer once again to Fynsk's *Last Steps* and, more precisely, to the chapter "The Step Not Beyond" that comments upon this plot by following it step by step and thereby bringing it into relief.

encounters, that describe paradoxical states of consciousness without subject, or that even take language as an object of description, as if the latter were more or less than a means of communication, rather a thing inert or living, empty or brimming with affects. Thus, for example, the difference between fragments evokes different "fear of language," one that would be incumbent on language that finds itself to be the subject of fear ("*From now on, it is the whole language that is afraid*"), the other that would make fear that upon which language opens when considered as something dead, a thing deprived of sense, rather than a subject of sense ("fear is a piece of language, something that it would have lost and that would make it entirely dependent on this dead piece" [59]). From one fragment to the other, from one typography to the other, language can pass from a condition of subject to a condition of object; it can be an affected subject or an affecting object. Less than a juxtaposition of multiple genres, *Le pas au-delà* thus seems to make the absence of a proper genre, of defined disciplines, the space where language multifariously unfolds without remaining within defined limits, the space where genre is transgressed *without even being able to constitute itself.* For these reasons, one can say that, in distinction to Kant's critical gesture that, as Greenberg recalls, uses logic to interrogate the limits of logic,[12] the critical gesture that one finds in *Le pas au-delà* proposes, rather, a critique of philosophical discourse wholly steeped in negativity (if one insists upon its Hegelian description), in what Michel Surya calls, in his book on Bataille, the death at work (*la mort à l'œuvre*) on the basis of what makes it impossible.[13] What is at stake in this critical gesture is not so much a question of critiquing philosophical knowledge on the basis of a fictional story; at stake, rather, would be *situating the "intensity" of the critique at the limit of all discourse,* in the *interval* between these different forms of expression, there precisely where the *incipit* invites us *to enter.*

Along with the consequences entailed by this questioning, by this critique of limits, let us attempt to understand more precisely how and why the limit of all discourse is in question in *Le pas au-delà.*

If *Le pas au-delà* is composed of a multiplicity of themes, there is nevertheless one theme that is, without exactly being central, still in a way at the origin of this multiplicity. It is, namely, the theme of death that we find already in the

---

[12]   According to Greenberg in "Modernist Painting": "Kant used logic to establish the limits of logic, and while he withdrew much from its old jurisdiction, logic was left all the more secure in what there remained to it" (85).

[13]   See Michel Surya, *Georges Bataille, la mort à l'œuvre* (Paris: Gallimard, 1987).

*incipit* and that recurs, in the infinitive form,[14] throughout *Le pas au-delà*. I said that death had a double valence insofar as it was a philosophical preoccupation that also contains a dimension of intrigue. Death is either the non being against which philosophical discourse is constructed[15] or the non being that accounts for the dialectic of being and permits one to understand that meaning is always a work, a product.[16] Death or non being is therefore not only an interesting subject for philosophy: it is that which makes philosophy possible, that which makes possible the purity of its discourse (in the case of Plato) and its aspirations to totality (in the case of Hegel). For Blanchot, however, precisely because death is not an object of thought, one cannot speak of death *itself*, in its noun form. If death is the "unfamiliar," it can no longer be apprehended by philosophy. Nor, therefore, can one still speak of death *itself* as an object that would have a certain status for thought and that would be a definite entity. Blanchot's point of departure is the fact that we are never contemporary to death. Death happens to us, rather, as the imminence of a *mourir* that, never coinciding with a present moment, pertains to an immemorial time, without a present of time. The impossibility of apprehending death thus overwhelms not only what grounds our knowledge but also what grounds our relation to time. One cannot know oneself to be dead. Nor, therefore, can one know what happens with death. Knowledge of death, belonging neither to the present nor to the future, belongs to a sort of future anterior: one knows that one will know death as something that happened without us, without a subject to witness it. Blanchot thus writes: "*I do not know, but I know that I am going to have known*" (124; italics in the original). There is no death in the present; there is the imminence of a *mourir* that will reach us only in a past that will remain without witness. There is no death as a finite moment that could be localized in time. Death never coincides with a present;

---

[14]  The infinitive form of the verb "to die," in French, is *mourir*. The infinitive form in French, however, can perform the function of a noun that, in distinction from "death" (*la mort*), is commonly translated as "dying." In her translation of *Le pas au-delà*, for instance, Lycette Nelson most often translates *le mourir* as "dying," which is not feasible here because the mobilization of the nominal function of the specifically infinitive form—*le mourir*—would be lost if translated by a gerund. Wherever English syntax allows a nominal use of the infinitive, I have given "to die" for *mourir*; everywhere else I have left the word in French.—Translator.

[15]  In this connection, one thinks of Plato's *Phaedo*, where philosophical language (dialogic speech) is constructed by withdrawing from death—which is why we read that "the one aim of those who practice philosophy in the proper manner is to practice for dying and death" (64a). Plato, *Phaedo*, trans. G. M. A. Grube, *Complete Works*, ed. John M. Cooper (Indianapolis: Hackett, 1997).

[16]  One thinks of the theme of the negative in Hegel, which is not that from which consciousness withdraws by eliminating but, rather, that through which consciousness occurs. In distinction from Platonic dialectic, Hegelian dialectic incorporates the negative.

there is only the infinitive of a *mourir* that does not begin and that does not end, that is, a *mourir* that has always already destroyed the possibility of time.

As we know through Derrida's decisive interpretation in "Living On," the theme of finitude in Blanchot must be read in terms of excess. Paradoxically, because death cannot be conceived as a limit, to live is not a finite determination either but, rather, a sort of "state" that is both lacunar and excessive (and therefore not exactly a "state").[17] The infinitive of the verb "to die" thus speaks to the infinite character of the ordeal constituted by finitude.[18] Since one cannot be contemporary to one's death, since *mourir* happens without event, without being fixed in time, to die would be "to die in relation to some immortality" (SNB 110).[19] The paradox of *Le pas au-delà* is that it does not situate the beyond (or immortality) in what frees us from finitude but, rather, in what renders finitude infinite, to borrow a formulation from Jean-Luc Nancy.[20] Thus, concerning "to die [*mourir*]," Blanchot says: "as if we only died in the infinitive" (94), that is to say, without subject (anonymously), without presence of time, and thus also without

---

[17] In "Living On," Derrida thus speaks of an "excess, which in life triumphs over life and in time is worth more than the eternity of life" (147). Jacques Derrida, "Living On," trans. James Hulbert, in *Parages*, ed. John P. Leavey (Stanford: Stanford University Press, 2011).

[18] For this reason, as one can infer from Derrida's analysis in "*Pace* Not(s)" ("Pas"), the "step beyond" (*le pas au-delà*) is not a step beyond finitude. Derrida has indeed brought out the polysemy of the words "pas" and "au-delà" in Blanchot, each of which can have the value of a noun ("pas" then designating movement and "au-delà," a region) or an adverb ("pas" then designating the negation of the beyond, while "au-delà" qualifies the noun "pas"). See Derrida, "*Pace* Not(s)," trans. John P. Leavey, in *Parages*, 39–40. If, however, there is for Blanchot no beyond to the here-below, one must also say, by contrast, that there is no here-below. The non-place of death, the infinitive of *le mourir* is indeed what precludes all present of time, all determination of a here, all fixation in a place. *Le pas au-delà* would then be an invitation to take a step outside all place, there where reference points are no longer possible, where there is no longer any path and therefore no movements, there where—because nothing can be fixed—"everything returns," as we read on numerous occasions. It is therefore problematic that, in certain translations (the English and Spanish translations in particular), the ambivalence of the words "pas" and "au-delà" have in a way been unmasked and fixed through the introduction of the adverb "pas" in the title (*The Step Not Beyond* or *El paso* (no) *más allá*). One must indeed remark that a reading of *Le pas au-*delà, and not its title, provokes an ambivalent sense. The French title is unequivocal. The "pas" in question is not an adverb (for which one would have to say "le pas *d'*au-delà"). Through these translations that add a word to the title in order to evoke the polysemy of the word "pas," it seems to me not only that Derrida's interpretation of *Le pas au-delà*, in addition to becoming authoritative as if no other interpretation were possible, is immediately fixed and no doubt banalized but also that we lose the simplicity of Blanchot's language and of the invitation made at the threshold of a book whose title alone (without any need for semantic complications through the addition of an adverb) poses the question of the threshold. For an explication of the translation of the title of this work in English, see translator Lycette Nelson's introduction, where explicit reference is made to Derrida's "Pas" (SNB xvi).

[19] On this subject, see also Jean-Luc Nancy's important study, "Blanchot's Resurrection," in *Dis-Enclosure: The Deconstruction of Christianity*, trans. Bettina Bergo, Gabriel Malenfant, and Michael B. Smith (New York: Fordham University Press, 2008), where the infinite character of finitude is analyzed in relation to the Christian problem of resurrection.

[20] Jean-Luc Nancy, *The Sense of the World*, trans. Jeffrey S. Librett (Minneapolis: University of Minnesota Press, 1997), 29.

end. The experience of the limit to which *Le pas au-delà* invites us is an experience of the infinite and, in this way, it is an infinite experience. Yet, if critique or, more precisely, *self*-critique is a reflection that concerns limits (of knowledge or of a discipline) and aims precisely at determining them, one sees that the critical exercise to which *Le pas au-delà* invites us proceeds inversely: from the thought of limits to the exhibition of their impossibility—from the thought of *la mort* (death) to the thought of *le mourir* (to die—dying); from *la mort* conceived *as* the finish and *at* the finish, to a *mourir* conceived as the impossibility of finishing, an encounter with the infinite. Henceforth, the invitation with which *Le pas au-delà* opens—"Let us enter into this relation"—is an invitation to enter what does not cease. It is indeed a question of taking a "step beyond": beyond the limits that constitute, at least according to Kant, the possibility of experience and of thought. Is it then a question of completely reversing the critical task that, at least according to Greenberg, characterizes the very task of modernism? Does the unlimited to which *Le pas au-delà* invites us not constitute the destruction of experience, of thought, and therefore of the possibility of critique?

## Kant's step toward Socrates

Blanchot's reference for critical thought in *Le pas au-delà* is not Kant, but Socrates, and we could even say that for Blanchot, in distinction from Greenberg, the first real modernist is Socrates. If Socrates does not, as Kant did, interrogate the limits of knowledge, it is through him, by contrast, that knowledge in its very possibility comes into question. Indeed, as Kierkegaard affirms in *The Concept of Irony with Continual Reference to Socrates*, Socrates's irony—characterized by the way he poses questions and, therefore, never says directly what he knows or what he thinks—does not manifest reserves of knowledge, but, rather, its suspension.[21] If Socrates never says what he knows, if he does nothing but pose

---

[21] For Kierkegaard, indeed, what characterizes the Socratic question is not necessarily articulating an answer but, on the contrary, being left before an emptiness. Thus, in distinction from speculation that comprehends a moment of reflection in itself (of self-return through which an appropriation, a knowledge, is produced), Socratic irony aims at no appropriation and, therefore, at no knowledge: "one can ask with the intention of receiving an answer containing the desired fullness, and hence the more one asks, the deeper and more significant becomes the answer; or one can ask without any interest in the answer except to suck out the apparent content by means of the question and thereby to leave an emptiness behind. The first method presupposes, of course, that there is a plenitude; the second that there is an emptiness. The first is the *speculative* method; the second the *ironic*" (36). Søren Kierkegaard, *The Concept of Irony with Continual Reference to Socrates. Kierkegaard's Writings, II*, trans. and ed. Howard V. Hong and Edna H. Hong (Princeton: Princeton University Press, 1989).

questions, it is because he only knows that he does not know. In this sense, for Kierkegaard, Socratic irony does not consist in reserving something unsaid: it consists in suspending everything said. By posing questions unceasingly, Socrates silences language and leaves us without answers with respect to the ground and possibility of knowledge.

The theme of "non-knowledge" is recurrent in *Le pas au-delà*, and, in its repetition, it returns in a distorted form. For instance, the sentence, "*I do not know, but I know that I am going to have known*" (SNB 106; italics in the original), returns several pages later in the following form: "*I don't know, but I have the feeling* [je pressens] *that I am going to have known*" (112; italics in the original). In its repetition, what belongs to the domain of cognition and certainty is modified with what belongs to the domain of feelings and emotions (the verb "pressentir" in French entails the idea of foreseeing, but also the idea of fearing). In its repetition, what is certain and should comfort escapes the mastery of a subject, hence the possibility of being a subject. With this distortion, the sentence returns uprooted from all proper place that would pertain to an author or a definite system of argumentation. It comes from elsewhere. If one analyzes the occurrence of this reference to non-knowledge, one realizes, for example, that the context of its repetition makes it a strange sentence that, without being dreadful, cannot be understood in relation to a prerequisite knowledge. Indeed, the fragment says: "I remember, knowing only that it belongs to a memory, this phrase: '*I don't know, but I have the feeling that I'm going to have known*' " (112; italics in the original). In this occurrence, the non-knowledge is not related to a knowledge, but, rather, to a memory. Yet, in distinction to a recollection that, without necessarily being objective, refers to an act, memory comes from elsewhere; it is always aleatory, not completely controlled. Thus, the context of this repetition, where an "I" claims to be in possession of a knowledge ("knowing only"), anchors knowledge not in the logical limits guaranteeing it, but, rather, in the indefinite character of a memory, that is, of what cannot be grounded or demonstrated, what always comes, that is, at random. The knowledge of non-knowledge thus comes from a knowledge that comes from elsewhere, over which one has no hold. This is why, in returning, non-knowledge is distorted. It no longer has a logical frame; it becomes a "feeling."[22]

From Blanchot to Socrates and from Socrates to Blanchot, the form and the meaning of self-critique returns and becomes distorted. If Socrates is nothing but

---

[22] On this subject, see the key role that Fynsk attributes to the passions in the chapter in *Last Steps* entitled "The Step Not Beyond."

irony, as Kierkegaard suggests, if the Socratic question presupposes no knowledge, and if Socrates knows only that he does not know, then the critical exercise's meaning and form come down to the same: in question is always and only the pulverization of everything claiming knowledge and, hence, the confrontation with silence.[23] Yet, as Hegel has shown (and after him—differently—Kierkegaard and Arendt), Socrates's silence constitutes an ethical moment before constituting a theoretical moment.[24] Critique discovers silence, and critique is exercised through silence, but silence also allows for understanding that thought is not only a theoretical exercise (assured of knowledge): it is the experience of an ordeal, of a relation. With Socrates, thinking requires this preliminary relation to silence through which one is uprooted from all preconceived knowledge. One can then say that, for Socrates, critique has an ethical dimension since it is through silence that the soul dialogues with itself, that an act of reflection is extracted from all presuppositions. Through silence, Socrates's empty knowledge, a self is born in a *relation* to itself, in a certain relation of friendship toward itself.

The way in which the theme of non-knowledge *returns* in *Le pas au-delà* also gives place to an articulation between ethics and critique, but one that is modulated otherwise. In order to understand this new articulation, let us first ask how non-knowledge in *Le pas au-delà* determines the critical exercise otherwise and, subsequently, let us analyze the ethical consequences of this new configuration of critique.

In *Le pas au-delà*, as we have seen, the theme of non-knowledge is explicitly linked to *le mourir*. *Le mourir* is the infinitive that returns due to the inability to die in the present, to be contemporary to one's death, to have knowledge of death. In this sense, "non-knowledge" in Blanchot does not reduce to an absence of knowledge, to a "negative result."[25] Like *le mourir*, it is infinite. It is not a lack of knowledge but, rather, what exceeds knowledge. This is why it returns throughout *Le pas au-delà*. It is not a finite moment of knowledge that could be either suspended (like Platonic *doxa*) or negated (like Hegelian

---

23    This is what Kierkegaard shows in his reading of Plato's *Protagoras*. For Kierkegaard, Socrates's non-knowledge is not a "negative result" through which knowledge would be denied; rather, it would remain of the order of knowledge. Cf. the chapter on "Protagoras" in *The Concept of Irony.*

24    For instance, one thinks of the way Arendt, in *The Life of the Mind*, describes what Plato called "the soundless dialogue … between me and myself" (185). Hannah Arendt, *The Life of the Mind* (New York: Harcourt, 1971). For Arendt, this interior dialogue, this "two in one," this means of giving birth to oneself in friendship is indeed a condition of thought. Thinking is indissociable from ethics in that thinking implies a self-relation. On the ethical moment represented by Socrates, see also Hegel's *Lectures on the Philosophy of History*, as well as Kierkegaard's *The Concept of Irony.*

25    See, again, Fynsk's "The Step Not Beyond."

negation). Non-knowledge not only resists knowledge; it also leads to the failure of knowledge. One of the fragments of *Le pas au-delà* indicates that non-knowledge is not determined as a function of a knowledge of which it would be the negative waiting to be overcome, the lack waiting to be filled. Rather, it disorients knowledge in relation to itself:

> There is an "I don't know" that is at the limit of knowledge, but that belongs to knowledge. Always, we pronounce it too early, still knowing everything—or too late, when I no longer know that I don't know, saying nothing and thus saying it.
>
> I know less about it than I know about it; it is over this being behind itself of knowledge that I must leap to reach—not attaining it, or ruining myself in it—non-knowledge [*le non-savoir*]. (63; translation modified)

If, to speak in Kojèvo-Hegelian terms, knowledge requires the negative (death) and if, as Blanchot stipulates, death as a finite moment is impossible, then the negative—non being, non-knowledge—is not the element of negativity (of overcoming non-knowledge), but rather that which, in knowledge itself, still "belongs" to it and prevents it from coinciding with itself. With Blanchot, knowledge is critiqued not only from within itself (and, in this respect, Blanchot does not differ from Kant), but through what prevents knowledge from returning to itself, from being knowledge of an object, all while being self-knowledge. In this respect, as in Socrates, critique in Blanchot leads to a silence, to a nothingness of knowledge, or rather to the knowledge put into question by the nothingness that constitutes it. In Blanchot, and in distinction to Kant, there is no project of determining the limits of knowledge; there is a threat of collapse.

Yet, can one identify Socrates's non-knowledge with Blanchot's? Are they two sides of the same figure of this "self-critical tendency" with which Greenberg characterizes modernism? What critical thought is at play in, and what modernist revolution takes place between, Socrates's irony and Blanchot's writing?

Blanchot and Socrates meet in the place of silence, of non-knowledge, but this silence is not of the same nature, for it does not have the same critical scope. Indeed, it is by understanding what differentiates these silences that we will be better able to understand how ethics and critique are articulated in Blanchot. Socrates's silence is the silence of irony, of a said that is unsaid, of a knowledge or belief in a knowledge (*doxa*) that is suspended. The silence in question in *Le pas au-delà* is the silence of a *mourir*, of the collapsing of language, of the interruption of knowledge. Indeed, if death does not happen as that about which one can speak and (from a Hegelian perspective) as that which allows us to speak, if there is only the imminence of a *mourir* that undoes the work of sense from within, then all sense, all language through which we make sense, and all knowledge in which sense is reflected and totalized are undone from within by this *mourir* that does nothing but silently echo sense. Not reducing to *la mort* (death), refusing the finite or finished character of *la mort*, *le mourir* is the negative that, while remaining essential to the work of sense and to the constitution of language, threatens sense with "collapse" (116). If *le mourir* is the impossibility of coming to term, then it is the infinite and amplified, but empty echo of sense always produced in limits, in words, in a reunified knowledge. This is why, concerning silence, Blanchot can, for instance, write: "Silence is not the refusal of words: silent from all words, from their reach, from their hearing, from that which, in the least word, has not yet developed itself in speaking ways" (132). Silence is not found in the suspension of language, in the fact of keeping quiet; *it is the echo of language*. Rather than being the limit of language or its negation, silence is for Blanchot what makes it not only inexhaustible but also unachievable: it is its empty and infinitely multiplied echo, but it is also that through which sense is never attained because it is never constituted. Thus: "*He enters, he speaks with the words that are already there to welcome him, feeling an equal pain whether he speaks or remains silent*" (41; italics in the original). The silence that is the echo of language is that which makes language both inaccessible and inexhaustible. To speak is impossible because the very thing through which meaning is constituted brings it back to its impossibility. If silence is the discovery of the impossibility of keeping quiet and of speaking, what ethics does it bear? Toward what friendship does it open?

Because silence, with Socrates, is the silence that uproots us from received knowledge, from *doxa*, it is the element of a possible *relation* to oneself. It makes possible thought insofar as it is "the soul's dialogue with itself."[26] Yet, because silence is, with Blanchot, the silence of language, it is no longer possible to master it, to make it an element of *self-relation*. This divergence concerning silence, then, questions the Socratic art of critique concentrated upon the theme of non-knowledge. If Socrates is critical of knowledge insofar as he knows only that he knows nothing, the question nevertheless concerns whether there can be a knowledge of non-knowledge. Socrates is the *master* of the question through which he pulverizes all received knowledge, but how

[26] Plato, *Sophist*, trans. Nicholas P. White, *Complete Works*, ed. John M. Cooper (Indianapolis: Hackett, 1997), 264b; translation modified.

to remain master before a knowledge that has become empty? Thus, in *Le pas au-delà*, the theme of non-knowledge returns in the form of a critique of critique, a critique made abyssal, a discovery of the impossibility of mastering non-knowledge, of saying *I* know only that *I* do not know: "I do not know; there is no 'I' to not know" (SNB 68). Just as non-knowledge always exceeds the knowledge that I can have of it, the silence upon which the question opens exceeds the mastery granted to the one posing questions. Silence, then, is not that through which an ego relates to itself, that through which the soul dialogues with itself, but rather the relation to alterity, to what exceeds the ego. Here, we see two different ethics sketched out, two different conceptions of friendship: while friendship for Socrates is the friendship of the dialogue that consists, finally, in a friendship toward oneself, friendship in Blanchot is not defined by terms of relation (of subjects, of friends); it is the very alterity of relation. It is the interval between us, that into which we are invited to *enter* at the threshold of a book that says "us" without any subject ever being identified. We thus read in *Le pas au-delà*: "Friendship: friendship for the unknown without friends" (133). Moreover, if silence is the silence of language, the silence of its impossibility (which is always, as we have seen, a double impossibility), then silence is that through which we enter into relation with *language as an other*. One of the fragments from *Le pas au-delà* expresses it in this way: "*I am not master of language. I listen to it only in its effacement, effacing myself in it, towards this silent limit where it waits for one to lead it back in order to speak, there where presence fails as it fails there where desire carries it*" (30; italics in the original).

From Blanchot to Socrates, we pass from critique—not as a project of limiting knowledge but, rather, as the discovery of an essential silence—to thinking and knowledge as an ethical moment of a self-relation. From Socrates to Blanchot, we pass from the relation to silenced language to the relation to language as a *silent thing*, from a relation with silence as the possibility of self-dialogue to a relation with silence as an encounter with alterity. Is it not, then, this other articulation of critique and ethics that will allow us to understand how the unlimited in Blanchot, the *mourir* that can only be said in the infinitive, can presage something other than a destruction of thought? And if the (or one of the) critical gesture(s) of *Le pas au-delà* consists in discovering language as something silent, to what is the reader invited from the *incipit*, from the moment it is said, "Let us enter into this relation"?

# With two hands

Let us return to the *incipit* of *Le pas au-delà*: "Let us enter into this relation." Even if allusion to death is made in the sentence that follows (the sentence that constitutes the first fragment in this writing marked by a lozenge), this *incipit* leaves us in the most complete indetermination. This relation might be death, but before it comes into question, one knows nothing of the invitation made to the reader—to the *us* that, without being named in French, is the first to be interpellated (the verb *entrer*, "to enter," in the imperative and in the first person plural, is indeed the book's first word in the original). In fact, upon following the book's first pages, one can, if not determine different relations (i.e., relations other than the relation to death), at least attempt to determine different facets of them. There is the relation to death, which I have already evoked; "the relation to the 'he/it [*il*]' " evoked rather quickly in the first pages of *Le pas au-delà* (3), which seems to be (although not reducible to) another name for the relation to the other; and the relation that cannot fail to strike the reader (since it comes without explanation) between the fragments' different typographies (at times in Roman font and at times in italics). Being different from one another in their visual aspect, the different topographies of *Le pas au-delà* indicate the space of a relation. Now, what is interesting is that all those differences are related to the reversal implied by the passage from self-critique to hetero-critique. They place us on the path of what Blanchot calls "the demand to write" (2), the path that implies a step beyond what one has traditionally understood by "relation." To conclude, let us attempt to understand what the *incipit* of *Le pas au-delà* signifies with respect to this demand.

As I have said, the movement of *Le pas au-delà* is not toward overcoming finitude. In question is not conceiving the beyond by breaking free from the finite world. The writing of *Le pas au-delà*, on the contrary, follows the path of finitude insofar as it escapes determination and the present character of nouns. Writing in this sense follows the line of the *mourir* that never ends. Writing has charge of what, in language, escapes the work of meaning that necessarily takes place as an act of determination, of de-fining. Like the "to die" that never takes place (and thus makes time impossible), "to write" belongs to the dimension of non-contemporaneity. "If to write [*écrire*], to die [*mourir*] are words that would be close to one another through the distance in which they arrange themselves," it is because "both" are "incapable of any present" (89; translation modified). The "demand to write" comes, as Derrida would say, from the trace, that is, from the fact that we are never contemporary to sense, from the fact that sense is always offset with respect to itself. Yet, to follow the line of *le mourir* cannot mean anything other than being situated in the interruption of the limits implied by *le mourir* (to die—dying) in its difference from *la mort* (death). Thus, while language produces the continuity of sense, writing "maintains," according to Blanchot, "an interval for *le mourir*" (93; translation modified). *Le mourir* is that which has been "erased" from sense "before being written," that which exceeds ("to die in relation to some immortality") before a limit can be defined. Paradoxically, the step beyond of *Le pas au-delà* speaks of crossing a line that can never be marked or, more precisely, a line that has been erased even before having been marked: it is indeed a matter of taking a step beyond *into what does not finish to the extent that it never took place*, a step that, therefore, can *never go* anywhere, that does not move and that is rather beneath than beyond. To die thus defines the movement of an "empty transgression" that "does not transgress the law" (since no limit is confirmed) but rather "carries it away with it" (106 and 101) (since to die, in distinction from the Law that poses limits, is unlimited). It is indeed because, as I have said, the "sinuous line of life" (94) cannot be traced without being immediately erased by a loss prior to all beginning that existence has an infinite charge. *Le pas au-delà* is in this sense the writing of a fissure, of what prevents the One from ever being in itself, what prevents the self from finding itself again in the unity of the "I think," what prevents a genre from recognizing itself in the truth of its borders. Thus, to follow the line of *le mourir* does not signify going straight to loss, to self-annihilation. The fissure constituted by *le mourir* is an interval between, a self-division. *Le pas au-delà*, indeed, invites us to enter into this interval between, there where the ego is already a relation to what forever divides it from itself and remains neutral, undetermined ("relation to the 'he/it' "),[27] where speech is born not from a meaning that can be developed in a continuous way but, rather, from what has always already interrupted speech and thus, paradoxically, prevented it from keeping quiet, where discourse no longer remains within the limits of a genre but, rather, already redoubles in different modes that no longer have the unity of a form. The different facets of relation that I have located in *Le pas au-delà* are therefore as many consequences of the fissure of the *mourir* defining "the demand to write."

If, however, writing consists in following the line of *le mourir*, it is nevertheless the ethical dimension of critique that allows us to understand this demand

---

[27]   "Il" can be used as an impersonal pronoun. It is not necessarily heard as a determined gender.

precisely. It is for this reason interesting to observe what characterizes the *relation* between the fragments in Roman font and those in italics. Indeed, the fragments in Roman font tend to adopt a mode of thinking that implies argumentation or that consists in posing a question, while others are citations (i.e., thoughts that repeat). The fragments in italics for the most part stage the relation that, while remaining undetermined, modulate this relation differently by using alternative narrative subjects and contexts. Sometimes, finally, the two types of fragments meet when, for instance, they stage dialogues wherein the space of the relation is once again in question. This composition indicates that thinking in *Le pas au-delà* happens through repetition. In fact, upon returning, thinking comes from somewhere other than an "ego" that thinks and whose thoughts would be unified by an "I." Now, repetition is not the space where thinking is eternally the same. The sentence, "I do not know, but I know that I am going to have known," returns not only, as we have seen, in multiple contexts but also in multiple forms. It is the object of a long explication in the middle of the book (112–114),[28] and it returns as a single, italicized sentence toward the end of the book. From the status of an utterance that comes from a determined argumentation and thereby claims a certain truth, it thus moves to resembling the subject of a rumor (124).

Yet, it is also worth observing that the italicized fragments are at times ways of reflecting thoughts that are apparently more ethical in their theoretical consequences. This is the case with the fragments that play upon the assonance between the two verbs in the infinitive, to write (*écrire*) and to die (*mourir*).[29] If "to die" is never to be able to begin (and therefore neither to end), and if "to write" is to follow the path of "to die," then the hand of the one who writes is always, for Blanchot, immobile: "To die [*Mourir*], like the hand that not far from the paper would hold itself immobile without writing anything or would even move ahead without tracing anything" (98; translation modified). Yet, the image of the hand returns on multiple occasions in *Le pas au-delà*, and one must grasp the *thought* of it in this return. The image returns, for instance, in an italicized fragment in which, this time, the hand is no longer the hand of the paralyzed ego-writer (who therefore can no longer be him- or herself), but rather the hand of *the* other or of *an* other: "*A hand that extends itself, that refuses itself, that we cannot take hold of in any way*" (106; italics in the original). The fragments in italics often replace the paralysis and, therefore, the solitude of *le mourir* in the

---

[28]    The fragment in question has been mistakenly divided into two fragments in the English translation.—Translator.

[29]    In French, "écrire" and "mourir" can be heard as the echo of one another because they rhyme.

context of *relation*. In what paralyzes it, the hand of the ego is already other. It is not the hand of a determined other but, rather, of what escapes all determination, whence the recourse to the neutral *il*, "it," in order to evoke alterity. The writer's solitude is therefore ethical; it is a relation to an "it" (*il*) through which a narrative word without ground, arriving like a rumor, echoes theoretical and coherent discourse. It is paralysis and therefore hell but, in the very site where it has no way out, it is a relation to the infinite of alterity. Because to write is to have charge of loss, because to write is to die, one can only write with two hands: in an isolation that is already relation, a paralysis that, unto itself, is an encounter with alterity and therefore, if not movement, at least upheaval. In the assonance between to write and to die, the thought of the hand is therefore double: the hand is irreducibly alone and, in this solitude, it has charge of the other irreducibly. Alterity does not save from solitude (the fragment is never the last word), but solitude cannot form a whole. It is an impersonal relation that, by preventing any fold back upon the self, opens onto an undetermined us. To use the words of *The Writing of the Disaster* here, the return of fragments prevents "thought" from "stopping at anything definite" (WD 33). Here "thought" does not represent that which is endlessly pursued but, rather the event of infinite fissure, of a duality that does not allow for the constitution of a unity and therefore of what belongs to the space of the return—there where what is repeated is what fails to be one. At stake in the return is therefore the impossibility of identity, of the one. As *Le pas au-delà* says, "it is less easy, more important perhaps … to think the leap from 0 to duality, the 1 thus giving itself as the forbidden, the between-the-two" (SNB 11–12). Whence the exergue of *The Infinite Conversation*:

> "But why two? Why two instances of speech to say the same thing?"
> —"Because the one who says it is always the other." (IC ix)

∗∗∗

One of the questions that can be posed in conclusion concerns whether Blanchot redefines or breaks free from the modernist project characterized by the intensification of self-critique. In addition to posing the problem of whether all art is not always, if not doomed, at least destined to self-reflect, it would be necessary to wonder if what art discovers in self-critique is not always the alterity of its materials, if it is not always the self as Other. Rather than taking this path, however, let us turn toward the question of how the demand to write engages philosophy in its critical task in a new way. On the one hand, as we have seen, the question of writing as Blanchot poses it makes possible a critique of critique because there is no self-reflection without a relation to alterity. On the other hand, however, the demand to write—far from being inscribed in a destruction of thought abandoned to that (infinity) which is no longer inscribed in the limits of experience—opens onto a thought that no longer takes place in the dialogue of the self with the self (Socrates) and that does not seek to posit the limits of either knowledge (Kant). The thought that emerges in *Le pas au-delà* is the thought of non-knowledge that returns, of the *mourir* that cannot be determined. This is why it is a thought that exceeds boundaries and demands being "unthought [*dé-pensée*]" (exceeding all measure, it does not return to a subject), as Blanchot writes in the wake of Bataille (SNB 68).[30] It is made unique through repetition and, upon return, comes from the other and therefore can only be a thought of the other. In this way, the critique of critique laid bare by the demand to write, far from destroying thought, indicates that thought is at once critical and singular in its ethical dimension. For that reason, *Le pas au-delà* is indeed a work of philosophy despite and even by virtue of these disclosures. Its narrative fragments interrupting (and interrupted by) theoretic reflections contribute to the renewal of the "self-critical tendency" that, according to Greenberg, makes Kant "the first real Modernist." It constitutes such a renewal, however, in showing that the critical task is possible only as hetero-critique. It constitutes such a renewal in returning to that other "first real Modernist" (if there is ever a sense in which one can say "first" and "real"), Socrates, he who had seen that knowledge can be critiqued only through the ordeal of its emptiness. It constitutes such a renewal, finally, in the interval-between that it exposes, which is also to say, in the way that it renews thinking and the experience of friendship that is the uncondition of thought.[31]

Translated by D. J. S. Cross

---

[30]   The French word "dépensé" contains the word "thought" (*pensée*) but means in fact "spent." The idea of "thought," thought as a "dépense," is therefore clearly associated with Bataille's notion of "dépense." It entails an excess.

[31]   This article is part of two research Projects funded by Fondo Nacional del Desarrollo Científico y Tecnológico (Fondecyt 1140113 and 1170580).

Part Two

# Blanchot and Aesthetics

# 7

# *Nescio Vos*: The Pathos of Unknowing in *When the Time Comes*

Jean-Michel Rabaté

*So he would have left*
*As the soul leaves the body torn and bruised,*
*As the mind deserts the body it has used. (…)*
*I should have lost a gesture and a pose.*
*Sometimes these cogitations still amaze*
*The troubled midnight and the noon's repose.*

T. S. Eliot, "La Figlia che piange"

*When the Time Comes* (*Au Temps Voulu*) occupies a special place among Blanchot's novels. It has been studied less often than other novels or short stories; since its publication in 1951 it has kept an aura of intractable obscurity given its mixture of confession and abstract speculation. It is not a coincidence that the enigmatic statements printed on the cover of the paperback issued by Gallimard in 1979—"At night, in the South, when I get up, I know that it isn't a question of proximity, or of distance, or of an event belonging to me, or of a truth capable of speaking, this is not a scene, or the beginning of something. An image, but a futile one, an instant, but a sterile one" (WTC 255)—were quoted by Jean-Luc Godard at the end of his 1993 film *Hélas pour moi*, a film presenting the mysterious possession of a young woman by a man who might be a god in disguise.[1] While no Zeus comes to impersonate Amphitryon for Blanchot, the plot of *When the Time Comes* partly rests on the issue of hospitality, or on the limits of hospitality: can two women who live together accept the return of the

---

[1] See Leslie Hill, "'A Form that Thinks': Godard, Blanchot, Citation," in *Forever Godard*, ed. Michael Temple, James Williams and Michael Witt (London: Black Dog Publishing, 2004), 396–415.

former male lover of one of them because he is in need of help? But this very question begs the issue of the possibility of reconstructing a linear narrative from the baffling sequence of scenes. This possibility can be demonstrated only by explicating the novel's riddles. To do this I will use information gathered about Blanchot's life in the past two decades, while taking into account the theoretical program that runs against the grain of a straightforward plot.

When Blanchot presented this novel as the central panel in his novelistic triptych, next to *Death Sentence* (1948) and *The One Who Was Standing Apart From Me* (1953), he added that all three texts are based upon the same experience.[2] What experience is this? Most readers have testified to their bafflement when discussing it, feeling lost in the detours and entanglements of a narrative that refuses to be a simple story. One of the first to state this impression cogently was Gerald Prince in 1976: "It is difficult to specify what happens in *Au Moment Voulu* because what happens cannot be pertinent: it does not develop in terms of a knowledge that we share with the text."[3] Prince looked to *Le Livre à venir*, in which he found the idea that a true narrative is not a description of an event, it is that event itself.[4] While this is true of *Au Moment Voulu*, nevertheless we can identify "events" and even stable "characters" despite the resistance to character development, classical psychology, and linear narrative.

If the "events" remain sketchy, we can piece together a tenuous plot: the narrator, who is not in the best of health, has come back to the Paris apartment that he shared in the past with a woman whom he calls Judith, even though this is not her real name. He discovers that she is now living with Claudia, her lover, a German singer. In spite of Claudia's initial reluctance, the two women put him up and help him weather difficult nights (he hurts his head, he faints several times, he runs fevers, he seems to forget where he is, he grabs bodies in moments of trance at night, etc.). The visitor recovers and stays with them in a tense, but joyful, cohabitation marked by verbal skirmishes with Claudia. Meanwhile Judith is mostly silent; she exchanges banal words with Claudia only, but often gazes at them or in space. The tentative harmony is broken when the narrator allows Claudia to come closer, almost seduces her, or perhaps she seduces him. This increased intimacy triggers an instant rejection. Judith shouts the words

[2]  Blanchot quoted by Christophe Bident, *Maurice Blanchot: Partenaire Invisible* (Seyssel: Champ Vallon, 1998), 306.

[3]  Gerald Prince, "The Point of Narrative: Blanchot's *Au Moment Voulu*," *Substance* 5, no. 14 (1976): 93–98.

[4]  Blanchot, *Le Livre à Venir* (Paris, Gallimard, 1959), 13, quoted by Prince, "The Point of Narrative," 98.

"Nescio vos," telling them that she does not know who they are. The outcome of the crisis is that she collapses into the arms of the narrator. The narrator warms up to her again, even if the paroxysm makes him return to his house in the South. There, he tries to write about these loaded moments, haunted by one image, a hallucinated vision of Judith sitting on his stairs at night.

Such a plot paraphrase is misleading in so far as it takes for granted the cliché of a lovers' triangle; my summary could evoke Godard's 1966 *Masculin Féminin*, an ironical analysis of the emotional entanglements of one young man sharing an apartment with three desirable women, with the result that no one is assured of having a partner. My reductive synopsis assumes that Judith and Claudia are lesbian lovers passing through a difficult patch; they would end up accepting a male intruder in order to invent new games once the man's attentions shift from one woman to the other. However, romantic clichés are avoided by Blanchot. One of the aims of *Au Moment Voulu* is to question the very idea of love as an "affair." This is stated after Claudia and the narrator begin to show signs of mutual interest, which elicits some body contact. Judith is supposed to be a very beautiful woman, whereas Claudia is not; soon, the narrator discovers beauty in her too: "Well, I said to myself, she is almost beautiful; up to till then I hadn't noticed it" (213). As he guesses, the two women play a private game involving seduction and jealousy; a few times, they come half-undressed next to him when they share the bathroom. Then Claudia states: "No one here wants to be connected to a story" (239). The narrator is struck by the implications of this sentence, and asks whether it applies to Judith; Claudia confirms this emphatically: they are all free to do what they wish. The meaning is clearer in French: *Personne ici ne désire se lier à une histoire*[5] suggests something like: "Nobody who lives here wishes to be caught up in a love affair." Blanchot plays on the triple meaning contained in *histoire*—a story, as in a narrative, a love story or an affair, and the broader History, evoked here by a few telling details.

This verbal knot linking personal incidents with a universal or abstract fate is tightened after the narrator has gone back to his Southern house. Reconsidering what took place, he tries to make sense of those precious moments of cohabitation in the Paris apartment. Writing these, he senses that his story will get undone, unraveled, or go backward; this is the condition for any truth to appear: "Things happened to me, to me and to the story, events that were more and more curtailed (in the sense that, just as I had become no one or almost no one as the traits of

[5] Maurice Blanchot, *Au Moment Voulu* (Paris: Gallimard, [1951] 1979), 108. Hereafter abbreviated as AMV.

my character weakened, the world was also readily merging with its limit), but this sort of penury of time was disclosing above all the exorbitant pressure of 'Something is happening,' a jealous immensity that could only curtail or suspend the natural progress of the story" (252). The story discloses its truth only if it can achieve a break with all stories. In this movement, the narrator unleashes an infinite "passion," which is identical with a concept of life. If "passion is living," the attendant paradox is that "the creature touched by passion also destroys the possibility that is life" (252). Hence, one reaches a disabused conclusion: "Anyone who wants to live has to rely on the illusion of a story, but this reliance is not permitted to me" (257).

Thus the whole novel deconstructs the logic of the stories and debunks the illusions on which we live. Its main mechanism is a Jamesian strategy of indirection in the clipped dialogues and nocturnal scenes. Most of the words exchanged have several meanings and are left to reverberate. These moments are then recaptured by commentaries. A latent Gothicism creeps in so as to suggest at times that the three main characters appear as ghosts who stage an apocalyptic confrontation between love and hate, life and death, faith and survival. The apparently neutral writing often unravels itself when it leaves room for verbal riddles and brilliant, fascinating images.

When Claudia says that no one wants to be involved in an affair, the statement might be construed as sad, disabused, or melancholic. However, what follows makes clear that it is the very impossibility of basking in the reassurance of romantic "stories" that generates joy, an excessive joy, a joy shared by all three protagonists. Their days in the apartment seem etched in the memory of the narrator and shot through by a sharp shadows and intense rays of light. All the most minute incidents, like asking for a glass of water, making a fire in the chimney, looking at a snowfall through the window, generate a strange exhilaration. The conventional story held in reserve by the plot could be deemed almost sordid: a man comes back to the woman he has loved in the past; finding her in a couple with a woman, he pretends to seduce the partner in order to wound the first lover. This backfires when the seduction triggers a crisis; he leaves, preferring to remain alone with his images. Such a summary misses the pathos of the book. The novel's pathos is not contained, as Prince and other commentators believe, in the reflexive neutrality of a narrative without object; the key to the story is not that the narrative of banal incidents reflexively turns into pure text, becoming identical with the act of storytelling. As Bataille observed in an early and insightful commentary to which I'll come back, the book's plot is marked throughout by the affect of joy, a joy that remains a joy of the outside, of future premonitions, of ethical awakenings.

A sentence following the passage quoted explains the link between an affect of joy and the scattered elements of the plot: "I must recall this: such days are not devoted to an unknown misfortune, they don't confirm the distress of a moribund decision; on the contrary, they are traversed by joyful immensity, a radiant authority, luminescence, pure frivolity, too strong for the days, turning them into a pure dissipation and each event into the image of a displaced episode (an episode that is not in its place, a sort of farce of time, belonging to a different age, a lost and baffled fragment of history)" (257). To this knot of joy and excess, Blanchot gives the name of "intrigue," a word that is not identical with "plot." It is repeated several times so as to be opposed to any "story." I will explore what the concept implies by referring to Emmanuel Levinas and Georges Bataille.

One should begin with Bataille's review of the novel in *Critique* (number 57, February 1952), "Silence and Literature," which begins by sounding an almost funny note. Bataille compares Blanchot with Wells' *Invisible Man*, and the 1933 film adapting the story: when the specter unwraps his bandages, one can perceive that there is just nothing.[6] This nothingness is represented by silence in Blanchot's novel. Bataille adds that it would be wrong to associate this nothingness with dread, horror, or anxiety, as some of Blanchot's essays might suggest. He insists that this is a very "happy book"—"there is no other book that offers such a description of happiness."[7] Bataille is aware that this happiness is not so readily perceptible because of the "confusion" already mentioned. He develops this with another filmic analogy: "the author's mode of expression introduces into literature a kind of perfect reversibility, in a way similar to that of a horse on screen, if one suddenly reverses the film."[8] The filmic metaphors complement each other: the deviant temporality of the narrative in which images radiate back and forth and constantly change their meanings is combined with the paradoxical appearance of a void where the author's face should have been.

Bataille's remark about the "reversibility" evinced by the text develops Blanchot's presentation of *Au Moment Voulu*. The *"prière d'insérer"* composed for Gallimard when he announced his novel before publication states this: "Of

---

[6]   Georges Bataille, "Silence and Literature," trans. Stuart Kendall, in *The Obsessions of Georges Bataille*, ed. Andrew J. Mitchell and Jason Kemp Winfree (Albany: SUNY University Press, 2009), Appendix, 197.

[7]   Ibid., 198.

[8]   Ibid.

this narrative, let's just say that what it relates is true. But it also approaches the moment when nothing is true, this point where nothing is revealed, where, in the midst of dissimulation, speaking is but the shadow of speech, this incessant and interminable murmur to which one has to impose silence if one wants, at last, to be heard." Accordingly, Bataille ends up quoting at length the novel, splicing together two different passages, the end of the paragraph beginning "It could be that I lived in the state of anxiety of a man obliged to take upon himself the anxiety and work of the day" (WTC 252) and a much longer section beginning with "Forgetfulness has not passed over things " (257–258). It is as if Bataille could not gloss or explicate but only quote a text deemed to be self-sufficient.

Bataille has seen that the novel multiplies reversals and contradictions, all the while asserting the infinite joy created by the "moment." Indeed, Blanchot's narrator writes: "That I have descended so far from myself, into a place that can be called, I think, the abyss, and that it should have surrendered me just to the joyful space of a festival, the eternal glitter of an image, this may seem astonishing, and this surprise I would share had I not felt the burden of this indefatigable lightness, the infinite weight of a sky in which what one sees remains, where the boundaries sprawl out and the distance shines night and day with the radiance of a beautiful surface" (258; translation modified). Indeed, the theme of joy and pleasure, recurring systematically in the novel, leads to considerations about what it enables. Above all, this supreme joy has ethical consequences: it ushers in a sense of freedom based on "opulent affirmation" (246). There is an inexhaustible excess in this affirmation, a "yes" brought about by a single moment of time but opening to a mystical timelessness. It joins the past moments of intimacy with an endless festivity in which the narrator perceives the "jubilant celebration of the future" (249; "*la fête jubilante de l'avenir*," AMV, 135). This joy is paradoxical, and one could be tempted to call it *jouissance,* Jacques Lacan's main concept, an intense pleasure pushed beyond the limit of the sexual orgasm, a radical enjoyment at the cusp between pleasure and pain. Such jouissance of the instant combines all the opposites, from activity to passivity, from day to night, from desire to loathing, from mortal fight to happy reconciliation.

The deviant logics of jouissance presuppose for its disclosure something different from the conventional plot; it has to be called "intrigue," a term conveying both the knotting of recurrent themes and the paradoxical effect of reversibility: "I don't think I've ever been unaware of it, I know I'm mixed up in a profound, static intrigue, one that I mustn't look at, or even notice, that I mustn't be occupied by and that nevertheless requires all my strength and all my time" (WTC 255). Then the narrator develops the meaning: "I spoke of an intrigue. It is true that this word is intended to fill a hopeless function, but even so, it expresses in its own way the feeling I have: that I am bound, not to a story, but to the fact that, as I am likely to have less and less of a story, this poverty, far from winning me simpler days, attracts what life I have left in a cruelly complex movement of which I know nothing" (256). The concept of "intrigue" launched by Blanchot in *Au Moment Voulu* has been explored in depth by Gabriel Riera in *Intrigues: from Being to the Other.*[9]

Riera takes Blanchot's novel as a starting point for analyses shared by Levinas and Blanchot. Intrigue can be defined as a "para-discursive and counter-narrative mode of writing,"[10] a writing that attempts to evoke—and fails, inevitably—the inextricable relation between two human beings. It fails because it can never fully domesticate the "not-assimilable strangeness that language harbors."[11] Blanchot had discovered this key principle of his work at the time of *Au Moment Voulu,* because this novel was exploring a past crisis in subjectivity, and had to give birth to a new concept of passion. Passion does not simply call up a tragic love story—for as we have seen, nothing highly dramatic takes place in the story, there is no murder, no sex, not even an explicit expostulation of jealousy. The intrigue promotes a concept of passion attuned to a deeper passivity; it is deployed in the novel's statement of an eternal and absolute love for an absent person who remains simply as an image that is not even a resemblance to one singular person: "That is why it is terrible to love and we can only love what is most terrible. To bind oneself to a reflection— who would consent to that? But to bind oneself to what has no name and no face and to give that endless, wandering resemblance the depth of a mortal instant, to lock oneself up with it and thrust it along with oneself to the place where all resemblance yields and is shattered—that is what passion wants" (WTC 258). Love and terror are intermingled, and passion looks like Rilke's angel bringing tidings from another realm where the dreadful and the horrific reign. However, the moment of this intermingling has happened thanks to an image without resemblance, a phrase to which I will return in a Nietzschean context at the end, noting here that this concept is sufficient to trigger a quest for meaning.

---

[9]   Gabriel Riera, *Intrigues: From Being to the Other* (New York: Fordham University Press, 2006). See above all pages 16–35 and 85–105.
[10]   Ibid., 12.
[11]   Ibid., 16.

Thus the strange flickering or excessive joy suggested on almost every page of the novel derives from the awareness that, for a moment, the three characters constitute a community, even though they know that it is condemned: "Naturally, this wasn't defensible, and we certainly weren't there in order to help make our little community stay on its feet: on the contrary, each of us was relying on the imminence of the ending—imminence that has nothing to do with duration—but leaned on it with such force that the edifice of an instant, founded on nothing, could also appear extremely solid" (221). This impossible community in which diffuse eroticism is rampant could not but attract Bataille. After the failure of diverse prewar groups like "Contre-Attaque," "Acéphale," and the Collège de Sociologie that he had launched, Bataille attempted to recreate smaller communities during the war. It was first in Paris from 1941 to 1943, with groups in whose hearted philosophical and political discussions Blanchot participated. This is how Blanchot met Denise Rollin, then Bataille's mistress, in her apartment rue de Lille in which meetings were held.

These biographical details contain in a nutshell the kernel of an "intrigue." In several essays from the 1950s, Blanchot used the term "intrigue" to present non-stories as offering original inroads into a subjectivity without a subject. According to Riera's analysis, the concept of intrigue designates the place where the act of writing resides, a writing intricately connected with disaster and the non reciprocal relation between subjects, sounding a theme that became central in Levinas's work. This is why Blanchot observes shrewdly in *The Writing of the Disaster* that for Levinas, in the end, one can speak of a "subjectivity without any subject" to define what had been called earlier the "subjectivity of the subject" (WD 30). This philosophical context is determining and I will return to it, but wish first to proceed more simply, to begin with more obvious remarks about the meaning of the text itself. I have been struck by the way most commentators diverge widely about the least details of the story. It is my belief that there is a basic plot in *Au Moment Voulu*, whose initial meaning derives from a biographical substratum. Of course, biographical elements do not exhaust the meaning of the text, but a careful consideration of how they have been rearranged will provide guidelines for subsequent philosophical extrapolations.

\*\*\*

Thanks to Bident's biography, we know that the main action of the novel is a recasting of the author's involvement with Denise Rollin, who was then living with her partner Marianne Oswald, a French-German singer. The erotic triangle forms a basic structure that the reversible non narrative complicates by inserting hyperbolic meditations. Blanchot stated that all was true in this novel, and indeed the setting is recognizable. Many details point to a precise geographical context; at the beginning, the narrator imagines that he might leave the apartment after a conversation with Claudia, feeling ready to go, and then imagines himself walking at night along rue de la Victoire in the direction of the Opera (WTC 219). Later we learn that their building faces the Paris synagogue whose bombing is recalled (227). The façade of the main synagogue had been partly destroyed in the night of October 2–3, 1941. The novel's action takes place sometime after the Second World War. Therefore the apartment has to be in the vicinity of buildings situated at 45 or 47 rue de la Victoire. It has to be high up, for at some point, Claudia points to landmarks like the church of La Trinité to the North, the Bourse to the South, and in between, boulevard Haussmann. Any Parisian will recognize the landscape of the Opera area with the *grands boulevards* nearby.

The real-life story behind the novel revolves around Denise Rollin, for whom Blanchot said he had written it. We know that Blanchot and Bataille had met at the end of 1940 and became immediately very close. Bataille had entered the life of Denise Rollin-Roth-Le Gentil early in October 1939. Because of Bataille, Denise broke up with her husband, a handsome actor, the father of Jean, their son, who was then 1-year-old. At the time, Bataille was striving to overcome the loss of Colette Peignot, a.k.a. "Laure." Laure who had already died (she died in November 1938) fascinated Denise who met Bataille after the tragedy. It is likely that the knowledge of the events underlying *Death Sentence*, hinging around Laure's last days, were conveyed by Denise to Blanchot. At the time of her involvement with Bataille, Denise's apartment on 3, rue de Lille, which would become Jacques Lacan's apartment in 1944, was used from 1941 to 1943 by Bataille to organize discussions at which Blanchot was present, as we have seen. It was there that Bataille read passages from *Inner Experience* to his friends. According to witnesses, Denise Rollin—close to André Breton, Jean Cocteau, and Jacques Prévert—was remarkable for her beauty—she modeled for several painters like André Derain, who left a beautiful portrait of her— and her attentive presence, that was as intense as silent. She followed Bataille to Vezelay with her son in March 1943. In Vezelay, Bataille met the young woman who was to become his second wife. He and Denise broke up at the end of 1943. She left the rue de Lille apartment to move to a sixth-floor walk-up on rue Vaugirard, which cannot be, however, the location of *Au Moment Voulu.*

Denise began a relationship with Blanchot in 1945. Blanchot's ill-health justified his move to the South of France one year later, which rendered the relationship more sporadic. Even when Blanchot lived in his house in Eze, near Nice, by the seaside, he would visit Paris regularly. All that time, in spite of their mutual love, Denise was not hesitant, not sure whether she wanted Blanchot in her life. Bident quotes her letter from the late 1950s: "It has now been fourteen years that I have refused myself to Maurice Blanchot who, however, was the person who had been 'destined' to me."[12] As Bident argues, Denise's wish to live an absolute passion to the end might have proved too hard for Bataille to bear. This uncompromising attitude could not but take Blanchot to task. Indeed, Blanchot's dedication to Denise keeps an ominous ring: "This book written for you in proximity to danger." What danger? Since the book was written after the war, the danger was not physical but moral, and its presence is at the core of *Au Temps Voulu*. A memoir written by Denise's son Jean makes it clear that she never stopped loving Blanchot; Blanchot reciprocated this all consuming passion mostly by writing to her thousands of letters, their curious epistolary passion preserving distance above all. When Denise died, her son Jean found on her desk a last letter to Blanchot—she hadn't had time to finish it. It began with: "I think of you every day."[13]

This knot of deliberately frustrated passion underlies one of the most obscure passages of the novel. It concerns Judith, who is compared with Abraham sacrificing Isaac. This paragraph has triggered considerable disagreement among interpreters. It appears almost detached from the rest of the narrative; it sounds less like a recapitulation or a conclusion, coming as it does after the incident of *Nescio vos!* and before the meditation on living alone in the South, than like a new beginning: indeed the text begins in the simple past ("*Je rencontrai cette femme*" [AMV 147]), as if it was the first sentence of the narrative that had started in medias res ("Because the friend who lived with her was not there, the door was opened by Judith" [WTC 203]). The tense here, moreover, contrasts with the preceding pages written in the imperfect ("*Lorsque j'ouvrais la porte ...*" [AMV 146]) or in the present ("*Il est vrai que je parle ...*" [AMV 146]). Here is the paragraph, divided into two sections:

12    Quoted in Bident, *Maurice Blanchot,* 275, my translation.
13    Jean Rollin, *Les dialogues sans fin, précédés de quelques souvenirs sur Georges Bataille, Maurice Blanchot et Michel Fardoulis-Lagrange* (Paris: La Mirandole, 1997), 29.

(1) I met this woman I called Judith: she was not bound to me by a relationship of friendship or enmity, happiness or distress; she was not a disembodied instant, she was alive. And yet, as far as I can understand, something happened to her that resembled the story of Abraham. When Abraham came back from the country of Moria, he was not accompanied by his child but by the image of a ram, and it was with a ram that he had to live from then on. Others saw the son in Isaac, because they didn't know what had happened on the mountain, but he saw the ram in his son, because he had made a ram for himself out of his child. A devastating story.

(2) I think Judith had gone to the mountain, but freely. No one was freer than she was, no one troubled herself less about powers and was less involved with the justified world. She could have said, "It was a God who wanted it," but for her that amounted to saying, "It was I alone who did it." An order? Desire transfixes all orders. (WTC 253)

The bafflement of commentators derives from their having attempted to read the two sections separately. Indeed, it is not easy to make sense of Blanchot's riff on Kierkegaard's lengthy meditations on the sacrifice of Isaac in *Fear and Trembling*. The motif modifies a trope that Blanchot was using in texts from the same period. Blanchot found a first inversion of the Biblical paradigm in Thomas Mann's *History of Jacob,* with which he begins the tetralogy of *Joseph and his brothers*. In his review published in 1942, Blanchot does not quote the text, but sums it up. He admires the way Mann presents a dying Isaak who believes that he has turned into a ram, the animal whose miraculous apparition saved his life when he was a boy. In his delirium, he starts bleating like a ram. Blanchot comments: "This primordial bleating, an allusion to the Paschal lamb, an echo of the prehistoric beast, the idol of the clan, echoes throughout the whole story."[14]

Another echo of the Biblical story appears in the first version of *Thomas the Obscure*, published in 1941. This takes place in the museum scene described in chapter XII, which presents Thomas's dalliance with Irene, a married woman who often takes lovers. Irene appears as rather hysterical. She is a close friend of Anne who is still alive then, but dies in chapter XIII. If chapter XIII presents a blueprint for *Death Sentence,* as has often been noticed, chapter XII announces the weird exchanges between Claudia and the narrator in *Au Moment Voulu*. The ironical treatment of the museum scene entails a rare (for Blanchot) exercise of ekphrasis: Thomas and Irene meet in the Louvre in front of Titian's *Woman*

---

[14] Maurice Blanchot, "Contes et Récits" (1942), in *Chroniques Littéraires du Journal des Débats*, ed. Christophe Bident (Paris: Gallimard, 2007), 140.

*with a mirror*. Irene is so moved by the portrait that she cries. Thomas, full of admiration himself, keeps a more joyful attitude. He displays the "joviality of a man for whom the sun revolves around the Bible is only a collection of adventure stories."[15] Irene then forces him to adopt the role of a little boy: "The more Irene, for reasons of a grown-up person … pushed him triumphantly into puerility, the more she felt that he was escaping again from the human race, and, joining the race of those who shout and scream facing a kidnapper because he is not a bohemian, was treating as equal, without admiration, with any difference in size, terrible dialogue of Isaac and Abraham, the equivalent of God for our older age. From the bottom of his mystery as a child, he exposed himself to the contagion of the strange good health, the reflection of abnormal images."[16] The syntax is curious, the wording tortuous; something seems to be missing. Moreover the entire chapter was deleted from the revised version in 1950. As Blanchot stated in a prefatory note, some of the pages of the first version were written as early as 1932. Now 1932 was the year of the notorious kidnapping of Lindbergh's son. What stands out is that Thomas identifies with Isaac. The famous parable of *Genesis* is presented as what remains of the fear of God after we know that we live in a godless world.

The three texts hinge around the sudden turn in the Biblical story when God, who is testing the faith of Abraham, substitutes a ram for Isaac at the last minute. What does it mean to assert that Isaac identifies with a ram, as Thomas Mann suggests? Why cannot Abraham-Judith see the son as a human being after the descent from the mountain of the sacrifice in *Au Moment Voulu*? Why does Thomas feel such a proximity to Isaac in *Thomas the Obscure*? We gather that for Blanchot, the story of Abraham and Isaac functions as a modern (since Kierkegaard, at least) substitute for the old belief in God (after Nietzsche, say). Judith, who becomes a sort of Abraham, cannot admit that her son is alive simply because of a miracle sent by God. She cannot erase the cruelty of the intended blood sacrifice; she sees the animal destined to be killed even after the miracle has granted a happy outcome. The rationale for this appears in the second section quoted.

If in *Au Moment Voulu*, the "mountain" and the land of Moria stand for Vezelay, a famous place of Christian devotion, asceticism, and ancient ritual, we can see the presence of Bataille in the parable. Vezelay was a sacred place even for him, while Bataille often appeared as the "Dieu-Bataille," as Laure would call

---

[15]    Maurice Blanchot, *Thomas L'Obscur* (Paris: Gallimard, 1941), 159. My translation.
[16]    Ibid., 160.

him.[17] Bataille had moved to Vezelay when he was in love with Denise Rollin, who had come with her son, but he went back to Paris being in love with another woman, fleeing her husband who had promised to kill him. Bataille, his daughter Laurence, Denise, and Jean Rollin had lived in Vezelay somewhat precariously from March 1943 to the end of 1943. After falling in love with Diane, Bataille returned to Paris late in 1943 but this was to break up with Denise. In Vezelay, he had acted as a surrogate father for Jean Rollin then aged 5. Rollin narrates how Bataille would tell him scary stories of wolves disguised as priests, or of young girls doing their first communion but being in fact baby wolves: "As far as I can go back into my memory, my first memories are those of a man bending over my cot. This man was talking, telling me stories to make me sleep … Other memories come back, images. This man and I, hidden in a corner, looking at the church on the little square of the village. Soon lots of little girls in white, with a veil on their heads and white gloves, stream out. 'These are big wolf babies (*bébés gros loup*),' he said. This phrase of '*bébé gros loup*' can be found in a short text, 'La petite écrevisse blanche' in Bataille's *Collected Works*, vol. IV, page 324."[18]

The return to Paris in 1943 was a sad moment for Denise and Jean; when Blanchot succeeded Bataille in the role of Denise's lover, he did not enjoy the same closeness with the mother and complicity with the son. Bident quotes Jean Rollin's memories of a sick, exhausted visitor who had trouble to reach their sixth floor walk-up, and of whom the concierge would make fun. Moreover, Jean had to remain silent and invisible when Blanchot came to visit.[19] The Isaac/Ram parable links the son Jean to Blanchot in several ways. In *Thomas the Obscure*, Thomas appears as a boy, even when he is about to become Irene's lover. He cheerfully accepts his own immaturity, which can be contrasted with the figure of a distant father-god who insists upon blood sacrifice. In 1943, Denise had moved to Vezelay hoping to recreate a family. More sacrifices would be required from her by Bataille, who was skeptical facing her "absolute" passion. However, after a while, back in Paris, Denise overcame her bitterness with the help of her female lover. Her remarks about Bataille quoted by Bident suggest that she judged him less untrustworthy than flimsy or "theatrical."[20] Meanwhile, her son had been changed too, if only because he had lost his substitute father. But the

---

[17]  Laure (Colette Peignot), *Les Ecrits de Laure* (Paris: Pauvert, 1979), 276.
[18]  Rollin, *Les dialogues sans fin, précédés de quelques souvenirs sur Georges Bataille, Maurice Blanchot et Michel Fardoulis-Lagrange*, 11.
[19]  Bident, *Maurice Blanchot*, note 1, 272.
[20]  Ibid., 274–75.

son had become a "ram" himself, because one might say, indeed, that he was her metaphorical phallus.

The "devastating" experience that lay in store for the Judith of Blanchot's story implies that she kept a ram instead of a son; this suggests that in her "jealous" and "avid" silence when she observes Claudia flirting with the narrator, she displays the attributes of a phallic woman: powerful, silent, shining, shameless, intense, and nevertheless "avid." Blanchot wanted to remain discrete about the private life of his friend Bataille, but other echoes can be discerned. At one point, the narrator wants to have something to drink, as he does often, but this time, instead of a glass of water, he requires alcohol. Claudia tells him that there is none; he replies: "There used to be!" The text goes on: "No doubt this allusion to a time when a young man (*garçon*) was in charge (*régnait)* here seemed to her to come from a very contemptible place, but one couldn't expect my thirst to be very considerate" (WTC 214). The word *garçon* is used once only; the term is curious if we think that the narrator must be in his late 30s. The term *garçon* links him with the son who remains invisible in the novel but was very present in the life of Judith's original.

Traces of the son merge with the ghostly presence of the narrator. Some dialogues imply that the narrator's very existence is "precarious," as when Claudia tells him: "I hardly believe in you" (243). The suggestion is that Denise (no doubt baptized "Judith" because of Denise Rollin's resemblance with Klimt's portrait of *Judith and the Head of Holofernes* hanging in the Belvedere in Vienna) has transformed her past ordeals into a joyful acceptance of fate, a stoical *amor fati*. Having gone to the mountain to sacrifice her son, she found that this would not be to obey God's commandment, whatever God's reasons were, but to be at one with her desire. What was first an absolute order to kill the person she loved most turned into a full assertion of her sovereign desire. The ram would thus be a Bataillean phallus turned against an acephalic male god, a god who will be sacrificed in his turn. The ram would stabilize a desire capable of "transfixing all orders." Thanks to her "ram," Judith, the traditional castrator of Holophernes, is free and can push away all obstacles. It is not by coincidence that Jean Rollin became famous as the director of post-Surrealist erotic films displaying sexy nude vampires.

In a sense, the parable of the ram suggests that Judith's attitude is similar to Claudia's posture when singing Robert Schumann's *Lied* "*Ich grolle nicht.*" The lyrics come from a poem by Heine that states a refusal to be angry or complain when one has been abandoned by an inconstant lover:

Ich grolle nicht, und wenn das Herz auch bricht,
Ewig verlor'nes Lieb ! Ich grolle nicht.
Wie du auch strahlst in Diamantenpracht,
Es fällt kein Strahl in deines Herzens Nacht.

We hear "Es fällt kein Strahl" in the context of Claudia's curious voice and her need to work more on such "classical" (AMV 71) pieces. This poem was adapted many times, the most famous version being Schumann's opus 48, number 7, from 1840; it is one of the songs of the *Dichterliebe* series. A literal translation might be:

I do not rage, even if my heart were to break,
Love lost for ever! I do not rage.
Even though you shine in splendid diamond light,
No sunbeam falls into your heart's dark night.

Marianne Oswald had made a name for herself by singing modernist cabaret songs. After her stay in America during the war, she tried a new repertoire of Romantic *Lieder,* here associated with Heine and Schumann. The darkness of the fickle lover's heart is not spurned or rejected but embraced in a general pardon, an assertion of power showing her overcoming loss and pain. Denise Rollin and Marianne Oswald—both Jewish, both wounded in love—were united less by an erotic passion than by a rejection of the world of men and their corrupted or contemptible values.

Claudia is based upon Alice Bloch, whose stage name was Marianne Oswald. She had been born in Sarreguemines at a time when it was a German territory. An operation on her throat as a child gave her a particular voice, low and hoarse, and she made the most of it. In the 1930s, she sang Kurt Weill and Bertolt Brecht's songs from the *Beggars' Opera*—a French Lotte Lenya, as it were. She developed a *Sprechgesang* style that was immediately recognizable. Her physical description in the novel confirms her identity (Marianne Oswald had globular eyes and high cheekbones). Her friends, the same as Denise Rollin's, included Jean Cocteau and Jacques Prévert. Prévert wrote the preface for the French version of her memoir *Je n'ai pas appris à vivre* published in 1948. Oswald never married, and was one time Denise Rollin's lover. Visiting the United States, Albert Camus discovered her memoir in English, *One Small Voice.* He liked it, contacted her, and he was instrumental in bringing her back to Paris. There she would sing again but with less success, which is reflected in *Au Moment Voulu;* after that, she would appear in radio shows and played small parts in films like *Les amants de Vérone, Le guérisseur, Notre-Dame de Paris*, and *Les Amants de Montparnasse*. What the narrator says about her peculiar voice can be paralleled with the story of Judith and her metamorphosed "sacrifice": Claudia's voice is "poor" at times, it becomes blank or indifferent, however attains to the sublime easily: "The pathos of deep registers has nothing to do with this event. I had heard voices harmoniously bound to desolation, to anonymous misery, I had been attentive to them, but this one was indifferent and neutral, hidden away in a vocal region where it stripped itself so completely of all superfluous perfection that it seemed deprived of itself: her voice was true, but in such a way that it reminded one of the sort of justice that has been handed over to all negative hazards (*à toutes les fatalités négatives*)" WTC 225). It looks as if Blanchot might have discovered his concept of the neuter by listening to Marianne Oswald singing Schumman's *Lieder*.

Claudia displays a certain animus against men, her "ram," like Judith. Claudia asks the narrator whether he would leave if requested; he agrees, but she interjects: "I don't believe you, all men are deceitful, all men lie. You lie too, I know it" (217). Would this show Blanchot as a feminist? Perhaps. However, lying or self-deception is shown to be universal in the novel. In that sense, Blanchot's final position in his text would call up that of Kafka whose work paradoxically transforms readers into liars struggling against lies and impostors half-aware of their ontological imposture: "Kafka's entire work is in search of an affirmation that it wants to gain by negation, an affirmation that conceals itself as soon as it emerges, seems to be a lie and then is excluded from being affirmative, making affirmation once again possible."[21] The text's own fictions are displaced, brought closer to the sharp but neutral voice of an impenetrable Justice, a Justice identical with a negated or negative transcendence. Its promise of future redemption creates a dazzling light facing which neither gendered psychology, ethical excuses nor narcissistic lures can offer a hiding place.

\*\*\*

A similar displacement of psychology can be seen in one of the bizarre moments of the novel, the scene when Judith screams "Nescio Vos" to Claudia and the narrator. Just like her "ram," Judith's "*Nescio*" keeps a Bataillean ring. "Nescio" seems to be a distant echo from Bataille's theory of Unknowing, a

---

[21]   See Maurice Blanchot, "La lecture de Kafka," in *De Kafka à Kafka* (Paris: Gallimard, 1981), 69, and "Reading Kafka," in *The Work of Fire*, trans. Charlotte Mandell (Stanford: Stanford University Press, 1995), 6.

theory that he was elaborating at the time. "Nescio vos" quotes from either Luke 13:27 or Matthew 25:12. One passage implies that "straight is the gate," that those who have chosen iniquity will be rejected by the Lord at the time of the final reckoning. The other insists on being prepared, and the five foolish virgins will miss the fateful date of reckoning. In both tales, the Lord says, "Nescio vos" (I do not recognize you). This sentence can be compared with Bataille's meditations. A passage from "The Consequences of Nonknowledge," a lecture given in 1951, the year *Au Moment Voulu* was published, seems relevant: "If you are facing a woman, as much as you know her, you hardly know her, in other words you have an understanding of her that borders on knowledge. Insofar as you seek to know a woman psychologically without letting yourself be carried away by passion, you distance yourself from her. Only when you seek to know her in relation to death do you draw nearer to her."[22] It seems that Judith has understood that lesson when she utters the terrible words and faints in the narrator's arms. The instant of the scream shows her in all her sublime beauty, for her "wonderful head" has been "uplifted" for an instant (WTC 248). Such a sublime moment operates a break with the previous entanglements and displays all the power of her phallic ram.

Judith's quote from the Latin Vulgate is construed as initiating a new and reciprocal *tutoiement*, *"l'intimité d'un tutoiement mystérieux"*: *"car elle était toi pour moi, et j'étais moi pour elle."* (AMV 134) This sounds counterintuitive: the Latin expression from the Vulgate states *Vos*, a plural "you." She does not utter *Nescio te*. The *Vos* includes Claudia and the narrator. However, having heard the words, the narrator concludes that he does not "know" Claudia either, thus identifying with Judith's position, as if the apocalyptic ring of the sentence had acted as a separating mechanism. If *Nescio vos* renews the mystical intimacy established in the pathos of distance that links him and separates him from Judith, it sounds the death knell of their little community.

The original trigger to a warming up in the exchanges between Claudia and the narrator was when Claudia suddenly decides to say *tu* to him. This happens at a moment when she assumes that he is interested in both of them ("Now, both of us!" [AMV 236; translation modified]). Reproaching him for never saying *tu* to anyone, she quotes a lusty proverb from her country: *"L'un lui dit tu, l'autre la possède"* (AMV 100), "One calls her 'tu,' the other takes her" (WTC 236). If the

---

[22] Georges Bataille, *The Unfinished System of Nonknowledge*, trans. Michelle Kendall and Stuart Kendall (Minneapolis: University of Minnesota Press, 2001), 115.

curious proverb is in German, it plays on *duzen* as opposed to *siezen,* the latter leading to *ziehen,* to pull, draw, or lay. This sentence ushers in a new *intrigue,* since the scene evoked entails for the narrator the gift of his passivity, a term that Levinas had already used a lot and that recurs in *The Writing of the Disaster.* The narrator only states: "do what you want," thus abandoning himself (WTC 237). Claudia dries his face soaked in sweat, and, in an echo of *Death Sentence,* acts like Veronica facing Christ. The scene leads to an erotic moment: the narrator seizes her twice; she lifts up his hands and lays them on her breasts. It is at the end of this frantic interaction that Claudia enters Judith's room, touches her arm and hand, which triggers the *Nescio* crisis. This crisis provokes a denouement. There, Judith identifies less with Christ than with the God of Abraham; she is not the sacrificed son, but the Lord when she screams the startling *Nescio Vos!* These "unforgettable words" are powerful enough to expel the narrator from the erotic triangle in which he had maintained himself. They are jealous and zealous at the same time, but also domineering and joyful. They embody "sovereignty" in Bataille's sense, a sense of lordship beyond any bondage, not afraid by death but also exceeding the Hegelian dialectics of the Master and the Slave.[23] This explains why these words retain an edge of murderous caprice: Salome is never far from Judith. Indeed, the two words reveal "the freedom of a pure caprice in which the taste for blood hadn't yet been awakened." (WTC 248) Judith has regained her sovereignty with just two words—then she rules and reasserts her sublime posture. The performative manifested by those two words is indeed sovereign; the speech act forces the narrator to leave the Paris apartment for good. Thereafter, he will be haunted by Judith, and not by Claudia, as some commentators (including Bident) believe. The syntax is clear enough: the underlined *la* in *"je la vis"* (AMV 137) refers to Judith as opposed to Claudia, who is named. The same subject is mentioned in the next sentence: *"Quand je la vis a nouveau ..."* (AMV 138), but this time the pronoun refers to a woman whose head is bent on her knees; the vision takes place at night in the South. This hallucination—we know that in fact "Judith" or Denise never came to the house in the South—is an "apparition" (WTC 251). The apparition is sufficient to disclose to the narrator's admission that this was the "willed moment." A simple, but pathetic, gesture is sufficient to embody a wordless ecstasy. The stooped figure of the woman who never stares back at the observer expresses neither expectation nor resignation;

---

[23] See Claire Niocheon, "Sovereignty," in *Georges Bataille: Key Concepts,* ed. Mark Hewson and Marcus Coelen (New York: Routledge, 2016), 125–35.

she is a mute figure of "melancholy dignity." Here lies her *Pathosformel*, to quote Aby Warburg's expression, an expression in which the ethical distance of Nietzsche is combined with a trans-historical form, a pattern deriving from the observation of similarities in expressive gestures observed in many cultures. Warburg thought that there was a universal language of pathos. The expression of *Pathosformel* ("formula of pathos") combines the expression of violent affects and comparative analysis founded on an encyclopedia of forms.[24] The formula of pathos deployed by Blanchot at the end of his novel supposes the pregnant function of a visual allegory that signifies a mutual and passionate avoidance, as if there had been a reciprocal agreement to remain in a productive and mystical non-relation: "Could I approach her? Could I go down? I didn't want to, and she herself, in her unwarranted (*illégitime*) presence, was accepting my look, but not asking for it. She never turned towards me and after I had looked at her I never forgot to go away calmly. The instant was never disturbed, or prolonged, or deferred, and maybe she didn't know me (*m'ignorait-elle*), and maybe she was unknown to me (*était-elle ignorée de moi*), but it didn't matter, because for one and for the other this instant really was the awaited moment, for both of us the time had come" (WTC, 250, AMV, 139). Lydia Davis was right to duplicate the terms in her translation of the concluding clause, in the original "*car pour l'un et pour l'autre cet instant était bien le moment voulu.*"

"Le moment voulu," this so-called "willed moment," is a phrase directly borrowed from Nietzsche. Blanchot exploits here all the echoes contained in Nietzsche's phrase; in an essay on Nietzsche, he had connected "*zur rechten Zeit*," the "free" choice of when to die, with the problematic of a *Wille* linking the cycles of rebirth with a decision to will, accept, and think through all the consequences of the eternal return. In his *Also Sprach Zarathustra*, Nietzsche had written "*Stirb zu rechten Zeit.*" Blanchot comments thus:

> Even when he condemns anxiety facing death, (Nietzsche) restores it under an even more ambiguous shape, that of joy and drunkenness. "One has to make a festival of one's death." One knows his "Die at the willed moment," which on the one hand is simply a Stoic apology for voluntary death, but on the other

---

[24] I have used it to analyze modernism in *The Pathos of Distance: Affects of the Moderns* (New York: Bloomsbury, 2016). Nietzsche's formulation in *Beyond Good and Evil* opposes the "noble" creation of true values to the slave morality whose spurious values derive from resentment. The "pathos of distance" expresses the regret facing the fact that men living in groups cannot be called "equal" but it soon leads to the idea of a "self-surmounting" or "self-overcoming" of man, thanks to which one ascends to the higher humanity of the "Overman." My contention is that *Au Moment Voulu* offers the most perfect exemplification of the "pathos of distance" in French literature.

hand conceals an anguishing temptation, for it recommends me to practice the impossible, linking my decision to a moment that no-one can recognize, the best moment, the willed moment that I could only perceive once dead, returning to the whole of my existence once completed, so that in the end the choice of the moment of my death supposes that I jump over my death and from there can look at my entire life, that I suppose myself already dead. (PF 288; my translation)

Indeed, if I *will* my death, this entails both that I am not dead yet and that I still consider my death as a possibility. Thus a strong will wants the privileged instant to take place not once only but be repeated again and again. If I will my own death to be an eternal cycle of returns, I will myself to be in the position of a ghost coming back to haunt the scenes evoked eternally. To this process, Blanchot gives the name of writing: a perpetual haunting. This idea is developed in "Two Versions of the Imaginary," an essay that allows us to link *L'Arrêt de mort* and *Au Moment Voulu*. In this dense essay, Blanchot departs radically from previous analyses of the image, particularly those of Sartre. For him, the question of resemblance is mediated by a meditation on what happens to an image, if it is to come "after" the object, as a cadaver comes "after" the living being. The image is presented as a *dépouille,* the mortal remains of someone whose resemblance is not really kept but lost by the semblance left behind, which calls up the lack of resemblance evinced by Judith in the novel. The image generates a series of paradoxes:

The resemblance of cadavers is a haunting obsession, but the act of haunting is not the unreal visitation of the ideal: what haunts is the inaccessible which one cannot rid oneself of, what one does not find and what, because of that, does not allow one to avoid it. The ungraspable is what one does not escape. The fixed image is without repose … We know that in spite of its so tranquil and firm immobility the cadaver we have dressed … is not resting. The spot it occupies is dragged along by it, sinks with it, and in this dissolution assails—even for us, the others who remain—the possibility of a sojourn. We know that at "a certain moment," the power of death causes it to leave the fine place that has been assigned to it. Even though the cadaver is tranquilly lying in state on its bier, it is also everywhere in the room, in the house. At any moment, it can be elsewhere than where it is, where we are without it, where there is nothing, an invading presence, an obscure and vain fullness. The belief that at a certain moment the dead person begins to wander (*errer),* must be ascribed to the intuition of that *error* he now represents.[25]

---

[25] "Two Versions of the Imaginary," *Station Hill Reader*, 422. Barrytown: Station Hill, 1999

Whereas *Death Sentence* is concerned with grasping the "certain moment," that is, the precise instant when death strikes, *Au Moment Voulu* inscribes that "moment" in a different continuity by transforming its image into a deliberate movement of errant haunting; this movement exceeds the boundaries between life and death, between living and surviving, by asserting an eternal or absolute time. The particular exhilaration that one feels bubbling among all the characters of the story is similar to that poison beloved by women murderers mentioned in the essay; after they have poisoned people, they take poison as their lover. Blanchot even quotes Poe and then Ludwig Feuerbach, the latter describing how a female poisoner who had already spent some time in jail was confronted with a bag of arsenic that she was asked to identify. Then "she trembled with joy, she experienced a moment of ecstasy."[26] Writing is this poison that carries with it its antidote, a joyful and excessive *pharmakon*.

The effort of writing to make the pathetically poisonous image survive will fulfill a similar function: by dint of repetition, the image immunizes the subject against the poison of despair born of absence and frustration. The image of the lost and haunting woman hovering between life and death mithridatizes the subject against the fear of loss and death. It fills the narrator's imaginary with a senseless joy, with the sporadic discharges of ecstatic illuminations. *Au Moment Voulu* stages the impossible story of the haunting by an image beyond love and death. The fascination for this image creates a black hole, an absence to which writing keeps returning, in the doomed but incessant effort to cover it with signs.

We have moved through a Hegelian progression marked by battles for love, domination and recognition in the Paris apartment, followed by a Bataillean affirmation of sovereignty. It is on the latter that the narrator meditates once he lives in the South. The dialectical reversals in the fight for erotic recognition have led to a Pyrrhic victory. Erotic seduction yields nothing, for it is extinguished by two words, canceled by the subsequent freeze on one image. The vision is a negative synecdoche because it abolishes all the rest as a *negativa pars pro toto*. It also signifies the abolition of time, according to the principle of reversibility mentioned by Bataille's review. Blanchot gives us here a perfect fictional equivalent of Nietzsche's doctrine of the eternal return of the same: "I think that this is the absolutely dark moment of the intrigue, the point at which it keeps returning to the present, at which I can no longer either forget or remember, at which human events, around a center as unstable and immobile as myself,

[26]   Ibid., 423.

indefinitely construct their return" (WTC 260; translation modified). What's more, as a startling testimony to Blanchot's skill as a writer, this personal pathos can be shared by readers. For us, too, awed by a gesture and a pose, such pathetic cogitations still amaze the troubled midnight and the noon's repose.

# 8

# Writing as *Überfluss*: Blanchot's Reading of Kafka's *Diaries*

## Michael Holland

*Là déjà le problème commence à naître. Qu'est-ce que ce serait cet "il" qui n'est plus de la troisième personne? Ce serait là le "il" de Kafka, ce serait là le "il" que Blanchot a essayé de retrouver. Bon, pour le moment on va pas trop vite.*

(Gilles Deleuze)[1]

The postwar period has been described as "the most fruitful phase in France's discovery of Kafka,"[2] and during those years, Maurice Blanchot played a significant role in that author's reception. Before then, there are no signs that he took any interest in Kafka. He was a writer whom Blanchot occasionally acknowledged, but only illustratively and as one of a number.[3] However, things will change after the publication of Jean-Paul Sartre's review of *Aminadab* in 1943.[4] This novel forms a pendant to *Thomas the Obscure*, which appeared the previous year and whose closing lines "as if the shame had begun for him" (TO 117)[5] clearly echo the last words of Kafka's *The Trial*: "as if he meant the shame

---

[1] "Now the problem is already beginning to appear. What would it be, the 'he' that is no longer in the third person? It would be Kafka's 'he', it would be the 'he/it' that Blanchot was in search of. But ok, for the moment let's not go too fast." Gilles Deleuze, "Anti-oedipe et autres réflexions," seminar given on 03/06/1980, transcribed by Méropi Morfouli. At http://www2.univ-paris8.fr/deleuze/article. php3?id_article=214.

[2] See Maja Goth, *Franz Kafka et les lettres françaises* (Paris: Corti, 1950), 250.

[3] In December 1941 Blanchot invokes Kafka's *Metamorphosis* to illustrate Kléber Haedens's point that a novelist does not need to create living human characters (Maurice Blanchot, *Into Disaster. Chronicles of Intellectual Life, 1941*, trans. Michael Holland (New York: Fordham University Press, 2014). In November 1942, reviewing Camus's *Myth of Sisyphus*, he includes Kafka in a list of writers—Sade, Melville, Dostoyevsky, Proust, Joyce, Malraux, Faulkner—"who have given to non-meaning the guarantee of an art coupled reasonably with the absurd" (FP 55).

[4] Jean-Paul Sartre, "*Aminadab*: Or the Fantastic Considered as a Language," in *Literary and Philosophical Essays*, trans. Annette Michelson (New York: Collier Books, 1962), 60–77.

[5] Maurice Blanchot, *Thomas l'obscur* (Paris: Gallimard, 1941), 232.

of it to outlive him."[6] The difference is that what outlives Joseph K lives on in Blanchot's Thomas beyond the novel's end, so that another novel is required in order to "be done with"[7] what Thomas embodies and signifies. If *Thomas the Obscure* is the novel of the failure of symbol, *Aminadab* is the allegory of what makes that failure interminable. Thomas enters a house in response to what appears to be an invitation from a young woman at a window. As he descends gradually deeper into the nether regions of the house, what Kafka calls "the shameful lowlands [*schändlichen Niederungen*] of writing"[8] open onto the abjection of the grave. As it proceeds, the novel adopts or acquires a number of features that recall Kafka's fiction, in particular *The Castle*, so that when Sartre asserts that "there is an extraordinary resemblance between [*Aminadab*] and the novels of Kafka"[9] he is right, even though the comparison he makes is designed to deny Blanchot's novel any originality.

Seemingly in response to Sartre's assertion, Kafka suddenly becomes a regular point of reference in Blanchot's critical writing. At first this occurs in passing, as if it is more Sartre's barb that concerns Blanchot than the author to whom he compares him. Hence this pointed remark in January 1943 with reference to Kafka's translator (suggesting he had had wind of Sartre's intentions): "To be associated with the writer who created the most solemn and incontrovertible images of human destiny is a merit that far exceeds the minor glories one may acquire through one's own writing."[10] Two years later he seems still to be smarting when, in an article on Melville, he reflects that "today, Kafka's name is inevitably mentioned in relation to everything that appears extraordinary."[11] A year later, in 1946, he will reveal how important Kafka has now become in his eyes: "Poetry had as its symbol Rimbaud, who stopped writing, for literature it was Lautréamont, who disappeared into what he wrote, and for the novel, Kafka, whose novels are unfinished."[12] Yet even in 1947, by which time he has begun to

[6]   Franz Kafka, *The Trial*, trans. Willa and Edwin Muir (Harmondsworth: Penguin Books, 1971 [1935]), 251.
[7]   In "After the fact" Blanchot refers to his wish to "have done with" the endlessness of what *Thomas the Obscure* imposed on him. See *Vicious Circles, Two Fictions & After the fact*, trans. Paul Auster (Barrytown: Station Hill Press, 1985 [1983]), 64.
[8]   *The Diaries of Franz Kafka*, trans. Joseph Kresh and Martin Greenberg (Harmondsworth: Penguin, 1972 [1948]), 213.
[9]   Jean-Paul Sartre, *Literary and Philosophical Essays*, trans. Annette Michelson (New York: Collier Books, 1962), 61.
[10]  Maurice Blanchot, "A Novel and a Tale of War," in *A World in Ruins. Chronicles of Intellectual Life, 1943*, trans. Michael Holland (New York: Fordham University Press, 2016), 36.
[11]  Maurice Blanchot, "L'Enchantement de Melville," in *La Condition critique* (Paris: Gallimard, 2010), 44.
[12]  Maurice Blanchot, "L'Enigme de la critique" (January 1946), in *La Condition critique*, 55.

pay sustained attention to Kafka's writing, the way Blanchot dismisses *Amerika* as "the least successful of his novels" contains a sideswipe at Sartre. In this novel, he says, "the strange is no longer that tunnel where, once you have entered it, all you can do is keep going ... with no hope of ever getting out of it."[13] Rather, the novel is one "you can enter or leave as you will; that is why the fantastic appears; it has the charm and sometimes the good grace of a caprice, but not the fateful quality of what is."[14] If this remark is designed primarily to differentiate between *Amerika* and Kafka's other novels, it also contains a pointed rebuttal of Sartre's use of the notion of the fantastic to dismiss *Aminadab*.

Sartre's observation must clearly have rankled: four years later, Blanchot is still reacting to it. However, the interest in Kafka's writing that it appears to have sparked off, or at least brought to the surface, very quickly takes center stage. A year after Sartre's review, in one of the last of his "Chronicles of Literary Life" entitled "The Literary *I*," Blanchot places Kafka alongside Goethe as an author whose development is marked by an increasingly objective approach to writing:

> we witness an author as exceptional as Kafka, who begins by keeping a diary in which all of his thoughts are direct confidences, then writes prose poems ..., and finally only succeeds in expressing himself completely through works in which he does not intervene, in objective "stories" ... that bear no relation to his personal biography.[15]

Blanchot describes this as "one of the great lessons of Kafka the writer." But the way he continues introduces an unexpected twist into his argument. Just previously, he has dismissed this lesson [*enseignement*] as one of "the most conventional lessons [*leçons*] of literary history": to see a writer progressing gradually from the subjective to the objective in his writing, he argues, is to propose an impoverished explanatory model. This brings him to the main subject of his article: "At first sight, Jouhandeau would appear to have chosen an entirely opposite development."[16] Over time, Marcel Jouhandeau has ceased to resort to the "alibi" of invented figures in his "Chaminadour" novels, and begun to portray himself and his family directly. Here Blanchot is not simply contrasting an "objectivist" model of narrative with a traditional subjective position. If Jouhandeau's writing displays this development, he goes on, it is

---

[13]  Maurice Blanchot, "Du merveilleux" (May 1947), in *La Condition critique*, 121.
[14]  Ibid., 122.
[15]  Maurice Blanchot, "The Literary I," in *Death Now. Chronicles of Intellectual Life, 1944*, trans. Michael Holland (New York, Fordham University Press, 2017). The original appeared as "Le *Je* littéraire" in *Le Journal des Débats*, June 1, 1944, 3.
[16]  Ibid.

because "*in himself* he has gone from a subjective stage to an objective stage" [my emphasis]. Whereas his alter ego M. Godeau was "more real" than his creator in the earlier works, Jouhandeau the writer is now "more symbolic" than his character. His "I" is therefore *more literary* than the characters of his earlier works.

If the paradoxical character of this claim makes it far from clear as it stands (pointing as it does, like all Blanchot's criticism, to changes going on in his fictional practice at the time),[17] it is also noteworthy that this paradox has as its counterpart a fundamental ambivalence in the way Blanchot thinks about Kafka. At one level, in response to Sartre no doubt, he seems to want to minimize Kafka's importance by focusing on Marcel Jouhandeau. True originality for a contemporary novelist lies in the creation of an objective *I*. This is no doubt a tactical move: as he moves away in 1944 from the novel toward the first-person *récit*, Blanchot appears to want to confine Kafka's writing to the third-person mode. But here lies the ambivalence: the example he uses in his article to illustrate the "great lesson" provided by Kafka is drawn not from his novels but from an entry in his *Diaries* dated September 19, 1917, to whose "remarkable form" Blanchot draws attention:

> Have never understood how it is possible for almost everyone who writes to objectify his sufferings in the very midst of undergoing them; thus I, for example, in the midst of my unhappiness, in all likelihood with my head still smarting from my unhappiness, sit down and write to someone: I am unhappy. Yes, and I can even go beyond that and with as many flourishes as I have the talent for, all of which seem to have nothing to do with my unhappiness, ring simple, or contrapuntal, or a whole orchestration of changes on my theme. And it is not a lie, and it does not still my pain; it is simply a merciful surplus [*Überfluss*] of strength at a moment when suffering has raked me to the bottom of my being and plainly exhausted all my strength. But what kind of surplus is it?[18]

---

[17] Considerable tensions are set up in Maurice Blanchot's writing after 1945 by the fact that he approaches literature simultaneously as a novelist and as a critic. As he searches for a language in which critical commentary can speak of literature, his own practice is the site of a protracted struggle to extricate narrative from the "endlessness" of third-person narrative, and shift it into that of the first-person *récit*. Over roughly five years, between the appearance of *Aminadab* in 1942 and the simultaneous publication of *The Most High* and *Death Sentence* in 1948, that transformation is slowly taking place. Even in 1948, *The Most High* retains many of the features of Blanchot's previous novels, notwithstanding the use of the first-person mode. Only with *Death Sentence* does he make a concerted break with the novel form, and set in train a series of first-person *récits* which will systematically expose the narrative "I" as merely a cipher, and locate subjectivity in narrative in the turbulent "space" between "He" and "I," where the one turns constantly into the other. It is this "space" that Blanchot's relation to Kafka serves to elucidate.

[18] *The Diaries of Franz Kafka. 1910–1923* (New York: Schocken, 1988, 384).

Like Jouhandeau, therefore, Kafka too discovered a "literary" *I*; he too described writing as a move to an "objective stage" within his own subjectivity. He "objectified" his suffering not by making it into the suffering of a novel character, but by writing "I am unhappy." Yet Kafka's "lesson," Blanchot goes on, is that what he called a "merciful surplus of strength"—the *Überfluss* released by writing—required, as it did for Goethe, more than lyrical effusion: its truth could only appear in what he calls "an objective fiction," in other words in a third-person novel. The mode of first-person writing that is "more than lyrical effusion"—Jouhandeau's "objective *I*"—is left out of account in Kafka's case.

It is clear that as his own fictional writing is seeking to cross the threshold of a new first-person mode, Blanchot's relation to Kafka is problematical. Not only does he allow Kafka's originality to be overshadowed by the ambitions of an interesting but far less original writer[19]; he appears either unwilling or unable to acknowledge that Kafka has already discovered that *I* can be an objective fiction, so that his "lesson" does not concern the move to third-person fiction, but what occurs in his *Diaries*. Writing at more or less the same time, Claude-Edmonde Magny observes that *The Trial* began as an *Ich-Roman* and then continued in the third person,[20] and in a footnote, she goes so far as to misread the September 19 diary entry when she writes: "Kafka notes that when he is unhappy, he cannot write to someone 'I am unhappy,' but just 'Er ist unglücklich,' which means that he is obliged in effect to choose between saying nothing about what he is feeling, or talking about himself in the third person."[21] Though Blanchot does not make the point as explicitly, he seems at this stage to be aligning himself with Magny's position. In the years that follow, this misreading will continue to influence his approach to Kafka.

***

[19] Reading Jouhandeau's *Uncle Henry* and *My Own*, the two books in which Blanchot discerns the emergence of an "objective I," one is hard put to find anything that breaks new ground in the way he describes. See "*Le Saladier* de Marcel Jouhandeau," *L'Insurgé* 8, no. 3 (March 1937): 5; "Chaminadour," *Journal des Débats*, 4–5 (August 1941): 3; "L'œuvre de M. Jouhandeau,"May 19, 1943, 3, and "Chaminadour," in *Faux pas*, trans. Charlotte Mandell (Stanford: Stanford University Press, 2001), 227–33.

[20] Claude-Edmonde Magny, *Essai sur les limites de la littérature. Les sandales d'Empédocle* (Paris: Petite Bibliothèque Payot/Boudry: Éditions de la Baconnière, 1945), 266.

[21] Ibid., 266 n. 4. The whole of Magny's argument in the conclusion to what in 1945 bore the title *Les Sandales d'Empédocle* emphasizes the third-person nature of Kafka's writing: "Even more symptomatic are firstly, the series of *Meditations* where, having first written 'Meine gesitige Armut …', he replaces it with 'Abrahams geistige Armut …', and elsewhere substitutes *er* for *Ich*; and also the Er *Auszeichnungen*, in which some fragments that begin in the first person end up saying *Er*" (ibid.).

In 1945, Blanchot enters the intense debates surrounding Kafka's work in postwar France with an article that strikes a note of considerable severity. He begins by deploring "the disorder in which Kafka's work is being presented to us," and denounces "opportunistic publishers" who have effectively pulverized Kafka's work, leaving it prey to "the disorder of multiple translations" and "the chatter of commentary." He sums up this situation as a "disaster." These are harsh words, and despite a passing acknowledgment of Pierre Klossowski's role in saving Kafka's texts from what he again calls a "disaster," the tone of the piece, which opens and closes with the assertion that Kafka's reception is based on a misunderstanding, is far from congenial. And in defending what he calls "this silent work," "these unpublishable books," and describing Kafka as "an enigma that wants to escape being seen," Blanchot sounds less like a critic than a jealous, possessive reader, determined to warn off others rather than allow them access to Kafka's work.[22]

In the second paragraph, however, a further intention becomes apparent. The misunderstanding he denounces concerns the widespread conviction that Kafka is "something more than a writer," even though he himself "wanted only to be a writer." The source of both of these viewpoints and hence of the tension between them is, says Blanchot, the *Diaries*. By their nature, they encourage critics to interpret this "something more" in non literary terms, and to turn Kafka's life into the true focus of his work. It is the case, he acknowledges, that *The Trial* and *The Castle* "refer us back endlessly to a truth outside of literature,"[23] and because of the *Diaries*, critics feel authorized to extract general truths about the human condition from them: "they foreground someone who has lived rather than someone who has written."[24] But things are more complex: if the novels contain a "truth outside of literature," that "outside" does not coincide with what we assume to be the domain of non literary truth, namely, rational thought. Why? Because according to Blanchot, "we begin to betray that truth as soon as it draws us away from literature, with which, however, it cannot be confused."[25]

---

[22]  Maurice Blanchot, "La lecture de Kafka," *L'Arche* 11 (November 1945): 107–16; "Reading Kafka," in *The Work of Fire*, trans. Charlotte Mandell (Stanford: Stanford University Press, 1995), 1–11. The references to "opportunistic publishers" and the "disorder of multiple translations" are omitted in 1949 from *The Work of Fire*. (In references to this work, the translation has frequently been modified.)

[23]  Ibid., 2.

[24]  Ibid., 1.

[25]  Ibid., 2.

Some years later he will make this point again with reference to *The Castle*: if K. may be said to attain a death that is not the imperfect one we have to be content with in life, but "another death, unknown, invisible, unnamed and what is more, inaccessible," this encounter takes place "not within the limits of the book," but in what Blanchot calls "the silence of what lies beyond the book," which he alters in 1970 to read "the silence of the absence of the book" (F 251). There is thus written into Kafka's fiction a relation between literature and what lies outside of it, which cannot be accounted for in rational terms, because that "outside," while being absolutely distinct from fiction, is accessible only through the fiction. Between the "outside" provided by rational thought and the "outside" onto which the fiction opens, no continuity exists: "Whoever stays with the story penetrates into something opaque that he does not understand, while whoever holds to the meaning cannot get back to the darkness of which it is the tell-tale light" (WF 4). One either reads the fiction, in which case all commentary becomes impossible; or one mistakes the "something more" encountered there for a general truth about humanity, and this means neglecting the fiction altogether.

If at first the *Diaries* appear to encourage the latter option, it is because "Kafka himself set the example by commenting occasionally on his tales and trying to clarify their meaning." But there is a difference in Blanchot's view: Kafka does not transpose his narratives onto a more accessible level: "the language of commentary embeds itself in fiction and is indistinguishable from it." Any rational perspective on the novels, including Kafka's own in the *Diaries*, is thus an illusion: "The *Diaries* are full of remarks that seem linked to a theoretical knowledge that is easily recognised. But these thoughts remain foreign to the generalisation from which they take their shape: they are there as if in exile, they fall back into an equivocal style that does not allow them to be understood either as the expression of a single event or as the explanation of a universal truth" (2). Each in their way, novel and diary expose the reader to an "outside" that cannot be accounted for in rational terms.

The question arises: where does this leave the critic? Whether approaching Kafka by way of his novels, or adopting the perspective provided by the *Diaries*, Kafka's reader cannot escape the domain of literature according to Blanchot. Nothing exists outside of literature except the outside onto which literature opens. In this situation, how can the critic even begin to speak about Kafka's work?

\*\*\*

This dilemma lies at the heart of Maurice Blanchot's activity as a critic in the years following the war. In the opening pages of "The Experience of Lautréamont" in *Lautréamont and Sade* he observes that "when it comes to the books that he loves best, the critic would prefer not to speak of them … The critic, because of this, is by nature given to silence" (LS 46).[26] And in "The Language of Fiction," which appeared in *The Work of Fire* in 1949, he repeats this idea: "Too many interpreters tell us too clearly what Kafka wanted, what he was, what he sought in his existence and his writings, for us not to want to return to silence a work that wished only for silence" (WF 81). The "silent work" he refers to in 1945 calls for silence on the critic's part. In Kafka's case, however, that critical silence is not a matter of choice: for him, as we saw, Kafka's novels are by nature inaccessible from any outside that does not lie within them, while his *Diaries* plunge the reader back into the fictional domain.

At the beginning of the essay on Lautréamont, Blanchot confronts this dilemma: even when an author's work leaves the critic with no rational standpoint from which to approach it, "commentary is inevitable" (LS 55). The critic must speak, even though he would prefer not to, and in Kafka's case, is unable to do so. This is not just a sterile and ultimately hypocritical paradox. The turmoil into which this dilemma plunges Lautréamont's reader offers an unexpected opportunity: "To read *Maldoror* is to go into a spin," and the reader is "a drunkenness launched into a headlong fall and an inertia that lets itself be engulfed." He continues: "In these conditions, how could he have the desire, and the means, to regain enough balance to discern where he is falling? He just plunges on. That is his commentary" (47–48). There are echoes here of Blanchot's description of what happens in Kafka's *Diaries*: "the language of his commentaries sinks into the fiction and is indistinguishable from it." And in "The Language of Fiction," he accepts that this must also be the activity of the critic: "we must plunge the interpretation back into the heart of the story, lose it there and lose sight of it, and grasp again the movement of the fiction whose details assert only themselves" (WF 83).

In suspending rational judgment, literature reserves the possibility for the mind of both writer and reader to be "something more" than either literature or rational thought, by allowing the mind somehow to enter a mode that Blanchot calls "commentary." What he claims vis-à-vis commentary no longer simply amounts to a paradox of the impossibility and necessity of interpretation, which

---

[26]   In references to this work, the translation has frequently been modified.

would at least allow the mind to keep its bearings. In escaping the rational mode, "commentary" is itself an escape, what Blanchot describes in "Reading Kafka" as "an escaping flood between … two streams" [*une nage fuyante entre … deux eaux*], making it something akin to Kafka's *Überfluss*: a yielding to the "something more" that literature contains, and which is at the same time a negativity that is accessible only in the silence or absence of the book. Commentary thus rides the tide of absolute negativity. In "Reading Kafka" Blanchot says: "Kafka's entire work is in search of an affirmation that it wants to gain by negation" (7). However, the negativity at work in it exceeds any rational frame. Its result is not the coexistence of different interpretations, but "for each theory, the mysterious possibility of seeming sometimes to have a negative meaning, sometimes a positive one" (6). Blanchot refuses to categorize this "mysterious possibility" in rational terms: "Even ambiguity does not satisfy us, for ambiguity is a compromise that seizes a shifting, changing truth, whereas the truth that is waiting for these writings is perhaps unique and simple …. Contradiction does not reign in this world" (5). And in "The Language of Fiction" he develops this idea: "The passage from yes to no, from no to yes, is the rule here, and any interpretation that avoids this (including the one that establishes this alternation) contradicts the movement that makes it possible" (83). And having offered a brief interpretation of his own of the story of K in *The Castle*, he concludes: "it is clear that such an interpretation seeks in vain to contain the ambiguity of a proposition in which assertion and negation are continuously threatening to achieve reciprocity. As long as it is couched in the well-defined form of an abstract thought, it escapes the verdict it renders" (83).

Commentary thus has no basis. Its inevitability is that of headlong plunge through the turbulent space that Blanchot evokes in relation to the reader of Lautréamont and the writer of Kafka's *Diaries*, in which absolute negativity is at the same time "something more." "In literature," he writes in "Literature and the Right to Death," "ambiguity is … abandoned to its excesses" (341). Commentary exists only in that mode. But the form it might take for his own critical writing remains difficult to grasp. In the years that follow, Blanchot will return repeatedly to the *Diaries*, pursuing his resistance to Kafka's use of *I* at one level, while at another, discovering in the *Diaries* the promise of a new and original literary mode.

✳✳✳

In "Kafka and Literature," written in 1949, Blanchot refers directly to Claude-Edmonde Magny's view that Kafka discovered the potential of literature when he saw it as a move from *Ich* to *Er*. This view, he says, has its limitations, because it omits to acknowledge that although Kafka's novels are about imagined characters, they are at the same time also about Kafka: "It seems the further he got from himself, the more present he became" (21). Blanchot appears to be moving toward a more complex understanding of the relation between subjectivity and objectivity in Kafka than he displayed in "The Literary *I*." Yet the dominant mode of Kafka's writing still remains firmly that of the third-person novel for him: "Fiction's narrative shapes a distance, a gap (itself fictive) inside the one writing, without which he could not express himself. This distance must become even deeper as the writer participates more in his narrative" (21). Consequently, he goes on, "it is not enough for me to write '*I* am unhappy.' As long as I write nothing else, I am too close to myself, too close to my unhappiness, for this unhappiness to become really mine in the form of language: I am not yet truly unhappy. It is only from the moment I arrive at this strange substitution, '*He* is unhappy,' that language begins to be formed into a language that is unhappy for me" (21–22). This is in effect what Claude-Edmonde Magny wrote in 1943, but it is not what Kafka said in his *Diaries*. If Blanchot can now acknowledge that Kafka is "more present," the more he writes *Er*, he still appears unwilling to grant any significance to the way Kafka's *Diaries* write *Ich*.

Yet in "The Paradox of Aytré," written in 1946, Blanchot has already begun to adopt a different approach. Once again, he cites Kafka's diary entry: "Kafka is amazed that man, at the height of unhappiness, can write 'I am unhappy.' Where, he says, does this excess of strength come from, that allows me to communicate my exhaustion without making it false?" (69). Here, Blanchot leaves aside the question of personal pronouns, to focus on Kafka's claim that writing produces an excess of strength: "perhaps what Kafka calls overabundance or excess is really a reduction, a retreat before my natural being, an emptiness both in regard to my sorrowful state and in regard to words" (69–70). And he concludes:

> He seems to believe that this awareness of unhappiness is, with regard to unhappiness, a kind of increase, a surplus, a plus sign that might be a challenge to the minus that unhappiness implies. But why? How could the fact that the darkness that torments me rises to a kind of transparency be some kind of good, and a remnant of luck? I see in it much more the first stirrings of a fundamental deprivation, and this destiny of mine of being always separated from myself, of not being able to hold on to anything and of having to let slip, between myself and what happens to me, an original silence, the silence of consciousness by which the sense that deprives me of it comes to each of my moments. (70)

There follows an extended reflection on the negativity that is deployed when I write "I am unhappy." The "silence of consciousness" that slips in between me and what happens to me if I simply *say* "I am unhappy" occurs in what Blanchot calls "a first emptiness" whose effects are entirely negative, but which "the fullness and security of ordinary language" will always seek to reduce to itself. At this level, the words display the same condition as any utterance. A simple negativity of a broadly Hegelian nature is at work alongside them. But then "The 'I am unhappy' enters literature" (70). Now, emptiness is deprived of the reassuring company of the fullness of language because, apart from the words that have acquired literary status, the rest of language has been nullified, since those words cannot be replaced by any others. It is "as if a new world really were beginning, a new field of language in the complete and definitive ruin of everyday language" (72). Out of absolute negation there emerges "something more." It is possible, says Blanchot, to wonder at this beginning and attribute it to an excess of strength, but in fact it is inseparable from an end. And making explicit the Mallarméan turn that he gives to Hegel's thought in this period, he goes on: "From one of its sides, poetry makes sense, but from another, it unmakes it … It dangerously connects the possibility of speaking with an impossibility that is so to speak its condition" (71). This echoes what Blanchot says about the emergence of an "objective" *I* in Jouhandeau: "As for the significance of such a change, it would be very dangerous to try to discover it,"[27] and in "Kafka and Literature" he describes the unrealizable "non-language" to which all language aspires as a "striving towards a dangerous horizon where it seeks in vain to disappear" (WF 22). If to write "I am unhappy" when I cannot say I am unhappy appears at an initial level to be a gift of fortune, at a second level, it exposes the writer to "an experience full of risk" before which the critic in his turn hesitates, because it also exposes the writer to "a silent stuttering [*ânonnement*] whose perfection does not prevent us from recognizing it as a lack" (71).

This analysis displays a much greater receptiveness to what is going on in Kafka's *Diaries* than has so far been the case. If the level of Blanchot's resistance to what the September 19 entry says remains constant, it has ceased to function as a mechanism for blocking what his own insight tells him about Kafka's "objective *I*," and exposed something about that *I* that overflows the bounds of the *Ich–Er* alternation entirely: a "silent stuttering" that turns the written *I* into the site of a perpetual interruption (which is precisely the mode of first-person

---

[27] Blanchot, "The Literary *I*."

narrative discourse that is being developed in *The Most High*, and especially in *Death Sentence* at the same time).

Blanchot returns once again to Kafka's *Diaries* in 1952, a year after the appearance of the complete German version, and pursues his critique of Kafka's positive interpretation of the role of writing. "Kafka and the demand of the work" begins with the following words: "Someone begins to write, determined by despair. But despair cannot *determine* anything: 'It has always, and right away exceeded its purpose.' (Kafka, *Diaries*, 1910)" (SL 57). Although this quotation comes from an earlier diary entry, Blanchot's intention from the outset in this article is to question further the relation that Kafka establishes between being unhappy and writing. On the one hand, writing can only arise out of "true despair" which, like unhappiness, reduces whoever experiences it to silence. But whereas in 1917 Kafka will present *Überfluss* as an arc linking the *I* who experiences unhappiness and the *I* who writes "I am unhappy," in 1910 it is experience itself that is characterized by an *excess* or *Überfluss* according to Kafka. The simple arc is absolutely interrupted as a consequence. *Überfluss* does not relate writing to experience in a productive manner; rather, it sweeps writing *and* experience (of despair, of unhappiness) away from any fixed basis on which a relation between them could be established: "the two movements—writing, despair—have nothing in common but their own indeterminacy." All that links them is a discontinuity within *Überfluss*.

Now, therefore, Blanchot is no longer arguing, as he did in 1949, that "I am unhappy" can only become literature by being transposed into the words "He is unhappy." If he can write in *The Infinite Conversation*: "as has been shown (*The Space of Literature*), to write is to pass from 'I' to 'he' " (IC 380), *The Space of Literature* also makes abundantly clear that the movement from "I" to "he" is traversed by another movement which is "much more profound" (SL 26), in which "I become no one" (28), "a faceless third person" (30), and which results in an "infinite dispersal" (33). This perspective is unchanged in *The Infinite Conversation*, where Blanchot says the movement from "I" to "he" leaves "he" not just "split in two" (IC 381), but mobile, fragmented, plural.[28] Hence, the *Überfluss* that Kafka attributes to his experience in 1910 does not only become the site of an interruption when it is repeated as writing. More than this, it calls into question the adherence to the personal—*Ich* or *Er*—that characterizes not just Kafka's 1917 diary entry, but Blanchot's own previous understanding of it:

---

[28] See *The Infinite Conversation*, trans. Susan Hanson (Minneapolis and London: University of Minnesota Press, 1993), 384, n.2.

"no one can say to himself, 'I am in despair,' but only 'You are in despair?'. And no one can affirm, 'I am writing,' but only 'Are you writing? Yes? Could you be writing?'" (SL 57; translation modified). The twofold indeterminacy that links experience and writing expels the mind from the domain of individual identity entirely, turning the unhappy or despairing subject who writes into nothing other than a dual question, the space of a twofold inversion or turning back that recalls the "silent stuttering" that Blanchot evokes in 1947, and renders experience, writing, and the relation between them fundamentally uncertain.

***

Despite Blanchot's sustained resistance to Kafka's use of *I* to write of his suffering, the priority he gives from the outset to the *Diaries* over the novels is maintained and developed over the coming years. In 1947 he readily acknowledges their literary importance. Kafka wanted to write like Flaubert and Dickens: "In his *Diaries* we see him constantly trying out descriptions of that type, and creating little scenes that use every means available to achieve precision."[29] And on two occasions in the 1950s he pursues his analysis of their originality. He begins a study of Henry James in 1954 by contrasting the way James uses his *Notebooks* with what Kafka does in his *Diaries*. The *Diaries*, he says, contain many drafts, "but these drafts are the work itself—sometimes a page or a single sentence, but this sentence is involved in the profundity of the story, and if it is an experimental search, it is the story's own search for itself, a path that the unforeseeable movement of novel writing can alone open up. These fragments are not materials that are later used" (BC 126). He cites Borges's claim that the subject of *The Trial* makes it one of the most admirable modern works, but then asks, "what is a subject?" In the case of *The Trial*, "The story of a man grappling with himself as with an obscure tribunal before which he cannot justify himself because he cannot find it is certainly worthy of interest, but it is scarcely a story, even less a fiction and, for Kafka, it was the basis of his life" (128; translation modified). And though he says no more about Kafka here, when he concludes that "the subject of *The Turn of the Screw* is—simply—James's art" (130), there can be no doubt that he also has Kafka in mind. Furthermore, by saying that the "subject" of *The Trial* is "scarcely a story, even less a fiction," but the basis of Kafka's life, he is again by implication pointing to the *Diaries* and their use of fiction as "the story's own search for itself" as the true center of Kafka's work.

---

[29]    Blanchot, "Du merveilleux," 121.

It is becoming clear now that Blanchot's reluctance to speak of Kafka's novels in 1945 was much more than a tactical move. And if his persistence in challenging Kafka's use of the pronoun *I* can be read at one level as a Bloomian "swerve," it is also motivated by a concern to identify the true originality of the *Diaries*. A year after the article on James, he returns to the issue. "The writer," he argues in "Diary and Story," "can keep the diary only of the work he does not write." Diary and literary work are radically separate; they cannot coexist; there is no continuity possible from one to the other. And generalizing a claim that he originally made about Kafka's *Diaries* he goes on: "this diary can be written only by becoming imaginary and by immersing itself, like the one who writes it, in the unreality of fiction." And he concludes: "This fiction does not necessarily have to do with the work it prepares." He then brings Kafka in again: "Kafka's *Diary* is made not only of dated notes that relate to his life, … but of a great number of drafts of stories, some of which are a few pages, most a few lines, all unfinished, though often already formed, and—what is most striking of all—almost none relates to another, none is the resumption of a theme already used, nor does it have a clear connection with the events of the day" (187).

The view of the diary being proposed here is complex and radical. The difference between the fictions in the diary and the work it prepares is complemented by a difference between the diary and the life of the person who keeps it. There is no simple relation between art and life for the writer. The diary does not belong to the writer's life, while his novel belongs to the world of imagination: the diary exists neither in the life nor in the work; it exists between them, borrowing aspects from each but reducible to neither. This can be understood simply, as Blanchot cites Marthe Robert doing, by seeing the diary as situated *structurally* between life and art. This is how he himself seemed to represent the relation in 1949, when he wrote that "Fiction's narrative shapes a distance, a gap (itself fictive) inside the one writing," so that the first-person language of the diary must be converted into the third-person form to have any validity. In neither case are the *Diaries* granted any independent existence. Now, however, the *fictive gap* that narrative opens up in the writer has found its own mode of discourse: "We also have the presentiment that these fragments constitute the anonymous, obscure traces of the book that is trying to be realised, but only in so far as they do not have a visible connection with the life from which they seem to come, nor with the work to which they form the approach" (187; translation modified). The "between" dimension that the diary occupies separates it absolutely both from the writer's life and from his art, and, in so doing, makes *separation* the only relation that exists between the two.

The description of the diary entry as one made up of fragments anticipates much later developments in Blanchot's thinking, but also recalls what he writes in 1945: "Kafka's main stories are fragments, and the totality of the work is a fragment" (WF 6). This introduces a lack which, he says, could explain the uncertainty that affects both their form and their content. But this lack is not accidental, which is to say it does not affect these works from without: "it is incorporated in the very meaning that it mutilates; it coincides with the representation of an absence that is neither tolerated nor rejected." At the heart of the ambiguity expressed here there is a lack, which, however, "is not a lacuna, it is the sign of an impossibility that is present everywhere and is never admitted" (6). As Blanchot will go on to show, what is simply impossible from a rational perspective opens onto a new and original mode of literary space. And as his own writing develops in the direction of what he will term "fragmentary writing," Kafka's *Diaries* will remain in the forefront of his attention.

✳✳✳

Superficially, Blanchot's interest in Kafka's *Diaries* could well appear to do no more than justify his own struggle to find a critical voice in the postwar era, and confirm his seemingly self-defeating claim that the sole mode in which the critic can legitimately express himself is that of silence. Unable to talk about Kafka's works, he falls back on what Kafka himself said about writing them. This would not seem to be a very promising move for a critic, and Tzvetan Todorov expresses what many readers of Blanchot have no doubt felt when he writes: "Numerous pages comment on Kafka's diaries and his letters, but only rarely is there any mention of *The Castle*. But surely it is because of the latter that we read the former."[30] In fact, Blanchot has discovered an entirely new project for the critic. Where Kafka's characters take him as he moves from *Ich* to *Er* is accessible only to Kafka and to the reader of his novels for as long as they are reading. Outside of the novel that dimension is inaccessible. There is therefore nothing that a critic can say about it. But readers of the *Diaries*, says Blanchot in 1959, occasionally have "the feeling of being close to crossing a threshold" (F 253). This does not lead to the intimacy of an individual *Ich*, nor is it the door to the

---

[30]  Tzvetan Todorov, "La réflexion sur la littérature dans la France contemporaine," *Poétique* 38 (April 1979): 136.

closed world of the novel. As he wrote a few years earlier: "the one who, in the work, leaves the objectivity of the stories for the intimate language of the *Diaries*, descends ... through an even darker night in which can be heard the cries of a man who is lost" (244; translation modified). At this threshold, the *Überfluss* which constitutes the new relation of self with self (the new subjectivity) that Kafka found in writing is encountered as a hyperbolic overflow of absolute negativity that turns writing into something akin to a gasp, a stutter, a cry of simultaneous agony and relief at being able to bring suffering into language.[31] It is to the *fragmentary* potential of this stertorous mode that Blanchot's writing will increasingly turn.

***

The foundational importance of Kafka's *Diaries* to Blanchot's project is confirmed in an opening footnote to "Kafka and the Work's Demand" in *The Space of Literature*: "His is ... not only a 'Journal' as we understand this genre today, but the very movement of the experience of writing" (SL 57). Earlier in the same work, however, what Blanchot terms the "recourse to the 'Journal'" is presented as a strategy that writers use to ward off what is most extreme about that experience: "The journal represents the series of reference points which a writer establishes in order to keep track of himself when he begins to suspect the dangerous metamorphosis to which he is exposed" (29). And he concludes: "Writers who keep a journal are sometimes the most literary of all, but perhaps this is precisely because in this way they avoid the extreme of literature" (29–30; translation modified). How do Kafka's *Diaries* avoid this avoidance? For Blanchot, they do and they don't, and this ambiguity reflects the extraordinary relation that he establishes with Kafka from the 1940s on, a relation of both proximity and distance which is reflected in the title that he gives in 1981 to his collected writings on the author: *From Kafka to Kafka*.[32] Kafka is Blanchot's constant companion, and in his last major work, *The Writing of the Disaster*, which appeared a year earlier, in 1980, Kafka is invoked increasingly frequently as the book reaches its close. At one level, he is made to epitomize the writer as

---

[31]  In *Kafka: Toward a Minor Literature*, trans. Dana Polan (Minneapolis and London: University of Minnesota Press, 1986 [1975]), Gilles Deleuze and Félix Guattari identify "the sub-humanness of becoming-animal" in Kafka's novels (23; translation modified), and say of his relation to German: "he will make it cry with an extremely sober and rigorous cry, ... use syntax in order to cry, ... give a syntax to the cry" (26).

[32]  Maurice Blanchot, *De Kafka à Kafka* (Paris: Gallimard, 1981).

Blanchot now sees him. The effort to undermine the power of what he terms "the One" is the focus of all writerly activity for Blanchot. It is, he says, "the combat of the disaster," and it is also "in a way, Kafka's combat" (WD 140). But only "in a way." Because Kafka's combat is also described as "for the One against the One," and then as "a sort of combat through literature for literature" (140–141). Present in the structure of these formulations is the same loop of *Überfluss* to be found in the title *From Kafka to Kafka*. But whereas for Blanchot, to write is to enter that loop and in so doing to interrupt it, the way he formulates Kafka's "combat" indicates that for him, Kafka remains in thrall to the One in the very act of struggling against it, and perpetually confined within the limits of literature.

In so far as the "combat of the disaster" is also "a combat for literature" in Kafka's case, it therefore falls short of its goal in Blanchot's eyes. It is certainly interminable: the hero of *The Castle* can never give up, however exhausted he becomes, because he cannot die: "the coming [*avènement*] of his death ... is changed into an interminable nonarrival [*non-avènement*]" (141). But a few pages further on, in what appears to be an allusion to Deleuze and Guattari's view of Kafka, Blanchot argues that to interpret what he calls "Kafka's trial" as a process that can overcome the transcendence of the One by endlessly reducing Law to laws and then to rules is possible only if one presupposes a fourth position, "that of the pre-eminence [*surplomb*] of literature itself," even though "literature refuses this privileged standpoint" (144; translation modified). Whereas for Deleuze and Guattari there is no transcendence in Kafka's novels, which they describe as "a limitless field of immanence,"[33] for Blanchot, what is interminable about them is the product of transcendence. In *The Space of Literature* he cites Kafka's use of the term *Tat-Beobachtung* ("a seeing of what is really taking place") in his *Diaries* to define what he terms "the strange, mysterious, perhaps dangerous, perhaps saving consolation that there is in writing,"[34] before observing: "Here literature is proclaimed as the power which frees ...; it is the liberating passage from the first to the third person, from observation of oneself ... to a higher observation, rising above mortal reality towards the other world, the world of freedom" (SL 73). Thus the endless task of combating transcendence endlessly presupposes what it combats. Because literature never ceases to ensure transcendence for Kafka, he is never quite the writer he has the potential to be in Blanchot's eyes. He repeatedly shies away from "the extreme of literature" that Blanchot terms fragmentary

---

[33]  Gilles Deleuze and Félix Guattari, *Kafka: Towards a Minor Literature*, Trans. Dana Polan (Minneapolis: University of Minnesota Press, 1986, 51, 86.

[34]  *The Diaries of Franz Kafka. 1910–1923*, entry for January 27, 1922, 406–407 (translation modified).

writing or "the writing of the disaster." Kafka "vacillates pathetically" (75), and he does so because of the priority he grants to life over writing: "It can be said that the debate with his father pushed the negative aspect of the literary experience into the background for him" (74). As a result, literature always appeared to him as a form of salvation, whereas according to Blanchot, "art is primarily the consciousness of unhappiness, not its compensation" (75).

If Kafka's *Diaries* contain "the very movement of the experience of writing" (whereas usually the journal provides writers with a means for avoiding that movement); but if for much of the time Kafka avoids that movement too in Blanchot's view, what is there specifically about the *Diaries* that allows him to make such a claim? The answer lies in the relation between I and I out of which any journal arises. While Kafka is all too ready in Blanchot's view to make the simple move from I to He that the novel allows, his *Diaries* never leave the domain of the I. And whereas the move to He does not call into question the underlying unity of the person—what Blanchot calls, in the fragment on "Kafka's combat" in *The Writing of the Disaster* "the transcendental 'I'" (WD 140)—the "I" of Kafka's *Diaries* offers a means of interrupting that unity and that transcendence with an *Überfluss* which unseats and dislocates the unitary subject.

This brings into perspective the seeming contradiction that allows Blanchot's own narrative practice to move in the opposite direction from the one he identifies in Kafka, abandoning novels in the third person in favor of the first-person *récit*. In a triptych of narratives written between 1948 and 1951, then in a further diptych written between 1957 and 1962, the relation between I and I is progressively made to accommodate the shifting, impersonal persistence of a third person which is neither He nor It: "the desert become our companion" as Blanchot writes in *The Infinite Conversation*, and which will come into its own in 1972, as the governing pronoun in the first of his two "fragmentary" works, that is, *The Step Not Beyond* (IC 171). This work, which begins uncharacteristically in autobiographical mode, with a reminiscence of the first words of Blanchot's first novel ("*he—the sea*") (SNB 1; translation modified),[35] immediately moves away from the autobiographical ("I will try in vain to represent him to myself, he who I was not") (2), toward a reflection on the third-person pronoun (he/it) that has now emerged as the impersonal subject of writing:

---

[35] Nelson chooses to translate *il* as "it" here, despite the fact that it refers to the protagonist of the novel, Thomas.)

If I write he/it, denouncing it rather than indicating it, at least I know that, far from giving it a rank, a role or a presence which would elevate it above anything that could designate it, it is I who, starting from there, enter into the relation in which "I" accepts solidification into a fictional or functional identity, in order that the game of writing may be played, in which he/it is either the partner and (at the same time) the product and the gift, or the bet, the stake, which, as such and as the principal player, plays, changes, moves around and takes the place of change itself, a displacement without placing and that is missing from any placing. (4)

Blanchot has at last made the move from "I" to "he" that he both endorses and resists in Kafka. By reversing that move, subsuming it within the endless movement between I and I to be found in Kafka's *Diaries*, then disrupting that continuum of *Überfluss* with an impersonal he/it that reduces I to no more than a function, "a canonic abbreviation, representing the law of the same, fractured in advance" (6), he simultaneously espouses Kafka's position entirely and introduces into it what Kafka himself excludes. "What Kafka teaches us," he writes in *The Infinite Conversation*, "is that storytelling brings the neutral into play" (IC 563). And all art, he writes elsewhere in the same volume "opens us up to a sort of neutrality where we cease being ourselves and oscillate strangely between I, He and no one" (366; translation modified). In this light, it is possible to see both *The Step Not Beyond* and *The Writing of the Disaster* as the diary that Kafka did not keep: the authentic diary of a writer and truly, the diary of a nobody.

# 9

# "I Hear My Destiny in the Rustling of an Oak": Blanchot's Char

## Kevin Hart

In 1953, one of his *anni mirabiles* for critical writing, Maurice Blanchot turns to René Char on two occasions, each time making a very large claim for his significance.[1] In the April of that year in "La Bête de Lascaux" he heralds him as "a poet linked with our destiny," and two months later in "Où va la littérature?" he is deemed to be, like Hölderlin, "Poet of the poet, poet in whom the possibility, or impossibility, of singing is made song." Char's poetry "answers" the German's over a century later, we are told, and in this contemporary Frenchman's writing we find "a form of experienced time [*durée*] very different from the time that simple historical analysis grasps."[2] On the first occasion Char is allied with Heraclitus, and his poetry is approached by way of the *Phaedrus*, while on the second occasion he is introduced with reference to Heidegger's elucidations of Hölderlin. The poetry is bookended by major philosophers at the dawn and evening of the West. Blanchot will value other French poets over the course of his long life, including Yves Bonnefoy and Louis-René des Forêts, but among his contemporaries Char will always have a privileged place, and not for purely literary or literary historical reasons.

[1] Blanchot had written on Char earlier. See his "René Char," *Critique* 5 (octobre 1946): 387–99; "René Char," in *The Work of Fire*, trans. Charlotte Mandell (Stanford: Stanford University Press, 1995), 98–110. The essay is an unimpressed review of Georges Mounin, *Avez-vous lu Char?* (Paris: Gallimard, 1946).

[2] Maurice Blanchot, "The Beast of Lascaux," in *A Voice from Elsewhere*, trans. Charlotte Mandell (Albany: State University of New York Press, 2007), 40, and "The Disappearance of Literature," in *The Book to Come*, trans. Charlotte Mandell (Stanford: Stanford University Press, 2003), 198. "La Bête de Lascaux" was first published in *Nouvelle Nouvelle Revue Française* 4 (avril 1953): 684–93, without the quotation of "La Bête innommable," and "Où va la littérature?" in *Nouvelle Nouvelle Revue Française,* 7 (juillet 1953): 98–107, with the reference to Char on 102. Blanchot had associated Char and Hölderlin a year beforehand in "L'Art, la littérature et l'expérience originelle," *Les Temps Moderne* 79 (mai 1952): 2210, which was reprinted in *L'Espace littéraire* (Paris: Gallimard, 1955), 277–333.

Nowhere in "La Bête de Lascaux," for instance, does Blanchot fold an appeal to the "primitive" art of the cave, which had been open to the public since 1948, into a case for Char as an exemplary modernist poet.[3] Char's collaborations with Braque, Kandinsky, Klee, Matisse, Miró, and Picasso, now all secure figures in the canon of modernist visual art, are nowhere mentioned.[4] At no time does he point to Char's schooling in surrealism, a movement he greatly prizes, as a prime credential for his standing in the pantheon of the avant-garde or as a representative of what we would tend to call these days "late modernism."[5] And he never dilates on formal concerns in Char's poetry—his lack of interest in *facture des vers* as prized by the Parnassians, his taste for *vers libre* and the prose poem (and even short prose texts), and so on—as distancing him from Symbolism, *l'art pour l'art*, and other literary movements that preceded him.[6] Rather, Blanchot figures Char by way of the philosophical, ancient and modern, and the political, with reference to the sacred.

Blanchot's reading of Char takes place in a context far broader than literary history, indeed far more capacious than literature, a category he will increasingly distrust, and wider even than history, which he regards Char's poetry as puncturing so as to indicate something neither truly ancient nor truly modern, a ceaseless hollowing of being as it becomes image in the act of writing, which he will name "the Outside" [*le Dehors*].[7] Note that Blanchot does not say "an image"; he has no commitment to imagism, unlike modernists such as Eliot and Pound, but is concerned with image as the state in which beings seem to disappear when captured by art, a borderless realm that fascinates us. "Our destiny," if we are mid-century French speakers, is to follow Char so that we may experience the Outside and thereby overcome any mistaken commitments to "being" or "unity" that we may hold. More than this is in play, as will become evident, but for now let us see how this is thought to happen.

\*\*\*

---

[3] Blanchot's interest in Lascaux, oriented by Bataille's study of the cave, continued. See his "Naissance de l'art," *Nouvelle Nouvelle Revue Française* 35 (novembre 1955): 923–33, translated as "The Birth of Art," *Friendship*, trans. Elizabeth Rottenberg (Stanford: Stanford University Press, 1997), 1–11.

[4] On Char's collaborations with visual artists, see Rosemary Lancaster, *Poetic Illumination: René Char and his Artist Allies* (Amsterdam: Rodopi, 2010).

[5] See Blanchot, "Reflections on Surrealism," in *The Work of Fire*, 85–97.

[6] Yet Char is perfectly capable of writing formal verse. See, for example, "Complainte du lézard amoureux," in *Oeuvres complètes*, intro. Jean Roudaut, Bibliothèque de la Pléiade (Paris: Gallimard, 1995), 294.

[7] For Blanchot's reservations about aestheticism and its relation with literature, see *The Infinite Conversation*, trans. and foreword Susan Hanson (Minneapolis: University of Minnesota Press, 1993), xi.

Blanchot prefaces "La Bête de Lascaux" with a central lyric from the sequence of the same name, "La Bête innommable." What appears to Char in the figure of the so-called unicorn in Lascaux is "mère fantastiquement déguisée,/La Sagesse aux yeux pleins de larmes" (fantastically disguised mother:/Wisdom, her eyes full of tears). Yet what first appears to Blanchot in reading Char's lyric poem is a particular sort of speech, impersonal, which Socrates identifies in the *Phaedrus*.

A written speech merely offers "the appearance of wisdom [δοξόσοφοι], not true wisdom [σοφίας]," Socrates insists, because it allows people to recite compositions by others and so seem "to know many things, when they are for the most part ignorant and hard to get along with, since they are not wise but only appear wise."[8] So writing can readily be abused, especially by Sophists, and can impair one's ability to learn. When used properly, as Socrates urges in a story about the invention of writing by Theuth in Thebes, Upper Egypt, it serves to remind oneself of something, not to replace memory (*Phaedrus*, 275a). It remains an external prompt, not an internal process. Truth itself turns on what is written in the soul of the learner, which knows to whom it should speak and to whom it should not speak (*Phaedrus*, 276a-b). Blanchot also tells us that Socrates "rejects no less forcefully—but with more reverence—another impersonal language, the pure speech that seeks to articulate the sacred" (VE 37). "Prophetic utterances" came from the oak at Dodona, Socrates says; it is the oldest of Greek oracles. He then observes to Phaedrus of those who went to listen to it: "The people of that time, not being as wise [σοφοῖς] as you young folks, were content in their simplicity [εὐηθεία], to hear an oak or a rock, providing only that it spoke the truth; but to you, perhaps, it makes a difference who the speaker is and where he comes from, for you do not consider only whether his words are true" (*Phaedrus*, 275 b-c). And Phaedrus, who had cast doubt on the authenticity of Socrates's story of the invention of writing, now agrees with Socrates about the dangers of written speeches. He also accepts the rebuke: if something is true, it is true regardless of who says it.

Of course, Socrates is being ironic when he says that Phaedrus and his friends are "wise" and that their forebears enjoyed a state of "simplicity." Léon Robin's translation from the Greek, on which Blanchot relies, has Socrates say, "You others, you moderns [*les modernes*], want to know who it is who is speaking

---

[8]	Plato, *Phaedrus*, 275a-b, in Harold North Fowler, trans. *Euthyphro, Apology, Crito, Phaedo, Phaedrus*, intro. W. R. M. Lamb, Loeb Classical Library (Cambridge: Harvard University Press, 1914).

and what country he comes from."[9] More important, though, is that Blanchot misunderstands Socrates almost entirely. As he reads the lines, Socrates says, "We are no longer … the kind of people who are content to listen to the voice of the oak or the stone [*Nous ne sommes plus … de ceux qui se contentaient d'écouter la voix du chêne ou celle d'une pierre*]," and infers from this reading that "everything that is said against writing would serve, as well, to discredit the recited speech of the hymn [*l'hymne*]" (VE 37). Yet Socrates is not contrasting the modernity of Athens with the primitive belief in the oracle that one finds in Homer and perhaps long before him. Nor is he saying anything about religious hymns, presumably the Homeric hymns to the gods or something like them.[10] Hymns might have been recited at religious ceremonies at Dodona, but for Socrates the place is important for the oracles uttered there in response to bronze tripods hanging from branches of the oak tree (and so murmuring when the wind caresses the tree). Instead, Socrates is doing two things. First, as we have seen, he is saying that truth is truth, no matter where it comes from and who declares it. And second, he is obliquely recalling that the priestesses in a state of ecstasy orally communicate the truths of the god.[11] The allusion to Dodona and not to a mystery cult such as the one at Eleusis probably goes by way of the story, preserved by Herodotus, that the priestesses there were originally from Thebes in Upper Egypt.[12]

Char feels kinship with Heraclitus, Blanchot recalls, and the final lines of "La Bête innommable" might remind us that he was known in antiquity as the weeping philosopher. The association with Heraclitus allows Blanchot to pass to Fragment B 93: "The Lord whose oracle is in Delphi [not Dodona, note] neither indicates clearly nor conceals but gives a sign" (ὁ ἄναξ οὗ τὸ μαντεῖόν ἐστι τὸ ἐν Δελφοῖς οὔτε λέγει οὔτε κρύπτει ἀλλὰ σημαίνει).[13] Socrates desires language to be human and dialogic, not to come from an unknown origin,

---

[9]   See Léon Robin, ed., *Platon*, Édition de la Pléiade (Paris: Gallimard, 1944).
[10]  See Apostolos N. Athanassakis,*The Homeric Hymns*, trans. and intro. 2nd ed. (Baltimore: The Johns Hopkins University Press, 2004). Other hymns may well have been performed, but most likely not Orphic hymns, most of which come centuries after Plato. See Apostolos N. Athanassakis and Benjamin M. Wolkow, trans., and intro., *The Orphic Hymns* (Baltimore: The Johns Hopkins University Press, 2013).
[11]  See Homer, *Illiad*, XVI, Trans. Anthony Verity (New York and London: Oxford University Press, 2012), 233–35. For Dodona, see Walter Burket, *Greek Religion*, trans. John Raffin (Oxford: Basil Blackwell, 1985), 114.
[12]  A. D. Godley, trans., *Herodotus*, 4 vols. Loeb Classical Library (Cambridge: Harvard University Press, 1981), II, 54–57.
[13]  See Char, "Heraclitus d'Éphèse," in *Oeuvres complètes*, 720–21, and T. M. Robinson, trans., *Heraclitus: Fragments: A Text and Translation with a Commentary* (Toronto: University of Toronto Press, 1991), 57.

which is precisely what oracular language is. There are times, especially in *L'Entretien infini*, when Blanchot will insist on a more radical dialogue between human beings than one finds in Socrates, and will value Char's commitment to fragmentary writing, but here, as in his earlier piece on the poet, he gravitates to oracular speech, which he will use to give substance to the claim that Char's verse is "linked with our destiny."[14] The oracular utterances at Dodona were not hymns; they were mostly replies in the positive or negative to questions written on a tablet, and consequently not quite the same as the famously ambiguous oracles at Delphi. In freely associating Dodona and Delphi, Blanchot pushes what we know of Dodona further than is warranted: "Voice of the oak, rigorous and closed language of aphorism [*aphorisme*]" (VE 51). So oracle converges on aphorism, doubtless by way of Heraclitus's dark fragments. (Yet we remember Char telling us in *Seuls demeurent* (1938–44) "L'oracle ne me vassalise plus" [The oracle no longer subjugates me] and wonder what its status would be for Blanchot.[15])

To be sure, some of Char's poetry is intensely aphoristic—we think of "Afin qu'il n'y soit rien changé," "Partage formel," *Feuillets d'Hypnos* and "Rougeur des martinaux," and, well after the appearance of "La Bête de Lascaux," *L'Âge cassant* (1965)—and individual sentences in lyrics and prose poems alike are also angular, incisive and have the air of the absolute. Yet Char's remarks have no kinship with aphorisms that state principles or that sparkle with pithy social wit. The connection between oracle and aphorism allows Blanchot to comment on the two at one and the same time. He does so by way of an unusual understanding of "prophet" [προφήτης]:

> The language in which the origin speaks is essentially prophetic. That does not mean that it dictates future events [*les événements futurs*]; it means that it does not rely on something that already exists—neither on an already accepted truth nor on a language that has already been spoken or verified. It announces, because it begins. It indicates the future [*l'avenir*], because it does not yet speak: language of the future [*du futur*], insofar as it, itself, is already like a future language [*un langage futur*], which anticipates itself, finding its meaning and legitimacy only ahead of itself, that is to say fundamentally unjustified. (VE 41–42)

---

14   See Blanchot, *The Infinite Conversation*, 73–74, and for his association of Char and the fragmentary, "The Fragment Word" in the same volume, 308–10. Also see "René Char," 107.

15   Char, *Furor and Mystery and Other Writings*, trans. and ed. Mary Ann Caws and Nancy Kline, intro. Sandra Bermann, foreword Marie-Claude Char (Boston: Black Widow Press, 2010), 49; *Oeuvres complètes* Paris: Gallimard, 1983, 133.

Prophetic language, in this sense, will remain important to Blanchot. Four years later, with André Neher's *L'Essence du prophétisme* (1955) in mind, he will consecrate an essay to its role in Judaism, and will comment on its dialogic structure.[16] God speaks to the prophet who then speaks imperiously to the people or a king.[17] One might well think that the same is true in Greek religion: the god speaks to a priestess who then delivers an oracle. Yet Blanchot insists instead on the oracle's grounding in an unknown origin, a murmuring of the sacred tree, and relates it to the "closed language of aphorism" (51). When responding to prophecy in Judaism, and unmooring it from positive revelation, Blanchot cites Rimbaud and Claudel; when speaking of Dodona, and bracketing belief in the Olympian deities, he invokes Char and retains talk of oracles. For all these poets, no doubt, "the chance of the poem is to be able to escape prophetic intolerance" (46). How that chance is concretely played out in the three poets is left unclear, but it is claimed that it occurs in an exemplary manner with Char.

Prophetic speech presumes nothing, Blanchot thinks; it speaks from a space it opens by itself and that can thereafter be occupied by other speech. As soon as Blanchot begins to clarify this oracular speech, however, he quietly starts to view Greece through a specific German lens. He evokes "the most tender break of day in which all the violence of a first clarity is declared" (46), and if we know our Blanchot, we think inevitably of Hölderlin's "Wie wenn am Feiertage": "Jezt aber tagts! Ich harrt und sah es kommen,/Und was ich sah, das Heilige sei mein Wort [But now day breaks! I waited and saw it come./And what I saw, the hallowed [Sacred], my word shall convey[18]]." In "Le Grand Refus" (1959) Blanchot takes Hölderlin to be wishing that his speech be holy. It is not holy now—it does not offer itself as the transcription of a private revelation, say—but it opens a space in which the holy may be witnessed. As we are told earlier, this prophetic speech says nothing at all, but in a sovereign gesture "makes this silence into the finger imperiously pointing toward the unknown" (VE 46).

Can modern poetry resemble oracular speech? It is written, of course, and therefore silent until read aloud. But can it indicate the unknown? Marina

---

[16]  Indeed, Blanchot will study Neher's work intently. See Éric Hoppenot, *Maurice Blanchot et la tradition juive*, avant-propos Éric Marty (Paris: Éditions Kimé, 2015), 188–97, 485–507.

[17]  See Blanchot, "La Parole prophetique," *Nouvelle Nouvelle Revue Française* 48 (janvier 1957): 283–92. It appears in English as "Prophetic Speech," *The Book to Come*, 79–85. The references to Rimbaud and Claudel may be found on pp. 85 and 84 respectively.

[18]  Michael Hamburger, trans., *Friedrich Hölderlin: Poems and Fragments* (London: Anvil Press, 1994), 395. Also see Blanchot, "The 'Sacred' Speech of Hölderlin," in *The Work of Fire*, 111–31. The placing of the comma in the second line is controversial, and one might contest the translation of "das Heilige sei mein Wort."

Tsvetaeva witnesses that some poetry, Pasternak's, opens a new future. "For in reality he isn't yet," she writes: "a babbling, a chirping, a clashing—he is all Tomorrow!—the choking cry of a baby, and this baby is the World."[19] Yet Char's poetry, for Blanchot, is not merely originating fresh literary possibilities in this world but is orienting us to the sacred (or, perhaps better, something that mimes the sacred). And here, for Blanchot, the sacred is not that which calls for veneration or worship; it has no power to redeem us; it has nothing to do with Magdalenian rites in the cave; and it is not quite *mysterium tremendum et fascinans*. It is not the "holy night" of Hölderlin's "Brot und Wein" but the spectral "*other* night" in which absence appears (SL 163).[20] It does not transcend the world but attracts us from an imaginary point that the world covers over. Nonetheless, it is unknown in a highly particular sense of the word. It is not simply the future, which is not yet known but will be known one day. Nor is it the sense familiar to us in Descartes, namely, of those things that exceed the capacity of the human mind but that, because of our limits, give us a negative certainty of them.[21] It exercises no power.[22] Rather, it is that which the known and the ordered have long hidden.

Is this how Char sees things? In part, yes. "Comment vivre sans inconnu devant soi?" (*How can we live without the unknown in front of us?*), he asks in the "Argument" of *Le Poème pulvérisé* (1945–47). The poetry to be written after the war will reject Parnassian perfection and surrealist freedom equally; it will not celebrate the deeds of the *maquis*; it will be a new poetry, without a literary model, yet one that remains answerable to the world he sees and feels. The "Argument" ends, "*Born from the summons of becoming and from the anguish of retention, the poem, rising from its well of mud and of stars, will bear witness, almost silently, that it contained nothing which did not truly exist elsewhere* [qu'il n'était rien en lui qui n'existât], *in this rebellious and solitary world of contradictions.*"[23] A poem consists of worldly things, Char thinks, but not the ordered world of the κόσμος.

---

19  Marina Tsvetaeva, "Downpour of Light: Poetry of Eternal Courage," in *Art in the Light of Conscience*, trans., intro. and notes Angela Livingstone (Cambridge: Harvard University Press, 1992), 23.

20  See Hamburger, *Friedrich Hölderlin: Poems and Fragments*, 270.

21  See René Descartes, "Rules for the Direction of the Mind," in *The Philosophical Works*, 2 vols., trans. Elizabeth S. Haldane and G. R. T. Ross (Cambridge: Cambridge University Press, 1972), I, 28. Jean-Luc Marion develops this train of thought in his *Negative Certainties*, trans. Stephen E. Lewis (Chicago: Chicago University Press, 2015).

22  See Blanchot, "René Char and the Thought of the Neutral," in *The Infinite Conversation*, 302.

23  Char, *Furor and Mystery*, 245; *Oeuvres complètes*, 249. We can get a clearer idea of Char's sense of *Le Poème Pulvérisé* by reading his glosses on the poems, which first appeared in *Arrière-Histoire du Poème pulvérisé* (Paris: John Hughes, 1972) and is now in the *Oeuvres complètes*, 1291–97.

Yet when Blanchot reads it, admiring its "furious ascension," it conjures the Heraclitean, primal Chaos, which precedes order.[24]

Blanchot relies on the Platonic interpretation of Heraclitus developed in *Theatetus* 152a–160e. The obscure philosopher of Ephesus can be read, perhaps more strongly, as a thinker of the deep unity of opposites, not primal flux, and in his poetry Char is sympathetic to this reading, as is apparent in his talk of "les loyaux adversaires" in *Fureur et Mystère*, which undergirds the imagery of hunter and hunted, man and woman, which runs throughout his writing. A more appropriate figure, given Blanchot's design, would be Cratylus who, according to Aristotle, was so committed to the idea that everything flows (πάντα ῥεῖ) that he "ended by thinking that one need not say anything, and only moved his finger."[25] That said, Blanchot follows Char very closely, right down to alluding to *Le Poème pulvérizé* in the context of his poetry as a whole. "This work has the force of the impersonal, but it is to the faithfulness of a unique destiny that it summons us, a tense but patient work, tempestuous and still, energetic, concentrated in on itself, in the explosive brevity of the instant, a power of image and affirmation that 'pulverizes' the poem and yet keeps the slowness, the continuity, and the understanding of the uninterrupted" (VE 47).

Three things need to be brought to the surface here:

1. For Blanchot, as for Bataille, the sacred is consequent on sacrifice: in the act of writing Char yields his empirical "je," and so, in a way, exposes himself to death, in order to let the sacred announce itself through him. "For isn't the writer dead as soon as the work exists?," he asks rhetorically in "La Solitude essentielle" (1953), then adds that after writing the author has "an impression of being ever so strangely out of work" (*l'impression d'un désoevrement des plus étranges*).[26] These remarks, and many others like them, serve to remind us that Blanchot tends to draw distinctions in an extreme manner, and that he frequently overdramatizes his main insights. Put less theatrically, the act of writing produces a poem, and the poem is itself and not the presence of the author or even a representation of what he actually thinks or feels: one ends up saying things in a poem of which one had not been conscious before it was composed. One begins writing as a

---

[24] See Char, *Hypnos: Notes from the French Resistance 1943–44*, trans. Mark Hutchinson (New York: Seagull, 2014), § 56; *Oeuvres complètes*, 189.

[25] Aristotle, *Metaphysics, I–IX*, trans. Hugh Tredennick (Cambridge: Harvard University Press, 1933), 1010a.

[26] Blanchot, "La Solitude essentielle," *Nouvelle Nouvelle Revue Française* 1 (janvier 1953): 78; *The Space of Literature*, trans. Ann Smock (Lincoln and London: University of Nebraska Press, 1982), 23.

"je" and is deflected into an "il," and this would be the case even if one were writing a narrative or a dramatic monologue: who the pronoun stands for does not matter. (Husserl would say that the sense of dislocation of self occurs because of awakenings brought about by way of passive genesis in the very act of writing.[27] And if we follow him, we have no reason to distinguish the "je" and the "il" so sharply.) If the emphasis on art and being derives from Heidegger, the insistence on sacrifice harkens back to Henri Hubert and Marcel Mauss, and the elaboration of the theory, quite unlike anything one finds in Anglophone literary modernism, goes by way of Greece, specifically the figure of Orpheus.[28]

2. This self-sacrificial act turns on a particular construal of the creative act, which Blanchot reprises later in the essay. "The work," he says, is "the struggling intimacy of irreconcilable and inseparable moments," which he calls "communication." This sense of communication is an unusual and complex one; it is reached by linking Heidegger and Laure, and it cuts its figure against the ordinary use of the word: the felicitous transmission of linguistic statements.[29] Instead, it is an attempt to reach beyond death to the sacred, which occurs in risking the apparently solid "je" in writing. The sacred, in this sense, is what Bataille (perhaps looking back to Rimbaud) calls "the impossible," since it exceeds our realm of possible experience. It goes without saying that we have no reason to think that Char would completely agree with Bataille on this point. Certainly he uses the same language, but at least in his later writings the sense is quite different: "L'impossible, nous ne l'atteignons pas, mais il nous sert de lantern" (We never attain the impossible, but it serves us as lantern).[30] With regard to *Le Poème pulvérizé*, Char says (specifically of composing "J'habite une douleur"), "J'ai pris ma tête comme on saisit une motte de sel et je l'ai littéralement pulvérizé" (I took my head as one takes a lump of salt and literally pulverized it).[31] What Blanchot sees as occurring in the poem, Char figures as having taken place mentally.

---

[27] On passive genesis, see Edmund Husserl, *Analyses Concerning Passive and Active Synthesis: Lectures on Transcendental Logic*, trans. Anthony J. Steinbock (Dordrecht: Kluwer Academic Publishers, 2001), esp. 119.

[28] See Martin Heidegger, "The Origin of the Work of Art," in *Poetry, Language, Thought*, trans. Albert Hofstadter (New York: Harper, 1971), 71, and Henri Hubert and Marcel Mauss, *Sacrifice: Its Nature and Functions*, trans. W. D. Halls, foreword E. E. Evans-Pritchard (Chicago: University of Chicago Press, 1981). Blanchot's "Le Regard d'Orphée" is contemporary with "La Bête de Lascaux"; it was published in *Cahiers d'art*, 28, 1 (1953), 73–75. See "Orpheus's Gaze," in *The Space of Literature*, 171–76.

[29] See Heidegger, "The Origin of the Work of Art," 71, and Laure (Colette) Peignot, "The Sacred," in *The Collected Writings*, trans. Jeanine Herman (San Francisco: City Lights, 2001), esp. 45.

[30] Char, *The Brittle Age and Returning Upland*, trans. Gustaf Sobin, foreword Mary Ann Caws (Denver: Counterparth Press, 2009), 25; *Oeuvres complètes*, 766.

[31] Char, *Oeuvres complètes*, 1294. Also see "La Bibliothèque est en feu," in *Oeuvres complètes*, 378.

At any rate, Blanchot adapts Bataille's idea in thinking of a particular moment in literary composition. In the act of writing there is a moment when the "je" is establishing the work in hand yet is, at the same time, being shadowed by the "il"; it is a time in which the "je" asserts its power to create, as though from nothing, and the creation itself, in coming into being, renders the writer increasingly powerless. This is communication, understood as the struggle between "the measure of the work that established a certain power and the measurelessness or excess of the work that strives toward impossibility."[32] (Char puts the same thing more memorably in "Impressions anciennes" when he says, simply, "Créer: s'exclure" and also in "À la santé du serpent" when, I take it, he addresses the poem he is writing: "Mon amour, peu importe que je sois né: tu deviens visible à la place où je disparais" [My beloved, it matters little that I've been born: you become visible just where I disappear].[33]) It is worth taking a moment to step back and explicate Blanchot's overly condensed expression.

In writing, Blanchot maintains, Char loses his empirical "je" but rather than dying produces a poem in which, *stricto sensu*, no living person speaks. It is not being that "speaks" in it but the Outside that murmurs just beneath, as it were, what we conventionally take to be the author's voice, this author who is born only in and through the poem. This murmur is the neutral "il" that has vanquished the authorial "je," and it is called a murmur and not a voice because what has been written turns on primary and secondary passive syntheses made in language: it seems as though one's consciousness is speaking without reference to oneself.[34] The "experience" in play is not anything represented by an aphorism, a number of verses or several lines of a prose poem; instead, the poem is itself experience, a passage for the author from one state to another, from "je" to "il," and an exposure to peril. There is a formal issue also in play, for the struggle is between a poem's drive toward a definite form, and the limitlessness from which it draws: the realm of image, which of course has no borders, in which sensuous or abstract being is hollowed out. If a poet retains mastery over his or her composition, if one does not remain open to what might come to be said by acceding to the imaginary point that becomes clearer as the "il" takes over and

---

[32]  Communication is a common theme in Bataille, especially in the early 1940s when, most likely, he elaborates on Laure's thoughts on the subject. See, for example, *Guilty*, trans. Bruce Boone, intro. Denis Hollier (Venice: The Lapis Press, 1988), 139. Blanchot takes up the idea in "L'Œuvre et la communication," *Nouvelle Nouvelle Revue Française* 12 (décembre 1953): 1064–71; *The Space of Literature*, 198–207.

[33]  Char, *Oeuvres complètes*, 742; *Furor and Mystery*, 283: *Oeuvres complètes*, 265.

[34]  See Blanchot, "Literature and the Right to Death," trans. Lydia Davis, *The Work of Fire*, trans. Charlotte Mandell (Stanford: Stanford University Press, 1995),330.

that fatally attracts then dismisses the "je," one might produce what could be taken to be a masterpiece, but it would have foreclosed on the unknown.[35] Of course, the question arises how a reader could ever know what has happened in the composition of a poem. It is usually hard enough for a poet to know himself or herself. Yet there is often a sense of surprise when one reads what one has composed: "Is that what I have really thought or felt?" Blanchot often appeals to writers, familiar with the psychology of composition, more than to practical critics who must respond solely to the words of a poem before them.

3. Char writes that poetry's purpose is "nous rendre souverain en nous impersonnalisant" (to make us sovereign by impersonalizing us); poetry touches upon "la plénitude."[36] Yet Blanchot approaches the matter otherwise. The sacred is encountered in the impersonal speech of the "il" which, unlike the one who says "je," occupies neither space nor time; it is neither internal (a "subject") nor external (another person). Hence the equivalent expressions "Neutral" and "Outside." Recall the *récit* of 1953, *Celui qui ne m'accompagnait pas*: "A speech? And yet not a speech, barely a murmur [*à peine un murmure*], barely a shiver, less than silence, less than the abyss of emptiness: the fullness of emptiness, something that one can't silence, occupying all of space, uninterrupted and incessant, a shiver and already a murmur, not a murmur, but a speech, and not just any speech, but distinct, appropriate: within my reach" (OWS 66–67/CAP 125–126). The sacred (or that which mimes it) is always anterior, never able to become a phenomenon like the burning bush or the Transfiguration. Yet poetry can open a relationship with the sacred.[37] Plato's attribution to Heraclitus of a primal flux is a figure for it, to be sure, but it is better to recognize it as *désœuvrement*, the state of being rendered idle, drawn toward the non-world of image, precisely by the triumph of the "il."[38]

＊＊＊

A decade after writing "La Bête de Lascaux," Blanchot returns to *Le Poème pulvérisé* but in a new spirit, with other things to see there. The first essay, "René

---

[35]   On the imaginary point, see Blanchot, "Encountering the Imaginary," in *The Book to Come*, 7.

[36]   Char, *The World as Archipelago*, trans. Robert Baker (Richmond, CA: Omnidawn, 2012), 61; *Oeuvres complètes*, 359.

[37]   See Blanchot, "How to Discover the Obscure?," in *The Infinite Conversation*, 40–48.

[38]   See Blanchot, "Heraclitus," in *The Infinite Conversation*, 85–92. Also see in the same volume his distinction between the narrator's voice and the narrative voice in "The Narrative Voice (the 'he,' the neutral)," 379–87. For Levinas on the *il y a*, see his *Existence and Existents*, trans. Alphonso Lingis, corrected ed. (Dordrecht: Kluwer Academic Publishers, 1988), 57–64.

Char et la pensée du neutre" (1963), passes from attention to the sacred and phenomenology to the thought of the Outside, while the second one, "Le Parole fragment" (1964), embodies his and Char's distaste for De Gaulle and the politics of the Fifth Republic. When revised for inclusion in *L'Entretien infini* (1969), this second essay also resonates with the irruption of *les événements de mai*.[39] The background for "Le Parole fragment" is plain: Blanchot had written "La Perversion essentielle" (1959), a fierce reflection on the Algiers putsch of May 1959, to which Char had responded, expressing his agreement.[40] What galls most about the power play is that it embodies "perverted values of the sacred" (PW 13): De Gaulle as savior of France. (One might note that Napoléon played the same role in the previous century.)

In the first essay Char's question is repeated: "Comment vivre sans inconnu devant soi?" An answer comes after the quotation: "Research—poetry, thought— relates to the unknown as unknown." The terms of the answer, especially in the final version of the essay, deserve close attention: "This relation discloses the unknown, but by an uncovering that leaves it under cover; through this relation there is a 'presence' of the unknown; in this 'presence' the unknown is rendered present, but always as unknown ... This relation will not consist in an unveiling ... The unknown will not be revealed, but indicated" (IC 300). We have heard a version of this argument before, in "Comment découvrir l'obscur?" (1959), the second part of Blanchot's engagement with Bonnefoy, in which the question of the relation between the sacred and poetry is explored.[41] If the first part takes its clue from Hölderlin's insight in "Wie wenn am Feiertage" that the sacred precedes manifestation, the second part broods on how poetry is experience of that anteriority, a relationship with the Outside or the "obscure."[42] Now, in passing from Bonnefoy to Char, we find a strengthened emphasis that phenomenology,

---

[39]   See Blanchot, "René Char et la pensée du neutre," *L'Arc* 22 (1963): 9–14, and *L'Entretien infini*, 439– 50. Also see his essay "Le Parole fragment," which first appeared in Italian translation as "La Parolo in arcipelago" in *Il Menabò* 7 (1964), 156–59, the journal being the sole publication under the sign of the *Revue internationale*. One of Blanchot's hopes for this venture was the leaguing of left-wing politics and fragmentary writing. The essay was modified and appeared as "Parole de fragment," in *L'Endurance de la pensée: Pour saluer Jean Beaufret* (Paris: Plon, 1968), 103–07. (Blanchot's essay was dedicated to Emmanuel Levinas to mark his concerns about Beaufret's reputed denial of the death camps.) Later, the same piece, recast again, and without the dedication, appeared in *L'Entretien infini*, 451–58. On the *Revue*, see Blanchot, *Political Writings, 1953–1993*, trans. and intro. Zakir Paul, foreword Kevin Hart (New York: Fordham University Press, 2010), 39–66.

[40]   See Blanchot, "La Perversion essentielle," *Le 14 Juillet* 3 (1959): 18–20, and Char, "Note à propos d'une deuxième lecture de 'La Perversion essentielle,' in 'Le 14 juillet' 1959," *Oeuvres complètes*, 744–45.

[41]   See Blanchot, "Comment découvrir l'obscur?," *Nouvelle Revue Française* 82 (novembre 1959): 867– 79. The piece was included in *L'Entretien infini*, 57–69.

[42]   See Blanchot, "How to Discover the Obscure?," 46.

even broadly considered, reaches a limit in considering the unknown.[43] The poetic word does not manifest being but points to the Outside, which is no longer coded as the sacred. (The influence of Derrida's deconstruction of presence in the mid-1960s is apparent in the placing of "presence" in scare quotes.[44])

"To write and to read this poem," he says in the second essay, "is to accept bending our listening to language toward the experience of a certain breaking up, an experience of separation and discontinuity" (IC 300). His remarks are partly directed against those French readers of Char who have found his fragmentary writing after the war frustrating.[45] These people are mistaken, Blanchot thinks, in part because they bring aesthetic categories to a work that fundamentally resists them. A fragmented poem "opens another manner of accomplishment—the one at stake in writing, in questioning, or in an affirmation irreducible to unity" (IC 308). We read poetry not for the consolation afforded by the beautiful but in order to grasp better how to be in relation with one another without those relations turning on the "je" as a center of power, and the best model is not of belonging to the homeland, as one finds in Heidegger (and later in Beda Allemann), but rather of being in exile from it.[46] Char's poetry asserts "a new relation with the Outside" (IC 308), in which neither the Same nor the Other absorbs the binary term. To be sure, this poem appears "like a block to which nothing seems able to attach" but then, reversing the train of his reasoning in "La Bête de Lascaux," he says that it is a "strange misunderstanding" to think that Char writes aphoristically, for the aphorism—he appeals to the etymology of the word [ὁρίζων]—"is closed and bounded: the horizontal of every horizon" (308), and Char's poetry is nothing if not open to the unknown (or, as Char would more likely say, the mystery of "le peuple dés prés").[47] Blanchot likes to quote Char's beautiful line, "Le poème est l'amour réalisé du désire demeuré désir" [The poem is the realized love of desire remaining desire].[48] Even the most polished poem still remains in a relation of longing for what has inspired it; it is a process as well as a thing.

---

[43]  Blanchot will propose a new mode of reduction to mark his difference from Husserlian phenomenology. See my essay "Une réduction infinie," in *Cahiers de l'Herne*, Blanchot special issue, ed. Dominique Rabaté and Éric Hoppenot (2014), 323–28.

[44]  See Blanchot, *The Infinite Conversation*, 452 n. 16. Also see Jacques Derrida, *Resistances of Psychoanalysis*, trans. Peggy Kamuf et al. (Stanford: Stanford University Press, 1998), 61–62.

[45]  A dissenting minority still contends Char's preeminence in modern French poetry. See, for example, François Crouzet, *Contra René Char* (Paris: Les Belles Lettres, 1992).

[46]  See Beda Allemann, "Le retrounement natal dans l'œuvre de Hölderlin," *Recherches et débats du centre catholique des intellectuels français* n.s. 24 (1958): 183–99.

[47]  Char, *Oeuvres completes*, 217.

[48]  Char, "Partage formel," *Furor and Mystery*, 117; *Oeuvres complètes*, 162. Also see Maurice Blanchot, "The Great Refusal," in *Infinite Conversation*, 47.

The Outside can only approach us; it never appears. Yet we discern it in many aspects of life: art, communism, everyday life, image, and the sacred. Talk of the sacred is quietly replaced in "Le Parole fragment" by a fresh sense of the political. What Blanchot now values is the spatial arrangement of *Le Poème pulvérisé*: it "accepts disjunction or divergence as the infinite center from out of which, through speech, relation is to be created: an arrangement that does not compose but juxtaposes, that is to say, leaves each of the terms that come into relation *outside* one another, respecting and preserving this *exteriority* and this distance as the principle—always already undercut—of all signification" (308). And once more Blanchot evokes Heraclitus, this time as Char's brother in thought, two thinkers of "Difference" separated by over two millennia. An analogy is proposed between difference in nature and in society, although the ground of the analogy is nowhere specified.

We must not forget the word "destiny" that sounds frequently in Blanchot. Doubtless he recalls Heraclitus's Fragment 119: ἦθος ἀνθρώπῳ δαίμων [a person's character is his fate (divinity)], but the word rings also for Char, language and France alike.[49] In "Comment découvrir l'obscur?" we are told that "Destiny" is "that which diverts from every destination and that we are seeking to name more directly in speaking of the *neutral*" (IC 50). Let us keep this in mind when reading a few lines from "La Perversion essentielle." Blanchot evokes De Gaulle as Symbol, "the visible presence of a great absent nation," who stands apart from power until René Coty, the last President of the Fourth Republic, appeals to him to become Prime Minister, which De Gaulle accepts on the condition of being given extraordinary powers, including the power to draft a new constitution:

> From this experience arose the consciousness of a sovereignty of exception that coincided, during the dramatic hours of the void, with the essential presence of the national destiny. What is characteristic here is the manifestation of this void: in 1940, nothing was more pathetic and more obvious; where France had been, there was nothing more than the void, and beyond this void of history, the almost visible, almost perceptible Destiny, as the very prophecy of her salvation. De Gaulle has held onto the horror [*hantise*] of this void, but also its intimate knowledge and the feeling of its necessity. He inscribed it into the Constitution. He made it legal in a way. For France to raise herself into a Destiny and for the power that represents her to become a sovereignty of salvation, she must become

---

[49]  Blanchot claims that language has a destiny in "Literature and the Right to Death," 328. See Robinson, *Heraclitus*, 69.

conscious of this void, which, owing to its institutions and its divisions, does not cease to threaten her. (PW 11)

If we step back from "La Perversion essentielle" and the two later essays on Char, we can make out what Blanchot urges his readers to think. To escape the grim politics of the Fifth Republic, that dark apparent destiny of France, we must turn to Char's poetry as marking the true destiny of France: a society marked by an openness to experience, to openness itself, and to the other in all its modes. It is unknown in the sense that the political, as envisaged here, has no precedent.

To return to the main argument: The wisdom at issue in "La Bête innommable," Blanchot believes, repeats the oracular language of Dodona. One does not have to go so far as to say that the unicorn is a "fantastically disguised" image of Gaea or Rhea, who, some believe, was worshipped at Dodona before Zeus was connected with the cult. All that is required is to twin the passing of the wind through the sacred oak tree with the rustling of the Outside, that "murmuring where nothing lets itself be heard" (*murmure où rien ne se laisse entendre*) (VE 50–51). The prehistorical beast depicted at Lascaux is an image of the Outside, covered over by generations of people who lack genuine wisdom; the tears of Wisdom, like those of Heraclitus, testify to our irretrievable loss of a consoling reality that is stable and unified, underwritten by a sense of the sacred that points to the gods or God. Char does this in the very writing of his poetry, Blanchot argues, and he even sees this conception of poetry rendered as a theme in some of the poems. The Outside is neither ancient nor modern, although Blanchot thinks, like Foucault, that a few writers have only recently become attuned to it.[50] There is no need to appeal to Char as a hero of the *maquis*. He is a poet of France's authentic destiny, a time to come that announces itself as unknown, as a "communism … beyond communism" (IC xii).

✱✱✱

We are now in a position to understand what Blanchot has in mind when he says that Char's poetry "makes rise up before us a form of experienced time [*durée*] very different from the time [*la durée*] that simple historical analysis grasps" (BC 198). It is time as image, time as fascination. And we can also see

---

[50] See Michel Foucault, "Maurice Blanchot: The Thought from Outside," in Maurice Blanchot and Michel Foucault, in *Foucault / Blanchot*, trans. Brian Massumi and Jeffrey Mehlman (New York: Zone Books, 1990), and Foucault, *The Order of Things: An Archeology of the Human Sciences*, n. trans. (New York: Random House, 1994), 384.

Blanchot's deeper investment in Char as French prophet. But we have yet to explain what is in play when he says that Char "answers" Hölderlin (*lui répond*). One could do this by way of a close reading of "Pour un Prométhée saxifrage," which is written "En touchant la main éolienne de Hölderlin," and which asks, "La réalité sans l'énergie disloquante de la poésie, qu'est-ce?" (What is reality without the dislocating energy of poetry?).[51] More economical, though, would be to follow the link between the two poets provided by Heidegger, as Blanchot himself almost suggests, and in doing so we can gain a fuller understanding of Char's achievement and why it cannot be contained by modernity and less so by an aesthetic-historical category such as modernism.

The principal commentary by Heidegger that Blanchot has in mind is "Hölderlin und das Wesen der Dichtung," first given as a lecture in Rome in 1936, published the same year in *Das innere Reich*, and eventually gathered in *Erläuterungen zu Hölderlins Ditchtung* (1951). Heidegger chooses Hölderlin, over and above arguably greater poets, to illuminate the "essence" (*Wesen*) of poetry. This is not an essence that would have universal, timeless pertinence, as if we could exfoliate Hölderlin's odes and then find what is essential to Homer's epics, Petrarch's lyrics, or Shakespeare's tragedies. Instead, Heidegger maintains that Hölderlin's poems provide "anew" the essence of poetry and in doing so determine a new age. "It is the time of the gods who have fled *and* of the god who is coming."[52] It will readily be noticed that Heidegger does not seek to assimilate Hölderlin to the politics of culture that was so loudly and darkly pronounced in Germany in the 1930s; his concern is otherwise, and is indicated by two quotations, one from "Brot und Wein" and the other from a Pseudo-Hölderlin, "In lieblicher Bläue": "wozu Dichter in dürftiger Zeit" and "Voll Verdienst, doch dichterisch, wohnet der Mensch auf dieser Erde."[53] The "time of need" is to be met, if at all, only by "dwelling poetically on the earth," that is, by standing before the gods. If this seems to be cultural nostalgia, it is not how Heidegger sees things. In a commentary on "Der Rhein" we are told, "Hölderlin is not the Greek world, but the future of the Germans."[54]

---

[51]   Char, *This Smoke that Carried Us: Selected Poems*, trans. Susanne Dubroff (Buffalo, NY: White Pine Press, 2004), 123.

[52]   Heidegger, "Hölderlin and the Essence of Poetry," in *Elucidations of 'Hölderlin's Poetry*, trans. Keith Hoeller (Amherst, NY: Humanity Books, 2000), 64.

[53]   Hamburger, *Friedrich Hölderlin*, 270, 714.

[54]   Heidegger, *Hölderlin's Hymns "Germania" and "The Rhine,"* trans. William McNeill and Julia Ireland (Bloomington: Indiana University Press, 2014), 231. Also see Heidegger, *Hölderlin's Hymn "The Ister,"* trans. William McNeill and Julia Davis (Bloomington: Indiana University Press, 1996), 54.

Heidegger nowhere specifies the linguistic extent of this divine interregnum, and we might well doubt if Emily Dickinson, G. M. Hopkins, and Alexander Pushkin, among others, experienced it to any great extent. Can one detect it in Wallace Stevens, Paul Celan, Federico García Lorca, or Eugenio Montale? Perhaps so—but in its specifics, barely, and at times not at all—and never with the pathos that weighs in Heidegger's meditation on art and in the final pages of Blanchot's *L'Espace littéraire*. That tonality seems to be specifically German, although for Blanchot it spills over into France, where it is reset, for he hears Mallarmé, Rimbaud, and, of course, Char speaking in its key. He is not wrong to do so, for in "Seuil" Char memorably evokes "l'abandon du divin" as a sense of a huge crack appearing in a dam (a metaphor for the human being).[55] In "Brot und Wein" Hölderlin evokes poets, like the priests of Bacchus, wandering from land to land. This is plainly not the case with Char, who remains rooted in his beloved Vaucluse. Instead, one finds in Char's poetry, Blanchot urges, a place where one can dwell, not in peace and contentment but in the grip of fascination.

That the natural world of the Vaucluse rivets Char is evident: we need only read "Quatre fascinants."[56] Blanchot goes further, however, seeing in the poetry— or at least some of it—an attraction to the Outside, the last vestige of the sacred in human history, in Char's poetry, and once one succumbs to its allure one loses hold of the fullness and direction of time. Rather, one lives the emptiness and stagnation of image: not exactly *la durée* as Henri Bergson conceived it but *la désœuvrement* as Blanchot diagnoses it.[57] Char responds to Hölderlin precisely by making his "sacred speech" ever more explicit, by living as a poet *avant le Dehors*. He is situated, for Blanchot, both in the space between the divine's turn away from human beings and our turn away from the divine, which is the opening of modernity, and in the space between the loss of the old gods and the arrival of the new.[58] The old gods spoke through the rustling of the sacred oak at Dodona, and the last god, who attracts us to the non-world of image, murmurs in Char's poetry.

\*\*\*

Blanchot seems to need Char in much the same way as Heidegger needed Hölderlin. Each poet supplies a sacred scripture for the thinker to explicate

---

[55] Char, "Seuil," *Oeuvres complètes*, 255.
[56] Char, *Oeuvres complètes*, 353–54.
[57] See Henri Bergson, *Time and Free Will: An Essay on the Immediate Data of Consciousness*, trans. R. L. Pogson (London: Allen and Unwin, 1910), 100–10.
[58] See Blanchot, *The Space of Literature*, 247.

and find there his own views glowing with "an alienated majesty."[59] Heidegger's Hölderlin became a symbol for a new Germany, for a *vaterländische Umkehr*, and the same is true of Blanchot's Char with respect to France. In order to do that, of course, one must be selective in one's reading. Lautréamont and Rimbaud are dropped from Char's heritage, leaving Hölderlin behind and center. The great fragmentary poem of *Le Poème pulvérizé* is surely "Le Météore du 13 août," yet the others are not written in that way and have powers of different kinds. More generally, if one reads Char in the mile as well as the inch, one finds a great many fine poems that play no role in Blanchot's construction of him, and that are arguably his main legacy. I am thinking of, among many others, poems that recall folk lyrics ("Quatre fascinants," "Quatre âges"), expansive love poems ("*Lettera amorosa*"), and other lyrics in verse and prose, such as "Congé au vent," "Sur le volet d'une fenêtre," "Compagnie de l'écolière," "La Sorgue," "L'Amoureuse en secret," "Le Martinet," "Le Bois de l'Epte," "Redonnez-leur," "Qu'il vive!," "Le Vipereau," "Allegeance," and "Les Inventeurs."

Char certainly saw the pertinence of Blanchot's criticism of his work, and we can perhaps discern the lineaments of his admiration of his friend in a poem he dedicated to him, "Le Partenaire mortel."[60] I read the poem to be about composition regarded as an erotic struggle between the poet (male) and the inspiration of the poem (female). Yet Char is also responding to composition as Blanchot conceives it. There are people whose secret "resides within the depths of the very secret of life," he writes. "They approach it. It destroys them. But the future which they have thus awakened with a murmur, notices and creates them. Oh labyrinth of utmost love" (*tient au plus profond du secret même de la vie. Ils s'en approchent. Elle les tue. Mais l'avenir qu'ils ont ainsi éveillé d'un murmure, les devinant, les crée. Ô dédale de l'extrême amour!*).[61] Here we can hear a lyrical echo of some lines in Blanchot's first essay on Char: "Inspiration is not the gift of a secret or a word granted to someone already present; it is the gift of existence to someone who does not yet exist."[62] An unusual echo, it reverses part of what it repeats. For Char, the secret that animates Blanchot and his writing, narrative as well as critical, is close to the secret of life itself, which I take to be, for Blanchot,

---

[59]    Ralph Waldo Emerson, "Self Reliance," in *Essays: First Series* (New York: A. L. Burt Co., 1900), 48.

[60]    For a somewhat different account of Blanchot's and Char's readings of one another, see Alain Milon, "Maurice Blanchot, lecteur de René Char?," in *Maurice Blanchot, de proche en proche*, éd. Éric Hoppenot and coordonné Daiana Manoury (Paris: Éditions Complicités, 2008), 209–20.

[61]    Char, "The Mortal Partner," in *This Smoke that Carried Us*, 97; *Oeuvres complètes*, 363. The dedication does not appear in the *Oeuvres complètes*.

[62]    Blanchot, "René Char," 99.

the Outside. To approach it directly, as Orpheus does with Eurydice, who is the inspiration of his poetry, is to lose it, and, as we have seen, to produce a new work is an act of self-sacrifice. It bespeaks extreme love. Although the poem is actually spoken by no one, its very articulation gives birth to a new person: the poet. And this particular poet, author of "Le Partenaire mortel," is for Blanchot the one who gives birth to hope for another France, one who breaks decisively with the politics of the Fifth Republic. Yet when Blanchot reads Char he also finds confirmation of his own thoughts on composition and the Outside. For some, reading might well be a "light, innocent Yes," but for Blanchot it is not always an entirely innocent activity.[63]

---

[63]  See Blanchot, *The Space of Literature*, 196.

# 10

# Neutral Conditions: Blanchot, Beckett, and the Space of Writing

Jonathan Boulter

*Perhaps first to carry a space of language to the limit from which the irregularity of another speaking, nonspeaking, space comes back.*

Maurice Blanchot, *The Step Not Beyond*

*In philosophical terms, space is neither subject nor object. How can it be effectively grasped?*

Henri Lefebvre, *The Production of Space*[1]

My intention in this chapter is to imagine Blanchot and Beckett as inhabiting a shared philosophical space, the space of the neutral. While it is tempting to read the idea of the neutral as a philosophical trope that is theorized by Blanchot and realized in the space of literature by Beckett, this will not, precisely, be my intention here. I am proposing that we read Blanchot and Beckett as both operating within the economy of philosophy and literature, as both having produced something that resembles philosophical literature, or literature *as* philosophy. It is my suggestion therefore that the neutral—a trope that in Blanchot is called the Neuter (*The Step Not Beyond*); in Beckett, the "neither"—becomes for both writers not merely something of a hermeneutical entry point into their work (as it surely is) but a condition of the writing of the work, as such. Thus, it is my interest here to examine how the neutral is figured within both writers. I will begin with Blanchot's essay "Where Now? Who Now?" and this critical assessment of Beckett's *The Unnamable* as an expression of the neutral: "There, language does not speak, it is; in it nothing

---

[1] Henri Lefebvre, *The Production of Space*, trans. Donald Nicholson-Smith (Oxford: Blackwell, 1991).

begins, nothing is said, but it is always new and always begins again" (BC 216). Blanchot here is, of course, asking us to understand, or at least attend to the possibility of, the ontology of the neutral: "it *is*." What I wish to suggest here is that the neutral is a category of being that can only ever mark the effacement of ideas like "category" and "being"; the neutral is not ever quite like Heidegger's notion of the "placeholder of being," but as a space of neither one thing nor another (as Blanchot reminds us is the etymology of the word), the neutral never quite is, never quite is not. Beckett, in his late prose-poem "neither," will use the phrase "unspeakable home" to figure the space of the non-ontology of the neutral; but his work, as Blanchot reminds us, has always tried to accommodate the burden of the neutral, and perhaps with some success. Blanchot's reading of *How It Is* as one expression of neutrality finds, as I read it, its perfect end point in an idea that is the main focus of my chapter. As he completes his discussion of the neutral, Blanchot writes, "Let us (on a whim) call it [the neutral] spectral, ghostlike" (IC 386). It is this idea, that the neutral, in fact the narrative voice, as such, is always already spectral, that perhaps allows us to begin, even retrospectively, to understand what both Blanchot and Beckett will come to mean by the neutral, and its critical place as the (aporetic) grounds of writing: the neutral, the unspeakable, both is and is not. The neutral exists only by virtue of its unspeakable effacement. To understand the neutral, in other words—and this understanding can only ever emerge from the space of writing—is to begin to understand being itself (and its possible reconfiguration within the aporia of narrative) as a kind of inescapable impossibility.

In his 1959 essay "Where Now, Who Now?," ostensibly an analysis of Beckett's so-called first trilogy of novels (*Molloy, Malone Dies, The Unnamable*), Blanchot makes an important early link between the concept of the neutral and the work of Beckett. Blanchot is clear that the approach to a neutral space is one that conditions the act of writing itself; the neutral, in other words, emerges out of an essential dialectic relation between author and work.[2] The neutral is a space that, in this case, Beckett himself, as writer, must enter and by entering give (compromised) life to characters (let us call them that, if only for the sake of convenience) who in turn emerge out of a space of neutrality to speak of the fact of being in, perhaps *as*, neutrality itself. It is, as Blanchot says, the work itself that

---

[2]  "Where Now? Who Now?" was originally published as "Où maintenant? Qui maintenant?" in *La Nouvelle Revue Francaise* (October, 1953). It was subsequently collected, with modifications in *Le livre à venir* (*The Book to Come*) in 1959.

demands that the author "become other" (BC 216) to himself; it is the work that "deprives this living man of the world by giving him the space of the imaginary to live in" (216). Blanchot's line of thinking follows crucially:

> that is, in part, in fact, the malaise of a man fallen outside of the world and, through this separation, floating eternally between being and nothingness, incapable henceforth of dying and incapable of being born, shot through with ghosts, his creatures, in which he does not believe and which tell him nothing, and which are evoked for us in *The Unnamable*. But that is still not the right answer. We find it rather in the impulse that, as the work strives to be accomplished, leads it towards that point where it is put to the test of impossibility. There, language does not speak, it is; in it nothing begins, nothing is said, but it is always new and always begins again. (216)

I am fascinated to notice how this passage begins with an eviction of the author, Beckett, having fallen "outside" of the world (does the neutral begin with a step beyond the world?), haunted by the essential spectrality of his "creatures," and while Blanchot indicates that he speaks here of Beckett, Beckett as author, it is equally clear that this condition of being between being and nothingness, being outside of the world, and of being incapable of dying and being born is the condition of the unnamable itself: "Where I am there is no one but me, who am not."[3] More precisely, and specific to our central trope of neutrality, the unnamable—and perhaps this is true of Beckett's condition as the writer in relation to this work—becomes that neutral space of the tympanum:

> perhaps that's what I feel, an outside and an inside and me in the middle, perhaps that's what I am, the thing that divides the world in two, on the one side the outside, on the other the inside, that can be as thin as foil, I'm neither one side nor the other, I'm in the middle, I'm the partition, I've two surfaces and no thickness, perhaps that's what I feel, myself vibrating, I'm the tympanum, on the one hand the mind, on the other the world, I don't belong to either.[4]

And it is here, in this neutral space of the tympanum, of not belonging to mind or world, that writing begins (and we cannot forget that the unnamable is a writer, of sorts): "How, in such conditions, can I write?"[5] This is a writing that is founded on an apprehension of neutrality, neutrality in essential relation to

[3] Samuel Beckett, *The Unnamable. Three Novels by Samuel Beckett* (New York: Grove Press, 1958), 348.
[4] Ibid., 376.
[5] Ibid., 295.

the nothing: "there, language does not speak, it is; in it nothing begins, nothing is said" (BC 216). But we must, of course, attend to Blanchot's deployment of this term "nothing"; we are obliged, to use a word crucial to both Blanchot and Beckett, to listen to the sense of "nothing" here. When nothing begins, *nothing* begins.

And it seems that for both Blanchot and Beckett, the nothing, the obligation to the nothing—an obligation that takes place in the tympanic space of the neutral, in the space between nonlocalizable mind and ungrounded world— is instantiated precisely as the entry into writing.[6] Perhaps unsurprisingly, Blanchot and Beckett, indeed within the span of a mere six years or so, both write crucial essays about the obligation to the nothing and the scene of writing. In "From Dread to Language" (1943) Blanchot writes: "Precisely that which causes language to be destroyed in him also obliges him to use language"[7] (GO 4); he continues:

> The writer finds himself in this more and more comical situation—of having nothing to write, of having no means of writing it, and of being forced by an extreme necessity to keep writing it. Having nothing to express should be taken in the simplest sense. Whatever he wants to say, it is nothing. The world, things, knowledge, are for him only reference point across the void. And he himself is already reduced to nothing. Nothing is his material. (5)[8]

In "Three Dialogues" (1949) Beckett uncannily echoes Blanchot.[9] Asked by his interlocutor, D, about what the writer prefers to create, beyond the "same old thing," B says:

---

[6] "Nonlocalizable" is one of Deleuze and Guattari's many metaphors for *becoming* (*A Thousand Plateaus*: 293); in some critical way the neutral, that which is neither one thing nor another, is always already a space of becoming. See Gilles Deleuze and Felix Guattari, *A Thousand Plateaus: Capitalism and Schizophrenia*, trans. Brian Massumi (Minneapolis: University of Minnesota Press, 1987).

[7] Blanchot's original reads: *Ce qui fait que le langage est détruit en lui fait aussi qu'il doit se servir du langage* (Blanchot, 1943), 10. Lydia Davis translates "doit" as "obliges" (Blanchot 1981: 4); Charlotte Mandell simply translates the verb as "makes": "That which destroys language in him also makes him use language" (FP 2).

[8] "From Dread to Language" (originally published as "De l'angoisse au langage") was published in *Faux Pas* (1943).

[9] From evidence in his letters we know that Beckett was aware of Blanchot's work at least as early as 1948 (107); we also know Beckett had read Blanchot's *Sade* by 1950 (210) and was attempting to translate part of that text in 1951 (219). Most importantly, Beckett was aware of Blanchot's "Où maintenent? Qui maintenant?" saying in a letter of 1954 that Blanchot's essay was "the big thing, for me" (442); in 1959, in a letter to Barbara Bray, Beckett recommends a translation of the same essay: "perhaps ce qu'on a fait de mieux on that gruesome subject" (222). See *The Letters of Samuel Beckett. Volume II: 1941–56*, eds. Lois Overbeck et al. (Cambridge: Cambridge University Press, 2011), and for the 1959 letter to Bray, see *The Letters of Samuel Beckett. Volume III: 1957–65*, eds. Lois Overbeck et al. (Cambridge: Cambridge University Press, 2014).

The expression that there is nothing to express, nothing with which to express, nothing from which to express, no power to express, no desire to express, together with the obligation to express.[10]

For Blanchot, what the artist "uses is an art in which perfect success and perfect failure must appear at the same time" (GO 8); for Beckett the artist's duty is to maintain a "fidelity to failure," a fidelity to an "expressive act, even if only of itself, of its impossibility, of its obligation."[11] It is within this nexus of impossible obligation, of failure, and fidelity to the nothing that writing, as such, emerges; it is here that the neutral space of writing—a space which works to efface the writer and the writing even as it comes into being—is announced. What both Blanchot and Beckett give us is an image of the writer bereft of world, bereft of expressive power, but compelled, obligated, to make something of this loss, even against his will, against his better judgment, against, perhaps, even his desire.[12] This is, crucially, an image of the author who is an *agent* of writing, rather than an active creator. Writing writes, and thus Beckett's question in *Texts for Nothing* 3, "What matter who's speaking?"[13]—a question both rhetorical and real; a question, moreover, as much about *writing* as about speaking—is answered in Text 5, with a vengeance: "I'm the clerk, I'm the scribe, at the hearing of what cause I know not"[14]; "That's where the court sits this evening, in the depths of that vaulty night, that's where I am clerk and scribe, not understanding what I hear, not knowing what I write."[15]

And yet writing occurs: the writing that Beckett produces and the writing that Beckett's subjects, in for instance, *The Unnamable, Texts for Nothing,* or *How It Is,* produce. Our task, as I understand it, is to think through the fact that writing does occur, against, as I say, the desire of the writer, but perhaps also the desires of writing itself. And what truly becomes our task here is to begin thinking through how Beckett—in this case, Beckett; perhaps, as does Blanchot, we could think also of Kafka, perhaps even of Sade; but here we are

---

[10]  Samuel Beckett, "Three Dialogues," in *Disjecta*, ed. Ruby Cohn (London: Calder, 1983), 139.

[11]  Ibid., 145.

[12]  Beckett's loathing of the process of writing is well known. In a 1958 letter to Alan Schneider Beckett writes: "I'm disgustingly tired & stupefied since finishing *L'Innommable* and writing seems more than ever before a quite impossible enterprise." See *No Author Better Served: The Correspondence of Samuel Beckett and Alan Schneider*, ed. Maurice Harmon (Cambridge: Harvard University Press, 1998), 47.

[13]  Samuel Beckett, *Texts for Nothing, Samuel Beckett: The Complete Short Prose*, ed. S. E. Gontarski (New York: Grove Press, 1996), 109.

[14]  Ibid., 117.

[15]  Ibid., 120.

tasked with thinking about Beckett—figures the subject of writing, the subject of writing who is, properly speaking, the object of writing, who emerges, displaced and decentered by the force of writing; subjected to writing, the subject speaks, but from an oblique position, from a position of hiddenness within the force of writing; "They'll clap me in a dungeon, I'm in a dungeon, I've always been in a dungeon, I hear everything, every word they say, it's the only sound, as if I were speaking, to myself, out loud, in the end you don't know any more, a voice that never stops, where it's coming from. Perhaps there are others here, with me, it's dark, very properly, it is not necessarily an oubliette for one."[16]

But hiddenness is perhaps the imprecise metaphor or figure for the space of the neutral, the space of the neutralized subject of writing, who in turn emerges from the space of writing. For what does the image of the dungeon or the oubliette give us? First, it immobilizes the writing subject, stills his movement; but stills him in *space*. Perhaps we need, if we are to comprehend the being of the neutralized subject—the subject, as in *Malone Dies* who is "neutral and inert"[17]—to unfold the economy of this *spatialized* neutrality. Because both Blanchot and Beckett seem, overtly or not, to insist on the spatialized nature of the neutral, of the neuter, even if the neuter offers itself as a deeply compromised figure of trajectivity.[18] If the neutral emerges within the step not beyond, it still is a step, a motion, even if only of its own impossibility. Because, as Blanchot tells us, the neutral "he/it" comes into being in space "at the border of writing" (SNB 6): "he/it, a word too many, which by a ruse we place at the border of writing, or the relation of writing to writing, when writing indicates itself at its own border" (6), and again: "Writing is not destined to leave traces, but to erase, by traces, all traces, to disappear in the fragmentary space of writing, more definitively than one disappears in the tomb, or again, to destroy, to destroy invisibly, without the uproar of destruction" (50). The fragmentary space of writing, we must insist, is still a space of writing. Beckett's metaphor of the dungeon or oubliette (an oubliette being a space of disappearance or the forgotten) metaphorizes the metaphorization of writing as a space of erasure.

---

16  Beckett, *The Unnamable*, 362.
17  Samuel Beckett, *Malone Dies. Three Novels by Samuel Beckett* (New York: Grove Press, 1956), 173.
18  I borrow the idea of the traject from Paul Virilio. In *Politics of the Very Worst* Virilio offers the idea of the traject as a way of moving away from the subject–object dialectic. The traject is the figure of movement; its being is defined, precisely, as "the trajectivity between subject and object" (39); the traject, neither subject nor object, thus is neutral. See Paul Virilio, *The Politics of the Very Worst*, trans. Michael Cavaliere (New York: Semiotext(e), 1999).

Blanchot will insist that writing, given its inevitable fragmentation of itself and its subject, seems to inaugurate some kind of initiatory trauma.

And perhaps it is here that we can understand Blanchot's turn to the idea of subjectivity without any subject in *The Writing of the Disaster*: "one ought perhaps to speak of a *subjectivity without any subject*: the wounded space, the hurt of the dying, the already dead body which no one could ever own, or ever say of it, *I, my body*" (WD 30);[19] crucially, Blanchot spatializes the idea of the disaster which is, as he says earlier, is the "limit of writing" (7): "Solitude or noninteriority, exposure to the outside, boundless dispersion, the impossibility of holding firm, within bounds, enclosed—such is man deprived of humanity, the supplement that supplies nothing" (30). Boundless dispersion: the subject dispersed beyond the boundary, measuring itself, perhaps, against the outside that can only confirm an essential solitude or noninteriority. And again, Blanchot's metaphors are spatial. The subject, who enters into the dangerous game of writing, allows himself to be dispersed within the ruthless space of writing that can only ever articulate the subject as always already beyond. And perhaps, as Blanchot will insist in *The Step Not Beyond*, the ultimate effect of this dispersal of the subject within the boundlessness of writing is an inevitable dispersion of the idea of space as such:

> Writing according to the fragmentary invisibly destroys surface and depth, real and possible, above and below, manifest and hidden. There is no hidden discourse that an apparent discourse would preserve, not even an open plurality of significations awaiting interpretive reading. To write at the level of the incessant murmur is to expose oneself to the decision of a lack that marks itself only by a surplus without place, impossible to put in place, to distribute in the space of thoughts, words and books. (SNB 50)

And yet. Spatial metaphors, deployed in order to speak of what cannot be conceptualized or naturalized—the neutral; the nothing—recur, insistently, like the return of that which is even beyond the spatial logic of repression. They recur in Blanchot just as they must, inevitably, in Beckett. As *The Unnamable* moves toward its inevitable, though compromised, conclusion the image of the prison

---

[19] Blanchot's figuration of subjectivity without any subject is a direct response to his reading of the figure of the Other in Levinas. In Levinas the Other's presence constitutes the self in the disturbing event of recognition and acknowledgment, what Levinas calls the "*traumatism of astonishment*" (73). Subjectivity, thus, emerges out of the relation to the Other, who in turn is constituted as a subject. Blanchot will maintain the idea of subjectivity—and, critically, the trauma of being—but will call into question its ultimate origin. See Emmanuel Levinas, *Totality and Infinity: An Essay on Interiority*, trans. Alphonso Lingis (Pittsburgh: Duquesne University Press, 1969).

occurs, recalling, of course, previous images of dungeons and oubliettes. Here we are given an image of a fantasy, a fantasy of the creation of the character, who must, as I have argued elsewhere, be the fantasy of the author calling himself into being, bound into boundlessness.[20] *The Unnamable*, an elaborate, aporetic, allegory of the obligation to create, essentially concludes with an extended fantasy of having a written identity, of having been given a place within a space that cannot support being, but merely archives the traces of being. Or is this a fantasy of what entering into the precisely *neutral* space of writing looks like for the writer, for Beckett (as for Kafka, De Sade, and the rest)? We observe immediately, again, how Beckett insists on the spatialization of the written/ writer, as he calls into being the prisoner now "riveted" to the neutral:

> Enormous prison, like a hundred thousand cathedrals, never anything else any more, from this time forth, and in it, somewhere, perhaps, riveted, tiny, the prisoner, how can he be found, how false this space is, what falseness instantly, to want to draw that round you, to want to put a being there, a cell would be plenty, if I gave up, if only I could give up, before beginning, before beginning again, what breathlessness, that's right, ejaculations, that helps you, that puts off the fatal hour, no, the reverse, I don't know, start again, in this immensity, this obscurity, go through the motions of starting again, you who can't stir, you who never started, you the who, go through the motions, what motions, you can't stir, you launch your voice, it dies away in the vault, it calls that a vault, perhaps it's the abyss, those are words, it speaks of a prison, I've no objection, vast enough for a whole people, for me alone, or waiting for me, I'll go there now, I'll try and go there now, I can't stir, I'm there already, I must be there already.[21]

What then is this space of nonarrival—"I can't stir … I'm there already"—if not a space of the neutral? Where before the unnamable would assume nothing— "neither that I move, nor that I don't"[22]—now the unnamable, in his prison, his cell, his vault—"perhaps it's the abyss"—cannot but speak of an existence in obscurity; this prison, this vault, this obscurity, this *false* space—a space that falsifies being as soon as it is articulated—is the space where voice is launched; here, speech emerges; here, in that allegorical space of the writer who is written into being even as he writes characters into being, writing emerges *in and as* a space that neutralizes both character and writer, writer as character; this is a

---

[20]  See Jonathan Boulter, *Beckett: A Guide for the Perplexed* (London and New York: Continuum, 2013).
[21]  Beckett, *The Unnamable*, 402.
[22]  Ibid., 301.

space, false, neutralizing, that can only claim a temporary, fleeting, hold on a being, Dasein (call it that), that can only survive as trace. "To respond to this demand of writing," Blanchot argues, again in *The Step Not Beyond*, "is not only to oppose a lack to a lack or to play with the void to procure some privative effect, nor is it only to maintain or indicate a blank between two or several affirmative enunciations" (SNB 50); rather, to respond to this demand, the demand of writing into the space of the neutral, to allow a character, a character-as-writer to emerge from this fatal space of the neutral is "to carry a space of language to the limit from which the irregularity of another speaking, nonspeaking, space comes back" (50).

But the question arises now with some urgency: what kind of being does the being within the space of the neutral have? Blanchot and Beckett cannot seem to rid themselves of the temptation to think of the neutralized subject; but equally they cannot rid themselves of the temptation to spatialize the neutral, to give a place to what is, essentially, beyond ontology. Let us here recall Blanchot: "The Neuter derives, in the most simple way, from a negation of two terms: *neuter*, neither one nor the other. Neither nor the other, nothing more precise" (74):

> The Neuter: paradoxical name: it barely speaks, mute word, simple, yet always veiling itself, always displacing itself out of its meaning, operating invisibly on itself while not ceasing to unwind itself, in the immobility of its position that repudiates depth. It neutralizes, neutralizes (itself), thus evokes (does nothing but evoke) the movement of *Aufhebung*, but if it suspends and retains, it retains only the movement of suspending, that is, the distance it creates by the fact that, occupying the terrain, it makes the distance disappear. (75)

The Neutral, neutralizing movement, yet moving toward the subsumption of itself; the neutral, caught in a space that effaces spatiality; the neutral: suspending itself, it retains the movement of suspension even as it cancels the distance it creates. How can we then understand this place? This space? How can we come to understand the possibility of the subject, written or writing, who occupies this space?

In *The Infinite Conversation*, Blanchot makes passing references to Beckett's *How It Is*; but these passing references, directing us as they do back to *How It Is*, perhaps alert us to that text's preoccupation with the spatialized subject; the subject who exists only insofar as it moves through an impossible space, closing distance between itself and the Other. And Blanchot will want us to remain alert to the neutralizing of the dialectic between *one* and the *other*, even at the level of the etymology of the word, the neutral: the neutral, he writes, "perhaps does nothing but take in this perversity of the other in making it still more perverse by the obscurity that covers it without dissipating it" (74). The neutral, in other words, becomes a space where the subject is neither one nor the other, but also can become a space where the other, as intimately conjoined with the one, yet simultaneously effaced, claims a perverse kind of attention: "The neuter takes the other back into itself under a light (but impenetrable) veil that seems only to force out of the other its incessant affirmation that a negative alone allows us to grasp: the other of the other, the un-known of the other, its refusal to let itself be thought as the other than the one, and its refusal to be only the Other of the 'other' than" (74–75). It is in *How It Is* that this relation—is this the relation of desire, simply?—is played out critically within a non-space of identity and writing. We recall that *How It Is* is divided into three sections: before Pim, with Pim, after Pim. The text moves the subject relentlessly through horizontal space toward its inevitable encounter with Pim even as it seems to recall memories, spatially located in the verticalized "above." The subject here in *How It Is*, in other words, is divided against itself; pluralized by virtue of having been separated from its own memories (we assume; *it* assumes), the subject, cast into this horizontal space of forward trajectory, is, in a perfect sense, neutralized by the separation from itself:

> life life the other above in the light said to have been mine on and off no going back up there no question no one asking that of me never there a few images on and off in the mud earth sky a few creatures in the light some still standing.[23]

Neither here, nor there, occupying a space that could, after Paul Virilio, be perfectly called the "trajective," the subject can only move, can only *be movement*, until the encounter with his other, Pim.[24] And it is here that the subject claims his other, fixes his other in this space through a violent act of writing. Deploying his can opener, he carves into Pim's back in an act at once definitional and brutalizing: "YOUR LIFE HERE long pause YOUR LIFE HERE good and deep long pause this dead soul what appal I can imagine YOUR LIFE unfinished for murmur light of day light of night little scene HERE to the quick."[25] Given the relentless logic of justice in the text the subject will, of course, find himself in the position

---

[23]    Samuel Beckett, *How It Is* (New York: Grove Press, 1964), 8.

[24]    The "trajective" is Virilio's term for the being that is neither subject nor object; the trajective is defined, or defines *itself*, only as movement, as trajectory: "I do not work on the subject and object"—that is the work of the philosopher—"but rather on the 'traject.' I have even proposed to inscribe the trajectory between the subject and the object to create the neologism "trajective," in addition to "subjective" and "objective" (*Politics of the Very Worst*: 39–40).

[25]    Beckett, *How It Is*, 96.

of being tortured (or imagine himself to have been tortured); what is given then, in *How It Is*, is a perfectly symmetrical image of exchange and definition: the other, othered, works in its turn to define the subject: positions, thus, of being Other are exchanged, effectively neutralized in this relentlessly trajective space that is, as always, a space of writing. This is a kind of writing that works to secure, against all security of knowing, the subject "in" his space: YOUR LIFE HERE; this exchange of positions, nullifying the other in space, is carried forward, as the text concludes, into the ultimate space of neutrality where the speaker, having since the outset of the text claimed the reality of this other (Pim), now denies the possibility of that mutually defining position of neutralized Othering. Now, as *How It Is* concludes, the speaker in his turn completes what, he claims, is an extended quotation (again we are in conventional Beckettian space here: the speaker is only a kind of scribe, conveying experience that is "overheard"); he asserts his essential solitude, just as he asserts his essential stillness:

> Only me yes alone yes with my voice yes my murmur … never crawled no in an amble no right leg right arm push pull ten yards fifteen yards no never stirred no never made to suffer to never suffered no answer NEVER SUFFERED no never abandoned no never was abandoned no so that's life here no answer THAT'S MY LIFE HERE screams good.[26]

With this denial—and we can choose to read it as only ever a denial of the essential facticity of suffering the subject wishes to disavow—comes the entry into, again, the neutral: no longer is the subject one who moves, nor is he one who does not move; it effaces that which it offers, can *only*, it seems, efface that which it offers, with its own proper voice, its solitary voice, the voice of the outside that can only ever mark a vanishing interiority.

And we have, thus, circled back to the essential question: what is this subject? Blanchot twice asks a similar question, after attending to the exigencies of reading *How It Is*: "But what is this voice?" (IC 330; 331). How are we to understand the subject, its voice, beyond our conception of the neutral, a conception that is consistently metaphorized as the spatial, metaphorized, and thus defined only as a series of deferred figures *for* the neutral, *of* the neutral? Can we move beyond the spatialized figuration of the neutral to arrive at a way of comprehending that which is and is not; there and here; there and not-there; speaking and spoken, a subject and a voice that both is and is not? My metaphors of movement and arrival perhaps betray the possibility of moving beyond figures of spatialization.

[26] Ibid., 146.

The figures of depth and motion, inevitably bound to Blanchot's conception of the neutral, suggest, perhaps, the impossibility of conceiving of the neutral as *other than* a spatial figure. And thus we arrive at a passage in *The Infinite Conversation*, a passage from chapter XIV, "The Narrative Voice (*The 'he', the neutral*)," which I wish to figure as crucial; this is a passage offered by Blanchot with a kind of unsurpassed clarity; a passage critically defining the economy of the neutral narrative voice; a passage which deploys, perhaps unashamedly we might say (Blanchot calls what follows a "whim"), spatial figures in its attempt to figure the spatial logic of the neutral voice; this is a passage, finally, that contains the maximum compression of Blanchot's thinking on the spatial logic of the neutral. I quote at some length, once again:

> Then again, without [the narrative voice's] existence—speaking from nowhere, suspended in the narrative as a whole—neither does it dissipate there in the manner of light, which, though itself invisible, makes things visible: radically exterior, it comes from exteriority itself, from the outside that is the enigma proper to language in writing. But let us consider still other traits, traits that are actually the same. The narrative voice that is inside only inasmuch as it is outside, at a distance without there being any distance, cannot be embodied. Although it may well borrow the voice of a judiciously chosen character, or even create the hybrid function of mediator (the voice that ruins all mediation), it is always different from what it utters: it is the indifferent-difference that alters the personal voice. Let us (on a whim) call it spectral, ghostlike.[27] Not that it comes from beyond the grave, or even because it would once and for all represent some essential absence, but because it always tends to absent itself in its bearer and also efface him as the center: it is thus neutral in the decisive sense that it cannot be central, does not create a center, does not speak from out of a center, but, on the contrary, at the limit, would prevent the work from having one; withdrawing from it every privileged point of interest (even afocal), and also not allowing it to exist as a completed whole, once and forever achieved. (IC 386)

Blanchot's characterization of the neutral calls to mind many figurations of the displaced, decentered, speaking/spoken subject in Beckett. Blanchot, of course, cites that critical instance of enclosure in *The Unnamable* to conclude "Where Now, Who Now?" giving Beckett the final word in his essay:

> I am in words, I am made of words, of the words of others, what others, the place too … I am everything else, a silent thing, in a hard, empty, dry, clean, black

---

[27] The original reads: "Appelons-la (par fantaisie) spectrale, fantomatique" (566). *L'Entretien infini* (Paris: Gallimard, 1969).

place, where nothing moves, nothing speaks, and that I am listening, and that I hear, and that I am searching, like an animal born in a cage of animals born in a cage of animals born in a cage of animals born in a cage. (BC 216–217)

One again may also be reminded of *Texts for Nothing* and its spectral, because decentered voice, speaking at the limit of what is, what was; speaking at the limit of constituting memory that fixes the subject in space—"Suddenly I was here, all memory gone"[28]—a here, that cannot be here, ever: "Elsewhere perhaps, by all means, elsewhere, what elsewhere can there be to this infinite here?"[29]; this is a voice that speaks at the limit of life and death: "if it's not me it will be someone, a phantom, long live all our phantoms,"[30] *as* a life constituted by neither place nor the materiality of bodies: "There is no flesh anywhere, nor any way to die."[31] The final lines of the final Text (13) summarize perfectly the decentered, spectral, subject in its limited and yet limitless positionality:

> And wonders what has become of the wish to know, it is gone, the heart is gone, the head is gone, no one feels anything, asks anything, seeks anything, says anything, hears anything, there is only silence. It's not true, yes, its true, and it's not true, there is silence and there is not silence, there is no one and there is someone, nothing prevents anything. And were the voice to cease quite at last, the old ceasing voice, it would not be true, as it is not true that it speaks, it can't speak, it can't cease. And were there one day to be here, where there are no days, which is no place, born of the impossible voice the unmakable being, and a gleam of light, still all would be silent and empty and dark, as now, as soon now, when all will be ended, all said, it says, it murmurs.[32]

Truth and not truth; silence and not silence; someone and no one; crucially, *here, which is no place*; and yet, as soon as this place, which is no place, is offered, as soon as this image of the non-place is offered, in a time that is not temporally limited—"here, where there are no days"—the relief of nontemporality, the relief of the possibility of nonbeing, is compromised by the insistence of some deeply compromised futurity: "now, *as soon* now." This place/space/time of the neutral can only ever be given as a hypothetical possibility of silence, in the future: *as soon now*. And why should this be? One answer, perhaps, is that despite the achievement of a kind of phantomic ontology ("I've given myself up for dead

---

[28]  Beckett, *Texts for Nothing*, 132.
[29]  Ibid., 123.
[30]  Ibid., 120.
[31]  Ibid., 113.
[32]  Ibid., 154.

all over the place"[33]; "Long live all our phantoms,"[34]), language still speaks a kind of neutrality into being: "all said, it says, it murmurs." What this "it" is, perhaps, is immaterial: whether "it" is the voice of the exterior, speaking the subject into compromised being or whether the "it" is a reflexive, neutral, yet still pronominal—and thus deictic—marker of the speaking subject, the subject, on the *verge* of the neutral, on the *limit* of the neutral, this "it" still calls a spatial subject into being, if only as a possibility.

One way, then, to characterize the neutral, the space of the neutral that Beckett's characters seem to inhabit, or for an instant attempt to inhabit, is that the neutral is, and can only be, a space of desire; it is an impossibility as long as the voice, as interior or exterior, marks the subject in the event of speech. As long as there is an agent, there, to be called into the deeply ungrounded house of being; as long as there is an agent, however compromised, the neutral is never fully neutral and writing, desperate to achieve that neutral space, is never realized, never *can be* realized. It is, thus, in late Beckett, in language—call it prose; call it poetry—that neutralizes grammar, as such, that the true space of neutrality opens as a possibility, within language. It is left to late texts, as *Ill Seen Ill Said*, or *Worstward Ho*, to give us a sense of the intimate connection between agrammatical language and spatialized being: "On. Say on. Be said on. Somehow on. Till nohow on. Said nohow on."[35]

It is not possible within the limits of this chapter to unfold the manifest and aporetic complexities of these last texts. Instead, in this concluding space, I will allow Beckett's "neither" (1976), a text that moves perhaps most fully and most successfully (before the late second trilogy) into the agentless space of the fully neutral, to stand as a transitional text:

To and fro in shadow from inner to outershadow
    from impenetrable self to impenetrable unself by way of neither
    as between two lit refuges whose doors once neared gently close,
    once turned away from gently part again
    beckoned back and forth and turned away
    heedless of the way, intent on the one gleam or the other
    unheard footfalls only sound
    till at last halt for good, absent for good from self and other
    then no sound

---

[33]   Ibid., 103.
[34]   Ibid., 120.
[35]   Samuel Beckett, *Worstward Ho, Nohow On* (New York: Grove Press, 1983), 89.

> then gently light unfading on that unheeded neither
> unspeakable home.[36]

What can be said about language without an agent? Without a subject? Perhaps, only, that "neither" enacts—as a kind of expression (but from nowhere, from no one)—an affect of agent-less desire. But what is the desire here, then? "neither" is of course a kind of lure, calling the reader, who in his turn, enacts the subjectless desire, to trace and track the spectral trajectory here from *shadow* to *home*. And there is a kind of movement here, a movement that is a shadow of desire's trajectory; we begin in motion—to and fro—we move into the neutral space of the "from" which is called into being in another spatial metaphor through the logic of the "by way." Is what is being given here a compressed image of being with and for the other? Is this an image of the shadowy relation between self and unself, modulated, as it can only be, in the space of impenetrable unknowing?

We may do well to recall Blanchot here: "The neuter takes the other back into itself under a light (but impenetrable) veil that seems only to force out of the other its incessant affirmation that a negative alone allows us to grasp: the other of the other, the un-known of the other, its refusal to let itself be thought as the other than the one, and its refusal to be only the Other of the 'other' than" (Blanchot 1992: 74–75). And as if acknowledging the abstraction, the impenetrability of the idea of the self and other relation, neutralized in the space of the neither, Beckett offers his first "concrete" metaphors: the refuge, the doors, metaphors which anticipate the final unspeakable, and perfectly nostalgic, idea of "home" which concludes the piece. Being with the other, defined as only trajective, is an endless oscillation between space, the space of welcome—the door—that refuses entry and endlessly invites entry: "beckoned back and forth and turned away." This is a space, perhaps, of a refused invitation to Being (can we suggest that "neither" is an allegory of Dasein? That it is "about" the movement of being itself?). And yet Being, at once heedless and intent (surely this is another way of speaking of neutralized desire: heedless and intent, but it *is* still desire), moving in space and yet unheard in that movement, finds its refuge (what Beckett in *Lessness* will call the "true refuge")[37] in stillness. And it is here, in the cessation of movement, in the cessation of trajectivity (and sound) that Being finds itself free from self and other, free from the compromise of being with others, *free, indeed perhaps, from the endless oscillation that produces even the neutral space of*

---

[36]  "neither" was written for composer Morton Feldman in 1976 and was originally published in the *Journal of Beckett Studies* in 1979. Quoted here in Beckett, *The Complete Short Prose*, 258.

[37]  Ibid., 197.

*neither one thing nor the other.* Beckett's final image, an image that can only be a figure of and for neutrality, the neither one thing nor another—which is the one space or another—is of home, the "unheeded neither." We should attend to the pairing of adjectives in these final lines: unheeded and unspeakable. The home, this neutral space, is, as I say, an image of and for neutrality. What does this mean? It means that the home is, we might say, almost indifferent, indifferent to the subject who may, or may not, approach it, move away from it, inhabit it, ignore it. The home is the unheeded neither: it does not mind if it is known just as it itself can, perhaps should be, indifferently ignored. Just as the self and unself move to and from each other almost indifferently via the neither in the opening of the text, so too the agentless agent of neutrality finds, or does not find, itself in the space of the home. And thus perhaps, like the unnamable who cannot be named, but is named in his unnamability, the home cannot find itself within the language of being, as such, but can only be located, linguistically, discursively, philosophically, in the deictic trace of absence. In other words, the home is unspeakable—unable to be spoken of—precisely because it is the space of the neutral. The neither is the trajective way between self and unself; the neither is the unheeded, unrecognized (because unrecognizable) space of refuge, the space where movement and trajectivity cease, where sounds cease: what remains, what endlessly can only ever remain, is the light—gently light unfading—forever illuminating what cannot be known.

# 11

# The Look of Nothingness: Blanchot and the Image

Jeff Fort

To what extent is a thinking and practice of "the image" constitutive of Blanchot's work? While no doubt a relatively infrequent topic in his essays, the image, as Marie-Claire Ropars-Wuilleumier aptly puts it, is "a marginal constant that accompanies the entirety of Blanchot's critical reflection"/"une constante marginale qui accompagne toute la réflexion critique de Blanchot."[1] But this margin is also "central" to Blanchot's writing, albeit in eccentric ways that can be difficult to trace. Known as a thinker of writing and of language—and of silence—and moreover as a writer who remains closer to obscurity and dim enigma than to the clarity of the contoured image, Blanchot nonetheless places "the image" at the heart of his reflections on literature and, no less so, of his fictional and recitical writings (as I like to call the texts he designated as *récits*). This chapter will delineate the place and importance of the image in Blanchot's thinking and writing practice, with a focus on the postwar period.

## Introduction: Blanchot and modernism? Wandering, an approach to the image

Before entering directly into this question, however, I would like to begin with a few words about Blanchot and modernism, in order to approach the central place of the image—for the latter turns out to be integral to what can be considered the most clearly "modernist" phase in Blanchot's writing.

[1] Marie-Claire Ropars-Wuilleumier, "Sur le désoeuvrement: l'image dans l'écrire selon Blanchot," *Littérature* no. 94 (1994): 114 113–24. Translations throughout are my own (though I have consulted existing translations); published translations are cited for the reader's reference.

It is not fortuitous that a discussion of Blanchot in relation to modernism would be drawn toward the postwar moment of his work, in *The Space of Literature* in particular, as well as *The Book to Come*, both of which include significant commentaries on some of the most canonical figures of modernism (Mallarmé, Rilke, Kafka, Proust, Woolf, Broch, Musil), or that the question of the image would be given a remarkable emphasis during that period. For it is there that Blanchot grapples most insistently with issues that can be identified as pertaining to a certain "high modernism," for example: the place of the subject in art, the quest for depth and interiority, non linear structures of time and space, problems of perspective in narration, the notion of truth in language and fiction, art as an excessive singularity with respect to restricted economies and technical processes, and as a search for its own essence. In a sense, however, Blanchot is not at all attempting to resolve these issues; rather, he is showing that they have reached an extreme point, not exactly a "post-," but a kind of nullity or self-nullification, a quiet implosion of their terms and moments, and no doubt also a radical dispersal and blanking out, a collapse "into" their endless outsides—or indeed into "the outside" in general. For example, time for Blanchot does not only become more complex, more layered, more dense and opaque, more unwieldy in its forms; it becomes more "simply" and more radically, but also more enigmatically, "the time of the absence of time" (SL 30/EL 25). This sort of highly equivocal formulation brings us directly into the type of dilemma that Blanchot faces us with at the juncture of modernism and some other stranger thing that modernism is becoming: does "the time of the absence of time" reinstall some retrograde remnant of eternity, or does it liquidate the very core and possibility of such a traditional notion? Strangely, it does both, as time devours itself from the inside and yet remains a distinct *form of time*, leaving precisely an empty but persistent shell, an indelible leftover and remnant—something called eternity, twisted around upon its own vacuity.[2] Likewise with the subject of art: for Blanchot, this "subject" (a word he doesn't really use in this sense), this artist or writer, is not a deeper or more interior or (again) more layered and richer entity through which an aesthetic object comes into being, but rather *no one*, or even better a mere "Someone," an impersonal being who has lost

---

[2]  I mean to evoke here, among other things, the mention in *Death Sentence* of a "shell of an enigma" (DS 3/AM 9) located at the very heart of the story, along with the death mask implicitly associated with it, and the "eternity" attributed to its gaze, in one of several occurrences of the word *eternity* (and variants) in the text. I will return to this below.

all capacity and mastery, including, as Blanchot often repeats, the power to say "I"—not in favor of a higher power or force that would speak through the neutralized artist, but rather as a mere erring image of itself and of the language it speaks, a ghost or a specter, a dead-living thing drawn on into an endless attenuation of sense. And, one can add, drawn toward an image, ever-receding, barely existing, which is the only thing that approaches a center or even something like a topographical moment in "literary space"—otherwise devoid of identifiable "features."

It is also worth noting that Blanchot's "modernism" is therefore not about innovation, but rather about radicality. Blanchot did not innovate narrative forms (as did, say, Faulkner or Joyce); nor did he "deepen" the subjective framework of literary writing/narration (as did the two just mentioned, along with Woolf, Proust). The canonical modernist writer to whom Blanchot is closest is Kafka; but what Blanchot really drew from Kafka was a resoluteness in wandering, in erring, and thus, in a way, in remaining with surfaces, endlessly shifting and continually permutating surfaces—a kind of horizontal allegorism without any keys, rather than a transcendent symbology. But after the novels (*Thomas the Obscure, Aminadab, The Most High*), and with the more and more attenuated narrative gestures of the *récits*, the scope of this wandering, and thus of any allegorizing tendency, became severely restricted, limited to the drifting repercussions of a voice that cannot stop. This voice is one driven by what Blanchot calls "fascination," and in particular a fascination before *the image*.

All this is to say that if Blanchot's work, at least during the postwar period up to the early 1960s, can be said to fall within some lineage of modernism, this is because it stretches the latter's terms and limits to an extreme point of rupture, if not outright destruction. Much like Beckett, and for reasons and in ways that are not dissimilar, Blanchot brings modernism to a terminal point, with tremendous rigor and focus, partly by converting deep interiority into irrevocable exteriority and exile, by turning it inside out and surveying the impossible topography that emerges, but also by resolutely going *nowhere beyond* this space. It is this nowhere beyond that gives Blanchot's work its understated pathos, its stubborn radicality, and the fatality of its incessant persistence.

If modernism was essentially a confrontation between a newly intensified techno-industrial modernity—the shrinking of experience, or perhaps its "destruction," but perhaps in a sense different from that of Benjamin—and the dwindling chances of an expressive, excessive and singular subjectivity, then

Blanchot was a modernist to the extent that he, too, resisted the former, while asserting something akin to the latter. But only something uncannily akin, like a long dead relative who continually returns to take up residence, and certainly not as a viable and substantial mode of (re)production. Blanchot's modernism, such as it is, was also predicated on a full knowledge that this battle, if it was one, had been irrevocably lost, and likewise on a duty to certify that loss, while nonetheless *refusing to capitulate*. For Blanchot, writing would be *in excess*—it would be without aim, goal, ground, or power; indeed it would work ceaselessly to evacuate such possibilities, and even possibility itself—or it would not be.

The image, and the artwork more specifically, are not simply one mode of this tension in extremis; it is rather precisely one of the forms of experience most directly at stake. Is there an image that is not immediately folded into a grinding dialectics of technical reproducibility, on the one hand, and, on the other, captured in the egological gears of psychology? The possibility of such an image, or inversely its fatality, is Blanchot's starting point.

## Blanchot's image?

Let us begin, then—or rebegin—with a very literal question: what is the image *of* Blanchot? Are there any images of Blanchot, to speak of? These questions will place us in the midst of Blanchot's equivocal relation to techno-aesthetic modernity, and to mass media, and thus of his highly strategic confrontation with the excesses of art and writing.

The second question just posed refers indirectly to the fact that, until recently, there were only a small handful of photographs (hardly more than two or three) of Maurice Blanchot circulating in public (which is to say, of course, above all on the internet). Two in particular were easily found and are quite well known. One is a portrait of Blanchot and Levinas, tightly framed, shot very slightly from below, showing two well-dressed young men during their student days in Strasbourg in the late 1920s. Unlike Levinas, whose look could be described almost as a glare, Blanchot's gaze is not directed at the camera but is rather drifting somewhere *just above*. It is unlikely that those present when this photograph was taken could have known that it would be virtually the only image of Blanchot to appear, in public, for many decades to come. Fast forward those many decades to another photograph, taken paparazzi style from a distance, showing a hunched old man dressed in black walking through the parking lot of a supermarket. The spiteful "gotcha" quality of this furtive gesture could be seen as a provocative response to a lifetime of "obscurity" and to an unwavering refusal to appear in public or, much less, to be photographed, filmed, recorded, or even interviewed. The interval between these two photographs (some sixty years) is one measure of the commitment to this refusal. And this is my point in posing this literal and material question: in a certain sense, Blanchot refused the image (and not only the image of himself). In an age when mass media representation was increasingly considered to be altogether inevitable, including for writers faced with the exigencies of publicity, Blanchot simply said no.[3] And he continued to do so, without exception. It was only after his death that a number of photographs of Blanchot were published in a compendium of writings and documents dedicated to the writer (in the Cahiers de L'Herne *Blanchot*).[4] These photographs call for comment in their own right, but for now I will say only that the images that appear in that publication serve, in my opinion, only to highlight the futility, in the end, of such a strategy, which is not to say that it was in any way unjustified. But this concrete refusal of the mediatic image does raise some complex and ambiguous questions at the outset regarding Blanchot's thinking and practice of the image *in writing*. First of all, what does Blanchot even mean by "the image" if he disjoins it from media and technicity? Does the writer's image that he evokes conveniently dematerialize images, problematically divesting them of any physical support and, therefore, any social and historical context? Do we have to do with an incisive critique or a self-protective, and perhaps deeply obfuscating, evasion (or both)? Was Blanchot's withdrawal from the public, from publicity, and thus from actually visible images, also a compromised subtraction from another even more encompassing and demanding dialectic, that between the writer and the specific material and technological conditions of his or her work? And if the image itself is not at all times technically and materially mediated—a question that remains very unclear in most of Blanchot's reflections on the image—then what on earth is it? Is it in the end not "on earth" at all? Are we quickly returning to a very equivocal kind of eternity after all?

The image *of* Blanchot, then, to the extent that there is one, already indicates some incompatibilities and tensions within a foregrounding of the image *as*

---

[3] An exigency of which Blanchot wrote that "publicity itself becomes an art" (BC 245) / "la publicité devient elle-même un art" (LV 334)—this in an age when, as Blanchot points out, the public itself is the basis for the writer's value. See "The Power and the Glory," the final essay in *The Book to Come*.

[4] I am grateful to Patrick Lyons for sharing with me the text of his insightful article, "Tracing the Obscure Image: Maurice Blanchot on Photography," in *French Forum* (Philadelphia: University of Pennsylvania Press, forthcoming).

*such*. For if Blanchot the author was so insistent on his own invisibility, this was very much in line with certain aspects of his writing, which both postulates and performs the author's impersonality, not to say destruction, and is itself turned toward nothing so much as its own (impossible) disappearance. Is the ultimate impossibility of this textual (not to mention public and visual) disappearance, which Blanchot also repeatedly thematizes, not in its turn profoundly linked with the question of technical processes of (re)production just evoked, as though the machinery of writing, in all its depersonalizing and effacing force, were not also the condition for the strange remnant persistence, the uncanny eternity, I have been calling up?

But there is another possibility to keep in mind as we enter into Blanchot's image-haunted literary space. It could be that a thinking of technology is linked at the deepest levels of Blanchot's work with precisely the most radical aspects of his thought concerning disappearance and effacement. Christopher Fynsk has commented richly and insightfully on the strange motto (if I may call it that) that traverses Blanchot's later thinking, especially in *The Step Not Beyond*: "Everything must efface itself. Everything will be effaced" (SNB 53)/"Tout doit s'effacer. Tout s'effacera" (PA 76).[5] Under this sign, beginning long before that text, we find one of the most insistent structural moments of Blanchot's writing, arrived at over and over from various angles and paths of approach, namely a radical hollowing of the present, a nullifying and evacuating of anything that could be considered "present" or "presence"—a nothingness that regards us from out of the heart of all possible experience. I do not believe that it is far-fetched to link this nothingness and vacuity in Blanchot not only with technology but also with the image. As evidence one can cite the first extensive text on images from Blanchot, his essay from 1950 on André Malraux's ambitious multi-volume work on the Musée imaginaire.[6] There Blanchot engages in a characteristically subtle and even-handed commentary on a project that, however, casts a thoroughly humanist glance over the totality of (re)produced artistic images in order to affirm the ever-widening value and virtues, the redemptive power, even, of art as a human and cultural *activity*. Not only does Blanchot in this essay introduce,

---

[5]  This fragment goes on to say: "to write is to go, through the world of traces, toward the effacement of traces and of all traces, for the traces are opposed to totality and always already disperse themselves" (SNB 53) / "écrire, c'est aller, par le monde des traces, vers l'effacement des traces et de toutes traces, car les traces s'opposent à la totalité et toujours déjà se dispersent" (PA 77). See Christopher Fynsk, *Last Steps: Maurice Blanchot's Exilic Writing* (New York: Fordham University Press, 2013), especially chapter 3, "Beyond Refusal: The Madness of the Day," and chapter 6, "The Step Not Beyond."

[6]  Blanchot's "Le musée, l'art et le temps" is collected in *L'Amitié*, 21–51; for English see ""The Museum, Art, and Time" in *Friendship*, trans. Elizabeth Rottenberg (Stanford: Stanford University Press, 1997), 12–40.

as a strange challenge to Malraux's optimism of culture, the image of the corpse that will have a significant place in *The Space of Literature* (to which we will return in a moment), he also links technological reproduction to the powerful forms of negativity that undermine this view.[7] And it is against this background that, at the end of the essay, he deals a final blow, writing—in direct response to a quotation from Malraux on art's ability to "negate our nothingness"/"nier notre néant"—that while "the image [may be] capable of negating nothingness, [it] is also the gaze of nothingness upon us"/"l'image, capable de nier le néant, est aussi le regard du néant sur nous," before concluding with a number of phrases that sound very much like the language of *The Space of Literature*.[8] The image, then, has a somber other side, devouring and groundless, a restless absence of presence itself: the image is also a gaze, and it looks at us from out of its/ our nothingness, irreducibly and perhaps originarily. If, at a certain level, "the image" for Blanchot is not visible, if it seems to brush toward a certain uncanny eternity, this may be because at bottom it is something that *becomes* visible only in its inevitable effacement, in the abyssal negativity of its native dissolution. Blanchot's subsequent major texts from this period, on the image and its "place" in literary space, provide further shape and articulation of this insight.

## Essential solitude: Becoming imaginary (Blanchot with Levinas)

The simultaneous importance and marginality of the question of the image in Blanchot's critical essays is indicated straightaway by its textual placement in the work that gives this question more direct attention than any other, *The Space of Literature*. "Essential Solitude," the essay which Blanchot placed at the opening of his most densely cohesive critical book, poses this question directly, but not until

---

[7]  In a related, but different, gesture, the essay that follows in *Friendship*, "Museum Sickness" (F 41–49) / "Le mal du musée" (A 52–61), aims a harsh critique at a complacent refusal of modern realities based on a "nostalgic memory of an unknown past" (F 48).

[8]  From there, in the final sentences of the essay, Blanchot writes of the image and nothingness:

> Elle [l'image] est légère, et il [le néant] est immensément lourd. Elle brille, et il est l'épaisseur diffuse où rien ne se montre. Elle est l'interstice, la tache de ce soleil noir, déchirure qui nous donne, sous l'apparence de l'éclat éblouissant, le négatif de l'inépuisable profondeur négative. De là que l'image semble si profonde et si vide, si menaçante et si attirante, riche de toujours plus de sens que nous ne lui en prêtons et, aussi, pauvre, nulle et silencieuse, car, en elle, s'avance cette sombre impuissance privée de maître, qui est celle de la mort comme recommencement. (F 40/A 51).

its final three pages—which then spill over into a long footnote, which in turn refers the reader to another essay "en annexes," the striking and enigmatic "Two Versions of the Imaginary." The question of the image thus literally bookends, or encircles, the tightly focused literary reflections of *The Space of Literature*, and provides a strange framing of the even more constant question of writing and the paradoxical conditions of its errant adventures.

Such a framing, however, operates less a marginal containment than a thoroughgoing contamination: literary space is image all the way through. This is expressed by Blanchot most radically, and in greatest proximity to the very materiality of writing, when he says (in the long footnote just mentioned) that literary language is not simply a language in which images take the upper hand or are deployed with particular skill, a *langage imagé*, but rather that it is itself an image, it is language become an image of itself, an image-language or language-image "that no one speaks" and whose words are "images of words and words in which things turn into images" (SL 34)/"images de mots et mots où les choses se font images" (EL 32). This phantomatic ghost-language—specter and double of its more functionally operative uses—this neutralization and deployment of language in its most radical element of sheer seeming, this apparent *shadow-language* is for Blanchot what marks out literary speech as such. Except that such a turn of language in fact bears no clear and distinctive mark that would separate it off from its surer and safer usages, and it is precisely here that literature insinuates its vertiginous becoming-image into all possible written worlds, and perhaps into all possible worlds period. In this sense, "the image" of literature—of a language-image as the condition of literary speech—has already overtaken writing as such even before the question of specific "visual" images arises, even before the entire problem of the relation between things and images is formulated. But perhaps (therefore) this is an unfitting way to pose the problem, for things have already been turned upside down, inverted, reversed or turned inside out, and brought before their more elusive image-like origins.

An illustration drawn from the text might help to clarify this strange transformation. Ordinarily we think of writing as a physical activity carried out by a human body, a real writer who uses a tool to inscribe words which, in turn, may introduce fictive images into a specific weave of discourse. The hand thus preexists the writing it does, which occurs as a stable process of movement and work based on this set of physical conditions. At one level, there is, of course, nothing false about this. However, without ever simply negating it, Blanchot rather playfully, and yet at bottom in all seriousness, turns it around: in one section of "Essential Solitude" subtitled "Persecutory Prehension," he says that the hand that writes, proceeding under a strange, uncontrollable, harassing compulsion, already "moves in a hardly human time, which is not that of viable action, nor of hope, but rather a shadow of time, [and it is] itself a shadow of a hand slipping unreally [*irréellement*] toward an object that has become its own shadow" (SL 25/EL 18–19). With this "object" (*toward* which …), we begin to approach the specificity of the image; but the point for the moment is that not only has language as a whole become a shadow and image of itself; the writer too, this person sitting at a table, has become a shadow—or at least the hand that writes has passed, maniacally, into such a state. For the other hand, says Blanchot, the non-writing hand, maintains the capacity to stop the "sick" hand that cannot cease. It remains on this side of the passivity and fascination into which the writer—the shadow-writer, the writer-image—has hopelessly wandered. And it is there that Blanchot draws some limit, at least, around what might otherwise appear to be an all-devouring *imaginaire*, or perhaps even a strange and remainderless idealism.

The image-space we are entering, however, does not constitute a form of idealism, despite the strange precedence of the image over things that is beginning to emerge—or if it is idealism, it is one in which "ideas" themselves have lost all solid ground and consistency, all stability and seat. First, in philosophical terms, the image in Blanchot is not linked in its own formation to a constituting subject engaged in a process of cognition and conceptualization. Here, rather, the image reigns—without a discernible law and without a system—and the writer, the closest thing to a subject in the vicinity, is in a position of extreme passivity, ruled over and yet entirely unbound. Nor, then, is the image a "mental image," a "representation" (idea as *Vorstellung*) conditioning the givenness of a world. Whence then the ontological priority of images over things? It is to be found in Blanchot's direct linking of images with the indefinite ground against and from which they appear—which, far from a remainderless and systematic constitution of all things, is itself a remainder that can never be dissolved, for it is the very ground of images: it *is* the given.

What is at stake, then, is rather a troubling relation not between reality and ideas, but rather between "reality and its shadow" (to quote the title of an important text by Levinas from this period), in which the shadow—the image—has always already unsettled the forms of stable constitution that have traditionally been invoked by philosophy. And in which the shadow, not reality, is what points the way to a more fundamental ground. We may note in passing that it is precisely here that these two thinkers are in league against a certain subjectivizing phenomenology, and (therefore) against a classical understanding of images; I will return to this point. For both Levinas and Blanchot, things do not precede their images, in the manner of model and copy; rather the link between model and copy has been scrambled, blurred, or even severed. "Being" has been neutralized, and one enters into the experience of what Levinas calls the *il y a*, a shadow world that is not secondary but rather uncannily prior and more "elementary" (a word used by both Levinas and Blanchot). But if a strange zone of shadow and image appears to take precedence over things and their world, far from a transcendentally constituting a priori, it is rather in the manner of an obtrusive leftover, a remainder, which appears (to quote Blanchot now) when "everything has disappeared"—when this "everything has disappeared" *itself appears* (SL 253/EL 340); or, in another formulation: it is "what there is when there is no longer world, when there is not yet world" (SL 33/EL 31); or yet again, as Levinas puts it, in very similar terms: "The exterior ... is no longer a world ... The disappearance of all things and the disappearance of the ego leads back to what cannot disappear, to the very fact of being in which *one* participates, willingly or no, without having taken the intiative, anonymously"/"L'extérieur ... n'est plus monde ... La disparition de toute chose et la disparition du moi, ramènent à ce qui ne peut disparaître, au fait même de l'être auquel *on* participe, bon gré mal gré, sans en avoir pris l'initiative, anonymement."[9]

This remainder is harassing and confining, and yet endlessly elusive, an exilic movement (Levinas refers to an *exotisme* in this sense) that leaves no place and no rest. To characterize this experience, Levinas evokes a number of affective experiences such as fatigue and insomnia, but also simply horror, the tragic guilt of Shakespearean characters, the inescapable bad conscience of a murderer— all of these as responses to Heidegger's notion of anxiety, which they do not simply elaborate or intensify, but rather oppose: "Horror of being as opposed to the anxiety of nothingness"/"Horreur de l'être opposée à l'angoisse du néant."[10] Levinas also writes (in the deliberately anti-Sartrian mode that occasionally marks this phase of his work):

> To be a consciousness is to be torn away from the *there is*, since the existence of
> a consciousness constitutes a subjectivity, since it is a subject of existence, that
> is to say, to a certain extent, a master of being, already a name, in the anonymity

[9]  Emmanuel Levinas, *De l'existence à l'existant* (Paris: Vrin, 1990 [1947]), 95.
[10]  Ibid., 102.

of the night. Horror is, in a way, a movement that will strip consciousness of its "subjectivity" itself … by precipitating it into an *impersonal vigilance* [or *wakefulness*].

Etre conscience, c'est être arraché à l'*il y a*, puisque l'existence d'une conscience constitue une subjectivité, puisqu'elle est sujet d'existence c'est-à dire, dans une certaine mesure, maîtresse de l'être, déjà nom, dans l'anonymat de la nuit. L'horreur est, en quelque sorte, un mouvement qui va dépouiller la conscience de sa "subjectivité" même … en la précipitant dans une *vigilance impersonnelle*.[11]

The "ontological" priority of the *il y a* is such that subjectivity, at least understood as consciousness, must undergo the violence of being, must be "torn away from it" and thereby given form and identity, against the indeterminate, shifting and threatening ground which, however, continues to haunt it, insomniacally and horrifically, and to which it *can always return*. Likewise for Blanchot literary space entails an experience of radical depersonalization, anonymity, errancy, groundlessness, and aimlessness from which the identifiable, namable, and active subject would have to emerge or escape, in order to be. The elements of passivity and captivity, not of freedom and expansiveness, are clearly foregrounded, as is the sense of an inescapable fatality, albeit before a fate that remains unknown.

At this level of questioning, then, the image in Blanchot—along with the question of literature in general—brings into play a kind of ontological "ground" which, however, renders the notion of *being* over to its fragmented dissolution and dispersion, in an experience that has no beyond, because this space of anonymity and *dépouillement* is the only beyond there is to get to. During this period of Blanchot's writing, one name for this beyond that is not beyond is *the imaginary*, and the landscape that it opens is strangely new: a place where philosophical reflection, pressed by thinkers like Levinas and Blanchot, has wandered into the outer confines of its constitutive margins, given over to experiences heretofore considered irrelevant to thought (insomnia, fatigue, horror, anonymity, fascination, etc.)—experiences normally treated in literature—thus making it into something radically different from what it has been. Heidegger's analysis of anxiety also moves in this direction, but not without returning, more or less safe and distinct, to this side of the swarming obscurities of writing—which by the same token is itself becoming something other than "literature." If in the 1950s Blanchot is content to use this term, it is in order to challenge philosophy on an indistinct border ground which the term itself already signifies.

---

[11] Ibid., 98; emphasis in the original.

## The imaginary and its others: Sartre and Heidegger

The language of "being" and ontology used above evokes Heidegger, of course, whose thought is a major preoccupation for both Levinas and Blanchot during this period. At the same time, on another flank, they also contest the dominance of Sartre's notion of engaged literature, as well as the version of "the imaginary" as articulated in the latter's work of that name, published in 1940.[12] When one looks closely at this book, with side glances at roughly contemporaneous texts by Blanchot and Levinas, it is difficult not to see Sartre—who usually appears so complex, so prone to intriguing opacities, so self-contradictory, by turns insightful and obtuse, both brilliantly provocative and mind-numbingly abstract—as a doctrinaire and flat-footed realist fixated on a thing called "consciousness" and its essential rootedness in and mastery of a pre-given world, a philosophical rationalist who appears innocent of even a cursory reading of Freud, having laid his bedrock in Cartesian evidences, proceeding then (after a deft leap over various Kantian abysses) to update them with adaptations from Husserl, whose own radical doubts and continual rebeginnings do not seem to have made much of an impression. If this seems unfair to Sartre (which it no doubt is—but let it stand as an index of this reader's frustration), then we might do well to evoke a much more measured, but essentially accurate, characterization of Sartre's discourse in *L'imaginaire*. The following is from Manola Antonioli's study of Blanchot, in a chapter on "Imaginaire et mimèsis":

> Sartre's question is this: what characteristics can be conferred on consciousness based on the fact that it is a consciousness that can imagine?
>
> The faculty of imagination is defined as the condition of the freedom of consciousness in relation to every particular reality; the imagination is constitutive of a "being-in-the-world" conceived at once as constitution and nihilation of the world. It ends up coinciding with the freedom of consciousness, as a transcending of the real. The unreal that is outside the world is the product of a free consciousness that remains in the world. The negative of the imagination is therefore immediately reversed into positivity, the apparent passivity of consciousness with regard to images gives way to the activity and freedom of

---

[12] See Jean-Paul Sartre, *L'imaginaire* (Paris: Gallimard, Folio Essais, 2005). Levinas's essay "La réalité et son ombre" ("Reality and its Shadow") was first published in Sartre's journal *Les Temps Modernes*, but its analyses are so directly antithetical to Sartre's position that the editors found it necessary to preface it with a two-page editorial disclaimer (signed simply "T.M."), carefully pitched so as not to undermine the obvious richness and brilliance of the piece, while clearly asserting the necessary distance. See Emmanuel Levinas, "La réalité et son ombre," *Les Temps Modernes* 4, no. (38) (1948): 771–89.

imaging consciousness, which, by way of the imaginary, only realizes its mastery over the object represented and of the world in which it operates, a mastery even more radical than in perception. The work of art, defined as an unreal [*un irréel*], can only participate in this dimension of mastery and activity.

The imaginary, which seems to withdraw the world from us, only serves to make it even more available for the freedom of a sovereign subject. The unreal is but a necessary detour for the self-affirmation of the real alone, that of a subject who is master of himself and of his world.[13]

This is an excellent description of precisely what Blanchot, in his own way, works to reverse and to undo. Indeed, nothing could be further from the "imaginary" evoked by Blanchot (who uses the term frequently), especially in terms of the strange space, the bottomless ground, into which he insists on drawing us in his analyses, not in order simply to liquidate the place of consciousness, freedom, and the relative mastery of objects and the world, but to reveal their radical dependency on the intractable paradoxes and fundamental irreality of *another* world—or even, in its most extreme formulation, "the other of every world" (SL 75)/"l'autre de tout monde" (EL 89–90). With this *unworlding* of the image, Blanchot turns away both from Sartre and, more importantly, from Heidegger, for whom even the abysses of anxiety and uncanniness, even the becoming-useless (the becoming-image) of broken things, leads not into an irreparably estranging collapse of all, not into "essential solitude," but rather into resoluteness and individualization (*Entschlossenheit* and *Vereinzelung*), and, thereby, heroically back to the world of possibility. From here, then, Blanchot turns us rather toward a region of captive fascination, in which images, distant and fleeting but inescapable, are but a thin margin of appearance on this side of nothing. Or, one might say, where they direct upon us the very look of *désoeuvrement*, the idleness and unworking, the passivity and powerlessness, in which any search for a work (an *oeuvre*) must abide and move.

## The image and fascination

The two pages of "Essential Solitude" titled "The Image" are extraordinarily dense and enigmatic, even within the overall landscape of *The Space of Literature*.

---

[13] Manola Antonioli, *L'écriture de Maurice Blanchot: fiction et théorie* (Paris: Editions Kimé, 1999), 74. My translation.

Blanchot writes in a brief introductory note to the book that if it has a center, it is somewhere in the vicinity of "The Gaze of Orpheus"—a gaze closely bound up in the paradoxes of the image of concern to us here; but if that is the book's approximate center, this short section on "The Image" is something like the brilliant and blinding surface enveloping it, its shell of light and vibration.

Having evoked fascination as that which "reigns" in the suffocating dispersion and exposure, the coldness and vertigo, the radical homelessness of literary space, Blanchot asks: Why fascination?[14] Why is fascination the experience or the force under or into which one falls when one writes? Fascination is "the passion of the image," as the *thing* is released into the distance and separation across which images must appear. But it is also precisely the experience, the way of seeing, in which the difference between near and distant collapses into a compulsive passivity of looking. And it is thus the "contact" of a distance that will not let go, that draws the gaze into something beyond itself, but something that is, again, but an image, and indeed ultimately *an image of itself*. If we read carefully, we "see" that the image, in "The Image," is the image of the gaze seeing itself, or even, in a sense, attempting to see itself seeing. It is in this sense, too, that it is impossible. Evoking again the distance and separation that make seeing possible, Blanchot writes:

> The scission that was the possibility of seeing, becomes, at the very heart of the gaze, frozen into impossibility. The gaze thus finds in what makes it possible the potentiality that neutralizes it, that neither suspends nor arrests it, but that on the contrary prevents it from ever having done, that cuts it off from all beginning, makes of it a neutral glimmer gone astray, a glimmer that does not go out, that does not illuminate: the circle of the gaze closed around upon itself.
>
> La scission, de possibilité de voir qu'elle était, se fige, au sein même du regard, en impossibilité. Le regard trouve ainsi dans ce qui le rend possible la puissance qui le neutralise, qui ne le suspend ni ne l'arrête, mais au contraire l'empêche d'en jamais en finir, le coupe de tout commencement, fait de lui une lueur neutre égarée qui ne s'éteint pas, qui n'éclaire pas, le cercle, refermé sur soi, du regard.

The loop or buckle evoked here indicates that we are indeed entering into territory that encircles an uncanny center, a center which, however, is thereby ruined not only of its function, but of its being what it is: the short circuit of fascination, of contact as distance, brings the image *into* the gaze itself, as though cracking open the kernel of an origin and inserting its object into the faculty

---

[14]  Quotations in what follows, unless otherwise indicated, are drawn from SL 32–33/EL 28–31.

(*puissance*) that would reveal it; the gaze itself closes on itself, showing not its fundamental structure but rather the neutralizing shadow of the light that makes its vision possible. Shadow of light: not as one share of a projected whole divided into light and shade, but shadow *of* light, light's mere "image" and glimmer of itself, in which the gaze can only turn on itself its own empty look. Blanchot goes on a few lines later to evoke the milieu that is "so to speak absolute" into which fascination draws one, along with "the gaze frozen into light" and a light that is in turn "the absolute shine [*le luisant*] of an eye that one does not see, that one yet never ceases to see, for it is our own gaze in a mirror … a light that is also an abyss." The gaze sees but the shine of an eye (running and bloodshot like those of Beckett's Unnamable, no doubt), not a face or a figure, only a dead gaze without a look which, in thus approaching the sight of its own seeing, merely sees blindly its still seeing blindness: fascination, writes Blanchot, is that

> in which blindness is vision still, vision that is no longer [a] possibility of seeing, but [an] impossibility of not seeing, impossibility turned into seeing, that perseveres—always and always—in a vision that never has done: a dead gaze, a gaze become the phantom of an eternal vision.
>
> en qui l'aveuglement est vision encore, vision qui n'est plus possibilité de voir, mais impossibilité de ne pas voir, l'impossibilité qui se fait voir, qui persévère— toujours et toujours—dans une vision qui n'en finit pas: regard mort, regard devenu le fantôme d'une vision éternelle.

*L'impossibilité qui se fait voir*: there are at least three ways to translate this crucial phrase, each of which gives a different shape to the knot of paradoxes that Blanchot is tightening here. First, "impossibility making or turning itself into seeing": not being able not to see becomes a different and strange kind of seeing, a seeing that emerges not from a capacity or faculty, a set of positive conditions, but somehow directly from an impossibility, from the negation at the heart of any capacity now turned into something that itself cannot be negated. With this we edge toward a very uncomfortable sort of endlessness, a problematic eternity, by way not of redemption but of non-mastery and compulsion. Second, "impossibility that makes itself see": this is the short circuit we have seen above, a collapsing of possibility into its neutralized power which, rendered unto passivity, is removed from the domain of mastery and action and given over to its own endlessness and futile perseverance. Third, "impossibility that makes itself *seen*": this is perhaps the most enigmatic, but likewise the most radical, moment implicated here. And while this sense is not the most visible surface meaning of Blanchot's phrase, being at most implicit, it resonates nonetheless in the midst of this "description" in which the relation to the image is located at the limit of both relation and image, where blindness itself appears to see and somehow *thereby to be seen*, and so to have an irreducible *look*. I believe that we do reach here a limit of what can be said or described, in the "process" or the deconditioning that Blanchot attempts to evoke by way of the fascinated gaze and its distant-intimate image. In a later passage, from the first sentences of "Two Versions of the Imaginary," we find a striking formula that can be said to schematize Blanchot's thought more generally in this regard: "What makes [the image] possible is the limit where it ceases" (SL 254)/"ce qui … rend [l'image] possible est la limite où elle cesse"—a limit identified in this case with a truth, an "indifferent ground," that exceeds the image and envelops it in its own disappearance (EL 341). In the pages of "Essential Solitude" this limit is made all the more manifest in being called, simply, "dead"—a dead gaze bound within a phantom of eternity. This sham of an afterlife, situated not beyond the world but rather "below" it (permanently *en deçà*), feels less like a theologically overdetermined escape from time, but also less like the poetic rendering of an underworld or purgatory of departed shades (as in Homer or Dante for example), than like a flattened stream of fake, futile, and compelling images.[15] It is a dead realm in which even the dead do not dwell and are not yet quite really dead. It is a realm of image corpses—and it is exactly in this sense that Blanchot proceeds from here in his peculiar "phenomenology" of the image.

## Dream and schema

In approaching the essence of the image, then, we are approaching the corpse. And we do so partly by passing through an endless displacement of images, as in a dream. In the last paragraph of "Sleep, Night" (after which "Two Versions of the Imaginary" immediately follows in the book's appendices), Blanchot calls up this unworld of image after image, using language that marks it as a reformulation of fascination itself, its vertigo and confusion:

---

[15] Could we say, then, moving too quickly, like a cinema-prison? Despite Blanchot's aversion to technically produced images, his descriptions of images in the automatism of their continual movement, their phantomatic presence-absence, their compelling and fatal force of capture, and their superficiality and emptiness all point very suggestively to an experience closely resembling that of the cinematic apparatus. Hence my suggestion, presented here only in outline, that Blanchot's thinking of the image may be inhabited by an originary technicity.

The dream touches on the region where pure resemblance reigns. There, all is semblance, each figure is another semblance, resembling the other and again the next, which in turn resembles yet another. One seeks the originary model, one would like to be sent back to a point of departure, to an initial revelation, but there is none: the dream is the semblance that sends one eternally on to another semblance. (SL 268)

Le rêve touche à la région où regne la pure ressemblance. Tout y est semblant, chaque figure en est une autre, est semblable à l'autre et encore à une autre, celle-ci à une autre. On cherche le modèle originaire, on voudrait être renvoyé à un point de départ, à une révélation initiale, mais il n'y en a pas: le rêve est le semblable qui renvoie éternellement au semblable. (EL 362)

With this Blanchot gives a schema for any movement through literary space: a search deprived of origin and goal, but impelled by and as a series of resemblant images (and indeed this schema recalls nothing so much as the plot of *Aminadab*).[16] This is Blanchot's eternity, or at least one version of it. If it borrows from the ancient tradition of the *nekuia*, the descent to the underworld, it deprives the latter of any outside insofar as it is itself already the outside, from which there is no path back to a world more real, to any "originary model."[17]

It is worth elaborating a bit further on the philosophical implications of this schema, in its undoing of the model/copy or the origin/semblance relation, partly as a way to approach, from a slightly different angle, the ontological priority of images already sketched, as this leads us toward the corpse and to the otherness of its world. Consider this dense formulation from the penultimate paragraph of "Essential Solitude," where in something of a summation Blanchot links fascination and the image once again to writing, a link that has been implicit throughout.

To write is to set out language under [the influence of] fascination and, by and in this language, to remain in contact with the absolute milieu, where the thing again becomes image, where the image, having been an allusion to a figure, becomes an allusion to what is without figure and, having been a form drawn out against an absence, becomes the formless presence of this absence, the opaque

---

[16] On the question of endless resemblance as a constitutive structure of Blanchot's thinking of the image, see Georges Didi-Huberman, "De ressemblance à ressemblance," in *Maurice Blanchot: Récits critiques*, eds. Christophe Bident and Pierre Vilar (Paris: Farrago/Léo Scheer, 2003), 143–67.

[17] On the *nekuia* as a schema for the deathly "experience" of literature for Blanchot, see Philippe Lacoue-Labarthe, "'Fidelities' and 'The Contestation of Death,'" in *Ending and Unending Agony: On Maurice Blanchot*, trans. Hannes Opelz (New York: Fordham University Press, 2015).

and empty opening onto what there is when there is no longer any world, when there is not yet any world. (SL 33)

Ecrire, c'est disposer le langage sous la fascination et, par lui, en lui, demeurer en contact avec le milieu absolu, là où la chose redevient image, où l'image, d'allusion à une figure, devient allusion à ce qui est sans figure et, de forme dessinée sur l'absence, devient l'informe présence de cette absence, l'ouverture opaque et vide sur ce qui est quand il n'y a plus de monde, quand il n'y a pas encore de monde. (EL 31)

Without attempting to untangle this taut and sinuous sentence, I would like to point to one important word: *redevient*, become again or, literally, *re-become*. Blanchot here describes, in a way that could be called "phenomenological" only if we radically redefine the term, a strange process of recession: writing under fascination draws back from world and things, not by drawing off copies of the latter in images that would thus be further removed from their origins and truth (the Platonic interpretation of images that still largely reigns), but rather things *re-become* images, they *turn back into* what they were "before" they were things, the images of themselves that somehow precede their existence as things. Writing under fascination enters one, so to speak, into a space in which the image-version of things shows itself not as derivative but as a precondition for things to be. It is tempting to bring such an "imaginary" into proximity with what Kant called the "productive" or "transcendental imagination"—and thus into proximity with the enigma of Kant's schematism—and there may be grounds for doing so, at least in some respects (more on this in a moment). But this would mean first recognizing the incompatibility of the notion of *production*, as well as that of the transcendental, in a space determined by *désoeuvrement* (one possible translation of which could be precisely "unproductiveness") and by indefiniteness, a non-determinacy that de-forms, undoes, and neutralizes the unitary formative power of any transcendental synthesis, to use Kant's language.[18] The fascinated language space in which world and things are both "no longer" and "not yet"—and are these in the mode of *images*—breaks the links between images and world/things. Indeed, in the sentence quoted Blanchot radicalizes

---

[18]  On links and similarities between Blanchot and Kant in terms of the imaginary/imagination, see Françoise Collin, *Maurice Blanchot et la question de l'écriture* (Paris: Gallimard (Tel), 1986 [1971]), 178–79; Antonioli, *L'écriture de Maurice Blanchot*, 77–79; and Jérôme De Gramont, *Blanchot et la phénoménologie: L'effacement, L'événement* (Clichy: Editions de Corlevour, 2011), 38. The respective chapters of these books also feature substantial analyses of the relation between Blanchot's treatment of the image in comparison (or in response) to that of Sartre.

this break as the recession goes even further. For there is another "step," back in the direction of the indeterminate: not only do things become the images that have preceded them, but images themselves refer or "allude" no longer to any figure but rather to what is "without figure"; they somehow turn back and away from figuration and toward the figureless (the faceless), so that their delineation as images no longer even evokes or vehiculates a presence-in-absence, but rather absorbs that absence, turns it toward one as such, effaces the contours of its form *as against* a ground, and obtrudes as formless ground made image.

The quoted sentence thus indicates the vertiginous receding movement into the "ground of the image," or *au fond des images*, to use Nancy's phrase.[19] It is in this ground that fascination becomes the force that, through and in language, presses this movement on, "reduces" things to images and strips images of figuration, thus making them images *of* nothing. And so it is that we confront in the image "the look of nothingess upon us"/"le regard du néant sur nous"— which is also our nothingness, from out of which we cast our vision, and ourselves take on a look, become visible, seen, aspected, looked at. At the same time, we should stress that this movement ruins any structure of intentionality in the phenomenological sense. Neither an after-image, nor a "mental image," nor a "consciousness," the image in Blanchot is an "opaque and empty opening" onto a no-longer/not-yet of world—and yet it is still somehow an image. And so here we are, if not at an origin, then at least at the site of a more than exemplary image-thing: for Blanchot's "image of" this image, and of the problematic space it opens, is that of a corpse, in its unsettling and unlocatable *resemblance*.

## The image/The corpse

In the first pages of "Two Versions of the Imaginary," Blanchot recalls this formless ground toward which fascination draws one, and from which things are drawn, calling it by various names: "the ineliminable residue of being" and "the elementary," but also a "sordid ground"/"fond sordide" and a "ground of impotence into which all falls back"/"fond d'impuissance où tout retombe" when things have "collapsed" into their images (the verb he uses here is *effondrer*, the falling out of the *fond*, the bottom or ground). He does this, first, in order to

---

[19] See Jean-Luc Nancy, "Masked Imagination," in *The Ground of the Image*, trans. Jeff Fort (New York: Fordham University Press, 2005).

evoke another less disturbing version of the image, one that would preserve us from the threat of this "sordid ground" of things by providing a certain mastery over them, keeping the nothingness at bay (as in Sartre's version): "the good fortune of the image is that it constitutes a limit alongside the indefinite" (SL 254)/"Le bonheur de l'image c'est qu'elle est une limite auprès de l'indéfini" (EL 341–342), so that the image even promises an appeasing back-world of dreams, as evoked by Hamlet (whom Blanchot cites in translation): "For in that sleep of death what dreams may come/When we have shuffled off this mortal coil" (SL 255/EL 342; *Hamlet*, act 3, scene 1). In a sense, the entirety of "Two Versions" can be seen as a reading of these lines, for the second way in which Blanchot calls on the bottomless ground of images is to lay that "mortal coil" restlessly to rest within it, to place it at the border between images and their elemental ground, as something of a disjointed link, at the point where, from a preservation of a world of things both real and unreal, they begin to turn their nothingness toward us, opening for us the void of their absence, their engulfing other side.

Enter, then, the corpse. Its role here is to disrupt the "ordinary analysis" (or "*analyse commune*") of the imaginary, which corresponds roughly with the Sartrian version, wherein "the image … is after the object and follows upon it; we see, then we imagine" (SL 255/EL 343). This version is in every sense *displaced* by the other one, driven by fascination into the self-enfolded distance of the corpse laid out right here. "Here," Blanchot writes—meaning in the spacing and distance between a thing and its image, and thus in fascination's collapse of this distance—"distance is at the heart of the thing … not the same thing at a distance, but this thing as distance … the strange heart of the distant as life and unique core of the thing" (SL 255)/"l'éloignement est ici au coeur de la chose … non pas la même chose éloignée, mais cette chose comme éloignement … le coeur étrange du lointain comme vie et coeur unique de la chose" (EL 343). The form taken by this distance is a strange and upsetting state of manifest *resemblance*, but a resemblance with nothing to resemble.

Where is the one this corpse used to be? Nowhere, precisely nowhere—nowhere other than right here, that is, such that "here becomes nowhere," *here* itself "becomes corpse," a "gaping intimacy," and the deceased, now unlocatable—permanently displaced from this unliving body—wanders at the limit between this world, with its all too visible corpse-display, and another one just behind it which, however, opens only onto nothing (where dreams may come, but with no pacifying force, and nowhere to stop their endless movement). This "behind" is a way to indicate the indiscernible gap between a corpse-image and the ungraspable leftover thing it is an image of—a minute gap of pure self-resemblance.

The nothing "behind" the image is thus nothing but the image itself, in its uncanny takeover of reality and world—which, after all, owe their very existence and form to "the elementary," the neutral indifference of which the corpse, as pure resemblance par excellence, gives an unsteady intuition. We are most emphatically, then, not in a world of originals (or models) and imitations (or copies), but rather one in which that relation, in order to be *set to work* in an elaboration of manipulable objects, has had to repress its conditions of deathly indifference:

> In the image, the object again brushes against something that it had to master in order to be an object, against which it edified and defined itself, but presently, now that its value, its signification, is suspended, now that the world abandons it to unworking [to unproductiveness] and sets it apart, the truth in it shrinks back, the elementary reclaims it. (SL 256)
>
> Dans l'image, l'objet effleure à nouveau quelque chose qu'il avait maîtrisée pour être objet, contre quoi il s'était édifié et défini, mais à présent que sa valeur, sa signification est suspendue, maintenant que le monde l'abandonne au désœuvrement et le met à part, la vérité en lui recule, l'élémentaire le revendique. (EL 343)

We can characterize these "two versions," then, in terms of a tension between the Sartrian interpretation of the image and a radicalization of Heidegger's thinking of uncanniness and anxiety. The Heideggerian element is evident in the quotation just given, in the suspension of value and significance, as well as in a subsequent paragraph that compares corpsely resemblance to the becoming-image of a broken tool—although instead of referring to Heidegger, Blanchot there quotes Breton (SL 258/EL 347).[20] This radicalization consists in making the image "fundamental," not as a world-constituting ground (nor as a formative schema), but rather, as we've seen, as an all-devouring de-constituting threat. "Only what has given itself over to the image appears, and all that appears is, in this sense, imaginary" (SL 259)/"N'apparaît que ce qui s'est livré à l'image, et tout ce qui apparaît est, en ce sens, imaginaire" (EL 348). In other words, to synthesize these points into their simplest and most radical form: everything that appears is, in a way, *a corpse.*

---

[20] He might also have referred to Duchamp, whose *readymades* bring similar questions into play, but to my knowledge Blanchot never mentions Duchamp in his published writing. Heidegger's analysis of the broken tool (a hammer) is found in *Being and Time*, section 16.

Put another way: everything that appears is imaginary, and the imaginary "itself" has *the look of a corpse*, in every sense. That is to say, it looks *like a corpse*, or *as a corpse does*. In the corpse the look thus opens a crack of indiscernibility between activity and passivity, subject and object. Moreover, the law of this look, this vision and appearance, lies in the death that, inherent in images as the condition of their visibility, draws a limit that marks vision itself in its underlying impossibility. In yet other words, and most explicitly, we can say that the image is structurally cadaverous because it compulsively mobilizes the lived space from which it is excepted while also presenting the gaze that it would be, in its animated looking back, as dead. The sordid ground has erupted, immeasurably, into the world posed "against" it, as against an ever-receding background.

## Death mask and index

Is it possible to glimpse along this strange border of figuration and (collapsing) ground the juncture in which a certain question of technology is played out in Blanchot, by way of the singular artifact of the death mask—an artifact whose technicity is all the more marked in its crude simplicity? I mentioned at the outset that Blanchot strategically avoided technical media, certainly where his person was concerned, but also, to a large extent, within his work. There are (for example) no radios or televisions in his fiction, no record players, hardly even a telephone, and only rare and passing mentions of cinema, and while photography plays an important role in *The Most High*, this is a fascinating exception.[21] Its single appearance in *Death Sentence* (to which I will return in a moment) is all the more striking for this reason. Likewise, as mentioned earlier, there is very little in his essayistic reflections addressing mechanical visual media. The broader reasons for this avoidance are worth interrogating.[22] But for our present purposes I would like to point to one specific, but consequential, figure: it is through the presence of a death mask—first in *Death Sentence* and then in a much later essay from 1992 that gives an autobiographical reference[23]—that

---

[21] For a fruitful discussion of photography in *The Most High*, see the article by Patrick Lyons, cited above.

[22] See Raymond Bellour's remark, echoed in my own comments above, that Blanchot's insistence on personal invisibility and silence had to do with a sensitivity to the growing "pressure" of mass visual media. Raymond Bellour, *L'entre-images 2, Mots, Images* (Paris: P.O.L., 1999), 327.

[23] Maurice Blanchot, "Anacrouse: Sur les poèmes de Louis-René des Forêts," in *Une voix venue d'ailleurs* (Paris: Gallimard, 2002), 15.

Blanchot's thinking on the corpse-image is linked most directly to the technology of image reproduction, thus introducing the latter into the living-dead core of Blanchot's writing, and not in a manner that could be neatly circumscribed, or that is in any way incidental. This artifact opens Blanchot's work as a whole onto the question of technology and the image, and it does so not only through the dead-body image, but also as the sort of ambiguous deathly *look* evoked already, as a disturbing visible aspect that looks back, one which is deliberately and directly inscribed into the very drive of literary writing. Elsewhere, the name of this look, of its female bearer, is Eurydice. Here, in *Death Sentence*, the death mask may well give the schema—or perhaps the problematic "schema-image"— of this writing.[24]

The death mask in *Death Sentence* begins its life, Eurydice-like, as the face of a dying woman. J's death in the first part of the narrative puts into play a dramatic and abyssal play of gazes and faces between her and the narrator, who appears to participate, strangely and unimaginably, in this death—both in its "arrest" and in its resumption, or assumption. Having stared into something he "should not have seen" (DS 21/AM 37) in J's dying face—something that he calls "the most terrible look that a living being can receive" (20/36)—he too bears the face or aspect of death: "Now then, take a good look at death" (DS 28)/"Maintenant … voyez donc la mort" (AM 48), says J., pointing her finger at him, not long before her return into death (while also performing the indexical gesture that will structure this story's enigmatic remnants). Later, in a prodigy of trans-narrative reproduction, the deathly woman herself returns, as it were, in the guise of N. or Nathalie, born somehow from the opacity and empty depth of what had happened before. Born, that is, again. Her name itself points in this direction, and the strange Christic resonance vibrating throughout the story, but multiply displaced and disfigured, is evoked already near the beginning of the narrative (9/19), when the narrator sees, in the cabinet of his dubious doctor, none other than a photograph of the Shroud of Turin, but with a woman's face—the beautiful, haughty, and "superb" face of Veronica *herself*—visible "behind" that of Christ: sub-imposed,

---

[24] I am referring to Heidegger's discussion of the schema and the "schema-image," in *Kant and the Problem of Metaphysics*, sections 19–23, trans. James S. Churchill (Bloomington: Indiana University Press, 1962), where Heidegger explicates this notion in part through the example of a death mask (in section 20), or rather, through the photograph of a death mask. Nancy's reflections on this moment in Heidegger's *Kantbuch* have been fundamental to my inquiries in this direction. See "Masked Imagination" in *The Ground of the Image*. I have proposed analyses of these texts and figures, in relation to Blanchot, in *The Imperative to Write: Destitutions of the Sublime in Kafka, Blanchot and Beckett* (New York: Fordham University Press, 2014), especially chapter 7, 248–63.

as it were, as the true subject of the image. This frozen dissolve (in the cinematic sense) shows that Veronica, with her "bizarre expression of pride"—the face of the woman who has always only tendered the face of another—is here pressing into the foreground, imposing a life in death (in photography) more sovereign even than the one impressed onto the Holy Shroud. She is overcoming the one who himself overcame death, and her emerging face is a prefiguration of the fixedly staring death mask that, in the end, opens and displaces the dimension of eternity occupied by the woman-thought (*elle, cette pensée*) who henceforth, as proclaimed in the text's last sentence, is "eternally there."

Death mask, photograph, holy shroud, Veronica's very own veil: this strange collection of curiosities has one remarkable thing in common. They can all be described—however fantastical or legendary their referents—as imprints, indexical images that imply, structurally (if not factually), presence, contact, and physical trace.[25] With the important qualification that photography is, at best, a kind of contact at a distance. But with this last phrase we have returned, word for word, to Blanchot's definition of fascination, which suggests even further that if these images are in some way images of "the image," it may be the photograph that gives this image in a privileged form, in its most precisely articulated and mechanically synthesized form. But like the rest of these images, and to an even greater degree, this form is marked and inhabited by absence and emptiness, an abyssal hollow that separates all vision from the present in which it sees *whatever* it sees, leaving it suspended over a ground (a sordid ground) containing nothing, in every sense. One name for this ground is *time: le temps*, but also a time that is once, *une fois*, in the voided formality—the effaced and blurred "content"—of its *one*. So that, finally, the indexical image would thus be a partially legible smudge *of that time*.[26]

Let us try to bring these statements into a little more focus. It is remarkable that Blanchot would mobilize such an iconography of indexicality, given the radical insistence one finds in his work on the impossibility of presence, the

---

[25] Another thing they have in common is that they are all evoked by André Bazin in his meditations on "The Ontology of the Photographic Image," in the essay bearing that name and elsewhere in his work—a fact which itself indicates a more than incidental convergence between Blanchot's images and the cinema. See André Bazin, "L'ontologie de l'image photographique," in *Qu'est-ce que le cinéma* (Paris: Cerf, 2000 [1985]), 9–17.

[26] It is worth adding that with the addition of time to the image itself, we enter on something more akin to cinema, a suggestion that I will have to leave to the side for now. For a reflection on Blanchot and the image that moves in the direction of cinema, see Raymond Bellour, "L'image," in *Maurice Blanchot: Récits critiques*, eds. Christophe Bident and Pierre Vilar (Paris: Farrago/Léo Scheer, 2003), 133–42.

emptiness and nullity of any present in time, the turn and return of a time that gives nothing but its movement of effacement and rebeginning. As mentioned above, this thinking becomes more explicit and elaborate in later works, especially *The Step Not Beyond* and *The Writing of the Disaster*, but it emerges already in the essays and *récits* of this earlier, more overtly literary period. What sense does an indexical image have for such a thinking? In an article that surveys some of the ground I am touching on here (the death mask, Heidegger's reference to it and to the schematism, Nancy's essay "Masked Imagination," and the indexical in Blanchot), Louis Kaplan has convincingly argued that Blanchot's apparently indexical images—and the death mask in particular—are not really indexical, precisely insofar as they have no localizable referent or temporal locus and indeed work to undo the very possibility of any such spatio-temporally structured referentiality.[27] At one level, this is undeniable. In fact, one can add that the very allusions one might muster in order to link Blanchot's death mask to a biographical indexeme (as we might call it) work precisely in the opposite direction: Blanchot's evocation in *Une voix venue d'ailleurs* of the death mask he owned and hung on the wall of his writing room, the legendary Inconnue de la Seine, is very likely not the true relic (as the story goes) of a desperate woman whose face floated up in all its beatific splendor from the deadly waters of the Seine, but rather a mass produced curio invested with a sentimental and romanticized story (and so also an artifact of rumor).[28] But the emptiness and non-referential status of Blanchot's indexicals is not merely a consequence of their referents being *fictional*; it is rather a question of the structural nullity of any relation a trace might bear to its "origin." The indexical emptiness of the death mask of the Inconnue, or that of Nathalie in *Death Sentence*, can be seen to render the structure of indexicality in general, at least according to Blanchot's most radical thinking of time, image (and language), and presence. Suffice it to recall in passing Derrida's analyses of supplementarity, the secondary of any

---

[27] See Louis Kaplan Kaplan, "Photograph/Death Mask: Jean-Luc Nancy's Recasting of the Photographic Image," *Journal of Visual Culture* 9, no. 1 (2010): 45–62. Kaplan argues further that photography should be understood less in terms of indexicality than in terms of exposure, and according to Nancy's rich reflections on this concept or condition. This is a plausible and highly pertinent argument. However, does not every photograph pose the question: *when* is (was) it exposed? Even if this question is strictly without response (or even when the response is in some sense "always already"), the very persistence of the question, along with its temporally indicative residue, stubbornly points us in the direction of the indexed *something* that a photograph shows.

[28] See Anne-Gaëlle Saliot, *The Drowned Muse: Casting the Unknown Woman of the Seine Across the Tides of Modernity* London and New York: Oxford University Press, 2015), 2–6. This work provides a comprehensive overview of the phenomenon of the Inconnue de la Seine and the mask's many appearances in art, literature, and culture.

posited origin or presence, the trace structure at the heart of these analyses, and the deconstructive action of writing *as technê*—all arguably inspired significantly by Blanchot—and we might well have the sense that it is a largely unavowed confrontation with technology and technical reproduction, or perhaps a thinking under their pressure, that leads Blanchot toward some of his most singular insights, perhaps to the very signature of his thought. Is Blanchot's relative avoidance of the question of technicity—and its nearly complete foreclosure in his explicit discourse on "the image" as a literary moment—something of an emblematic seal placed, *en creux*, over the deeper conditions of his writing? I am not suggesting that Blanchot avoided a more frontal treatment of technology in order to preserve an intact and intimate inwardness (in the manner of a certain modernism, evident at times for example in Rilke); much rather that a very strange experience of language, of the language-image, may have pressed the figural aspects of his work into forms that appear to *touch the real*, not in order to capture it, but as a way to manifest its ultimate vacuity, its preformed destiny in effacement and disappearance. But also that perhaps he *failed* to do this as thoroughly as his more programmatic statements appear to indicate.

The reason for this failure may have to do with the insistence, despite everything, of the indexical image, the indelible specter of temporal singularity that, for its part, cannot fail to haunt such an image (perhaps any image at all). I cannot here enter into the details and logic of this failure—and the unending failure of failure that twists and ties it into paradox. Instead I will end by pointing again to the troubling appearance—within the public sphere, the realm of publicity and publication—of the photographic specter of Blanchot himself.

The *Cahiers de l'Herne* devoted to Blanchot features some twenty-five photographs in which the writer appears, at greater or lesser proximity, alone or with companions, including the double portrait with Levinas I mentioned at the beginning.[29] Given Blanchot's well-known attitude, the editors must justify this decision. Their reasoning is worth citing: "We know to what extent Blanchot cut himself off and effaced himself from the world of Letters and from mediatic visibility. It is not a question here of simply disregarding all that Blanchot thought concerning this essential anonymity borne by writing."/"On sait combien Blanchot s'est retranché et effacé du monde des Lettres et de la visibilité médiatique. Il ne s'agit donc pas de faire fi de tout ce que Blanchot

---

[29]  Cahiers De L'Herne, *Blanchot*, eds. Eric Hoppenot and Dominique Rabaté (Paris: Editions de L'Herne, 2014). The quotations that follow are from pages 11 to 12.

a pensé de cet anonymat essentiel que porte l'écriture." They pertinently evoke Blanchot's remarkable essay "The Power and the Glory" as evidence that he understood quite well the stakes, and the impossibility, of complete invisibility and anonymity in relation to publicity—indeed he goes so far as to say in that essay that the "rumor" and "murmur" of the public, of publicity itself, is not separate from *but rather lies at the heart of* literary language, of the listening that hears this language and the voice that speaks from out of its indistinct ground. In the end, the editors state that it is "to give back to the writer his embodiment, his necessary historicity"/"pour rendre à l'écrivain sa part d'incarnation, sa nécessaire historicité," adding: "for it is indeed this singular and exemplary historicity that we must think in order to be capable of situating the work and thus to preserve its active encitement to write after it, to write with it or against it"/"car c'est bien cette historicité singulière et exemplaire qu'il nous faut penser pour être capable de situer l'oeuvre et ainsi en préserver la part active d'incitation à écrire après elle, à écrire avec elle ou contre elle." Without entering into a commentary on the images themselves, this justification strikes me as highly pertinent, both to our concerns, as readers of Blanchot with no desire to dehistoricize or disembody a complexly situated author, and to Blanchot's, as a writer who encountered, and cannily countered, the intense pressurization of literature under the force of modern mass publicity and its technical systems. This encounter passes by way of the image—and is figured specifically by indexical images that play on the relation between technically wrought evacuation (of presence, of lived experience) and "ineliminable residues" (of what *was once*). Located in this problematic relation is our attachment to the sense that indexical images deliver the emanated singularity of a once present past (as expressed by Roland Barthes, for example[30]). It is this link that Blanchot sought in writing to sever from inscription itself, and in this sense he strove with all his resources— and with an inexhaustible lack of resources—toward a true atheism, a form of writing, and a way of living on earth, without deified or unified transcendence, and without unicity of time. For is this link of *emanation*, so dear to Barthes— and no doubt, at bottom, to us—not ultimately of a theological nature? And is Blanchot's emphasis on impersonality and anonymity not aimed in part at the "glory" of the writer, of art, and of the image? Blanchot's emptied indexicals may well provide a way to undo this mystical link, not in the name of reason, but for

---

[30]  Roland Barthes famously calls up the "emanation of the referent" that a photograph "literally" reveals. See Roland Barthes, *Camera Lucida: Reflections on Photography*, trans. Richard Howard (New York: Hill and Wang, 1981), 80.

the sake of a different thinking and experience of time. And yet, despite every aim at loosening it, this attachment stubbornly persists: we see the pictures, they stare back at us, and there he is, still there in having been. The "still" of this remnant figure and face, of this indeterminate but sollicitous residue of time, is perhaps the kernel of Blanchot's historical dilemma, in which the demand for impersonal poetic singularity confronts the irrevocable shattering of its possibility as world—or (to put it even more enigmatically) where the demands of thought, as eternal return, confront the impossibility of a living face. But if Blanchot's "image" was in some sense always moving, it has now begun to catch up with his ghost—now so visibly, so seemingly and eternally there.

# 12

# "The Call of the Anterior": Blanchot, Lacan, and the Death Drive

### Allan Pero

Perhaps one of the most remarkable surprises of twentieth-century French thought, with its imbricated, complex sets of intellectual and artistic networks, is that contemporaries Maurice Blanchot (born 1907) and Jacques Lacan (born 1901) would seem to have had so vanishingly little to do with each other. Virtually nothing has been written about their relationship (which, admittedly, appears to be that of passing acquaintance), and only slightly more about their shared intellectual interests. Although they do make occasional, respectful references to each other's work (Lacan calls Blanchot "simplement comme le chantre de nos Lettres" ["simply the bard of our literature"] in *Séminaire IX*), they offer no sustained engagement with each other's ideas.[1] Indeed, they each appear in each other's biographies (Elisabeth Roudinesco's *Jacques Lacan*, and Christophe Bident's *Maurice Blanchot: Partenaire Invisible*) merely as part of a litany of names in the French cultural firmament.[2] That said, their shared interests were many, and those interests certainly warrant attention. Blanchot's well-known fascination with death, as a site of (im)possibility, of limit-experience, of an experience veiled by pulsions like repetition, by the blandishments of errancy, finds its intellectual antecedents not only in writers like Mallarmé, Sade, Levinas, and Bataille, but also in psychoanalysis.

In *The Space of Literature*, Blanchot invokes Freud as a means of addressing the problem of death as error sustained, repeated, as that which "is precisely the impossibility of being for the first time," but wants to distinguish sharply the

---

[1] Jacques Lacan, *Séminaire IX, de 1961–62: L'Identification, de Jacques Lacan*, 604; translation mine.

[2] Elisabeth Roudinesco, *Jacques Lacan*, trans. Barbara Roy (New York: Columbia University Press, 1997), 166; Christophe Bident, *Maurice Blanchot: Partenaire Invisible* (Paris: Champ Vallon, 1998), 49, 145, 247, 336, 442, 471, 559.

repetition that inheres in our fascination with death from Freudian complexes, which for Blanchot "are the experience of beginning again" (SL 243). That is to say, Blanchot works to hive death off from the "closed wound" of the complex, which finds its enjoyment in its failure, in the anguished pleasure of needing to repeat, in answering the cry of "Again, again!" heard by a particular being. The danger of conflating death and the complex is that it will "ruin death as possibility" by domesticating it, by giving it a location and origin (SL 3). Blanchot's insistence upon bracketing death in this way is an understandable one, given Freud's largely gestural discussion of the death drive—a concept for which he has been much maligned, even as he himself expressed much doubt and hesitation about its potential. For example, recall Freud's discourse about Rome in *Civilization and Its Discontents*. In mapping the history of discontent, of civilization's war on love, Freud enjoins us to wander about the city of eternity, around the havoc of the Roman quadrata, to pace the teeth of the Aurelian wall, and the Servian rampart of regression; each of them broken, burnt, rebuilt dozens of times, ruins piling upon ruins, the bleached stones of the mind. He asks us to search, with the gaze of Morpheus, the pentimento of its every architecture, in which the Palatine, the Sabine, the Latins, the Etruscans, the Goths, Augustus, Nero, Hadrian, and Agrippa occupy the same ring as the angling St. Peter. We are asked to hover over its metonymies, its strange contiguities, the legends of its unforgotten desire, ever deferred by the hive of culture. The ruins that persist are the memory-traces, the unconscious spatial history of a city that has duly repressed it through its persistence as a site of civilization. In this moment, Freud almost unwittingly transforms Rome into death's space, and becomes dizzy at the thought of the complex metonymies, the doublings that inform the "same space ... [having] two different contents."[3] At the same time, we should hover over this comparison; the metonymies, the spatial juxtapositions, are precisely those of unconscious desire; the city's history surfaces in fragments, articulates itself as ruin and building, trauma and reconstruction. But he cannot. And he stops.

In his hesitation, Freud throws away his allegorical prize—of death's possibility—and warns us to turn back, too—to remember time from space, history from geography, and (of course) ego from unconscious—for we rebuild by both destruction and design. In doing so, he asks us to choose time and

---

[3] Sigmund Freud, *The Standard Edition of the Complete Psychological Works of Sigmund Freud, Volume XXI (1927–1931)*, trans. Joan Riviere (London: Hogarth Press, 1981), 63.

repetition—in short, desire—over what Blanchot calls "death's space" and its freshening possibility, its immovable ambiguity.

In Lacanian terms, desire is metonymic, indeed sustained in its deferral by the ongoing project of civilization itself. But its history registers itself in strange contiguities that we attempt to explain and narrate. In Freud's hesitation to continue the thought he has opened up, however, we see what is for him a horrifying insight: our unconscious relation to civilization is part and parcel of wanting to go "beyond the pleasure principle." This has occurred because of the rift between the pleasure principle and the world, in the gap between the potential for happiness and the creative and civilizing pursuits from which this happiness is to be derived. Hence, we encounter the reason for the subject's desire to find "intense enjoyment" from that which in some way tarries with the negative of stasis or inertia that produces mere "contentment." The pleasure principle is thus *a law*; one is permitted a kind of enjoyment (i.e., pleasure—not *jouissance*), but there is a limit or prohibition (the legal dimension of this prohibition is what prompted Freud, in *The Interpretation of Dreams*, to call it the "unpleasure principle").[4] But the pleasure principle is not enough. It is the death drive, we are told, that gets in the way of the homeostatic balance produced by the law of the pleasure principle; the death drive is the ambiguous space "beyond" that would seem to throw the psychic system into flux.

But for Lacan, the death drive is not flux; it is the site of radical loss—of loss *as* satisfaction, and, paradoxically, loss *as* impossibility. In his late work, Lacan theorized the loss at the heart of the big Other, a loss that indestructibly drives life.[5] That is to say, the death drive, like Blanchot's concept of death both as possibility and impossibility, is not linked to repetition—or rather, it is uncoupled from repetition. Repetition is instead one of the lures desire sets for us, to help us avoid what he describes, in his reading of Freud, as "the call of the anterior"—what I will nominate as the call of the death drive (SL 242). If desire sustains itself by avoiding satisfaction (the circuit of repetition around the object of desire ensures that no repetition is perfect, and thus defers satisfaction), then the death drive offers what would seem to be impossible: the radical attainment of satisfaction without achieving its goal.

---

[4]  Sigmund Freud, *The Standard Edition of the Complete Psychological Works of Sigmund Freud, Volume V (1900–1901)*, trans. James Strachey, Anna Freud, Alix Strachey, and Alan Tyson (London: Hogarth Press, 1981), 574.

[5]  Ellie Ragland, *Essays on the Pleasures of Death: From Freud to Lacan* (London: Routledge, 1994), 87.

If desire hides the satisfaction of the death drive from us, then we can understand why Blanchot would resist the blandishments of repetition. From the perspective of the doubleness of death, Blanchot's privileging of death's space in the act of writing is driven by the ambiguity that inheres both in life *and* literature's relation to death. In his paraphrase of Hegel in "Literature and the Right to Death," Blanchot says that literature itself is "the life [that] endures death and maintains itself in it" (GO 41). Leslie Hill reminds us that this phrase "is susceptible to two radically divergent readings, depending on whether death is a triumph or a defeat, as the apotheosis of the labour of negation, or the rending apart of being by its own unmasterable limits."[6] In sum, death makes literature possible, and the negativity that paradoxically makes it possible— that is, that signs and their referents do not have an impermeable one-to-one correspondence—is also a site of impossibility, one that is radically other, and utterly outside experience. (Or, more properly, it is the experience of what Blanchot calls "The Outside.") For Blanchot, literature occupies a liminal zone between death as possibility and its impossibility. In other words, one writes in order to be able to die, and yet the ability to write comes from the anticipation of death: "*Write to be able to die—Die to be able to write*" (SL 94). But how does Blanchot help us contend with this paradox? By exploring how the writer can create the space for the work in death's space in providing shelter from death for him- or herself as a writer. In effect, Blanchot gives the lie to the banal notion that one writes to be immortal; one writes but to free oneself from "the wretched regret that one cannot be oneself for longer." To hide from death, one must in a sense "hide in it" because death itself is "the deep of dissimulation" (95).

By way of comparison, the satisfaction of the death drive is of a different register. The death drive finds its satisfaction not in whatever truth it encounters, but in the negativity that persists as a result of its *not* having attained its goal—that is, the goal remains elusive, even as satisfaction does not. This is why repetition ceases to be the concern of the death drive; in desire, repetition is bound up in the subject's achieving its goal (the subject's failure thus sustains desire, which is why the desire for something always produces the desire for something else). But in the death drive, satisfaction comes in the disappearance of desire as lack, and in the transgressing of desire's limit. Another way of putting it is to say that the death drive is a limit-experience, one whose satisfaction comes from an encounter with impossibility, with satisfaction's impossibility, of making the

---

[6]   Leslie Hill, *Blanchot: Extreme Contemporary* (Routledge: London, 1997), 112–13.

impossible—death—possible. This is why Blanchot says, in speaking of Kafka's work, that

> one must be capable of satisfaction in death, capable of finding in the supreme dissatisfaction supreme satisfaction, and of maintaining, at the instant of dying, the clearsightedness which comes from such a balance. Contentment is then very close to Hegelian wisdom, if the latter consists in making satisfaction and self-consciousness coincide, in finding in extreme negativity—in death become possibility, project, and time—the measure of the absolutely positive. (90)

The "balance" that Blanchot refers to can be understood as the inhabiting of the limit; "self-consciousness" is, in this context, the limit of consciousness the self can experience, and it can experience that consciousness only in negativity—a negativity that writing in death's space can provide. If we bring death's space (the space of the work) and the death drive (the pulsion of satisfaction) together, we see that in terms of the death drive, experiencing satisfaction is to comply fully, to discharge oneself completely in the name of the work's demand. That is why the death drive is not, as Lacan famously, even notoriously avers, a question of biology, but of culture.[7] The work's demand—not the demand writers make on themselves, but the demand the work-as-anterior makes on them, of dread's insistence that they write in the space of their unworking (or *désoeuvrement*)—is the moment when writers confront "a region anterior to the beginning where nothing is made of being, in which nothing is accomplished. It is the depth of being's inertia [*désoeuvrement*]" (SL 46). The paradoxical space of the work—which insists upon the inertia, or the unworking of the being who produces it—is outside chronological time, outside the workaday concerns of life and the jottings in the daily journal. Not that the writer is simply "lost" in the act of creation, or has simply "lost track of time" in the midst of composition—rather, the temporality of the work is simultaneously prior to its origin and utterly anticipatory. In effect, the work's demand occupies a radical outside, one of time's absence, one of fascination cut off from the present, from presence: if it has a temporality at all, it is the future anterior of distress, of anxiety, of ambiguity. As Blanchot puts it, the void of fascination is a space where "it is as if there were no beings except through the loss of being, when being lacks" (29). That is, the fascination of time's absence is not prompted by the lack-in-being (which

---

[7] Jacques Lacan, "Function and Field of Speech and Language in Psychoanalysis," in *Écrits: The First Complete Edition in English*, trans. Bruce Fink, Héloïse Fink, and Russell Grigg (New York: Norton, 2006), 264.

would be desire); instead, it is lack or loss of being itself (an encounter with the drive). At the level of writing, it is an attempt to respond to the fascination of, to paraphrase W. H. Auden, "making nothing *happen*." I have named the space of time's absence a "future anterior" not in the sense that it comes to some dialectical synthesis or conclusion about its fascination (something that Blanchot warns us against) (30), but rather that it is a losing of oneself in the incessant murmur of language as Outside, as Other, as "Other Night." Lacan describes the experience thusly:

> I identify myself in language, but only by losing myself in it as an object. What is realized in my history is neither the past definite as what was, since it is no more, or even the perfect as what has been in what I am, but the future anterior as what I will have been, given what I am in the process of becoming.[8]

According to Lacan, this "becoming" is determined by being lost in language, not by remembering or discovering one's history; more important, becoming is predicated on a past that is also forever lost, even as the future itself can only be the projected abolition of what one already is; it is determined by the aleatory, radical unknowability of "what I will have been." If for Blanchot the work is the space of fascination, it is also an intervention by the Other Night (not the night of sleep and rest, but the night of inertia, of being's unworking), whose incarnation is "Present Midnight," the "hour at which the present lacks absolutely, [which] is also the hour in which the past touches and, *without the intervention of any timely act whatever*, immediately attains the future at its most extreme" (SL 114; emphasis in original). This hour is the exteriority—or limit-experience—of the future anterior: in the evacuation of the present, the past radically becomes the future: one in which that which was will have become that which will forever be.

In his reading of Mallarmé, Blanchot detects "the motionless sliding which causes things to move forward at the heart of their eternal annulment" (114). One way of understanding this rather gnomic insight is to link it to Mallarmé's famous line "*Un Coup de dés jamais n'abolira le hasard*"; that is, "A throw of the dice will never abolish chance."[9] Here we encounter the important difference between the contingent and the aleatory: we are not governed by absolute contingency; its power is qualified by the aleatory, which, etymologically, means "dependent on a throw of the dice." In other words, the throw of the dice

8   Ibid., 247.
9   Stéphane Mallarmé, *Collected Poems*, trans. Henry Weinfield (Berkeley: University of California Press, 1994), 125–41.

itself—not the act of throwing—will make a decision, and reveal its outcome: boxcars, snake eyes, or what have you. But the very possibility of producing that outcome—in the case of Mallarmé, the work—is dependent upon chance, and not upon a particular act on the part of the subject. In throwing the dice, the subject gambles with his own abolition; it is chance that intervenes, not the subject. In terms of producing the work, Blanchot insists that *Un Coup de dés* grants the work "its last chance, which is not to annul chance, even by an act of mortal negation, but to abandon itself entirely to chance, to consecrate chance by entering without reserve into its intimacy, with the abandon of impotence, *'without the ship that is vain no matter where'* " (SL 117; emphasis in original). The work of psychoanalysis is akin to this very logic. The function of analysis "is not," as Lacan proceeds to explain, "as people maintain, simply to be received by the subject as approval or rejection of what he is saying, but truly to recognize or *abolish* him as a subject. Such is the nature of the analyst's responsibility every time he intervenes by means of speech."[10] If we compare Blanchot and Lacan's contentions, we discover some uncanny parallels: the interventions are made not by the subject, but by the Other (the Other Night, Chance, the Analyst); the space of writing, like the space of analysis, is one of a future anterior, utterly cut off from the present—the breath is held, as the site of the "will have been" reveals itself as a becoming, the articulation of a destiny that only death, or the lack of being, makes possible. Indeed, Blanchot himself views "the voice … not simply [as] the organ of subjective interiority, but, on the contrary, the reverberation of a *space* opening onto the *outside*" (IC 258; emphasis in original).

By retaining the notion of death as possibility, Lacan is accorded a specific kind of praise in Blanchot's *The Infinite Conversation*. Blanchot sees Lacan's return to Freud as a reimagining of the role of analyst as "profound other [*autrui*]" who "frees psychoanalysis from all that makes it an objective knowledge or a kind of magical act" (235). I contend that the radicality of Lacan's intervention into analytic discourse redounds upon Blanchot's understanding of the limit-experience. If the analyst assumes the position of *objet a*, around which the "real in the symbolic" can be experienced by the analysand's desire as "knowable" or experiential *jouissance*, then the death drive takes on the features of another, Other *jouissance* that occupies a site of radical impossibility in a pre-symbolic real, "the impossibility of being for the first time," beyond the seductive reach of complexes and beginnings. In other words, the analyst becomes *l'autrui*, one who

---

[10] Lacan, "Function and Field of Speech and Language in Psychoanalysis," 248; my emphasis.

does not merely "negate" symptoms, but instead embodies a particular space of the outside, the *il y a*, where death's infinite silence, its truth, can be heard, beyond the clamor of desire's ensnarement in repetition. It inculcates, through the experience of the impossible, that is, the Other *jouissance*: not psychosis, but possibility. Lacanian psychoanalysis is, for Blanchot, an instantiation of the infinite conversation.

The intimacy of psychoanalysis is, of course, one constructed largely through transference, and is marked by silence in the same way that Blanchot argues that the task of writing is "to silence" that which "cannot cease speaking" (SL 27). In this way, silence is one of the ways in which the incessant murmuring of the analysand in psychoanalysis and the call of the anterior in writing are by turns echoed, recognized, or abolished. However, in making a connection between the act of writing and psychoanalytic practice, we have reached a potential objection to my linking of death's space to the death drive; the analyst does not "write" the analysand into existence, whatever interventions the analyst might make. Even though Blanchot himself makes the comparison between psychoanalysis and his theory of the *autrui*, we must approach this stumbling block carefully. There is the work and its demand, just as there is analysis and its vicissitudes; there is the writer, unworking herself in death's space in order for the work, however humble, however inadequate, to appear, even as the analysand dismantles herself in order for the truth of her symptom, of her relation to it, to shift and become something adequate to being able to live. But what of the analyst? The analyst occupies a peculiar space and role in this schema: the analyst occupies the position of the work's demand, of the demand that analysis makes on the analyst. The analyst embodies, symptomatically, the demand of the work. That is, in the transference, the analyst embodies the symptom, the *objet a*, for the analysand, in effect separating demand from the death drive. But the cost of the analyst taking on this role for the analysand is that the death drive is brought back by the analyst.[11] The identification with the analyst produces a gap or chasm between demand and the death drive; the analyst must then occupy that gap that separates them, and mediate the analysand's discourse in the death drive's name. Blanchot is thus correct when he speculates that "it is the dangerous duty of the psychoanalyst to seek to suppress this speech [a 'speech as a depth without depth'], suppressing that which in fact opposes all supposedly normal conduct and expression—but

---

[11]   Jacques Lacan, *The Seminar of Jacques Lacan, Book XI: The Four Fundamental Concepts of Psychoanalysis*, ed. Jacques-Alain Miller, trans. Alan Sheridan (New York: W. W. Norton, 1981), 273.

also suppressing himself, thereby meeting up again with death, his truth" (IC 237). The analyst's desire is not the desire the analysand attributes to him/her. In this regard, the analyst rejects the notion of being "the subject supposed to know."[12] The desire proper to the analyst is one that is in solidarity with the death drive. The space the analyst occupies—allied as that person is with the death drive—is the space of listening. As Gerald L. Bruns puts it, "psychoanalysis is, like philosophy, unresponsive, that is, structurally repressive with respect to the impossible or indestructible. Its job is to negate what is outside the negative."[13] The analyst listens with this task in mind, just as Blanchot asserts that the "poet only speaks by listening. For he lives in the *separation* where the still wordless rhythm and the voice that says nothing but does not cease to speak must become power to name in him alone who hears it, who is nothing but attunement to it, a mediator capable of informing it" (SL 226).

But the demand placed upon the analyst is complicated by its seemingly sadistic dimension; that is to say, the psychic pain of psychoanalysis, which is an effect of creating a space for the unconscious to speak, inverts the logic of neurotic fantasy ($\$ \lozenge a$), in which the subject of desire ($\$$) attempts to contend with the other as surplus *jouissance* (*objet a*). Lacan's discourse of the analyst places the analyst, as the agent of analysis, in the position of *objet a* and the analysand, as the subject of desire (the matheme for which is $\$$) in the position of the other. On the surface, this relation is precisely the same formulation as that of sadistic fantasy ($a \lozenge \$$).[14] In other words, the analyst stands as the embodiment of both the other's desire and the figure of the law at the same time; the "sadism" of analysis comes in making the analysand's desire an ontological problem for it—a problem that the analyst, as the "subject supposed to know" is presumed to "resolve." The important, crucial difference between sadistic fantasy and the analyst's discourse is that the latter is a social link that works toward the analysand's unconscious knowledge. The lower positions of the analyst's discourse—the "unconscious" of the social link between analyst and analysand—are truth (occupied by the matheme $S^2$, "knowledge") and production (occupied by the matheme $S^1$, "the Master Signifier"). The truth of the analysand's unconscious knowledge does not reside in the analyst, but can be known only obliquely, through a "meeting up

---

12  Ibid., 235.
13  Gerald L. Bruns, *Maurice Blanchot: The Refusal of Philosophy* (Baltimore: Johns Hopkins University Press), 236.
14  Jacques Lacan, "Kant with Sade," in *Écrits: The First Complete Edition in English*, trans. Bruce Fink, Héloïse Fink, and Russell Grigg (New York: Norton, 2006), 653.

again with death, his truth" that hystericizes the analysand's discourse such that the unconscious may be permitted to appear.[15] But the path to its appearance implies both a suffering and a duty to be faithful to one's desire. There is a link, therefore, between suffering as *jouissance* and duty as an ethical injunction. The work of psychoanalysis and of its demand are the stuff of what Georges Bataille calls "inner experience." Lacan himself wittingly uses the term to capture Daniel Schreber's analysis in his *écrit* "On a Question Prior to Any Treatment of Psychosis";[16] significantly, Lacan insists that Bataille's term "inner experience" cannot be understood as a synonym for psychosis; in its very poetry, its reliance on metaphor, inner experience is much more akin to the limit-experience that Lacan associates with the questions prompted by analysis than with the virtually unyielding metonymies of psychosis.[17] As Blanchot aptly puts it in his short essay on Bataille's text, "Inner experience is the answer that awaits a man, when he has decided to be nothing but question. This decision expresses the impossibility of being satisfied" (FP 37). By positing herself as "nothing but question," the analysand makes desire and *jouissance*—and their attendant suffering—the objects of analysis. In order to understand better the implications of the analyst's discourse, we will now turn to the texts by Blanchot and Lacan that engage with the work of Sade.

As is well known, Blanchot writes of Sade in dialectical, often encomiastic, terms as one whose work is marked not by excess, but by an excess of reason—that is, Sade does not write to convince; rather, "we are offered as it were to a manner of understanding that escapes us and yet draws us on" (IC 218). The reason this form of thought eludes our grasp is that reason itself is held by Sade to a kind of rigor that will not allow the lures of truism and nature to trip it up. Blanchot goes on:

> One of Sade's truths is that reason is capable of an energetic becoming and is itself always in the process of becoming, being essentially movement. And one can say as well that this is the impulse that moves his work—an impulse that is certainly inordinate, but because to be reasonable is first of all to be so excessively. (219)

Here Blanchot is following Hegel in his approach to Sade—that "the madness of writing" is reason in its extreme (217). This inordinate impulse drives

---

[15]  Jacques Lacan, *The Other Side of Psychoanalysis: The Seminar of Jacques Lacan, Book XVII*, trans. Russell Grigg (New York: Norton, 2007), 33–35.

[16]  Jacques Lacan, "On a Question Prior to Any Treatment of Psychosis," in *Écrits: The First Complete Edition in English*, trans. Bruce Fink, Héloïse Fink, and Russell Grigg (New York: Norton, 2006), 485.

[17]  Jacques Lacan, *The Seminar of Jacques Lacan. Book III: The Psychoses: 1955-1956*, trans. Russell Grigg, ed. Jacques-Alain Miller (New York: Norton, 1993), 218–19, 227–28.

Sade's own commitment to the "permanent state of the republic," which he calls "insurrection," rather than to the foundation of the French republic, as revolution's final stage (223). The state is not the goal: the goal is satisfaction. The movement that drives reason in Sade is thus not the logic of desire, with its laws, its objectives, and its repetitions, but the death drive.

In terms of his own discussion of Sade and the state, Lacan invokes and slightly alters Père Ubu's "Long live Poland, for if there were no Poland, there would be no Poles."[18] Here we see the limits of analytic deduction. For as anyone familiar with the history of Europe over the past 235 years would tell you, Poland did not exist as a political, mappable entity for over half of that time. In other words, the notion that one's "Polishness" is apparently indebted to "Poland" as a transcendental category of nation is obviously a false one. For example, readers of the first volume of Witold Gombrowicz's *Diary* would have noticed that this anxious relationship to Poland is a constant theme of this text of exile, and its argument anticipates, in some ways, Lacan's "Kant with Sade" by almost ten years. Gombrowicz criticizes those Poles who "do not know how to act toward Poland" precisely because they lose themselves in the very act of slavishly exalting the Polish state;[19] in other words, the only proper Pole is a Pole in exile—a Pole *without* a Poland. I suspect that Lacan invokes Alfred Jarry's line here because, of course, Poland ceased to be a state during exactly the period (1795) when Kant and Sade were most active. Kant insists upon struggling against the pleasure that might "get in the way" of the unconditional acceptance of the good, while Sade struggles against the conditions placed upon enjoyment *tout court*. For Blanchot, Sade's radicality resides in the rejection of historical violence (which continues to structure state-sanctioned violence) and the embracing, in the absence of already-sullied values of good and evil, of an "energy," "a relation to the principle to which affirmation and negation answer when they are pushed to their fullest measure and identify with one another" (IC 223). But when we bring Kant and Sade together, the freedom of the ethical act in Kant opens up new possibilities for *jouissance* (which is, of course, Sade's reason-driven obsession). The capriciousness of *jouissance* is a freedom toward which one must strive; liberty, in Blanchot's reading of Sade, must, in order to be enjoyed, remain forever in movement.

---

[18]  Lacan, "Kant With Sade," 647.
[19]  Witold Gomborwicz, *Diary*, trans. Lillian Vallee (Chicago: Northwestern University Press, 1988), 6.

Lacan comes at the same problem in a different way—through Kant. Breaking free of the natural order (Sade's dream of limitless *jouissance*) is the ethical act in Kant: this is Lacan's main point. But Lacan does not attempt to install Sade as the ethical thinker *par excellence*, nor is he suggesting that Kant, with his categorical imperative, is really just a Sade in celibate bachelor's clothing. Rather, it is the relation to the ethical that binds them together. This ethics is not structured by a discourse of reciprocity or intersubjectivity. Why? Because desire, as desire of the Other, marks the relation between subjects through the arbitrary intervention of the Master Signifier ($S^1$); thus, any fantasy of mirroring between one subject and another is already marked by distortion, by anamorphosis. It is thus not a relation of equivalence or reciprocity, because the Other is in the dominant position over the subject. The reason for this resides in the split in the subject that is the recognition of subjectivity, that one is *subject to* the Other. Otherwise, one is seduced by the fantasy that, as subject, one names the other. This is what Lacan, in "Kant with Sade," tries to show in the pun "Tu es" (You are) and in what "is evoked out of the lethal depths [*fonds tuant*] of every imperative."[20] Since pain is a crucial marker of ethical experience, it is for Kant and Sade a radical encounter with nature. Both attempt to transcend natural law: Kant, through his notion of radical autonomy, and Sade, through his notion of radical enjoyment. Sade is not saying, for example, that one should just break the received social rules around pleasure. Instead, one should be prepared to break one's fidelity to one's pleasure. Desire, as Lacan tells us, will trick us with its "will to *jouissance*" by generally choosing pleasure over enjoyment—it "disappears under pleasure's sway."[21] So Sade's point is that if nature seems to be the limit, then that limit must be broken too. Kant's point is that an ethical act is a rupture within the law itself. A moral act is simply following the rules. Thus, one does not love one's neighbor as oneself without addressing the evil in oneself or in the other—otherwise, one risks becoming a sadist, not a Sadean, as it were. We can now return to the problem of avoiding the snares of the good, of the law, and the love of one's neighbor. One way is not to confuse altruism with love of one's neighbor (hence Lacan's invocation of this doctrine near the end of the *écrit* in his reading of Pierre Klossowski's *Sade, My Neighbour*, and Freud).[22] One must instead be prepared to confront the *jouissance* of the Other, that aspect of Otherness that

---

[20]    Lacan, "Kant with Sade," 650.

[21]    Ibid., 652.

[22]    Ibid., 666–67.

cannot be reduced to cuisine or couture, or what have you. Indeed, trying to consume the *jouissance* of the Other—of the real of the Other, in other words—is another erotic lure veiled by a fantasy of self-sacrifice. In other words, attempting to confront the *jouissance* of the Other may actually be simply a way of hiding or betraying one's own *jouissance* or preventing the Other from gaining access to her own *jouissance*. This is what Lacan means when he says, "I retreat from loving my neighbour as myself because there is something on the horizon there that is engaged in some form of intolerable cruelty. In that sense, to love one's neighbour may be the cruelest of choices."[23] Such a conclusion almost inevitably leads him to confront Kant with Sade.

Sade prompts us to confront the *jouissance* of evil, of the limits of what we are prepared to confront, to bear, about the subject's relation to the other. The point of *jouissance* is the recognition of other *as* other. This relation is in part structured by our investment in a part object, the *objet a*, is that it is not the person, but in the negativity of the Thing (the Thing is another way of framing the *objet a*). The distance between the other and the Thing is traumatically suspended in the moment when "It (that is, the Thing) speaks." (For Blanchot, it is the *il y a*, that experience in which the subject finds herself outside being, utterly alienated from her existence; the ontological certainty of "there is" metastasizes into "there is … no-thing.") In late eighteenth-century France, the Thing speaking may very well have been freedom of the other. "With Sade," Blanchot calls our attention to "a very high form of paradoxical truth—we have the first example … of the way in which writing, the freedom to write, can coincide with the movement of true freedom, when the latter enters into crisis and gives rise to a vacancy in history. A coincidence that is not an identification" (IC 222). It points toward, in other words, the radical negativity of the relation between the object and the negative space that makes its appearance and speech possible; it is the enjoyment or satisfaction that comes in the unpleasure that occurs in the return of the repressed—a satisfaction that coincides with the subject, but resists or defies identification.

In their different ways, both Blanchot and Lacan demonstrate that ethical reason—or the madness in reason—in Kant meets Sade's excessive reason at the crossroads of freedom. Both thinkers exhort us to alienate ourselves from a particular, dearly held notion of ourselves, and submit ourselves to an abstract

---

[23] Jacques Lacan, *Ethics of Psychoanalysis*, trans. Dennis Porter (New York and London: W.W. Norton, 1992), 194.

principle that rejects the desirous lures of the good, the law, or even the love of one's neighbor.[24] This is the paradox of freedom's *jouissance*: it is the surplus of enjoyment that is derived from desire's symptom, even as one suffers as a result of it. It is, in other words, the satisfaction that comes from suffering for one's desire. One would then assume that the removal of the obstacle to enjoyment—the law of the father—would make more enjoyment possible. But as Lacan insists, following Freud's *Totem and Taboo*, the murder of the father does not "open the path to *jouissance*," but instead "strengthens the prohibition."[25] The act of murdering the father becomes not a means of ensuring more satisfaction, but accruing a debt that is inscribed in the symbolic order. The relentless demands of the superego become all the more pronounced the more one tries to submit to its edicts. Prohibition, then, becomes crucial to enjoyment in that enjoyment itself can become a rut (or drive?). Prohibition is thus the "all-terrain vehicle" that makes enjoyment possible.[26] Prohibition is thus the link between desire and the law; desire is produced by the prohibitions set up by the law—the law of a father who is always already dead. This is why Lacan insists that the symbolic father, the father of the law and desire, is always a dead father.[27]

So the question remains: How does one answer the demand of the work, the demand of analysis itself? By saying. By saying—or trying to say—everything. Just as Blanchot, in his theorization of Sade, characterizes his writing as the excess of reason—the madness that Bruns explains is "an exigent madness" or "the noncoincidence of reason with itself [rather] than its breakdown or failure"[28]—one of the other earmarks of this excess is, as Blanchot reminds us, a kind of duty: this is what Sade means when he insists that "philosophy must say everything" (IC 229). It is precisely this alien or foreign element of reason—its noncoincidental dimension—that Lacan sees as the basis for the duty that psychoanalysis entails for the "I," the analysand: "Will it or will it not submit itself to the duty that it feels within like a stranger, beyond, at another level?"[29] That is to say, will the analysand submit neither to the authority of the analyst nor to the pathological duty of the obsessional neurotic, but to a duty born of

---

[24]   Alenka Zupančič, *Ethics of the Real: Kant and Lacan* (London: Verso, 2000), 82.
[25]   Lacan, *Ethics of Psychoanalysis*, 176.
[26]   Ibid., 17.
[27]   Jacques Lacan, "Subversion of the Subject and the Dialectic of Desire in the Freudian Unconscious," in *Écrits: The First Complete Edition in English*, trans. Bruce Fink, Héloïse Fink, and Russell Grigg (New York: Norton, 2006), 698.
[28]   Bruns, *Maurice Blanchot*, 189.
[29]   Lacan, *Ethics of Psychoanalysis*, 7.

pure desire—one that sacrifices one's idea of oneself to this "stranger" within and beyond? For Lacan, this sacrifice means following one's desire in the same way Sade asks us, in reading him, to follow reason—to its limit. The limit, at desire's lip, is the site where conscious speech yields to unconscious enunciation, where desire is purified in its sacrifice to the death drive; it is, as Lacan puts it in *The Ethics of Psychoanalysis*, "the second death"—a space of fundamental suspension of transformation;[30] in *Séminaire IX*, Lacan singles out Blanchot's *L'arrêt de mort* for praise as "the surest confirmation" of what he was saying in *The Ethics* about the second death (translation mine).[31] It is the juncture at which Kant and Sade, despite all they might teach us, both fail; psychoanalysis is neither a discourse of absolute self-fashioning, nor is it an absolute submission to or identification with the other; instead, it is the agonizing, alienating coincidence of the two. This is the pain of psychoanalysis. Through the analyst as *autrui*, the analysand strikes at the very heart of her desire. One must traverse one's fantasy—the fantasy that sustains one's desire—in the name of freedom. For Blanchot, this is the fascination at the heart of the story of Orpheus and Eurydice.

As we know, Orpheus, the poet and musician, descends into the underworld to rescue his beloved, Eurydice, from death. Hades is so impressed by Orpheus's music that he agrees to allow Eurydice to return to the world, on one condition: as they make their ascent, Orpheus cannot turn back to look at her. But when his anxiety becomes too great, he breaks his promise, and loses her forever. When Blanchot returns again and again to the allegory of Orpheus and his lethal gaze, he is confronting the demand made on the subject—the annihilation of the heart of Orpheus's desire—by traversing the fantasy that sustains his desire, namely, Eurydice's return. In *The Infinite Conversation*, Blanchot turns to the myth one more time: "Eurydice is the strangeness of the extreme distance that is *autrui* at the moment of face-to-face confrontation; and when Orpheus looks back, ceasing to speak in order to see, his gaze reveals itself to be the violence that brings death, the dreadful blow" (IC 60). When we think about it, one of the profound truths of the Orpheus/Eurydice myth is that mourning is an ethical duty that one cannot avoid. In losing Eurydice, in living with and singing of her absence, Orpheus is confronting what it means to experience the "no-thing" that has taken up residence in his heart. If, in Blanchot's parlance, Eurydice and the analyst are in the position of *autrui*, then Orpheus is the analysand, saying

---

[30]  Ibid., 20.
[31]  Lacan, *L'identification*, 604.

"everything" in the hope of sustaining his desire. But if we push the analogy further, we discover something more important. If the analysand, in his anxiety, continually turns back to look at the analyst, then he is "ceasing to speak in order to see," and is doing violence to the death drive to sustain a desire for an other who is nothing but absence. In this respect, the lesson in Orpheus's anxious turning around is not "don't look back," but rather that he, like the analysand, *must* look back:

> But not to turn toward Eurydice would be no less untrue. Not to look would be infidelity to the measureless, imprudent force of his movement, which does not want Eurydice in her daytime truth and her everyday appeal, but wants her in her nocturnal obscurity, in her distance, with her closed body and sealed face—wants to see her not when she is visible, but when she is invisible, and not as the intimacy of a familiar life, but as the foreignness of what excludes all intimacy, and wants, not to make her live, but to have living in her the plenitude of her death. (SL 172)

That is to say, in looking back, Orpheus, like the analysand, is traversing the fantasy, going beyond its limit, and, in doing so, betraying the desire that was holding him back from doing the painful work of psychoanalysis; he enters the space of the second death. In terms of the future anterior, the past and future have collapsed into a suspended present: Eurydice is already dead, and will be dead again. This is the point at which desire and the death drive are linked; Orpheus, in betraying Eurydice, chooses death over desire, satisfaction over the goal. He sacrifices his desire for the sake of the work. If the analyst is Eurydice, then she only seems to be the source of the pain of loss; she is not—it resides in her absence. She, like the analyst, can be addressed only obliquely, since the source of the pain that comes is the radical unworking of oneself—in the call of the anterior, in the name of death.

# 13

# "Unmade According to His Image," or, Night for Day: Blanchot and the Blacknesses of Cinema Figure

Kevin Bell

*Don't guess what I'm going to say. That's a fucking rotten habit you have. It's what's wrong with your films. You can't let anything happen. You coax it along … You still think you're breaking the law …* How many times have I told you to ignore the law?

Bill Gunn, *Black Picture Show*, 1975

*What for me had to be destroyed was a certain kind of ethnographic veracity—which had characterized black films up to that point. Which was that people "told it as it was," "told it straight," and you were supposed to feel the injustice from the celluloid. "We're poor, we suffer and this is it … you know, look at our kitchen, got no food in it …" all of that; that whole documentary tradition we absolutely wanted to destroy … to draw a line which said from this point on, there had to be some reflection about the nature of these images.*

Filmmaker John Akomfrah of the Black Audio Film Collective, interviewed 30 October 2012 on its 1986 documentary *Handsworth Songs.*

\*\*\*

When, in "Literature and the Right to Death," Maurice Blanchot consolidates the figure of the Jacobin insurrectionist as a nexus between the experience of death and the experience of freedom—and in the same essay, observes the writhing involution that alone inaugurates and sustains non-mimetic writing as a different flexing of the same relation—he plots *and* vaporizes the central coordinates of an entire cultural field that is secured only by its own dialectical theater of oppositions and definitions, themselves animated and bound by the motor-force of Hegelian/Kojevian recognition formulas.[1]

Foregrounded in Blanchot's atomizing of that definitional field is what gets buried in its establishing as the epistemological horizon of the modern Western world. This would be all sense of the originary impasse of "interminable and incessant" anxieties, intensities, and alterities against which such ordering formulas are drawn and set into place. The anterior excessiveness of unknown force necessitating whatever imagined stabilizations these anchoring rivets might provide—discursively codified as these are in the forms and practices of personifications and roles—processed and denuded as these are of disruptive potentials—and *fast-tracked,* as these are in the practical development of other, more pliant tendencies, by the institutions of control within which they are continually re-molded and re-tooled—this "nocturnal" impenetrability of depth and density, within which these presumptive bonds and contracts are necessarily pre-voided, is, across Blanchot's evaluations of the programmatic orders of Western capitalist modernity, receded to the point of disappearance.

What emerges through the impress of his thought, however, is the degree to which literature—and the "poetic image" at work therein and elsewhere—only become so in their ongoing traversal of the "terrifying" randomness of this immersive space; the zone by which modernity's referential matrices of concepts, values, positions, schemas, and strategies are always already liquefied by force of what comes *precedent* to their defensive systematization as such.

Blanchot's writing never separates from the gravitational pull of this suspended surplus, nor from what it holds in continual suspension itself—the daylight operations and predications of what he frequently termed "the world of action"; or, in one instance, "the imperialism of light." He is conditioned by discernment of an alternate, always de-legitimated rootedness in what this self-installed empire disowns as its inert, non-historical, non-rational other, fit only for either subjection to or disqualification from the accrediting authorities of reason, canonicity, and right—all explained by logics of transparency and *light*—itself now wired through the representational circuitry of Western world

---

[1]  See Maurice Blanchot, *The Work of Fire*, trans. Charlotte Mandell (Stanford: Stanford University Press, 1995), 318–22.

orders as the defining ideal and arbiter of thought and action. In *The Infinite Conversation*, Blanchot amplifies the Nietzschean antipathy to this installation, with Nietzsche's words triggering Blanchot's own challenge:

> *"The world is deep: deeper than the day can comprehend:"* Nietzsche does not content himself here with calling up the Stygian night … why, he asks, this relationship between day, thought and world? Why do we say confidently, of lucid thought, the same thing we say of the day and thus believe we have in our grasp the power to think the world? Why would light and seeing furnish us all the modes of approach that we would like to see thought provided with in order to see the world? … Why do we see essences, Ideas and God? But the world is more profound … Why this imperialism of light? (IC 162)

Blanchot moves not only beyond the ocularcentrism by which this self-proclaimed "world" confines itself to this metaphysical field of vision and understanding, but toward the amputated "profundity" animating the vastness beyond those boundaries, the discarded depth and force refused entry to the self-anointed empire of light.

Accessing several of Blanchot's critical instruments, perhaps most crucially his notions of the poetic image and the "Outside," "neutral," or "il y a," this chapter investigates a few shapes created within one such amputated sphere, that of the more radical or experimental constellations of black-diasporic film and writing, still essentially occluded from the spectra of Euro-American critical theory's own historical networks of analytic engagement. But it is within these particular constellations' unique terms of *refusal* to understand or measure themselves within the discourses of cultural reproduction by which they are always already disfigured and discredited that such works are continually poised in the neutral insistence of the "*other* night." Which is to say that they develop in the involuntary, absolute, and irreversible movement of detaching from any organizing regime of reference or memory established beyond the internal logics and temporalities of their own opening and articulation; that such works not only evacuate the theoretical premises of those networks' authority and competence, but that they also draw into an orbit of not-so-distant "friendship"[2] with Blanchot's own insurrectionary impulsion toward an art that eviscerates every law of proprietary fixity—an art thus realizing its most revelatory intensity

---

[2]  Denis Hollier renders Blanchot's notion of friendship in a way that resonates with the modes of linkage this essay wants to draw. "Friendship is the means through which I relate not to the clarity but to the obscurity of the other" (19). Denis Hollier, "Blanchot, Speaking in Tongues: Otherness in Translation," *Paroles Gelees* 15, no. 2 (1997): 11–29.

in the paradoxical powerlessness of its "grasp of that imaginary point where the world can be seen in its entirety" (WF 339).

In "Literature and the Right to Death," the surging of this dispersive force is adduced by Blanchot as the originary deluge that is subsequently frozen into the gridding of discursive order by the identifying function of language. Revising Hegel's insistence on language's negation of its referential objects ("Adam's first act, which made him master of the animals, was to give them names, that is he annihilated them in their existence"), Blanchot writes:

> Hegel means that from that moment on, the cat ceased to be a uniquely real cat and became an idea as well. The meaning of speech, then, requires that before any word is spoken, there must be a sort of immense hecatomb, a preliminary flood plunging all of creation into a total sea. God had created living things, but man had to annihilate them … and man was condemned not to be able to approach anything or experience anything except through the meaning he had to create. He saw that he was enclosed in daylight, and he knew this day could not end, because the end in itself was light, since it was from the end of beings that their meaning—which is being—had come. (WF 323)

No predication or proposition outlives the violence with which the outward movements of its own initial experimentality are mired in a referential network of positional differences that amount only to equalizations, "enclosed in daylight." The inscriptive force of representation's amputative aspect is not limited to marking merely the phantom-limb afterlife of either the severed "referent" or its abstraction in name. Instead, it is by way of such violence that the system of interchangeable reductions is itself formulated and grounded, modernity's incessant transacting of positions oriented not so much by fluctuations of sensibility, impulse, or intensity as by a governing logic of finitude and designation. It is what Blanchot means when he writes, in the essay's next paragraph, "Therefore it is accurate to say that when I speak, death speaks in me. My speech is a warning that at this very moment death is loose in the world, that it has suddenly appeared between me, as I speak, and the being I address: it is there between us as the distance that separates us, but this distance is also what prevents us from being separated, because it contains the condition for all understanding" (WF 323–324). But it is the totality of this cultural arc by which to realize—as does Blanchot's own unique image of the imprisoned writerly *practice* of the Marquis de Sade—the urgency of dis-inhabiting the idioms of that enclosure and of disentombing one's own thought; to think the Outside, the other of "the world of action" from within the continual re-assemblage of cultural determinations and representations cementing its coherences. "To write is to break the bond that unites the word with myself," reads a line from "The Essential Solitude" (SL 26). For Blanchot, writing is the involuntary drop from functionalized being, measured time, and calculated movement into an alien contingency of "interminable, incessant" recession of everything already known or given—a space of necessarily transfigurative movement—necessary futurity—in language, image and thought.

## At least they'll see the black

By way of cinematic example, one *optic* disarticulation of this mimetic bind is provided by an introductory sequence in a film antecedent and, to some degree influential to a couple of works discussed later: Chris Marker's 1982 essay documentary *Sans Soleil*. Its interventionary power inheres in its visual isolation of the addiction to continuity that organizes the death-bound linguistic/cultural frame of identity and exchange Blanchot describes. Its opening sequence is itself one of the most frequently cited in reflections on the film—perhaps most recently by the Jamaican-born poet Claudia Rankine, who uses the pivotal line from the scene as the epigraph to her 2015 book *Citizen*.

Marker's organizational structure is direct—an unidentified woman narrates a series of letters from a cameraman (the final credits reveal his name as Sandor Krasna) who sends her film images and correspondence from random points throughout his travels around the world. Its first image is a shot of total blackness. This quickly cuts to a second image whose terse elaboration in the narration—in which it is referred to as the *first* image—introduces a conceptual focus orienting the allo-representational logic of the entire film.

> The first image he told me about was of three children on a road in Iceland, in 1965. He said that for him it was the image of happiness and also that he had tried several times to link it to other images, but it never worked.
>
> He wrote me: "one day I'll have to put it all alone at the beginning of a film with a long piece of black leader; if they don't see happiness in the picture, at least they'll see the black."

All figuration, all organization; all difference, all shape, and indeed all light proceed from the depth, duration, and disorientation of black; a black now vested by the cameraman's writing with an interpretive force that blackness is always said to block. It is a black now laced with a valence of significative power, of which blackness has always been designated the absolute effacement. Does this narration mean what it implies—that the duration of blackness is no longer strictly the duration of negation or even discontinuity—no longer a mere framing device by which to set off the world of light—which is to say, the world of experience, of history, of thought—of Enlightenment? Or does it mean that black is meant to disrupt *precisely* such an unimpeded flow of presuppositions and is therefore indispensable to knowledge's dialectical self-realization—by way of "its" "other?" Does the sequence of cuts disclose in less than a minute the movement from "nothing to everything" (or its inverse) that Blanchot, again in "Literature and the Right to Death," argues is ultimately at stake in the project of literature (WF 316)?

To think this sequence with Blanchot suggests the question not to be the relation of the image of ocular blackness to the specific meaning or depiction of the "image of happiness," but the relation of blackness to the question of the power and function of the figural image itself. Which suggests that to fasten critically upon such an interval or suspension as Marker's black leader is to have already ejected from the resolution imperatives of the cinematic idioms the film leaves behind. Blanchot finds in the obliterative or suspensional function of the poetic image both its essential value and its critical point of disappearance—a dispossessing of any capacity to fix its meaning at the core of its allure, at the root of its exercise and extraction of the force of the *fascination* that undoes its beholder and renders him or her simultaneously helpless before that image and alien to the "known" self and its world:

> What happens when what is seen imposes itself upon the gaze as if the gaze were seized … the gaze gets taken in, absorbed by an immobile movement and a depthless deep … what fascinates us robs us of our power to give sense. It abandons … the world, draws back from the world, and draws us along … Whoever is fascinated doesn't see, properly speaking, what he sees … Fascination is fundamentally linked to neutral, impersonal presence, to the indeterminate They, the immense, faceless Someone. Fascination is the relation the gaze entertains. (SL 32–33)

For Blanchot, the poetic or figural image is the precise marking by which the monumentalizing impulse toward re-capture of lost reality or presence is itself scattered forever, the social obligation to "preserve face" and designation dissolved as the price/reward of the new relation. Stupefaction before the image brings to a momentary dead-stop the performative habituations of a social constituted by market and ritual cycles within which it would be apprehended only from the point of view of consumption and reproduction.

That such stoppage would result from the imagistic obliteration of face and the disconnection of light suggests a deep connectivity between Blanchot's insistence on the disabling force of "the neuter" or "il y a" *inhering in the figural*—and revolutionary potentialities in the social—for it is in the interval of uncertainty opened by the image, a duration and a space in which all the cues and props, all the terminologies and signaling systems of anthropomorphic/subjectivist familiarity are powered off, that the "profound" immensities of the other night, wishfully discarded by the rationalist orderings of "world" make themselves most acutely felt. Gerald Bruns renders the relation from several angles; this one emerges in an incisive characterization of Blanchot's "appropriation" of Emmanuel Levinas's formulation *il y a* (there is), itself described by Levinas as "this impersonal, anonymous, yet inextinguishable 'consummation' of being, which murmurs in the depths of nothingness itself." For Bruns,

> The *il y a* is not anything, but neither is it nothing; it is being from which everything has been withdrawn; being without substance and without light. The *il y a* is nocturnal; not a night that passes into day but night which excludes every passage, including the movement of day into the night that brings sleep. Sleep enables us to finesse the night. By contrast, the *il y a* is the interminable, incessant night of insomnia, a night of pure vigilance without anticipation or release, a night that persists through the day. Insomnia is the experience of impossibility, not just the impossibility of sleep but the impossibility of the day.[3]

---

[3] Gerald L. Bruns, *Maurice Blanchot: The Refusal of Philosophy* (Baltimore and London: Johns Hopkins University Press, 1997), 59. Moreover, for a particular sense of the reflective power of a very similar figure in Blanchot, see one of Leslie Hill's usefully comprehensive considerations on the *critical* functionality of "the neuter" in *Maurice Blanchot and Fragmentary Writing: A Change of Epoch*. Proceeding from Blanchot's attempts to distill and theorize Nietzsche's evident tendency toward contradiction in the progression of his own writing, Hill offers the following: "Blanchot's purpose, however, was not to identify inconsistencies as such in order to resolve them, or even allow them to cancel each other out. His strategy was rather to search for a vanishing point, a *point de fuite*, indicative not of the power or potency of conceptual thought (i.e., what it can), but far more radically, its impossibilities, weaknesses and erasures (i.e., what happens when it exceeds its horizon of competence). The approach then is not so much hermeneutic as hyperbolic; the aim being to push Nietzsche's assertions to the limit, to that extreme point where something other than the regularity of the concept is exposed, an otherness that escapes conceptual explication and can only be inscribed by way of a logic of supplementarity, that is by a logic of both subtraction and addition, according to which every articulation, by dint of the fragmentary, is no sooner affirmed than withdrawn, such that withdrawal features henceforth as a species of affirmation and affirmation as a species of withdrawal, the one erasing the or overwriting the other in a ceaseless movement of dispersion. Such logic has no proper name, which is why it can receive, provisionally at least, the modest, unassuming title of the neuter, the neuter that has no centre, unity, or self-identity, but which nonetheless, exceeding positive and negative alike, cannot but be affirmed, which speaks in language, but is not identifiable with any single word or expression or concept, for it precedes and outstrips all available terms, which it hollows out, displaces and re-marks" (36). Hill, *Maurice Blanchot and Fragmentary Writing: A Change of Epoch* (London and New York: Bloomsbury, 2012).

"At least they'll see the black" offers hope that the black leader induces an insomniac anxiety of hermeneutic indeterminacy—one that the ideal picture of happiness might have softly narcotized, had it hit its desired mark. Blackness in this instance is not only made to break frame in its frequent role "as" the frame by which to center the image of radiant plenitude embodied by the three girls; it is made also to dis-inscribe the experience of spectatorial time or duration itself. Krasna can be said to equate the image of the girls with the black leader so as to make them as timeless, as unreadable, as un-colonizable by discourse as is the effect of marking he seems to project that the blackness will make. The slow-motion film image of the girls is allowed to unfold in silence; but the narrator speaks during or over the quick cut of blackness, which again, at this point, appears relegated to the function of framing. But in conscripting the black leader to function instead as a default or substitute image should that of the girls fail to transmit his ideal *as such*—as if it were a fixed object of exchange, ready for delivery or pickup—Krasna's line suggests the disruptive, re-inscriptive power of visual blackness to be secured by the gravity of its very appearance, the meaning of which is presumably incapable of being missed because it is never so burdened with messaging. Optic blackness, culturally criminalized for its refractory non-responsiveness to interpretative appropriation, appears now to find the very movement of its ongoing recession to be the fugitive differential of nocturnal force that Krasna's default option invokes.

But the *other* night is always other. (SL 155)

For Blanchot, something in non-mimetic writing's very initiation is exerted by this amorphous anteriority without legible authority—something that actually impels its futurity, since it turns away so blithely from the conventions it has previously absorbed; something unassimilable to any prescribed economy of cognitions or schematizations. This means that from the operational point of view of Blanchot's world of action, structured by contractual models of relation and quantitative metrics of appraisement, in which culture industries are established and inventories of cultural memory are stocked, depleted, and replaced (or not), that such essentially transient figuration as the literature he explores emerges already stripped of currency, without any pretense of purchase or value. Consigned to simultaneous ignition within what, from the work's perspective, must be felt as a double-void—that of the banal impositions and pressures of daylight order and, its fearful, un-articulable subjection to the *other* night's impenetrable presence—the other of the routinized practicum cohering the order of day's labor and night's rest—the material consistencies of poetic image—shape, velocity, color, rhythm may only enkindle upon the concrete conditions these same elements abrade in their inability to be absorbed into reproductive social orders.

## No more stories

Essentially free of dialogue, narration, and any imposition of human likeness, Christopher Harris's 2000 black-and-white experimental documentary, *Still/Here*, engineers an anti-auratic film alterity from out of the architectural rubble of St. Louis, Missouri's, decimated North side.

Contoured extensively within and around a few of the more than 6,000 abandoned and disintegrating houses and buildings concentrated in this single quadrant of St. Louis, *Still/Here*'s sequencing of lengthy visual shots accompanied by unanticipated sound projections short-circuits the prevailing postmortem documentary approach to film treatments of social catastrophe. It inverts the scenography of residential and commercial ruin into nonverbal exploration of a curving in time precipitated by a complete breakdown in space. This is to say that the film's images are evidence of this space having been significantly populated at one moment, and of its having been completely deserted at another moment whose arrival is never disclosed—is itself disappeared, a black hole in the organizational center. Its arrhythmia of collisions, frictions, and tensions between visual and aural elements *within* each frame of the film documents only the impossibility of reducing the sources of such destitution into a narrative of determinations, timelines, and outcomes.

Each shot sculpts its own singularized arc of temporality, allowing its compositional elements of sight and sound to emerge, recede, pulsate, or waver in relation to other elements in the shot. None are made to explain anything, and these interpenetrations of image and sound never tangle themselves in the default traps of the hyper-subjectivist American documentary scene, with its stock arrays of testimonial victims, villains, heroes, and academic talking heads to map out a prefabricated range of spectatorial personifications, "debates," and constituencies with which to identify. The film does not ask after "lives," personas, or narratives of any recognizable kind at any point, but instead constructs figures, shapes, and relations of visuality and sound that emerge sharply in the uninterrupted absence of bodies, faces, and the abiding film injunction that documentary retrofit itself to the cut and conventions of story. Harris ignores the injunction to amputate the excess/overflow of forgotten, trashed territories and objects, allowing them to luxuriate in non-belonging.

*Still/Here*'s visual images are instead volatilized into slivers of interpretative possibility by incisions of incongruent sound. Hard, disembodied footfalls and voices superimposed over each other while accompanying an image of sunken, pulverized rows of hundreds of seats in the rubble-filled, black interior of a deserted, old movie theater; or a massive field of grass quivering in a gentle breeze—accompanied by the sounds of telephones and doorbells ringing without end; or the brick frame of a three-story house standing erect and still—with an even taller and extremely lush tree jutting boldly through its absent roof, seen while a high-speed splicing of voices from assorted talk-radio shows call in to spill their own interiors all over the scene.

By way of example, sixteen minutes into the film, the camera gazes outward onto the traffic of a city street from the dark, interior perch of one of its buildings. The camera sees daylight not through an open window, but directly through a massive hole—perhaps half its space—in the center of the brick and mortar wall of the theater itself. The view of the street below is partially occluded from within by a growth of weeds springing up from *inside* the baseboard underneath this hole—and from without, by the back of the marquee lettering suspended on the other side of the wall. This marquee introduces the building as the Criterion, once a classically art moderne movie house, now so completely rotted out that wild vegetation has taken deep root along the margins of its auditorium. The weeds are visible across the lower part of the screen, their leaves and stems only curling into the shot intrusively after intermittent exhalations of wind from outside.

In a subsequent shot, eight minutes later, another interior angle shows the deeper rows of the nearly 700 crumbling and broken seats inside illuminated by a broad shaft of sunlight projecting through the wall's hole—which now, from the perspective of a camera now drawn back for a fuller shot of the room, is revealed to have eaten away nearly half the wall itself.

The first shot, from behind the marquee and the weeds, is accompanied by a sonic overlay of public conversations and laughter, bodies rustling into theater seats, and interminable, hard-cadenced footsteps on a wooden floor; the sounds perhaps of an audience settling into their seats for a performance, or mingling outside in some auditorium lobby. In the second shot, of the unimpeded sunlight pouring into the auditorium through the gaping wall, the only sound imposed is an increasingly loud rumble, which might be thunder, or an airplane passing overhead.

In each of these shots, the imposed sounds of social and physical activity detonate whatever totalizing intent or "message" might be implied by the primary focus, in each cut, of the doubled cavity at the center—the massive breach in the theater wall and the black hole in the cavernous strangeness and empty drama of the images themselves. In this instance, the indistinguishable voices and infrequent footsteps undermine the reality of what they underscore— nothing is happening here. But something else, outside the program of the narratorial, is. Nothing is happening in this space—but the image itself testifies that while many different, contrasting, opposed things *have* transpired in the spaces, the superimposed sounds unsettling the visual stillness demonstrate that much more could be, breaking the cinematic/documentary trancing into linearized "history" away into the recognition of the continual self-splitting that alone constitutes the fabric of this film—a parting from doctrine, and an imparting of an unanticipated mode of imparting; a listening that is a studying, that is a refusal, that is a forgetting, that is an abandoning, that may be a mode of revelation, that is assuredly a cinematic futurity; a division opened by the multiple gestures that comprise the shot—a splitting presented as a (w)hole that releases a host of genealogical elements from prior relationships without grounding any of these formal gestures in the mimetic fields of denotation or value.

Instead, the film shapes sensorial arcs of what Edouard Glissant termed *non-history*, by which to document a single cluster of what Blanchot sees as that expanse of "profound" materialities lying outside Enlightenment territories of mastering discourse; questions of what is triggered cinematically by the apparently unseen eviction of the always already unseen.

What the film leaves in place is the mute blankness of the shock—the incommensurability of the (non)event it takes as its central object—the open incomprehensibility of local disaster underscored by the drifting character of its seemingly random organization of images and the wavering quality of its optic segues between shots. Its essential practice is contrapuntal, in the sense that it lingers so extensively upon interior spaces, only to avert the un-articulated premise/promise that these interiors conceal some transcendent explanation. The time devoted to exploration of these architectural interiors at once invites and refuses countenance of subjective *interiority* axiomatically presumed not to exist where black people in the United States are concerned.

It is not merely that the negativity at work within the image scatters, defers, or frustrates meaning, but that it announces itself so jarringly while leaving so pristinely undisturbed the immobility of the visual image. What I argue here is not that this undecidable impasse—what art historian Georges Didi-Huberman terms this *rend* in the fabric of the image—is finally a matter of appealing to a poetics of unreason. It is rather to follow a discipline of ongoing self-displacement in attention to the neutral silences of explanation laid down by the film; of listening into the paradoxical presentation of a dispersed history that can be falsified only by restitutive disposition. Instead of adjudicating between isolated visual/sonic images and generalized impositions of meaning, the opacities and overdetermined figures attract the fascination allowing their images repeated escape. They draw judgment's resolve out of itself and turn it back toward the black holes providing the sole substance of any shot and leave it there, unable to distinguish meaningfully between figural invention and the disorientations of reality.

Harris's filmic figuration of the filmic boneyard offers more than elegiac comment upon the disappearance of a generally unobserved cultural landmark and the equally submerged networks of people it served. It rips this object away from the representational mausoleum of urban or destitution in which standard documentary account would have it interred, and situates it within another logic of formal improvisation that extends the life of creative impulse for which the Criterion once provided space. The Criterion is no longer simply a ruined shrine before which to mournfully genuflect, but is converted into a prismatic element of filmic disclosure and withdrawal at once, in which image moves beyond representation into a detonating of all such presupposition, making plain that the experience of breach or rend or nothingness is the basis of interpretive praxis. The massive breach in the theater wall is only one graphically direct statement among several of this overarching theme.

So the nonappearance of any live human face or figure in *Still/Here* is both poetically and theoretically consistent with the particular time, space, and matter of the annihilation it takes as its subject. Harris's work reformulates and attests to a reality upon which so many other forms in explorative or radical black aesthetics subsist—the critical intersection of material destitution with conceptual transfiguration. In this remarkable gloss from Amiri Baraka, there also appear to be rhetorical as well as conceptual intersections with Blanchot:

> The Negro could not ever become white and that was his strength; at some point, always, he could not participate in the dominant tenor of the white man's culture. It was at this juncture that he had to make use of other resources … And

it was this boundary, this no man's land, that provided the logic and beauty of his music.[4]

The imperatives of subjectification and racialization, which presume to lend basis to the ethic of reclamation through which conventional American documentary approaches such absence or loss, are deserted completely in Harris's film in favor of an exploration of a doubled "no man's land"—the emptied ruin of the North Side, and the abandoned traditions of formal representation by which to account for the first. At this point, one might imagine a conceptual horizon drawn by thinkers as disparate as Baraka and Jacques Rancière. In *The Future of the Image*, Rancière writes:

> To investigate something that has disappeared, an event whose traces have been erased, to find witnesses and make them speak of the materiality of the event without canceling its enigma, is a form of investigation which certainly cannot be assimilated to the … representative logic of verisimilitude …[5]

Twenty minutes into *Still/Here*, the spectator is before the image of the exterior brick wall of what was once a large, likely multifamily, house somewhere on the North side. The large hole in this wall—which perhaps suggests nothing so much as a Magritte painting of the outline of a transparent man in a bowler-hat standing in profile—forms the center of a definitively contoured, personalized structure whose presence embodies a functional void, a vacated history, a useless ruin. The wall holds up nothing, contains nothing, apart from long grass and weeds growing through the interior floor. Isolated filmically, not only from the context of the rest of the block, but from the very idea of its own function as boundary, this disintegrating wall becomes the puzzlingly porous chalk outline of the photographic "crime scene" speculated by Walter Benjamin. Whatever clues are made available from this image are scrambled hopelessly in the multiple breach of its figurality at the level of the visible—a house which is not a house, a hole which is a center, a wall which keeps nothing out or in precisely because there is nothing to be kept in or out. And with all these elements working autonomously beneath the superimposition of sounds that are scrambled even more multiply, the shot's drift into non-intelligibility might be thought a final locale of the film's "non-reason."

---

[4]  Imamu Amiri Baraka, *Blues People: Negro Music in White America* (New York: William Morrow and Co., 1963), 80.

[5]  Jacques Rancière, *The Future of the Image*, trans. Gregory Elliott (New York and London: Verso, 2007), 129.

In looking at it, we are made to linger within the paradox of the "rend" central to the experience of Didi-Huberman's aesthetic image—the point beyond which an image is defined by its inability to be absorbed into any available logic of production and the point at which this incompatibility begins to generate alternative logics, outcomes and ideals. This convergence invests the scene with its critical, which is to say, its playful character; in other words, the understanding that the sonic breach of the scene—the figural/interpretive ruination of the ruin it projects at its ocular center—is the pivotal element of its intelligibility. "It is not a matter of appealing to a poetics of unreason," Didi-Huberman writes. "The 'world' of images does not reject the world of logic, quite the contrary. But it plays with it, which is to say … that it creates spaces there—in the sense that we speak of 'play' between the parts of a machine."[6]

The spectator is again situated before the connective wirings and gear-shifts of this filmic machine, as the fixity of the visual image is cut by the superimposition of a jumble of radio-call in sentence fragments, answered telephone rings, partial dialings, dial tones, and then an infuriating automated loop of recorded "response" instructing the caller:

> Thank you for calling the St. Louis Housing Authority. If you know the extension of the person you are calling, press "pound." For the Section Eight division, press "one." For the human resources division, press "two." For the legal division, press "three." For the finance department press "four". For the Re-development Department, press "five." For the Procurement Department, press "six." For the Housing Operations Division, press "seven." For Executive offices, press "eight." Or press "zero" to be connected to an operator ….Thank you for calling the St. Louis Housing Authority. If you know the extension of the person you are calling.[7]

These cuts constitute aural images whose intervention into the visual projection creates and exploits exactly such crevices in the parts of the machine. Each intersplicing of sonic overlay is a provisional opening of an articulation of a desire, intensified by that very partiality—by that desire's incapacity to even fully communicate itself. The desire is both thematic—note the fractal longings for coherence and exploration as one of the few discernible fragments tries to describe the incommunicability of "what goes on in one's head"; yet another mentions that someone died because he left the boundaries of his neighborhood—

[6]  Georges Didi-Huberman, *Confronting Images: Questioning the Ends of a Certain History of Art*, trans. John Goodman (University Park: Pennsylvania State University Press, 2005), 142.
[7]  Christopher Harris, *Still/Here* (Marietta, GA: Cinepost, 2000), 23, 34.

and figural; note the sensory overload of the three-minute scene itself during which the camera does not move, a scene hopelessly saturated with incomplete utterances which augment, even as they divert, spectatorial attention toward and away from the visual image; broken utterances which fragment, disorient, and redistribute the enormity of absence in which the film originates. The very length of the shot itself situates in dialogue both the textures of duration and the isolated instants of which it consists. Edouard Glissant's evocative revision of Benjamin's flashing moment of danger juxtaposes the character of endurance structuring all survival with the fleeting or flashing character of discovery and transfiguration—to which all existence presumably aspires:

> We no longer reveal totality within ourselves by lightning flashes. We approach it through the accumulation of sediments. The poetics of duration … reappears to take up the relay from the poetics of the moment. Lightning flashes are the shivers of one who desires or dreams of a totality that is impossible or yet to come.[8]

If, as we look into this image from *Still/Here*, we also send Glissant's formulation into conversation with Didi-Huberman's logic of the rend—"the negative force within the image"—we become able to see how a filmic assemblage of lived collapses and catastrophes can be made to re-inscribe, not by re-collecting and cohering those collapses into narrative edifices of authoritative meaning, but by splintering them even further apart, beyond the points of recognizability or even cognition, by such means of randomized aural artifice as are instrumentalized here, opening reflective impasses that intersect the experience of incomprehension with the critical construction of "new" affective, perceptual, and memory networks whose archives of material are presently hidden in plain sight.

## The other of the law

In Blanchot's *own* image of Sade are inscribed the extremities of force, helplessness, solitude, urgency, and possibility, made to coexist however anxiously, in the movement of writing itself. Blanchot's Sade is locked away in a tower in complete isolation—"a tolerant man, rather shy, obsequiously polite: but he writes, all he

---

[8]   Édouard Glissant, *Poetics of Relation*, trans. Betsy Wing (Ann Arbor: University of Michigan Press, 1997), 33.

does is write" (WF 321). Generating fresh images obsessively, caught up in a constant opening and reopening of time, each new scenography propelled by what Blanchot identifies as "one of Sade's ambitions: to be innocent through culpability; to use his excessiveness to smash apart, for good, the norm, the laws which could have judged him" (LS 41). Blanchot writes elsewhere that Sade

> turns the most bizarre, the most hidden, the most unreasonable kind of feeling into a universal affirmation, the reality of a public statement which ... become(s) a legitimate explanation of man's general condition ... He is the man for whom death is the greatest passion and the ultimate platitude, who cuts off people's heads the way you cut a head of cabbage, with such indifference that nothing is more unreal than the death he inflicts, and yet no one has been more aware that death is sovereign, that freedom is death ... He is negation itself; his oeuvre is nothing but the work of a furious negation, his experience the furious action of a furious negation driven to blood, denying other people, denying God, denying nature. (WF 321)

It is by way of this unlikely detour through Sade that my argument winds into a different set of stakes, first in consideration of a moment in the work of poet Claudia Rankine, mentioned earlier in the section devoted to Marker's *Sans Soleil*, and whose own images open another window into the future of Blanchot.

In her 2004 multi-genre text *Don't Let Me Be Lonely* (2004), Rankine draws a certain relation of likeness between Sophocles's Antigone ("the character, not the play," Rankine reminds) and Osama Bin Laden. Conjoining the pair with Sade and Blanchot is the quavering fragility and final ferocity Rankine names in the imparting of "breath to breathlessness":

> Overnight Osama Bin Laden becomes a household name. Laden, I am told, rhymes with sadden, not lawless. If I close my eyes I can see him. He is of course being represented as Satan. He is a terrorist. His commitment to his interests extends beyond his need to be alive, perhaps beyond need or life itself.
>
> In college, when I studied Hegel, I was struck by his explanation of the use of death by the state. Hegel argued that death is used as a threat to keep citizens in line. The minute you stop fearing death you are no longer controlled by governments and councils. In a sense you are no longer accountable to life. The relationships embedded between the "I" and the "we" unhinge and lose all sense of responsibility. That "you" functioning as other, now exists beyond our notions of civil and social space.
>
> So terrorists embody that state of beyond; they are that freedom embodied. They bring life to that deathly state of lawlessness, breath to breathlessness. They

carry those whose lives they touch over into that breathless realm. Antigone, the character, not the play, by Theban definition was a domestic terrorist. Hegel uses her as an example. She identified with the dead, was willing to walk among them. In the course of the drama, even though she has many lines left to speak in the play, Creon eloquently describes her to her sister as already dead. So it is, was, already, with Osama.[9]

"Breath to breathlessness" is the exhalation that does not merely *restore* breath to the site of its dispossession but instead seems to detoxify that space. It is an interventionary exhalation in that it infuses the recipient with an interruptive gust that scatters the "deathliness" of its inhabitation by the state, and fills it with the breath of the Outside, or the "beyond" of everything posited—in this way dissolving the logic of finitude binding the "we" as well as the "I." Such breath re-animates a self now made *other* or alien to that state. It is a body that no longer lives within the law, and within whom the law can live no longer, having been expunged by a neutral non-cognition of the law; by "lawlessness."

In this sense, Rankine's terrorists fall into relation with what Blanchot sees as the revolutionary dimension of Melville's "Bartleby," who is continually walled in by the law, yet at no moment controlled or contained by it because impossibly innocent and indifferent to the law's capacity to instill fear of its repressive flexing. Like Bartleby, Rankine's terrorists are poised to "unhinge" the structuring relations of the social because their lives are not structured by fear of losing their hinges; they are located "beyond" dialectical play of recognition, because they have been moved beyond all fear or anxiety of their own self-loss; lifted out of a social sphere kept self-coherent by its fear of death under the law. Neither "legitimate" nor "illegitimate," her terrorists emerge from depths unknown to the system of law and judgment, which encloses thought in a repeating matrix of entombing designations and oppositions, such as legitimacy and illegitimacy, possession and non-possession, citizen and criminal, winner and loser.

Animating Rankine's terrorists, as well as Sade's or Blanchot's, is what such a figure breathes, in and as the alternate state of "beyond"; as the embodiment of a zone left ideologically un-inscribed, constituted doubly by its detachment from the demand that it replicate an administered ideal, and, by its willingness to lose the life of that body before losing the life of that detachment from what had subordinated it. This "state" of beyond is no more an antagonistic counterforce

---

[9]  Claudia Rankine, *Don't Let Me Be Lonely: An American Lyric* (St. Paul, MN: Graywolf Press, 2004), 84.

to the death-based Hegelian model of state embodied by Creon, than are Blanchot's Outside or Neuter conceived as oppositions to the negating system of language in which finitude structures the horizon of cultural possibility. Breath to breathlessness exceeds and undoes the tight disciplinary organization of a state held in place by steady ingestion of a logic of sanctioned repression, collectively recirculated into atmospheric permanence.

The death in freedom, freedom in death that at once induces and threatens to undo every gesture structuring every performance and program of unity, possession, and propriety—beginning with that of a prospective "I" and perpetuating it differently in every step in the making of any social relation—is the material of this outside; the non-volitional but ever-decisive quantity of pressure that can be exerted by one who has "lost death" (IC 34); a figure, again Bartleby-like, who seems to have emerged *from* death or even as one bearing death in himself.

This unmanageable, nocturnal force is palpable, in Blanchot's analysis, not only in the flash and the sustenance of radical violence that threatens to scorch the pretense of one's grasp of his or her "given" circumstances, but in the abyssal modes of writing that are disjoined from any tendency toward reproducing, recovering, redeeming, or even referring properly within the systems that produce and contain them. This is writing in which Blanchot reads "disaster" because the legibility of its difference is found only in the ongoing expansion of the abyss opened by writing's incapacity to assign any final designation to its drifts, their shifting velocities and their internal rigors—as the organization of Rankine's writing and the inability of her terms to *not* gesture beyond what is given demonstrate. It is in this sense that for Blanchot, the question of radical insurrectionary violence relates directly to that of writing.

In its narrative replay of what may have been a primal scene in the critical and creative arcs of imprisoned black revolutionary theorist and writer George Jackson's published works, what follows might lend texture to an interval in his transvaluation of the Western world order of his time—which is to mark the very opening of that project, perhaps with Blanchot, perhaps not—as a particular mode of unworking the world of action. But in their very different refusals of that world, and in their yielding to the images in which they are at once lost, and in which they may come at least momentarily, into the most complete realizations of how that world operates and why it must be abandoned, Blanchot and Jackson might be said to cross paths. In the night.

June 7, 1970
I haven't seen the night sky for a decade. During the early sixties in San Quentin, "lockup" meant just that, twenty-four hours a day, all day, a shower once a week, and this could last for months …. On a shower walk one day in '63, a brother called me to his cell for an opinion on this work he was doing on his walls. He had drawn in *the night sky* with colored pencils and against it, life size, lifelike (he was good), female comrades—some with fluffy naturals like my sister Angie, some with silky naturals like my sister Betsy. He had worked on it for three months. It was enormous—beautiful, precise, mellow. When he finished the last strokes the pigs moved him to another cell and painted over it, gave him a bad-conduct report and made him pay for the new coat of paint. That brother didn't draw much any more last time I saw him. Some political cartoons, abstracts in book margins. Life's a tale told by an idiot. Have you read any Shakespeare? I really enjoyed him when I was young. Macbeth is timeless, put him in a Brooks Brothers or a uniform and he'd fit right into the seventies. But you read all that stuff when you were in high school. I keep forgetting your background (class). Forgive me, sister, forgive the parochialism I sometimes slip into, habits formed in being, and addressing myself to, the hindmost.
From Dachau with love-

George[10]

The literal whitewashing of the drawn-in night sky, whose intrusion of warm familiarity leads Jackson's usually obsidian prose into rhapsodic reconstruction of scenes from his life before imprisonment at age 18, seems to include in its own neutralizing sweep the melancholic mode of his narrative energy at that point, the colorless efficiency of state penal machinery perhaps too deadening and too commonplace in his experience to warrant poetic analysis. But while the bloodlessness of this effacement of face is a matter of routine in the repressive materiality of state authority, it also performs for Jackson a dis-installation of ideology's *affective* operation—one within which, as suggested by his letter's initially redemptive language and tonalities, Jackson may have been still too deeply ensnared to realize in 1963. The caged mirage of the vivid night sky, replete with anthro-personifications that might be found in a Jackson family

---

[10]  George Jackson, *Soledad Brother: The Prison Letters of George Jackson* (Chicago: Lawrence Hill Books, 1994), 312–13.

album, is itself no more than an illusory respite from the continuity of solitary subjection that defined nearly eight of his eleven years in the California state prison system. Only later does he appear to recognize in this night sky an image by which to mark his relation to a past and to a material world outside walls that is itself, part of the very fabric of capitalistic reproductive power that the Jackson of 1970 is bound to incinerate.

What distinguishes this letter is not so much the emergence of an anomalous sentimentality in Jackson's narration. What lifts it out of mimetic anecdote and into individuating *event* is a subtle movement of consciousness that the letter formally reconstructs without recounting outright. It is not merely that Jackson is reactively angered by witnessing a gratuitous abuse of state power, but that he is *detoured,* radically re-inscribed by the guards' material whitewash of his own nostalgic enthrallment with a fixed portrait of the past. His discernment of the deeper representational stakes of the erasure is signaled by the shift or acceleration of referential play at the level of his own language. This is initiated by the Macbeth citation underscoring his awareness of the absurdity of the prison-house theater of gestures in which the guards reassert their domination, not only by an arbitrary destruction of a source of pleasure for the incarcerated, but by finding yet another technique of affective neutralization, aimed at the destruction of any reflective or imaginative connection the imprisoned might find with systems of value not installed by the state.

At the same time, the very retrievability with which this night sky is represented suggests its deep continuity with the daylight operations for which it provides such innocent "cover." That this illustrated night does not challenge but instead relieves the harshness of the conditions in which it appears—at least from the perspective of its captives (*this* reality becoming, of course, the episode's pivotal one)—does not appear to trouble the George Jackson of 1963—at least not as that Jackson is re-animated by the writerly Jackson of June 1970.

It may be for this reason that the irreverent discontinuity of the letter's final lines *sends up* the melancholy linearity of its first part, emptying the very logic of story drawn-in by its opening section. It is through the unplugged, sardonic disjuncture of its conclusion, in which the nostalgic, rhapsodizing "I" is displaced by its seemingly sudden remembrance, that his entire narration, indeed his very presumption to write and to be read comes to depend upon his having forgotten his "place" as the "hindmost," the abject, black criminal brute he is seen and said to be by white America. The unexpected whiting-out of the drawn-in night sky snaps Jackson's backward-looking reverie and redirects attention to his own circumstances and beyond, this, in the sense that Claudia Rankine envisions Antigone's most concentrated attention to move far past the immediate, and to drift mutely and inexorably toward the world of the dead.

The membrane of white paint, paid for with the prison "wages" of the anonymous artist himself, is the sediment along which Jackson suggests the movement of his own ongoing transfiguration of consciousness. The completeness of its nullifying function seem to anticipate the completeness and depth of Jackson's own contact with whatever otherness rips him from recognizability during the prison uprising he allegedly sets into motion, on August 21, 1971, leaving several guards dead. He is said by his closest friends in San Quentin to have had "no expression on his face" during the approximately thirty minutes of bloodshed; described by fellow prisoner John Clutchette as having had "a blank look in his eyes," and appearing to be "in a daze … he wasn't saying anything, wasn't talking to anybody." Clutchette finally remembers only an alien otherness having overtaken Jackson's face: "That day when I looked at him and looked at his face … he just looked like someone I didn't know anymore. He just looked like, I don't know, 'what the hell', or something, I don't know."[11] According to prison authorities, Jackson is eventually shot by guards after running out of a side door and sprinting toward a distant wall, nearly thirty feet high.

In *The Writing of the Disaster,* Blanchot describes *inattention* in the following terms:

> the distantness that keeps watch beyond attention, ensuring that attention not be limited by causing attentiveness merely to something, indeed to someone— indeed to everything. Inattention neither negative nor positive, but excessive, which is to say without intentionality … mortal inattention to which we are not free—or able—to consent, or even to let ourselves go (to give ourselves up); the inattentive, intensely attractive, utterly negligent passion which, while the star shines, marks—under a well-disposed sky and upon the earth that sustains us—the push toward, and the access to the eternal Outside … There … in the clearness bereft of light, sovereignty suspended—absent and there, always there—refers endlessly to a dead law which in its very fall, fails yet again, the lawless law of death. The *other* of the law. (WD 55)

From an image of Jackson's doomed push toward an impossible outside, an experimental film or poem composed from the materials and dispositions

---

[11]    As recounted by Clutchette in the documentary film by Ken Swartz, *Day of the Gun* (USA: KRON-TV, 2003), 93 min.

considered here might be prompted to investigate how it could be, that for all the frequency with which modern Western philosophy and critical theory have told us that we finally know nothing of death, aside from the bar of finitude it imposes on the living, that we appear to know even less of freedom—and the urgency of its neutral destruction of the "deathly" discourses we incessantly ingest. But in the work of creating such an image, it would seem imperative at some early point to consult the writing of Maurice Blanchot.

Part Three

# Glossary

# Disaster

William S. Allen

In 1943, in the introduction to his first collection of essays, *Faux Pas*, Blanchot discusses the relation between language and anxiety, or anguish (*angoisse*). This relation takes place as anxiety, profound anxiety, gives rise to language, just as language, and the failures of language, give rise to anxiety. The failures of language refer to its constitutive inability to provide certainty as sentences convey ambiguity not just in their meaning but also in their status, something that further sentences only exacerbate. Does this sentence describe my situation, or make it into something else; is it expressing my anxiety, or displacing it? Writing brings this anxiety to a pitch of acuteness that involves the writer's existence, since it is language that articulates existence or fails, leaving it undefined and inarticulate. Hence, writers are drawn to anxiety as the focus for their most urgent demand, that of articulation as such, which nevertheless cannot be achieved. Writing thus becomes the site in which this mutual instability is experienced, an instability of existence as much as of language, which are its two interlinked sides, for just as the writer requires anxiety, so "anxiety, which opens and closes the sky, needs the activity of a man sitting at his table and tracing letters on a piece of paper in order to manifest itself" (FP 4/12; translation modified).

The terms used here mark it as Blanchot's earliest form of the disaster, which would reappear thirty years later in *L'Écriture du désastre* as an encounter in which a child looking through a window sees "the sky, the *same* sky, suddenly open, absolutely black and absolutely empty, revealing (as though the pane had broken) such an absence that everything has always and forever been lost in it" (WD 72; translation slightly modified). Nothing has changed, the window has not broken, but everything has been utterly transformed, for in this experience language, like the window, has shown itself to be neither opaque nor transparent but disastrous, since in it "is affirmed and dissipated the vertiginous knowledge that nothing is what there is, and first of all nothing beyond" (WD 72/ED 117). The disaster is not an event. It does not take place in the order of things that happen but is discovered as that which has taken place, as the experience of this utter lack of grounds for meaning, the lack of any transcendental unity or order, an experience that language conveys but that is not limited to language, which is its other, mortal side.

In his discussion of the meaning of orientation in thinking, Kant ascribes a phenomenological basis to abstract thought by claiming that through our physical orientation to the sun and the stars the larger definition of existence is guaranteed. By knowing that the sun rises in the east, it is possible to define one's position and direction, and by analogy to this sense of orientation the idea of god develops to provide a transcendental ground for thinking, a pole star toward which thought tends. The idea of god is necessary for Kant, as without it thought would have no unity or order, and although it is abstract, it remains rooted in concrete experience and so is not merely speculative. But in a sky that has become absolutely black and absolutely empty there is no possibility for orienting thought, no unity or order to ground meaning or knowledge. The disaster is not simply due to a lack of orientation: as the word implies, it is not the absence of stars that is referred to but rather the disaster, the unlucky or misfortunate star. Without any fixed star to which thinking can orientate itself there is only deviation and the accidental.

Kafka's fragments on the hunter Gracchus guide Blanchot's reflections on the other side of the disaster as they convey the existential situation of the accident. Gracchus is hunting a chamois in the Black Forest when he slips and falls to his death, but then the disaster (*Unglück*) happens: although he dies he somehow carries on living, as if he had missed his appointment with death, for by accident his "death boat went off course [*verfehlte die Fahrt*]."[1] Gracchus drifts on and as he is unable to die, but not able to live, death is disappointed: it is no longer the point toward which life tends when it cannot eliminate the endlessness of dying. Without its central organizing guidance, life is only contingent and accidental, disoriented, disastrous. The unexpected (*inattendu*) aspect of this scene, which recalls Blanchot's own experience of fatal disappointment in 1944 (in which his last-minute escape from a firing squad was marked by a feeling of lightness that he later described as "the instant of my death henceforth always in abeyance

---

[1]  Franz Kafka, *Nachgelassene Schriften und Fragmente* I, ed. Malcolm Pasley (Frankfurt am Main: Fischer, 1993), 309.

[*en instance*]" [IMD 10–11]) is, as he wrote in reference to the encounter with the empty sky, "the feeling of happiness that immediately submerges the child, the ravaging joy," which suggests a form of rootless ecstasy in which one is no longer subject, an abstract sublime where the experience of endlessness as such is undergone, which is thus the evacuation of experience (WD 72/ED 117).

To some degree this disorientation coincides with the disenchantment inherent in secularization, the fundamental lack of grounds distinctive of modernity, and also the language-skepticism found in Hofmannsthal and Mauthner. But the focus of Blanchot's most extensive treatment of this issue, in *L'Écriture du désastre*, is precisely that of the relation between writing and the disaster where, as he had said, the nothingness of what lies beyond is both affirmed and dissolved. The disaster does not refer to a simple nihilism of values but to a radical displacement in which meaning is subject to an extreme contingency such that it occurs but its value or status cannot be guaranteed. Given this lack of ground, the form of writing starts to fragment as it cannot legitimize itself from one sentence to the next, and each new beginning is subject to the same uncertainty. The disaster has always already happened. It is never present, never complete; it is not something that can be experienced but is rather the evacuation of experience insofar as it leaves it undefined and without any historical sense. It is thus that it comes to affect the space of literature, as writing undergoes a loss of order and unity in the attempt to respond to the eccentricity and aporias of a field that cannot end or begin. Such a writing of disaster is not merely disruptive of the relation between thought and language, but imposes a thinking of its possibilities as a perspective without interests, a rigorously disinterested expanse without ground or direction.

# Fragmentary Writing

William S. Allen

Fragmentary writing is not concerned with aphorisms or epigrams; it is not a form of writing that neatly encloses itself according to an aesthetics of wholeness. Nor does it operate microcosmically, as in the thought of the German Romantics, by representing the possibility of the whole in the part. Instead, fragmentary writing emerges as writing discovers its own incompleteness: the lack of any form or essence that would guarantee its development. Aphoristic writing has a long history that Blanchot discusses through such figures as Pascal, Schlegel, Nietzsche, and Wittgenstein, but when he turned to fragmentary writing in the late 1950s it was for a complex of reasons that bore their own consequences. To understand this change it is necessary to understand the approach to literature that had previously occupied him, as it is out of this approach, and its limitations, that the fragmentary demand arose.

The change that marks Blanchot's early writings is the transformation from the novel (*roman*) to the narrative (*récit*) that is demonstrated in the reshaping of *Thomas l'Obscur*, which was republished in 1950, a decade after the first version, and at a quarter of the size. Blanchot's concern, as was spelled out in the preface to the new version, was to refine the earlier version so as to draw out its center or source. This point is repeated in the preface to *L'Espace littéraire* and in his analyses of the *récit* in *Le Livre à venir*, where it is a question of orienting writing toward its own center, from which its space and form can then be derived as the approach, the site, and the event of its own occurrence. It is the peculiar intensity of this reflexive space that makes the narratives of the early 1950s so distinctive, but as the decade moved on a number of changes took place that made Blanchot reconsider this relation of writing and space. Some of these changes were extra-literary, insofar as they involved the major social issues that were affecting France and Europe at the time, which drew him into a greater concern with the political and with the necessity of rethinking the form of relation as a relation without coercion or necessity. Other changes were literary in that writers had emerged, particularly Beckett, Robbe-Grillet, and Duras, who appeared to be approaching writing in ways that were similar to his own works. But these issues simply brought to a head the pressure that had been developing in his own writing, where the question of form was becoming more and more problematic.

For alongside these external pressures, writing struggles to present itself and substantiate its relation without falling apart under its own internal pressure. The status of a sentence lacks certainty without continuation, but nothing guarantees the form of that continuation, and so the sentence starts, and then stops. It seeks a relation, or to make a point, but in doing so finds its appearance dissembling or undermining that attempt and so it breaks off. But writing cannot cease. Even in its failure, each sentence calls for a further attempt and so it goes on, fragmentarily, in a logic that has been explored by Lyotard in *Le Différend* in terms of the aporetic contingency that arises between phrases, where "to link is necessary, but a particular linkage is not."[1] Such an aporia is familiar from Beckett's works, and Blanchot also finds an extreme tension in writing between the inability to go on and the inescapability of going on. The problem that both writers are focusing on is that of the skepticism of relation that language exposes. If language in the narrative is attempting to say its own event by broaching its relation, then the form of the narrative comes under pressure as this attempt finds that there is nothing that subtends it. As a result, the movement of language falters and is forced to start again, repeatedly. The center that writing had sought is beyond it, just as its relation is outside its possibility, hence the reflexive form of the *récit* is no longer appropriate.

But in this discovery something else is found, as the interruption of the sentence leaves it exposed to this exteriority: the outside as the source and the obstacle of its expression, the narrative step or block (*pas de récit*) that is (its) halting progress. The sentence posits a relation that is then negated, but this does not occur without remainder, and what is left is neither posited nor negated but fragmentary. A relation without relation, as Blanchot will say, as is found in states like waiting or forgetting, a neutral relation, without center or point but eccentric and endless. For if one sentence cannot guarantee its relation to the next, then the possibility of conjugation is lost and the relation of thought to

---

[1] Jean-François Lyotard, *The Differend: Phrases in Dispute*, trans. Georges Van Den Abbeele (Minneapolis: University of Minnesota Press, 1988), § 136.

reality that is guaranteed in language is also lost. So, in coming up against this aporia, thought and writing come up against an absence that is the loss of the *logos*, of the self-certainty of presence. Writing in fragmentation leads into what is not, into its own breakdown as well as to the experience of its groundlessness. Fragmentation affects not only language, but also thought and existence.

The rupturing of existence and thought reveals that fragmentation is not merely textual, since it concerns a negativity that disrupts the necessity and coherence of presence. Considering the writings of Heraclitus and René Char, Blanchot suggests that this instability can be found in the way that poetry exposes thinking to a dissembling and indeterminacy of sense between things and words, and a deferral or displacement of relation between subjects and objects. Rather than appearing and announcing itself in a reflexive moment of self-generation, poetry fragments by diverging from its own annunciation as thought and writing encounter an ambivalence at the point of their occurrence that leaves them incomplete or unannounced, subject to error. Fragmentary writing is already over and always to come as it opens onto a relation without end, whether materially, ethically, or temporally, but also to an end without relation, an endless aporia of thought, language, and existence.

# Community

Joseph Albernaz

That such a notoriously reclusive and solitary writer as Blanchot should take up "community" as a key theme is surprising only if one has never glanced at his texts on the matter, which present a radical and influential reimagining of this seemingly traditional concept. Community had been an important, if somewhat submerged, leitmotif in Blanchot's work until 1983, when in the slim book *The Unavowable Community* he confronted the term directly. Blanchot's thought of community intersects unavoidably with many of his other conceptual signatures, and in addition the term has become something of a watchword in an oblique but unmistakable philosophical and political dialogue involving thinkers like Georges Bataille, Jean-Luc Nancy, Jacques Derrida, Giorgio Agamben, and others—a dialogue, perhaps an infinite conversation, that is still ongoing.[1]

Blanchot's *The Unavowable Community*, we learn on the first page of the book, was written in the wake of an essay on Blanchot's close friend Bataille by Jean-Luc Nancy, which soon became Nancy's book *The Inoperative Community*. *The Unavowable Community* is divided into two sections: the first, titled "The Negative Community," discusses community through the lens of the life and work of Bataille, while the second section, "The Community of Lovers," involves reflections on the May 68 movement in France and a reading of a cryptic novella by Marguerite Duras. For Blanchot, community never designates the existence or experience of a shared identity, essence, substance, or trait. On the contrary, if something like community or sharing is possible, it is possible only in and as the absence or ruin of such phantasms: "The absence of community is not the failure of community: absence belongs to community as its extreme moment or as the

---

[1] Jean-Luc Nancy has just recently published a volume reflecting on his and Blanchot's engagement with community, thirty years after their original essays and books on the concept. See Jean Luc Nancy, *La Communauté désavouée* (Paris: Galilée, 2014).

ordeal that exposes it to its necessary disappearance" (UC 15). In reviewing Bataille's various projects and mini-communities both political and intellectual, Blanchot finds the mysterious Acéphale group to have been the most decisive, owing to the latter's emphasis on community through impossible sacrifice and death. Blanchot is quick to point out, however, that for Bataille sacrifice does not necessarily mean killing, but rather an exposure and self-abandonment to the experience of a limit: sacrifice is "the infinite exigency it exposes itself to in what opens it to the others and separates it violently from itself" (15). Similarly, death is nothing but the paradigmatic figure of finitude, a finitude simultaneously ownmost and co-exposed (to put it in the Heideggerian terms Blanchot was constantly thinking in). Indeed, if one had to condense Blanchot's difficult conception of community into a single word, that word would likely be *exposure*: "The community is not the place of Sovereignty. It is what exposes by exposing itself" (12).

Because community names an exposure that can never be a common project—it is in fact the "without project" (30)—Blanchot almost always refers to it negatively. Community is tied to lack, exclusion, death, absence, limit, abandonment, finitude, and so on; it is also what constitutively eludes calculation, measure, and work: "In common we have: burdens. Insupportable, immeasurable, unsharable burdens. The community does not secure itself against such disproportion; it has always left behind the mutual exchange from which it seems to come. It is the life of the nonreciprocal, of the inexchangeable—of that which ruins exchange" (WD 87). As we might expect, another negative marker Blanchot associates with community is its traditional antipode, *solitude*—yet here Blanchot often imbues solitude with hints of communal possibility, referring to solitude as "common" or "shared." Hence "a being is either alone or knows itself to be alone only when it is not" (UC 5).

Blanchot wrote about community with an awareness that the very word itself seems ravaged and hollowed out, especially after a century that saw the twin horrors of Stalinism and fascism, both of which vowed to found a community based in some shared social substance. And yet, Blanchot still attached a special importance to the possibilities evoked by the word "communism"—he refers, for example, to a "communist exigency" at the opening of his discussion of community (1). Along these lines, it is difficult to overstate the significance of the evanescent events of May 68 for Blanchot; in May 68, "what mattered was to let a possibility manifest itself, the possibility—beyond any utilitarian gain—of a *being-together* that gave back to all the right to equality in fraternity through a freedom of speech that elated everyone" (30). This "being-together" was not the result of a project, plan, work, or even a resistance, but was simply being-together itself, exposing new possibilities for community through everyday acts of speech and gathering together outside in the streets to do nothing.

Despite its apparent abstraction and its emphasis on negativity, non-production, and deprivation, Blanchot's concept of community does not involve a withdrawal from actual politics. That community is unavowed and unavowable does not mean that action in the world is renounced. Blanchot does relate the unavowable nature of community to Wittgenstein's famous "one must be silent," but with the crucial caveat that "one has to talk in order to remain silent" (56). Thus the unavowable community "carries an exacting political meaning," claiming and leaving us responsible for imagining and "opening unknown spaces of freedom" which confront us with the utmost urgency. The communist exigency reveals that the fullness of our present ("present without presence"[2]) is shot through with the absence of the work and the absence of the gods, as Blanchot, following Hölderlin, puts it. These unavowable absences are just the exposure to the open interval where community can come through, only to dissolve and depart again, in that rhythm which is sometimes hard to distinguish from disaster—but also from the everyday.

---

[2] "Between the liberal capitalist world, our world, and the present of the communist exigency (present without presence), there is only the dash of disaster, an astral change" (PW 93).

# Désoeuvrement

Michael Krimper

Blanchot deploys the concept of *désoeuvrement* at multiple junctures in his writing without fully defining the term. At one point, he asserts that the concept of *désoeuvrement* is among those in his lexicon that defy all conceptualization.[1] It refuses fixed meaning, grasp, and determination. To gloss a concept that defies conceptualization would already amount to a daunting task, but what complicates things further is that Blanchot's technical use of *désoeuvrement* proves to be considerably difficult, if not impossible, to translate into English. Though we can more or less translate the common French usage of *désoeuvrement* as "idleness," "doing nothing," or "unemployment," Blanchot extends its semantic range beyond any state of "inaction" or "being unoccupied." Ultimately, this is because he puts into play the negation (*dés*) of the root noun (*l'oeuvre*) in the word *dés-oeuvre-ment*. Within this configuration, the concept of *désoeuvrement* opposes not only the concept of *travail* in the sense of work as "productive activity" or "labor," but also the concept of *oeuvre* in the sense of the "literary work" or "artwork" (*l'oeuvre d'art*). Such an opposition between "work" and what we might call for shorthand "non-work" (*désoeuvrement*), furthermore, does not involve a dialectical operation of contradiction as much as an irreconcilable movement of contrasting forces and tensions. The immeasurable current of non-work under question for Blanchot would seem to insinuate itself into the overall work undertaken by humanity in the modern era. It would seem to run counter to the dialectical labor of the negative whereby human being strives to transform the totality of the given for the sake of achieving its own self-realization and fulfillment in the course of Western history.

---

[1] See Maurice Blanchot, "Tomorrow at Stake," in *The Infinite Conversation*, trans. Susan Hanson (Minneapolis: Minnesota University Press, 1993), 420.

Yet the term "non-work" only approximates Blanchot's dynamic use of the concept of *désoeuvrement*. What makes *désoeuvrement* arguably impossible to translate from the source to the target language is that its meaning oscillates between the passive pole of idleness, on the one hand, and the active pole of the refusal of work, on the other. The translation of *désoeuvrement*, then, must signify the suspension of ordinary work coupled to an altogether different way of (non)working, no longer governed by the dialectical principles of mastery, appropriation, and realization. While some readers of Blanchot have consequently chosen to render *désoeuvrement* into English as "worklessness," others have coined the promising term "unworking" (at the same time many other translations have proliferated, most notably "inoperativity"). Nevertheless, even if "worklessness" and "unworking" retain the negation of the root noun "work," they still slightly distort the equivocal meaning of *désoeuvrement*; for whereas "worklessness" accentuates its passivity, "unworking" accentuates its activity. Indeed, if the concept of *désoeuvrement* is untranslatable into English, then it is because the target language lacks a word for its irreducible ambiguity: "worklessness" and "unworking" at once.

In order to sketch the active-passive ambivalence of *désoeuvrement*, let us briefly consider some of the ways in which Blanchot applies the term in *The Space of Literature*. There, he begins to experiment with the concept of *désoeuvrement* in at least two interconnected ways. First of all, it bears on the social predicament and experience of the writer in modernity, which, in Blanchot's view, is characterized by exclusion. The writer, he argues, is excluded not only from work in the everyday sphere of productive activity and labor, but also from the work of literature itself. Insofar as a writer like Kafka assumes the infinite demand of the work, he inevitably becomes exhausted by the impossibility of the task, and, at the limit, is given nothing to do but submit to the experience of being strangely "out of work" (*désoeuvrement*) or workless (SL 23). The writer becomes the "inert idler" (*le désoeuvré*) cast outside and deprived of the work (24). And yet, for Blanchot, the activity of writing is paradoxically borne out of such an experience of sheer passivity, powerlessness, and exclusion. To write is to undergo the depersonalizing experience in which the "I" is abandoned to the work, in which "I" am dispossessed, and at which point "one" cannot help but write without end. For Blanchot, it is precisely the impersonal and anonymous experience of *désoeuvrement* that animates the creative production of the work (*l'oeuvre*).

This brings us to the second and much more well-known way that Blanchot uses the term *désoeuvrement*, designating the fragmentary dispersal and undoing of the work. The concept of *désoeuvrement*, in this sense, bears on the contestation of the work from within the work, above all the contestation of its identity, unity, and totality. Perhaps Blanchot's rewriting of the myth of Orpheus stages this non-dialectical movement of *désoeuvrement* in its most condensed scene. According to Blanchot's version of the myth, Orpheus desires to reach the origin and essence of the work beyond the possibility of its accomplishment. Orpheus, more specifically, wants to transgress the prohibition against looking at his deceased lover, Eurydice, in the underworld—the prohibition that would otherwise enable him to complete the work and to ascribe a meaning to his creative activity, but only on the condition that he turns away from its source of concealment. However, when Orpheus puts everything at stake by looking back and breaking the interdiction, he sees nothing. He sees nothing, that is, but the enormous presence of Eurydice's absence, the endlessness of dying, the inessential and insignificant non-foundation of the work. Drawing on the non-revelatory gaze of Orpheus, Blanchot traces and retraces, as he puts it, "the ordeal of eternal inertia" (*l'épreuve du désoeuvrement éternal*) at the heart of the work (173). And reading Mallarmé, he similarly lays bare the profound emptiness and silence of the "inertia of being" (*désoeuvrement d'être*) at the heart of the work (46). What Blanchot's literary interrogation of the essence and origin of the work hereby lets us glimpse is the worklessness out of which the work is generated, as well as the unworking that destines the work to irremediable ruin, thereby indicating elements of difference, discontinuity, and plurality in excess of the whole.

Throughout his writing, Blanchot does not stop trying to think the active-passive movement of the work, or the absence of the work, at times under the sign of *désoeuvrement*, at other times with another distribution of mobile and fluid terms. Without settling on any fixed definition, genealogy, or filiation, he subjects the concept of *désoeuvrement* to constant modification and mutation, later to be taken up and elaborated otherwise by Jean-Luc Nancy, Philippe Lacoue-Labarthe, and Giorgio Agamben, among many others.

# The Neuter/The Neutral

## John McKeane

The notion of *le neutre* plays a major role in the later writings of Maurice Blanchot. It has a status similar to other terms he commonly uses—the *œuvre* or the fragment, for instance—while being less immediately relatable to discourses such as literature and aesthetics. Indeed, despite a superficial similarity to concepts in fields as diverse as journalism and physics, gender studies and grammar, *le neutre* proves more recalcitrant to understanding than a good deal of Blanchot's notions. However, there are various ways to begin to read this notion. Growing out of initial usages in adjectival form and as "neutrality," and translatable both as "the neuter" and "the neutral," the term appears in Blanchot's reading of Heidegger and Levinas in the 1950s.[1] As one of the conclusions of *Totality and Infinity*, Levinas adopts a strong position against "the philosophy of the Neuter," namely, a thinking where Being, as what is neither one being nor another, is presented as the Neuter. Blanchot responded to his friend's thinking by asking, "Is this not a rather shameful Neuter?"[2] And indeed, much of his later thinking will be informed by *le neutre*; he does not wholly accept Levinas's account of external forces that entirely efface beings; for Blanchot, *le neutre* goes beyond such neutralizations.

---

[1] Leslie Hill lays out the discussion in *Blanchot: Extreme Contemporary* (London: Routledge, 1997), 127–42. Other useful critical approaches to the topic are Christophe Bident, "The Movements of the Neuter," trans. Michael FitzGerald and Leslie Hill, in *After Blanchot: Literature, Criticism, Philosophy*, ed. Leslie Hill, Brian Nelson, and Dimitris Vardoulakis (Newark: Delaware University Press, 2005), 13–34; and Jacques Rolland, "Pour une approche de la question du neutre," *Exercices de la patience*, 2 (Winter 1981): 11–45 (11).

[2] Maurice Blanchot, "L'étrange et l'étranger" (1958), in *La condition critique : Articles, 1945–1998*, ed. Christophe Bident (Paris: Gallimard, 2010), 278–88 (287); my translation. Blanchot was responding to a Levinas article from 1957 in which the material of what would soon become *Totality and Infinity* is explored.

One text where Blanchot sets out his thinking on the matter is a dialogue named "The Relation of the Third Kind (Man without Horizon)" (IC 66–74). Here the author moves through three types or kinds of relation: the first is where the Same dialectically dominates the Other, without itself changing; the second is an inversion of the first, with the Other now able to alter the Same, thus bringing about a fusional relation; and the third mode of relation is that referred to by Blanchot as a "neutral relation" (73). Here, there is neither dominance nor fusion, but instead something like a dynamic spacing. Neither term in the relation occupies a fixed position; instead, the neutral produces a movement or difference, and is said to be "*always separated from the neutral by the neutral ... always elsewhere than where one would situate it ... always on the hither side and always beyond the neutral*" (305; italics in the original). This sense of dynamism is reflected by the dialogue format employed by Blanchot during this period, from the philosophical dialogues collected in *The Infinite Conversation* where the interlocutors work through the unfolding and ultimately unworking of dialectical thought, to the ethically attuned *Awaiting Oblivion*, a multilayered text in which recounting, among other things, a misfiring dialogue between a man and a woman. *The Step Not Beyond* continues to think in these terms; its rich vein of italicized fragments works through the notions of fiction and dialogue, presenting unnamed interlocutors discussing an unknown topic, alongside the meta-discussion of how their relation is constituted. In these texts, Blanchot's thinking on *le neutre* often situates itself outside straightforward epistemological frameworks; *le neutre* can begin to be thought not through knowledge but in terms of the unknown.

Of course, though, Blanchot is as much reworking as inventing an epistemology here, for the injunction *to know that one does not know* lies at the beginning of philosophy. Accordingly, the adoption of a format strongly marked by Plato's writings is part of a process that saw Blanchot insist more centrally on the philosophical background already present in his pre-1960s work. Indeed, he suggests that the way philosophy moves from opinion to truth, from the particular to the general, is similar to the movement of *le neutre*:

> In a simplification that is clearly abusive, one can recognize in the entire history of philosophy an effort either to acclimatize or to domesticate the neuter by substituting for it the law of the impersonal and the reign of the universal, or an effort to challenge it by affirming the ethical primacy of the Self-Subject, the mystical aspiration to the singular Unique. (IC 299; translation modified)

On a first reading, this passage simply dissociates *le neutre* from philosophy. However if we read more closely, we see Blanchot implying that it has been at least possible to use the impersonal and the universal—those frameworks imposed upon us, especially within the context of philosophy's prominence in French education—to carry out a similar task to that of *le neutre*. What's more, the refusal to philosophize, insisting on the ethical nature of the Self, is also spoken of here as a rejection of that same *neutre*. Blanchot does signal his concern over these statements as a "simplification that is clearly abusive"; he nonetheless suggests that ultimately, *le neutre* is complicit, if not with the actual history of philosophy, then at least with the spirit of philosophy: a questioning without end.

For Blanchot *le neutre* is "that which cannot be assigned any gender, escaping position as well as negation" (F 220). While one moment of his work paints it as complicit with philosophy, at other times its sympathies are said to lie with literature. Here too the movement goes beyond the subject or the self in order to encounter an alterity, a radical otherness that is not simply another subject or self. We can see this when in *The Space of Literature* Blanchot famously compresses the act of writing into the movement from *je* ("I") to *il* ("he"/"it"). This is taken up in the later article "The Narrative Voice (the "he," the neutral)," where we read that "narration that is governed by the neutral is kept in the custody of the third-person 'he,' a 'he' that is neither a third person nor the simple cloak of impersonality" (IC 384). By way of examples, Blanchot mentions the readings of Flaubert, Kafka, and others, as impersonal writers, and we can also turn to the third-person protagonist of Blanchot's short narrative, which otherwise it would be tempting to class as referring to himself, *The Instant of My Death*. Thus literature distances the writing subject from him-, her-, or itself, while preventing this self from being merely replaced by any Self simply redefined more broadly. For Blanchot, the aim is to move beyond seeing writing either as an expression of the individual self, or as any vehicle of that more broadly defined Self, for instance the community. As the expression of neither self nor Self, *le neutre* thus opens up a space of writing beyond something that Blanchot understood only too well: the fear of the Other.

# Passivity

Patrick Lyons

The lengthy meditations on *passivity* that appear throughout the pages of *The Writing of the Disaster* first appeared in the review *Le nouveau commerce* under the title "Discours sur la patience (en marges des livres d'Emmanuel Lévinas)."[1] As such, Blanchot's notion of passivity can be read alongside Levinas's in its affirmation of responsibility and ethical openness toward the Other. Blanchot pushes further, however, emerging with a unique concept more readily attuned to the study of writing and literature than it is to ethics. Levinas is useful to consult on articulating the significance of passivity, but Blanchot's notion of passivity deserves consideration on its own terms.

The elusiveness of Blanchot's notion of *passivity* is not unlike that of the *neutral*: both command incessant attention from his readers, yet withdraw as soon as they are sought. As with many of Blanchot's notions, his particular understanding of passivity hinges on a movement of defamiliarization that overturns the word's common use. As such, it helps to underscore this common usage, if only in order to look past it. *Passive*, as it is commonly understood and used, is the clear opposite of *active*. Set against Blanchot's use of the term, however, this oppositional, negative definition falls apart. Similar to several other of Blanchot's fugitive concepts, passivity designates something always-prior to a customary binary logic. His reasoning is quite simple: how can a subject ever be passive, if passivity precludes its own enactment? Even in our attempts to conceive of passivity we are, effectively, always-already active. If we consider passivity in light of its practical impossibility, we come to know it as a fugitive concept that grants a slippery trace of an *outside*, which designates a

---

[1] Maurice Blanchot, "Discours sur la patience (en merges des livers d'Emmanuel Lévinas)," *Le nouveau commerce* 30–1 (1975): 19–44.

fragile limit between the knowable and the unknowable. Passivity, in this sense, represents what might otherwise be called "infinite passivity: perhaps only because passivity evades all formulations" (WD 16).

In turn, perhaps the clearest illustration of Blanchot's understanding of passivity is found in his meditations on Melville's *Bartleby, the Scrivener* throughout *The Writing of the Disaster*.[2] As Melville's narrator (a Wall Street lawyer advertising need of a new scrivener) recounts, a slight young man named Bartleby arrives at his offices in search of work. As the story unfolds, Bartleby's unsettlingly passive presence (or present-absence, perhaps) weighs heavily upon both the productivity of the narrator's offices, and the soundness of his mind, eventually leading to Bartleby's forced removal from the offices and subsequent death in prison. The narrative motor behind these events, paradoxically, is Bartleby's own radically passive existence in the face of work, sociality, and self-preservation. Not only does Bartleby's passive resistance pair neatly with Blanchot's notion of *infinite passivity*, but his occupation draws the concept into the realm of writing. "Refusal," Blanchot writes, "is said to be the first degree of passivity" (17). Yet to agree with Blanchot's understanding of passivity, this must then be a particular type of refusal, one that precludes (rather than relies upon) the *act* of refusal, that is, a passive refusal, emblemized in Bartleby's mantra: "I would prefer not to." For Blanchot, Bartleby's words register as something of a speech *non*-act: "an abstention which has never had to be decided upon, which precedes all decisions and which is not so much a denial as, more than that, an abdication" (17). Put otherwise, Bartleby's utterance may be thought of as an *infinitely passive* refusal in that it is intransitive: it does not refuse anything in particular; rather, it refuses to engage in the act of negotiation, or refusal: "'I will not do it' would still have signified an energetic determination, calling forth an equally energetic contradiction. 'I would prefer not to … ' belongs to the infiniteness of patience; no dialectical intervention can take hold of such passivity" (17). Through its reliance on the conditional ("I would …"), Bartleby's statement hovers in indecision, further exaggerated by the placement of *prefer* (*prae*: before; *ferre*: bear), which recedes into the slippery, prior passivity evoked above, *vis a tergo*. As such, Bartleby's conditional preference refuses to take a stance on anything, refusing the act of refusal itself, asking us as readers to struggle toward a thought of *infinite passivity*, even if it always slips away, or

---

[2]  For a deeper engagement with Blanchot's interest in Melville's *Bartleby*, see Ann Smock, *What Is There to Say* (Lincoln: University of Nebraska Press, 2003).

stands before. Further, the particular status of the 'I' here (an 'I' that *would*, not one that *will* or *can*) refuses stability or closure. If we call to mind the outcome of Melville's story, Bartleby's passive refusal crystalizes Blanchot's understanding of passivity's preclusion of a coherent, essential model of subjectivity, one built upon stability and closure. As the story progresses, Bartleby drifts into obscurity, eventually disappearing altogether, dying of *preferred* starvation in prison, seemingly as a result of his passive refusal. Returning to the openness to alterity innate to passivity, Bartleby's sustained passivity in the face of work and sociality results in his unraveling and disappearance, suggesting passivity's work of subjective *désoeuvrement*: "When the subject becomes absence, then the absence of a subject, or dying as subject, subverts the whole sequence of existence, causes time to take leave of its order, opens life to its passivity, exposing it to the unknown, to the stranger—to the friendship that never is declared" (29). As such, passivity is aligned with death and anonymity, a working against the coherence of a notion of sovereign subjectivity, and drawing, therefore, upon the act of writing.

While Orpheus may be Blanchot's patron saint of writing (crossing through death, turning to see the ghostly trace of a vanishing Eurydice, just as the writer flirts with the outside through literary language), Bartleby appears to be his next of kin, offering a different perspective through what Blanchot deems "'pure' writing, which can only be that of a copyist (rewriting)" (145). The work of the scrivener points to the citational nature of all writing, stressing its rapport with passivity through its fixation with the copy as its end goal, rather than overlooking it in the pursuit of creative novelty. "Pure writing" comes from the "passivity into which this activity (writing) disappears, and which passes imperceptibly and suddenly from ordinary passivity (reproduction), to the beyond of all passiveness: to a life so passive—for it has the hidden decency of dying—that it does not have death for an ultimate escape, nor does it make death an escape" (145). Bartleby's copying is a writing whose action is passiveness, producing nothing beyond writing itself, courting the edge of the *outside* with keen proximity, a writing folded back over itself, a "pure act" of passivity. As he writes, "Passivity: we can evoke it only in a language that reverses itself" (14).

# Literature

## Audrey Wasser

The irony of a glossary entry on Blanchot's notion of literature is that "literature," for Blanchot, names something impossible to define. Still, it is possible to elaborate on this impossibility, and much of Blanchot's writing is devoted to doing so. With philosophical precision and poetic finesse, Blanchot spells out the contradictory expectations that twentieth-century readers and writers bring to an experience of literature. He draws on his training as a philosopher, especially on his readings of Hegel and Heidegger, and he reflects on his own experience as a fiction writer, essayist, and critic with a care that comes from the intimacy of a personal struggle with the written word.

What is so difficult about defining "literature"? Blanchot begins "Literature and the Right to Death" by noting that the question "What is literature?" has caused some surprise for receiving meaningless answers (WF 302). The problem has to do, in part, with our critical belatedness: we cannot approach the question of literature innocent of the ways it has been asked and answered—or not answered—before. Blanchot's work is thus densely allusive to this critical legacy, with major touchstones including Mallarmé, Paulhan, and Sartre in the French context; the Jena Romantics, Hölderlin, Rilke, and Kafka in the German. The question is deceptively simple, moreover, even "childish" as Jean Paulhan called it, insofar as its answer seems self-evident. Blanchot's work is challenging to read precisely to the degree it seeks to undermine this self-evidence. Finally—for reasons I explain below—the question "What is literature?" is ill-suited to the approach of the natural scientist or philosopher, which begins from a perspective external to the object. Blanchot thus describes the way the question unfolds from within literary writing itself: the way each work poses anew the question of its own being, its own right to existence, and its own conditions of possibility.

"Let us suppose that literature begins," he writes, "at the moment when literature becomes a question" (300).

The question of literature is "peculiarly ours, central to our times" (SL 211). It is a *modern* question. Why? Literature encounters a loss of status in modernity, no longer serving the aims of religion or the political project of a people. This loss is, however, at the same time a strange gain, for it forces literature back upon itself, following "a movement which, in varying degrees and along diverse paths, draws all the arts toward themselves, concentrates them upon the concern for their own essence" (219–220). Interestingly, Blanchot's claim about the recursivity of the arts in modernity finds an echo in the writings of his near-contemporary Clement Greenberg, the American art critic who similarly identifies modernism with a self-interrogation revealing the limits and powers of each medium; painting, famously, investigates the flatness of its surface. For Blanchot, romantic and post-romantic literature investigates the limits and powers of language.

Language in its everyday use entails negation. "For me to be able to say, 'This woman', I must somehow take her flesh and blood reality away from her, cause her to be absent, annihilate her" (WF 322). Language names things, and, in so doing, names their limit (determining them with a concept) and names their absence (being able to function in their stead). While in ordinary communication, language disappears in the act of negating, in the literary work language has the potential to shine forth, to cease being merely a support for representation and to become visible in its own right: "a non-transitive speech whose task is not to say *things* (not to disappear in what it signifies), but to say (itself) in letting (itself) say, yet without taking itself as the new object of this language without object" (IC 357). This visibility cannot be secured once and for all, however, for it is a visibility made of negation, and of a negation that cannot stop disappearing into meaning. This undecidable wavering between appearance and disappearance, or between the non-transitive and the transitive use of language, constitutes language's "ambiguity."

Just as language is divided between these two aspects, the transitive and the non-transitive, so is the literary work divided between two sides or "slopes." One slope is concerned with meaning, and with the negation of things inherent in meaning-making. Seeking to "destroy language in its present form and create it in another form," the literary work distrusts words, going so far as to apply the movement of negation to language itself (WF 314, 330). The other slope of literature is concerned with "the reality of things … their unknown, free, and silent existence," and ultimately with the reality of language in its material (and paradoxically silent) existence (ibid.). Here we encounter the double demand of the work: the demand to extend the limits of language, on the one hand, and the demand for what lies outside of language, on the other. Because the work cannot decisively free itself of meaning, and because the meaning it seeks cannot free itself from language, each slope finds itself turning into the other.

"The Gaze of Orpheus" from *The Space of Literature* explores this double demand by means of the myth of Orpheus in Hades, recounting the inspiration that compels the artist to explore unknown regions, just as Orpheus is compelled to seek Eurydice in the darkness of the underworld. And it describes the work that, capturing this inspiration and rendering it sayable or visible in the light of day, necessarily betrays it, just as Orpheus betrays Eurydice by turning to look at her. The work is actual, and belongs to the realm of space and time; its inspiration is measureless, and belongs to "the pure night of … possibilities" (WF 307). The work cannot come to be without sacrificing the obscurity of what inspires it. Nevertheless, this inspiration can be disclosed only within an existing work.

Literature, in short, is "infinitely problematic" (SL 172). Blanchot reveals the space of the work as one of contradiction and risk. We enter this space not by theorizing, but by encountering within each work the constitutive tensions that make it up. Within the work, the "liveliness" of the question of literature insists and persists, in this space where nothing is guaranteed—but everything is possible (211).

# Outside

Audrey Wasser

"The outside" is a domain of radical alterity opened by the autonomous functioning of language in modernity. Though the term is a spatial one, it points to an aspect of experience that cannot be situated spatially. The term makes its way across multiple registers in Blanchot's work—the linguistic, the phenomenological, and the ethical-political. And it has an important afterlife in the next generation of thinkers, most significantly in the writings of Michel Foucault and Gilles Deleuze.[1]

An element of non-relation, "the outside" eludes the simple binary oppositions inside/outside, interior/exterior. Nonetheless, it is helpful to begin an explanation in these terms. Thus, we might say, "the outside" refers to what is excluded from language; it can also refer to what is excluded from representation, from conceptual thought, from the work of art, from the law, from politics, or from a relation to the other. In each case, what is excluded relates essentially to what excludes it. And in each case, it is offered as a limit-experience, one that cannot be grasped by the senses or bound by space and time. The exteriority at stake in the outside, in other words, cannot be conceived according to a "tranquil spatial and temporal continuity" (IC 161). Rather, it has a time and space proper to it: its time takes the form of an absence of time that Blanchot calls "the interminable" or "the dispersion of a present," and its space takes the form of an immediacy that Blanchot calls "fascination" or "passion."[2]

---

[1] See Michel Foucault, "Thought from the Outside," trans. Brian Massumi, in *Foucault/Blanchot* (New York: Zone Books, 1987); Gilles Deleuze, *Foucault*, trans. Séan Hand (Minneapolis: University of Minnesota Press, 1988); Gilles Deleuze, *Cinema 2: The Time-Image*, trans. Hugh Tomlinson and Robert Galeta (Minneapolis: University of Minnesota Press, 1989), especially chapters 7–10.

[2] See, for example, *The Space of Literature*, trans. Ann Smock (Lincoln and London: University of Nebraska Press, 1982), 26–34, and *The Infinite Conversation*, trans. Susan Hanson (Minneapolis: Minnesota University Press, 1993), 45–48.

When we speak, something falls outside of speech. Maybe it is our motivation for speaking; maybe it is the external world produced as an effect of reference. Blanchot does not specify the content of the outside because he is interested in it as a structuring condition: language cannot, by definition, realize non-language (WF 22). The impossibility of bringing nonlanguage into language is nevertheless felt from within as an uncertain vacillation between limit and origin: "as soon as something is said, something else needs to be said" (ibid.). Ordinary speech names things and falls silent; speech from the outside has already begun and continues ceaselessly, "an indefinite murmur" (IC 159).

The outside is not "the beyond." An experience of the outside is unique to modernity, insofar as this experience cannot be explained by transcendent notions of God, Man, or the afterlife. The outside belongs to an epoch marked by the death of metaphysics, for it cannot be located within the purview of Being or absolute spirit. Nor does it entertain a dialectical relationship to Being: neither nonbeing, negation, nor contradiction, it is an "interruption that does not bring together" (161). It is neutral, neutrality itself, a version of what Blanchot calls "the neuter."

In *The Space of Literature*, through his reading of Kafka, Blanchot links art to "what is 'outside' the world … this outside bereft of intimacy and of repose" (SL 75). The outside is at stake in an experience of literature in different ways. The writer withdraws from the world in order to create, and her creation falls outside of the authority, industry, and progress that belong to other kinds of human activity. This experience of the outside is, in turn, betrayed once the work is realized; the writer now finds herself "exiled from [the] work" (81). For the reader, finally, the work opens a new experience of the outside insofar as its language, in its ambiguity, equivocates between meaning and thing, where "thing" indicates something uncognizable, "an outside deprived of an inside" (WF 165).

*The Infinite Conversation* offers a more robust treatment of "the outside," connecting it to a radical conception of writing that opens onto questions of ethics and politics. Here Blanchot envisions writing as a sheer force of dispersal, going so far as to describe writing as "outside discourse, outside language" because it does not operate in the service of communicative speech or conceptual thought (IC xii). Rather, "through its own slowly liberated force … [it] seems to devote itself solely to itself as something that remains without identity, and little by little brings forth possibilities that are entirely other: an anonymous, distracted, deferred, and dispersed way of being in relation" (ibid.). In this way, writing points to a domain of relations that escape totalization—it points to the outside, where relations escape even relationality in the ordinary sense. For the outside is "what accords neither distance nor retreat ... without ceasing to be radically different" (46). It shelters the irreducibility of the other *as* other. Thus, Blanchot can claim that the outside is the region of community, articulating the thought of a community that would be without communion or fusion.[3]

Everyday language names the possible, and supports "our relations in the world and with the world [which] are always, finally, relations of power" (42). Yet something else in language—call it "writing," "poetry," or simply "another center of gravity" of language (65)—moves toward the impossible, and "announces itself according to a measure other than that of power" (43). This measure is that of the outside.

---

[3]  See Maurice Blanchot, *The Unavowable Community*, trans. Pierre Joris (Barrytown: Station Hill Press, 1988), 7, 10.

# Friendship

Aïcha Liviana Messina

Although there is not a systematic approach to the topic of friendship in Blanchot's work, a definition of friendship can be proposed. For Blanchot, friendship corresponds neither to the Greek idea of reciprocity that depends on the idea of symmetry between the I and the Other, nor to Montaigne's idea that friendship is a mere mystery that has no explanation, that friendship happens, in Montaigne's words, "because it was him … because it was me." Closer to Nietzsche's conception of a "stellar friendship" in which the friend's distance and unpredictable becoming (*devenir*) are cherished, for Blanchot friendship is a relationship to the unknown that escapes any form of presence and that therefore is not related to personal qualities or to particular persons. Yet, whereas in Nietzsche the friend's distance is part of the unpredictable dimension of the becoming that leads close friends to choose different paths, in Blanchot distance is a quality that is inherent to proximity. What makes friendship stellar, shining in its distance, is not the fact that friends *might* change, as if they were once present or known, but rather that they are of themselves other, inaccessible unknown. Hence, Blanchot evokes a "friendship for the unknown without friends" (Blanchot 1992, 133). Along these lines, friendship does not form a closed circle of friends allied to and identified with one another. Rather, it happens as the rupture of this closed community. Yet, in this context of otherness where friends relate to one another as unknown, are not all friendships equal and all friends the same? With this "friendship for the unknown," do we not run the risk of neutralizing the singularity of each friend, namely, of ignoring the presence of friends in the end?

Blanchot's writings are indeed punctuated by the evocation of singular friendships. At the end of "For Friendship," a little essay first published in 1992 by way of a "pre-text" for Dyonis Mascolo's *A la recherche d'un communisme de pensée*, Blanchot speaks of his friend Emmanuel Lévinas, author of *Totality and Infinity*, as "the only friend" "whom I call *tu* and who calls me *tu*" (PW 143). In this text, Blanchot also describes the encounter with his friend Robert Antelme, "almost timid but certainly intimidating" (PW 137), who would later publish *L'espèce humaine* in 1947. Curiously, in a text that one would expect to address the author of the book prefaced, Mascolo, with whom Blanchot shared, in crucial political moments such as the Algerian War and May 1968, political reflections as well as political forms of militancy, Blanchot evokes other friendships instead.[1] Yet, this violence that Blanchot seems to engage in a text dedicated to friendship ("*for* friendship") indicates that friendship is singular inasmuch as it is not a limited and confined experience but, rather, an infinite exigency. Lévinas, the "only friend" "whom I call *tu* and who calls me *tu*," that is, the only friend with whom Blanchot claims to have a relationship of familiarity, is also the one whose thought construed the thinking of proximity as inaccessible, as the opening of an infinite distance. He or she (or it) "whom I call *tu*," who is familiar, is the Stranger, the Unknown. In the same token, the friendship with Mascolo should not be located where one expects it to be, namely, in comradeship or militancy. Whereas comradeship is an exigency focused on the present moment and during which differences seem to be erased (2010, 141), friendship can only exceed present determinations; it can only call for irreducible differences. It is neither acquired nor reached. It can only be addressed, "*for* friendship."

"Friendship for the unknown without friends" describes an exigency rather than an acknowledged fact. It is a relationship to the infinite and therefore an infinite exigency. Now, the infinite of this exigency is measured precisely by finitude, which should not be bypassed. A moving essay, "Friendship," written after the death of Blanchot's friend Georges Bataille, helps us illustrate this idea. In this essay that gives its name to the entire volume of *Friendship*, first published in 1971, Blanchot affirms a tragic truth: not only does death put an end to life and therefore to a friend's proximity; it puts an end to the distance that characterizes friendship. It puts an end to a friend's speech but also to the very silence that is the in-between of friendship. With death, "what was close to us not only has ceased to approach but has lost even the truth of extreme distance" (F 292). The death of a friend is without any sort of redemption, not even the redemption that memory makes possible by maintaining present remembrances. Hence, friendship, this infinite exigency, entails forgetfulness as the refusal of a memory

---

[1]  I thank Luis Felipe Alarcón for directing my attention to this detail (and many others).

that would maintain the illusion of a presence. But how can forgetfulness be an act of friendship? Is not forgetfulness, if not a sign of cynicism, at least a sign of indifference? Again, with forgetfulness, are we not doomed to lose the singularity of each friendship?

Blanchot's call for forgetfulness belongs more to a suspicion concerning memory than to a belief in the possibility of forgetfulness. As Blanchot says in the wake of Nietzsche's *Dawn*, forgetfulness is "unproven" and "improbable" (WD 105). If forgetfulness is not doomed to be a part of memory, then it has to happen passively, without a subject's being aware of it. Thus, forgetfulness remains unproven. Friendship's exigency does not therefore *end* in oblivion. Yet, while oblivion is as unavoidable as it is improbable, it allows the exigency that friendship be defined with more precision. "Friendship for the unknown without friends" is certainly the affirmation of separation, of the friend's distance and otherness, but it is also an exigency that relates to the present in its finitude and irredeemability. Oblivion is therefore nothing other than the finitude of time that opens the space for friendship in the fragility that makes each friendship singular. It is the beating heart of the "unknown" that constitutes friendship. It is the "unknown without friends" that makes each friendship singular in the infinity of an exigency that can relate only to the finitude of time.

# Index

neutral, 13, 23, 25, 36, 71, 73–4, 85, 103,
106, 109–10, 113, 115, 119, 135,
137, 144, 156, 181, 192–3, 196,
203–18, 221, 226, 228, 232–3, 236,
239, 265, 268, 274, 279, 281–2, 284,
292, 303–5, 307, 316, 319
New Criticism, 30
Nietzsche, Friedrich, 5, 36, 55, 70, 109–10,
113, 152, 159, 161, 265, 319, 321
nihilism, 101, 289
nothingness, 23, 32, 75, 101, 113, 131, 145,
205, 224–5, 228, 237–8, 269, 274,
289

Orpheus, 6, 8–9, 14, 57–9, 61–6, 73–5,
78–9, 191, 201, 232, 261–2, 301,
309, 313
Oswald, Marianne, 149, 155–6
outside, 6, 90, 94, 100–3, 108–9, 111,
114–16, 118, 124, 145, 168–70, 184,
192–7, 199, 201, 205, 209, 213–14,
220, 230, 235, 250–5, 259, 265–6,
279–80, 283, 292, 307, 309, 315–17

passivity, 3, 107–8, 146–7, 158, 227,
229–33, 240, 300, 307–9
Paulhan, Jean, 29, 83, 311
Pound, Ezra, 7, 184
Proust, Marcel, 19, 27–8, 79, 86, 96–7, 221

Rabaté, Jean-Michel, 65–7, 73, 79
Rancière, Jacques, 275
Rankine, Claudia, 15, 267, 278–80, 283
refusal, 3–4, 66, 98, 107, 115, 212, 217,
223, 265, 273, 300, 305, 308–9, 320
repetition, 7, 14, 48–9, 87, 112, 115, 124,
129, 136, 138, 161, 247–50, 254, 257

Rilke, Rainer Maria, 23, 27–8, 62–4, 77,
147, 224
Rimbaud, Arthur, 34, 164, 188, 191,
199–200
Rollin, Denise, 11, 148–9, 153–5
romanticism, 21, 61, 70, 90, 97, 105,
108–9
Ropars-Wuilleumier, Marie-Claire, 219
Rousseau, Jean-Jacques, 84, 93

sacred, 12–13, 152, 184–5, 188–91, 193–7,
199
Sade, Marquis de, 52–3, 84, 207, 210, 247,
256–61, 266, 277–9
Sartre, Jean-Paul, 9, 14, 28, 36, 81–3,
87–91, 106, 160, 163–6, 230–1, 238,
311
Schumann, Robert, 154–5
Second World War, 1, 7, 12, 102, 115,
149
Socrates, 11, 128–33, 138, 185–7
subjectivity, 12, 97, 147–8, 167, 172, 178,
209, 221, 228–9, 258, 309
surrealism, 12, 110, 117, 184

Todorov, Tzvetan, 177
transcendence, 85, 97, 101, 156, 179–80,
245
transgression, 15, 28, 31, 99–100, 102, 105,
108–9, 124, 135

Valéry, Paul, 27, 35, 45
violence, 4, 99–101, 103–6, 108, 113–14,
117, 188, 229, 257, 261–2, 266, 280,
320

Wittgenstein, Ludwig, 291, 297

Lightning Source UK Ltd.
Milton Keynes UK
UKHW020035140121
377022UK00008B/202